CW01023064

Dispensati Today, Yesterday, and Tomorrow

by Curtis I. Crenshaw, II and

Grover E. Gunn, III

This is a letter to our dispensational brethren from two former dispensationalists, both having attended Dallas Theological Seminary.

"He must reign until He has put all His enemies under His feet" (1 Cor. 15:25)

Reprinted 1986

Reprinted 1987 with minor changes

Reprinted 1989 with critique and response

Reprinted in 1994 with updates added by
Crenshaw in the Introduction and in
Chapters 1-8 regarding the new movement
in dispensationalism

Reprinted 1995

ISBN: 1-877818-01-1

To my faithful, beloved wife, Ruth, who is also a friend. We have now shared over a quarter century.

(I also thank God for my grandmother, Connie M. Nave, who is now with the Lord and who taught me my first verse: " . . . those who honor Me, I will honor . . ." [1 Sam. 2:30] and for my mother, Frances Gillespie, who prayed for years that I would develop a love for studying. Her prayers are answered!)

Table of Contents

Foreword

The major issue facing the church of Jesus Christ in every age is, "What is the gospel?" Without the right answer to that question there is no assurance that life, death, or eternity means anything. The proper way of finding the right answer is of major importance. Is it to be found within our own opinions? What about the opinions of the majority? How are we to be sure that we know what the true meaning of life is?

A word from God, since he is outside our mental and historical processes, would provide a sure answer to the question. If God has created all things, and the Bible assures us that he has, then he is the determiner of the meaning and focus of life and history. He knows what all of it means, and he is actively working out his purposes in the course of history. God has graciously given us in the Bible his plan for history, so that we do not have to wonder or guess at what he is doing.

For the last hundred years an elaborate system of Bible interpretation has provided an answer to the question of the meaning of history that is contrary to what the church has historically held to be the teaching of Scripture. That system is known as dispensationalism, and it has become very popular and widespread; so much so that many people hold to its tenets without knowing much about the system or that there is an alternative.

In this book Curtis Crenshaw and Grover Gunn, who formerly adopted dispensationalism wholeheartedly, examine the teachings of dispensationalism in the light of the Scripture. There is always the danger in such an examination of erecting "straw men," that is, not presenting accurately an opposing view, or the danger of critiquing the opponents arguments that are the easiest to disprove. But Crenshaw and Gunn have done the church a great service by quoting extensively from the writings of the major spokesmen of dispensationalism, carefully and honestly comparing those views with the Bible, and showing that dispensationalism is not the teaching of Scripture. Because of their intimate and extensive knowledge of that system, and because they themselves were not easily convinced to leave it, they neither caricature opposing views, nor give "easy" answers. They go to the heart of the system, show its foundational principles, and demonstrate that it is contrary to Scripture.

The issue before the reader is not a few minor disagreements between those who hold basically the same position, but whether dispensationalism provides us with God's good news and plan for history, or instead, the opinions of man imposed on the Bible. What is at stake is the saving gospel of Jesus Christ and the sinner's assurance that he is living according to God's gracious plan for history. Ultimately, the question is not what has the church believed throughout the centuries, or even what Curtis Crenshaw and Grover Gunn believe, but what does God say in his Word. This book is a faithful presentation of the Word of God, and I commend it to you with the prayer that God will use it to recover his church from the errors of dispensationalism.

Daniel R. Morse (former professor, Reformed Theological Seminary; now senior pastor of Immanuel Reformed Episcopal Church in Memphis, TN)

Preface

I have close friends who adhere to a dispensational system of doctrine. With thanksgiving I acknowledge that we are brothers in Christ. I believe that we need more unity in His body and that men will know we belong to the Lord by our love for one another. Biblical love, though, does not imply that we close our eyes to our differences. On the contrary, we must confront one another with Bible in hand and with a spirit of humility. I ask my dispensational brethren to receive this book in love, for it was prompted by a desire to be true to God's Word and by a zeal to share these truths with the brethren.

I used to be a dispensationalists myself. My knowledge of covenant theology was secondhand and faulty, and this is true of dispensationalists in general. After graduating from Dallas Theological Seminary, I helped to translate an Old Testament interlinear in Wilmington, Del., and out of the some dozen men or so on the translation team I was the only dispensationalist. I thought this was a good time to test my dispensational mettle if I could find a foeman worthy of my steel. They were more than worthy and knew my theology much better than I knew theirs. Indeed, their "steel" was "sharper than any two edged sword" and pierced my straw man armor with ease. My mosaic of the Scripture was destroyed by their consistent unity. If you are a dispensationalist, have you read the covenant theologians *firsthand*?

Here I feel constrained to make some observations based on my thirty-one years as a dispensationalist. My dispensational system and hermeneutic was one of distinctions, finding distinctions in everything I examined, yet I distinctly missed the unity of the Bible in God's covenant of grace in Christ. My unifying element in theology — whether systematic or biblical — was eschatology, by which standard we tested the orthodoxy of others. For example, when we applied for a ministry in a church or Bible college, the first thing that was settled was our eschatology. If this was "wrong," the application was voided. Any new Christian we met was regarded with great suspicion if he were not dispensational, premillennial, and pretribulational; we would have little to do with one who "spiritualized" the Bible. We could split eschatological hairs with seeming erudition but sadly we knew little of the "weightier matters of the law" such as God's decree, predestination, effectual calling, regeneration (logically follows faith, we said), repentance and faith (we said repentance was not necessary iv

for salvation and held to mental assent for faith), sanctification (an optional second work of grace begun by obeying some imperative, we were taught), justification (not broken law and judgment but God's love for each sinner, we thought), the place of the law of God, theology proper, etc. These things had little emphasis in seminary. We were taught to give out the "gospel" by exhorting sinners to invite Christ into their lives in such a way that denied the lordship of King Jesus in salvation — a very dangerous thing in light of Galatians 1:8, 9.

We were thoroughly programmed to deprecate others — especially the covenant theologians — who needed to justify a system, while we played the ostrich to evidence that threatened us. While suffering from dispensational monomania, we accused others of bending scripture to justify a system. I now say to my dispensational brethren: Could it be that we, too, suffered from myopia?

Curtis I. Crenshaw

Acknowledgments

I gratefully acknowledge that many people have helped in the production of this work. First, my wife, Ruth, has been patient in the many hours this project has taken, and has made helpful suggestions. Secondly, Thomas M. Frye read the manuscript and made accurate observations that were incorporated. Charles Turner, no mean writer himself, made excellent improvements in the style though the final result is mine (alas, I wish I could blame it on Charles!). May God grant that someday I could write as well as he! Also, without Richard Woodward the project could not have been done, as he made time and money available to me to complete it. Dan Morse has read the work and suggested changes, which have been made. Teresa Johnson read my chapters (1-8) for the 1994 edition and tried to correct my mistakes. Any errors remaining are mine.

Finally, 18 years have passed since I was graduated from Dallas Theological Seminary, and although I have learned much from others since those seminary days, I still want to acknowledge my debt to the Dallas Theological Seminary professors who taught me to love the Bible as the infallible Word of God, inerrant from cover to cover, to love the triune God of the Bible as the only God, to love the Lord Jesus as God and man in one Person forever, and to love the original languages of Greek and Hebrew. Their labors here were faithful and true and will reap their reward in due time. Though we may disagree in many areas now, we are still brethren; my love and respect for them remains.

Curits I. Crenshaw

Introduction to the Original Edition

by Curtis I. Crenshaw

Before we critique dispensationalism, I must note that there are many kinds of dispensationalism. There is hyper-dispensationalism, a view that says the church started in the middle of the book of Acts or at Acts 28. Therefore, only a few of Paul's epistles apply to the church today; the rest of the New Testament is Jewish and belongs to Israel.

Next is classical dispensationalism (Mr. Gunn's excellent term), as represented by Scofield and Lewis Sperry Chafer, with Israel on the earth and the church in heaven, and "the twain shall never meet," two ways of salvation (works in the Old Testament and faith in the New Testament), with Chafer holding to two New Covenants. This view dominated from the late 1800's to the 1950's.

Then neo-dispensationalism (again Mr. Gunn's term) emerged, being promoted by such men as Charles C. Ryrie, John F. Walvoord, and J. Dwight Pentecost. These men hold that Israel and the church shall be together after the millennium, claim only one way of salvation in both testaments (faith), and one New Covenant. Dallas Theological Seminary is the primary promoter of this view.

I must now turn to another question: How to approach dispensationalism. There are many weaknesses we could tackle in dispensationalism. We could challenge dispensationalists to establish why they read so many Old Testament "kingdom" passages into Revelation 20? What identifies Revelation 20 with these Old Testament passages? In addition, how do they know that Revelation 20 is speaking of the Second Coming? These things are just assumed. If the church is a parenthesis, when did it start and how do they know? When will it end and how do they know?

However, these things are peripheral. The truth or falsehood of dispensationalism stands or falls with three things, of which all dispensationalists are agreed: (1) its "literal" hermeneutic, (2) the distinction between Israel and the church, and (3) the parenthesis theory. These three pillars are what we are challenging. If these three supports are successfully challenged, then all forms of dispensationalism will be vanquished.

Some peripheral aspects of dispensationalism have been addressed, not because they are determinative, but because many think they are so important. Such addenda are: When did the church begin, the kingdom Christ offered while on earth, what a dispensation is, the rapture, unconditional covenants,and so forth.

I trust too that the chapter on the implications of dispensationalism, which is the real practical and dangerous part of the system, will be helpful, too.

Each writer has written and edited his own part, being solely responsible for it, and each retaining the copyright to his respective work.

Mr. Crenshaw quotes from the NASB and the NKJV while Mr. Gunn uses the KJV.

Introduction to the 1994 Edition

by Curtis I. Crenshaw

It has been almost a decade since Grover Gunn and I first went to print with this book. It has now gone through five printings, and this is the third edition. My section has been slightly altered and another chapter added (chapter 8) on antinomianism in dispensationalism.[1] This book was not going to be reprinted again, but the demand has been so great that we have happily complied. We have been delightfully surprised to see how many Bible college and seminary students have called and written to thank us for helping them out of dispensationalism. Pastors also have consistently ordered it to help their people see the fallacies of the system and to help those coming to their Reformed churches from a dispensational background. The movement is almost always from dispensationalism to the Reformed view and rarely the reverse.[2]

Gracious Endorsements of Our Book

There have been gracious comments about our book from some scholars. Most notably, Bruce Waltke, the former head of the Old Testament at Dallas Theological Seminary who is no longer a dispensationalist, has said: "Contributors should have dialogued with, not ignored, the influential and well-researched work by Curtis I. Crenshaw and Grover E. Gunn, III."[3] Waltke was referring to the many contributors to the book defending dispensationalism just listed in the footnote. This political response of silence to our book has been

---

[1] I have written a separate volume against their view that one can have Jesus as Savior without Lord entitled, *Lordship Salvation: The Only Kind There Is*. It may be ordered from the publisher at the front of the book.

[2] Also people convert from Arminianism to Calvinism, and rarely the reverse.

[3] Waltke said this in Craig A. Blaising, *Dispensationalism, Israel and the Church* (Grand Rapids: Zondervan, 1992), p. 354. Blaising did not contact Mr. Gunn or me to discuss what the purpose of this new book should be, which he wanted to do for us.

basically Dallas Seminary's only response. This political response was safe, for if they had said anything, our book would have been noticed. By the blessing of God, though, it has been noticed quite well for years.

Another scholar, whose endorsement is also on the back cover, is John H. Gerstner who said of our book: "Curtis I. Crenshaw and Grover E. Gunn, III, made a notable contribution in 1985 with their *Dispensationalism Today, Yesterday, and Tomorrow.* Coming from two scholars who knew Dispensationalism from the inside as students at Dallas Theological Seminary, this volume is a thorough study of crucial Biblical passages with an especially fine examination of eschatology and a masterful defense of the Reformed faith."[4]

Other Books Against Dispensationalism

Gerstner has an excellent critique of dispensationalism, *Wrongly Dividing the Word of Truth.* This book is must reading for those interested in the on-going discussion. Gerstner is hard hitting and very insightful, often tying up the opponents in logical knots. As in the case of our book, dispensationalists generally do not respond to Gerstner.

Vern S. Poythress wrote *Understanding Dispensationalists* in 1987, published by Zondervan. He has two excellent chapters on what "literal" means and how dispensationalists often do not know themselves. He indicates that the Israel/church distinction determines their hermeneutic, not the reverse. He also discusses classical dispensationalism and other variations within the movement. We agree with Poythress and also with Willem A. VanGemeren[5] that the Israel/church dualism gives rise to their hermeneutic and not the reverse.

It has been my contention for some years that this dualism in dispensationalism is gnostic[6] with its heavenly versus earthly ideas, spiritual versus material, individual versus covenant or community,[7]

---

[4](Brentwood, TN: Wolgemuth & Hyatt, Publishers, Inc., 1991), p. 254. The publisher has gone out of business, but Gerstner is coming out with an updated version with another publisher. The title will be *Wrongly Dividing Wrongly Dividing.* This is not a typo.

[5]Blaising, p. 345.

[6]See the most excellent book by Philip J. Lee, *Against the Protestant Gnostics* (New York: Oxford University Press, 1987).

[7]In dispensational churches the individual is sovereign over the church so that discipline is seldom administered. The individual simply goes elsewhere when trouble arises at his church.

political versus spiritual, Christ versus Satan,[8] and escapism motifs. Dispensationalism comes to the Bible with these dichotomies already in place, and these distinctions *will* be seen; it is simply a matter of how. With most dispensationalists these dichotomies also lead to others: justification (heavenly) versus sanctification (earthly), faith (heavenly) versus works (earthly), spiritual Christian (heavenly) versus carnal Christian (earthly), position (heavenly) versus practice (earthly), grace (heavenly) versus law (earthly) — all of which are based on man being sovereign over God in his "decision" for Christ. In each dichotomy the heavenly either cannot affect the earthly or can do so only at man's behest. Indeed, it is because man is sovereign that these dichotomies arise, for if God's grace were irresistible then the heavenly would necessarily affect the earthly.[9] For the Reformed and the Bible, the heavenly necessarily affects the earthly with the heavenly being sovereign.

Another book that usually goes unmentioned is *House Divided: The Break-up of Dispensational Theology*, by Greg L. Bahnsen and Kenneth L. Gentry, Jr., published by ICE in Tyler, TX. Bahnsen's part discusses the ethical question and Gentry's the eschatological question. This is an excellent addition to the literature, and one that must be reckoned with, for the ethical problems of dispensationalism are substantial and only considered in summary fashion in my part of the book.

Dispensationalists Respond

There is a book now by dispensationalists, seeking to answer some of the problems raised, letting everyone know where they are in their on-going development: *Dispensationalism, Israel and the Church* (see footnote 3). There are numerous dispensational authors of the book, and responses by Willem A. VanGemeren, Bruce K. Waltke, and Walter C. Kaiser, Jr. Dispensationalists have been bludgeoned so much over their "literal" hermeneutic that they confess that now they have abandoned it, and most of the book is given to the exegesis of particular texts regarding Israel and the church.

---

[8]Of course there is a true spiritual war, but in the Bible Satan has lost while in dispensationalism he wins, at least in this age. Thus we have ethical dualism with Christ's people and their ethic existing alongside Satan's seed and their ethic instead of the Christians reigning over the world and Satan.

[9]When students of the Bible come into the doctrines of grace (TULIP), they nearly always leave dispensationalism, for one of the sustaining presuppositions of the dichotomies is gone.

In the index of persons, conspicuous by their absence are Gerstner and his book, Bahnsen and Gentry's book, and our book.[10] As I have pointed out in one of my chapters, dispensationalists do not take criticism well, tending to ignore it and to parrot one another's caricatures and statements of those who differ with them.

The inherent weaknesses in dispensationalism have not really been changed, such as the assertion that Israel and the church are distinct (with all the implications for two ways of salvation) and continued antinomianism. They are so blind to their antinomianism that they do not even address it, except for a few comments by Kenneth L. Barker in his chapter.[11] Crucial is the doctrine of union with Christ, by which one is saved if he is in union with Jesus and lost if not, and especially that Christ is the covenant Head of the people He represents, obeying the law for them, dying for them, and being raised bodily from the grave for them. The book does not develop this belief or explain how these new dispensationalists understand union. If there is one covenant Head, it would seem that there can only be one covenant people, not one covenant Head and two peoples (which would make God a bigamist, having two brides). If there is no salvation apart from union with Jesus, then Old Testament saints must be in union with Him; and if in union, they are in the church. Thus the Israel/church distinction, Arminianism and antinomianism, and union with Christ are problems they left in place. One wonders why they do not address these in a separate book since they did not in this one. Perhaps the reason is that they are so taken up with eschatology that they have no consensus in soteriology. I have seen untold dozens of books by dispensationalists on eschatology but none by a compendium of dispensational scholars on soteriology.

Yet Craig Blaising, the editor of *Dispensationalism, Israel and the Church*, thinks that something significant is taking place in dispensationalism. The following are their concessions: the former distinction

---

[10]Blaising mentions our book in a footnote with a typically irrelevant and wrong comment.

[11]There are two chapters on Jesus and the law, but these do not address antinomianism directly. They do, however, continue antinomianism in that the moral law in the Old Testament is either played down or negated. Barker, on the other hand, seems to be theonomic! He disclaims this in one paragraph after giving several pages of arguments for the Old Testament law being for today unless specifically abrogated, using the same arguments that Dr. Greg Bahnsen does in his work, *Theonomy*. Barker simply asserts he is not theonomic; he does not explain where he differs with Bahnsen.

between the kingdom of heaven and the kingdom of God is gone (p. 12); two entirely separate peoples of God, one earthly and the other heavenly, are no longer adhered to; only one new covenant exists, not two; Israel and the church are now in the same covenant; eternal distinction between Israel and the church is now only a temporary distinction (p. 25); the church is not a parenthesis (pp. 146, 225); Jesus did not offer a millennial kingdom when He came; the Davidic covenant is not exclusively Israel's but also the church's; the literal hermeneutic is defunct (p. 29); and finally, Blaising confidently asserts that though dispensationalism used to be man centered on two peoples it is now Christ centered (p. 383). Blaising is especially hard on the "literal" hermeneutic as espoused by Charles C. Ryrie, John F. Walvoord, and J. Dwight Pentecost (p. 30ff).

It is true that the Ryrie/Walvoord/Pentecost view that Jesus offered the Jews the millennial kingdom while on earth is apparently now rejected for the more Reformed view that Christ fulfilled the Old Testament promises from day one by inaugurating Israel's covenants. It also true that now this new breed of dispensationalists see the church as fulfilling "in some sense" the promises to Israel. However, this ostensible Reformed view is fatally compromised by seeing the church as still somewhat a parenthesis in God's program, by a continued distinction between ethnic Israel and the church in the so-called millennium, and all the dichotomies mentioned above.

Blaising says that all these considerations "have led to the search for a new definition of dispensationalism" (p. 32). Blaising confesses about their new book: "The present book of biblical studies finds its identity precisely at this point: *the hermeneutical reexamination of the relationship between Israel and the church, which in turn contributes to the process of self-definition currently underway in dispensationalism*" [emphasis his].[12] Earlier Blaising had confessed: "The importance of this work for the self-understanding of late twentieth-century dispensationalism cannot be overstated."[13] We wonder if other dispensationalists will follow these new beliefs, and if so it will take at least a generation and more likely two generations for the implications to ripple down from seminary to pulpit to pew. Meanwhile, our book is still necessary as this new movement has not yet spread very far.

---

[12]Blaising, *Dispensationalism, Israel and the Church*, pp. 33-34; see also the footnotes on p. 249.

[13]Ibid., p. 23.

Even further, there are now many brands of dispensationalism. There is the old classic brand that is still adhered to in some circles, which was popularized by C. I. Scofield and Lewis Sperry Chafer.

Then there is neo-dispensationalism, which John Walvoord, J. Dwight Pentecost, and Charles Ryrie have promoted for some years. This view is still by far the predominant view, promoted by the vast majority of Bible colleges throughout the country and by many seminaries world wide. Neo-dispensationalism is also held by the vast majority of dispensational pastors, most of whom are probably not even aware of what is taking place in the new dispensational movement.

Hal Lindsey has a popular following that no scholar takes seriously, especially with his helicopters in the book of Revelation and constant newspaper exegesis whereby he updates his listeners every Saturday on a national call in talk show with the latest "last days" events in light of the current news. Since his books have sold over 30 million, his following is substantial.[14]

There is also the dispensationalism of the charismatic groups, such as Pentecostals, Assemblies of God, Churches of God, and even the Word of Faith movement. These movements tend to be either classic or neo-dispensationalism, though they have their own modifications peculiar to their groups.[15] Now we have "moderate" or "progressive" dispensationalism as espoused by those in this latest book. Of course there is hyper-dispensationalism, popularized by C. F. Baker, especially in his *A Dispensational Theology*[16] and by C. R. Stam in his writings. One wants to ask: Will the real dispensationalism please stand up? The differences between the major views may be summarized as follows:

---

[14]At the 50th anniversary of Dallas Theological Seminary, Hal Lindsey was invited to speak. Many of the professors were so embarrassed at his newspaper, imaginative exegesis that they said he would never be invited back again.

[15]I have written a major work exposing and refuting the beliefs of the leaders of the Word of Faith movement with a biblical presentation of the truth. The leaders include E. W. Kenyon, Kenneth Hagin, Kenneth and Gloria Copeland, Paul and Cheryl Crouch, Benny Hinn, Fred Price, Charles Capps, Oral Roberts, and others. The book may be ordered from the publisher in the front of this book and is entitled *Man as God: The Word of Faith Movement*.

[16]Ryrie invited Baker to speak to our theology class in seminary, and we studied and refuted his views.

Table 1

	Hermeneu-tic	Israel/church	Old Test. Justification	Union with Christ	New Covenant
Classic Dispen	Literal	Eternally distinct	by works	OT saints not in union	Two New Covs.
Neo-Dispen	Literal	(same)	by faith though not in Christ	(same)	Two aspects to one new covenant
Moderate Dispen	Not literal	Only distinct during millennium	by faith & usually not in Christ	unclear though implied OT saints not in union	One new cov.

Table 2

	Millennium	Church a Parenthesis	David Cov.	Holy Spirit	Law-Grace
Classic Dispen	Christ offered	Yes	Not for church	OT saints not permanently indwelt	Absolute dichotomy; church not under OT law at all
Neo-Dispen	Christ offered	Yes	(same)	(same)	There was grace in the OT; church generally not under OT laws
Moderate Dispen	Not offered	Somewhat	Church partakes	(same)	Grace in OT; OT laws may be for today

The problem of dispensationalism defining itself is compounded by the fact that Charles Ryrie, Zane Hodges, and Jody Dillow are still writing books,[17] and these men represent neo-dispensationalism —

---

[17]All three have written books in response to John MacArthur's excellent books against antinomianism: *The Gospel According to Jesus* and *Faith Works*. The books of the antinomians are: Charles C. Ryrie, *So Great Salvation* (Wheaton: Victor Books, 1989); Zane C. Hodges, *Absolutely Free!* (Grand Rapids: Zondervan Publishing House, 1989); and Joseph C. Dillow, *The Reign of Servant Kings* (Miami Springs: Schoettle Publishing Co., 1992). I have written a book defending

not the newer moderate kind.

In contrast to this, the Reformed have always held to the concept of "Reformed and always reforming." This means there is a core truth that does not change ("Reformed") but also that we develop in our understanding of Scripture ("Reforming"). We hold to one covenant of salvation in which Jesus is the Head of His one people, that He obeyed, died, and rose for them alone (TULIP), that Israel is the bud and the church the flower, that the whole Bible is to be used, and so on. But dispensationalists are changing at the very core of their beliefs, if we believe Blaising accurately represents the new movement. The "literal" hermeneutic and the consistent and eternal distinction between Israel and the church were considered the *sine qua non* of dispensationalism for at least 100 years — now apparently they aren't. Ryrie would view their changes as a radical departure from dispensationalism:

> If the Church does not have a new covenant then she is fulfilling Israel's promises, for it has been shown that the Old Testament teaches that the new covenant is for Israel alone. If the Church is fulfilling Israel's promises as contained in the new covenant or anywhere in Scripture, then premillennialism is weakened. . . . we agree that the amillennialist has every right to say of this view that it is "a practical admission that the new covenant is fulfilled in and to the Church."[18]

Apparently J. Dwight Pentecost would agree, who recently confessed to "being deeply disturbed by developing trends in dispensationalism."[19]

The dilemma dispensationalists face and are trying to solve has no solution apart from the Reformed one, which is how to reconcile two distinct peoples of God with the *one* salvation accomplished by Jesus in union with His *one* people. If there is only "one faith, one Lord, and one baptism," then there is only *one* people of God, *one* way of salvation, and no dichotomy between Israel and the church, between Old Testament and New Testament law, and so on. In short, dispensationalists find themselves on the horns of a very sharp dilemma: If the Old Testament saints were saved in the same way as New Testa-

---

MacArthur and attacking the antinomians, entitled *Lordship Salvation: The Only Kind There Is*, which may be purchased from the publisher in the front of this book.

[18]Charles C. Ryrie, *The Basis of the Premillennial Faith* (Neptune, NJ: Loizeaux Brothers, 1966), p. 118.

[19]Blaising, *Dispensationalism*, p. 251, footnote 13.

ment ones, then they were regenerated, believed in the coming Messiah, had the Holy Spirit permanently, were in union with Christ as their Head, and did works by God's grace. Therefore, we must ask, What possible difference could there be between Israel and the church? But if the Old Testament saints were not regenerated, did not believe in Jesus, did not have the Holy Spirit permanently, or were not in union with Christ, then we necessarily have different ways of salvation and two peoples of God. Dispensationalists must move from a man-centered, end time, millennial focus to a consistent Christocentric focus or else there is no solution to their self-definition.

There is also virtually nothing in their new book on the pre-tribulational rapture of the church. Indeed, this unique doctrine was based on a consistent distinction between Israel and the church, the parenthesis theory of the church, a literal hermeneutic, that the church did not partake of the Davidic covenant or the New Covenant with Israel, so that when God again begins to deal with Israel, the church must be removed. However, if all these beliefs are either gone or compromised, then it would seem that the pre-tribulational rapture would be gone as well.[20]

We agree with Bruce K. Waltke's assessment of the new book on dispensationalism:

> . . . it does not augur well for the future of dispensationalism. What remains distinctive to dispensationalism pertains to the "not-yet" aspect of the kingdom. The truth that ethnic Israel retains a place in God's redemptive history is not distinctive. . . .[21] At issue is whether or not God has two "true peoples" (true Israel and the church) and whether true Israel has a future role in redemptive history different from the church. If one envisions a Jewish millennium in which the kingdom will be restored to ethnic Israel in the land, the term *dispensationalism* will still be useful. If ethnic Israel's role is only its remnant status on a permanent equality with the Gentiles in the one true people of God with no distinctive role in the land beyond the Parousia, then the term *dispensationalism* ought to be dropped.[22]

---

[20]This may prove difficult for professors at Dallas Theological Seminary who yearly have to sign the DTS doctrinal statement agreeing to the belief.

[21]Indeed, postmillennialists have argued for centuries for a future for ethnic Israel, but this is not tied to the land and not as a separate people but as part of God's one covenant people.

[22]Ibid., p. 354.

Waltke's comments are to the point, but I do not think dispensationalists have really left their roots, as we shall see throughout my section of this book you are reading. Their hermeneutic is still intact though modified; their dualism between the earthly and the heavenly is still there; their Arminianism and antinomianism have not changed; and their view of Old Testament salvation remains basically the same. They are still pursuing eschatology and self-definition rather than overcoming these weaknesses. They simply cannot find themselves. We wonder about animal sacrifices, which the older dispensationalists said would be reinstituted during the so-called millennium, which in light of Hebrews 10 is an abomination. Do these new dispensationalists hold the same? They do not say in this new book. In dispensationalism one can go from the extreme of a Zane Hodges who is blatantly Arminian and antinomian[23] to a John F. MacArthur, Jr., who is Reformed in his soteriology. We do not find such swings among the Reformed, who are, by definition, not Arminian or antinomian.[24]

Since dispensationalists have no formal confession of faith to unite them, I predict that they will either degenerate into many competing camps or hopefully become Reformed (at least more of them).

May the sovereign Triune God be pleased to use this volume to His glory. Amen.

---

[23]The two go together.

[24]There have been some hyper-Calvinists who were antinomian, but these were rare and often Baptists (such as many Primitive Baptists of today).

Chapter One

The "Literal" Hermeneutic

The hermeneutic one uses in interpreting prophecy will determine what he sees. If one understands a literal hermeneutic one way, Israel could not refer to the church nor vice versa; but if literal is understood differently, then Israel and the church could be identified or at least overlapped. This latter concept of literal would certainly rule out a pre-tribulational rapture of the church, since such a concept is predicated on the "church" being removed so God can finish with "Israel." In this chapter we investigate what "literal" means.

As a former dispensationalist I was mesmerized with the literal hermeneutic, the way in which we interpreted the Bible. I was satiated with the confidence that this principle of interpretation was the cornerstone of any true approach to Scripture, and paraded it before all as the bedrock of the dispensational method. This "literal" approach produced in me a calm lethargy to anything the covenant men could say. Any argument they could muster was disarmed in advance with such statements as: "They do not advocate a literal hermeneutic." No one seemed to know precisely what literal meant, but it was always a key word if one wanted to decidedly abolish the opponent. There was a mysticism that shrouded the term, giving it force but little content; it was a fetish of the highest order.

But precisely what does "literal" denote? Dr. Charles C. Ryrie stated that literal ". . . gives to every word the same meaning it would have in normal usage, whether employed in writing, speaking or thinking."[1] Even further, he calls it the "grammatical-historical inter-

---

[1] C. C. Ryrie, *Dispensationalism Today* (Chicago: Moody Press, 1969), p. 86.

pretation" or the "normal way words are understood."[2]

Such comments, however, do very little than restate the problem, for then one must define "normal." Actually it is not so much the formal definition of the term that is objectionable as it is the application of the rule, which allegedly leads to a strong distinction between Israel and the church, resulting in two peoples of God.

Their essence of literal may be better described than defined. It is an insistence that two different words — like Israel and church — *must* denote two distinct entities, and a belief that prophecies, especially Old Testament ones, must be understood only from the Old Testament perspective, not also from the New Testament perspective. To elaborate, if the Old Testament said that Israel would inherit the land forever, this means that national ethnic Israel must have the geographical land spot in the Middle East forever.[3] If one should say that Israel is now a spiritual nation over the whole earth (1 Peter 2:9, 10), that the "land" promise is expanded to include the whole earth (Rom. 4:13), or that the "land" the Old Testament saints anticipated was a heavenly New Jerusalem (Heb. 11:13-16; 12:22; Gal. 4:25, 26), this would violate their concept of literal.

Ryrie adduces three reasons for the dispensational idea of literal. First, ". . . prophecies are to be normally interpreted (i.e. according to the received laws of language) . . . ."[4] But what, it may be retorted, are "the received laws of language" and what is the "sound philosophy of language"? Such statements express an extreme naivete concerning the contemporary philosophical scene and concerning the supposed autonomy of man.

Concerning the philosophical milieu: Since Ludwig Wittgenstein's studies in linguistic analysis, no two philosophers have surfaced such "laws" on which they can agree nor a "*sound*" philosophy of language. The debate still rages, and even in Colin Brown's three volume *Dictionary of New Testament Theology* there is a lengthy article on the differing opinions of such a philosophy (see the article under "Word").

Concerning the supposed autonomy of man: Such statements further indicate that the dispensational hermeneutic is derived from a

---

[2]Ryrie, p. 87.

[3]"Forever" for dispensationalists usually entails one thousand years, not quite forever.

[4]Ryrie, p. 87.

humanistic concept of literal. By assuming the sovereignty of man and the neutrality of philosophy and facts, Ryrie has "straight jacketed" Scripture with his humanistic notion of literal. He has, on his own authority, "rigged the game" so that now he can confidently predict the outcome. God could not equate Israel and the church if He wanted to do so, for this would violate the "sound philosophy of language." Thus he has determined — before entering Scripture — not only *how* God can teach but also to a great extent *what* He can say. But this is only Dr. Ryrie's first reason.

His second reason for the literal hermeneutic is:

> If one does not use the plain, normal, or literal method of interpretation, all objectivity is lost. What check would there be on the variety of interpretations which man's imagination could produce if there were not an objective standard which the literal principle provides?[5]

In response, two things may be noted. On the one hand, the literal method is no check on imagination, for then one must ask how far to go with the literal. As incredible as it may sound, one dispensational author actually states that God has a body since the Bible speaks of God's hands and arms.[6] One professor at Dallas Theological Seminary said that Ezekiel 38 and 39 prophesied horses and swords to come out of Russia to attack Israel in the future and horses and swords they would be — not tanks or planes. (I do not understand these chapters to so predict anything of Russia).

On the other hand, what is the "objective standard" to which Ryrie refers? It seems to be a philosophical rationalism imposed on Scripture from the reader's mind. This seems to be the case as noted from the conversations I had with Dr. Ryrie in seminary and from the course I took from him entitled "Dispensationalism." A major part of this course was a study of hermeneutics, and a large part of the semester was devoted to Dr. Fuller's dissertation, *The Hermeneutics of Dispensationalism*. We always spoke of a literal hermeneutic, but we never precisely defined this nor did we exegete Scripture to derive it. It was always a "philosophical necessity." Is this "objective"? Is the standard for interpreting God's inerrant Word found in errant man?

Ryrie's third reason is: "The prophecies in the Old Testament concerning the first coming of Christ . . . were all fulfilled literally.

---

[5]Ryrie, p. 88.

[6]F. J. Dake, *Dake's Annotated Reference Bible* (Atlanta: Dake Bible Sales, 1965), p. 280 in the New Testament.

There is no non-literal fulfillment of these prophecies in the New Testament.''[7] This pithy remark is so often repeated among dispensationalists that it has virtually become a proverb. And yet this is precisely the reason I am no longer a dispensationalist. What is the apostles' hermeneutic? How did they apply the Old Testament to Christ? Ironically, a course I took at Dallas Theological Seminary entitled "The Old Testament in the New Testament" taught by S. Lewis Johnson, began to open my eyes to the fallacies of the dispensational hermeneutic.[8] At this juncture it may be helpful to investigate some New Testament passages to see what the apostles' method of Old Testament interpretation was, and then I shall use this same hermeneutic to make some suggestions concerning the relationship of Israel to the church.

---

[7]Ryrie, p. 88.

[8]For an excellent discussion of how the dispensationalists evolved their hermeneutic, see George M. Marsden, *Fundamentalism and American Culture* (Oxford, 1982).

Chapter Two

The Apostles' Hermeneutic

Matthew chapter two affords several opportunities to observe the apostles' hermeneutic. Matthew adduces from Scripture that Jesus is the promised Messiah, and in chapter two he conjoins four quotes from the Old Testament. The first quote is Matthew 2:5, 6 from Micah 5:2 (5:1). In the New Testament context Herod inquires where the Christ will be born, and the unanimous response of the Jews is Bethlehem, for so Micah had prophesied. Micah the prophet speaks of the Messiah in 5:2-5a, using exalted thoughts that could only refer to Jesus. In the previous context Micah had spoken of God's judgment on heathen neighbors (4:9-5:1), and now he predicts that the One to come will rule the earth, whose "goings forth are from long ago, from the days of eternity." Such language refers directly to Christ and to His eternal existence. Therefore, this first application of the Old Testament to Christ is direct, or what the dispensationalists would call literal, being pure prophecy about Christ alone in straightforward language.

The second quote in Matthew (2:15) echoes Hosea 11:1, which in turn reflects Exodus 4:22 and other such passages in Exodus. Christ exits Egypt from where He had been hiding from Herod who was murdering the infants. But Hosea and Moses refer to the nation of Israel when they say, "Out of Egypt did I call My Son." How, then, could Matthew say that his quote refers to Christ coming out of Egypt? The answer is that the nation of Israel was a type of the Messiah. The conclusion is that this is a typological fulfillment. In fact many Old Testament persons (David, Joseph), places (tabernacle, temple), and things (sacrifices, lambs) are types, divinely designed to prophesy of the coming Messiah.

Thirdly, when the infants were killed by Herod, Matthew speaks of the event as a fulfillment of Jeremiah 31:15, reflecting Genesis 37, when Rachel wept for her children. What has the murdering of infants in Christ's time to do with Rachel's loss? It is very unlikely that Rachel is a type of Mary and Rachel's children types of Mary's children. Why? Because Mary's children are not killed and the Old Testament types are designed to point to Christ Himself — not usually to some lesser figure. However, the circumstances between the two events are similar. Therefore, it must be concluded that the fulfillment is analogical, the New Testament circumstances being *like* the Old Testament ones.

Finally, Matthew says that Christ resided in the city of Nazareth so that the prophets might be fulfilled: "He shall be called a Nazarene." Which prophet said this? Commentators have searched everywhere to find this quote but remain nonplussed. Matthew uses the word prophets (plural) probably indicating a reference to the sense of what they said. (Did Jesus take a Nazarite vow?) This is probably a fulfillment according to sense.

Matthew then gives four different kinds of use in chapter two: direct (v. 5), typical (v. 15), analogical (vv. 17, 18), and according to sense (v. 23). In each instance — except the direct or "literal" — Matthew says the Old Testament prophecy was *fulfilled*.

There is at least one other way the New Testament writers use the Old Testament concerning the Messiah, and this is found in Hebrews 1:10-12. This passage is quoted from Psalm 102:25-27, and the Old Testament context speaks only of Yahweh. The author of Hebrews applies the passage to Christ (see 1:8, 9). When an Old Testament text that only speaks of Yahweh is applied to Jesus, this may be termed the eschatological Yahweh fulfillment.[1]

There are, therefore, five kinds of fulfillment of the Old Testament in the New Testament as applied to Christ. It may be helpful at this point to devise a table of all the New Testament passages that apply Old Testament texts to Christ's first coming, and notice the kinds of fulfillment. (We follow the New Testament in canonical order, with each change in the New Testament books noted by putting the book in bold print.)

---

[1] S. Lewis Johnson, Jr., Notes from class at Dallas Theological Seminary, 1976.

Summary of Old Test. Prophecies About Christ

New Testament	Old Testament	Fulfillment
Matt. 1:23	Isa. 7:14	Direct (typical ?)
2:5	Micah 5:2	Direct
2:15	Hosea 11:1	Typical
2:18	Jer. 31:15	Analogical
2:23	OT in general	According to sense
4:1-4	Deut. 8:1-3	Analogical (typical ?)
10:35, 36	Micah 7:6	Analogical
11:5a	Isa. 35:5ff	Analogical
11:5b (Luke 4:18, 10)	Isa. 61:1	Direct
12:18-21	Isa. 42:1-4	Direct
13:35	Ps. 78:2	Typical
16:27	Ps. 62:12	Typical
21:4, 5	Zech. 9:9	Direct
21:9	Ps. 118:26ff.	Typical
21:42 (Acts 4:11; 1 Peter 2:7; Rom. 9:33)	Ps. 118:22	Typical
22:43-45 (Acts 2:34; Mark 12:36; Luke 20:42, 43)	Ps. 110:1	Direct
24:30	Dan. 7:13, 14 (See Zech. 12:10, 14)	Direct
26:31	Zech. 13:7	Direct
27:9, 10	Jer. 18:2; 19:2, 11; 32:6-9: Zech. 11:12,13	According to sense from Jer. & Direct
27:34	Ps. 69:21	Typical
27:35 (Mark 15:24; Luke 23:34; John 19:24; 27:39)	Ps. 22:18	Typical
27:39 (Mark 15:29)	Ps. 22:7	Typical
27:43	Ps. 22:8	Typical
27:46	Ps. 22:1	Typical
Mark 1:2	Mal 3:1	Direct
1:3	Isa. 40:3	Direct
11:9, 10 (John 12:13)	Ps. 11:25, 26	Typical (Esch Yah?)
12:11	Ps. 118:23	Typical
12:36	Ps. 69:21	Typical

New Testament	Old Testament	Fulfillment
14:18 (John 13:18)	Ps. 41:9	Typical
14:24	Isa. 53:12	Direct
	Ex.24:8	Typical
14:27	Zech. 13:7	Direct
14:34	Ps. 42:5, 11	Typical
14:62	Ps. 110:1; Dan. 7:13	Direct
Luke 22:37	Isa. 53:12	Direct
23:46	Ps. 31:5	Typical
John 2:17	Ps. 69:9	Typical
3:14	Num. 21:9	Typical
6:31, 35	Ex. 16:15; Num. 11:7-9	Typical
7:42a	2 Sam. 7:12	Typical
7:42b	Micah 5:2	Direct
12:15	Zech. 9:9	Direct
15:25	Ps. 35:19; 69:4	Typical
19:28	Ps. 22:15	Typical
19:29	Ps. 69:21	Typical
19:36	Ex. 12:46	Typical
19:37	Zech. 12:10	Direct
Acts 1:10	Ps. 69:25; 109:8	Typical
2:25-28 (Acts 13:35)	Ps. 16:8-11	Typical
3:22, 25	Deut. 18:15, 16, 19	Direct
4:25, 26	Ps. 2:1, 2	Direct
8:32, 33	Isa. 53:7, 8	Direct
13:37	Ps. 2:7	Direct
Rom. 9:33; 10:11 (1 Peter 2:6; Matt. 21:42; Mark 12:10; Luke 20:17; Acts 4:11)	Isa. 28:16	Typical
10:13	Joel 3:5	Esch. Yah
11:26, 27	Isa. 59:20, 21	Direct
1 Cor. 5:7	Ex. 12:11	Typical
2 Cor. 3:16	Ex. 34:34	Esch. Yah
Gal. 3:16	Gen. 13:15; 17:7; 24:7	Typical
Phil. 2:10, 11	Isa. 45:23	Esch. Yah
2 Thess. 1:9	Isa. 2:20	Esch. Yah

New Testament	Old Testament	Fulfillment
2:8	Isa. 11:4	Direct
Titus 2:14	Ps. 130:8	Esch. Yah
	Ezra 37:23	Typical
	Deut. 14:2	Typical
Heb. 1:5	Ps. 2:7	Direct
1:6	Deut. 32:43; Ps. 97:7 (LXX)	Esch. Yah
1:8, 9	Ps. 45:6, 7	Typical
1:10-12	Ps. 102:25-27	Esch. Yah
2:5-8	Ps. 8:4-6	Typical
2:12	Ps. 22:22	Typical
2:13	Isa. 8:17, 18	Typical
5:6	Ps. 110:4	Direct
6:19	Lev. 6:12	Typical
10:5-7	Ps. 40:6-8	Typical
1 Peter 2:8	Isa. 8:14	Typical
2:22	Isa. 53:9	Direct
2:24, 25	Isa. 53:4-6	Direct
2 Peter 1:17	Ps. 2:7	Direct
	Gen. 22:2	Typical
	Isa. 42:1	Direct
Rev. 1:7a	Dan. 7:13	Direct
1:7b	Zech. 12:10	Direct
2:26, 27	Ps. 2:8, 9	Direct
3:7	Isa. 22:22	Typical

This table covers most of the direct quotes or strong allusions to prophecies of Christ's first coming cited in the New Testament from the Old Testament (I may have missed some). Out of 97 Old Testament prophecies only 34 were directly or literally fulfilled, which is only 35.05 percent. Did not Ryrie say *none* were fulfilled in a non-literal manner? Do not the New Testament writers apply texts to Christ that one may be tempted to question (if he has a rationalistic concept of literal)? Whose concept of fulfillment should be used, Man's or God's? Someone may say that the apostles had esoteric insight into the Old Testament so that no one today could mimic their approach. However, we would respond that the Apostles' hermeneutic is used on the basis of Scripture, whose hermeneutic would the objector use? S. Lewis Johnson, the former New Testament department head at Dallas Theological Seminary, concludes the same in his excellent book:

> Since they [the apostles] are reliable teachers of biblical doctrine, they are also reliable teachers of hermeneutical and exegetical procedures. It is just this that is lacking in so much of our biblical interpretation today. Failing to examine the methodology of the scriptural writers carefully, and following too abjectly and woodenly the limited rules and principles of human reason's presuppositions, we have stumbled and lost our landmarks along the pathway toward the understanding of Holy Scripture. *Scriptura sui ipsius interpres* [Scripture is its own interpreter] is the fundamental principle of biblical interpretation. The analogy of faith pertains to both doctrine and exegesis.[2]

Or again this dispensational (?) writer concludes:

> In the final analysis the biblical interpreter is interested not only in what the inspired author meant but also in what God meant. Therefore, *the New Testament understanding of the Old Testament is the true understanding of it* [emphasis added], because it supplies the reader not simply with what Moses and the prophets understood but also with what the Holy Spirit understood, gave to them, and empowered them to write down.[3]

In *Dispensationalism, Israel and the Church* the claim is made that the literal hermeneutic is no longer a part of the evolving, progressive dispensationalism, that it has been dropped. We would like to believe this, but in reading the book we discovered the idea is still solidly entrenched. Repeatedly we read that ethnic Israel will still inherit the land for this is the "literal" fulfillment of the Old Testament promises.[4] At other times the use of the "literal" method of interpretation controlled what the new brand of dispensationalists saw. For example, in Luke 22:16 when the Lord said that He would not eat the Passover again "until it is fulfilled in the kingdom of God," this is said to have no reference to the Lord's Supper since the Supper is not mentioned specifically.[5] To bring other passages to bear and draw the

---

[2] S. Lewis Johnson, Jr., *The Old Testament in the New* (Grand Rapids: Zondervan, 1980), p. 83.

[3] Johnson, p. 94.

[4] Blaising, *Dispensationalism, Israel and the Church*, pp. 93, 94, etc.

[5] Ibid., p. 59.

obvious inference would violate the "literal" interpretation.

Repeatedly we observed that the writers of this new dispensational book would not draw the obvious inference but required God to say something specifically before they would conclude the text taught something. A sample of this is Carl B. Hoch, Jr., who wrote that Paul did not mean to teach in Ephesians 2 that the church is the new Israel but only that Gentiles *share* in the promises with ethnic Israel.[6] The reason for this conclusion is that Paul did not specifically say the Gentiles were now *members* of Israel or *in* Israel. "Paul . . . cannot be arguing for a Gentile incorporation into Israel. . . . Paul never writes of Gentiles as 'in Israel' in any of his letters."[7] In other words, the "literal" hermeneutic led this author to twist Paul's statements that Gentiles are now *fellow* citizens with Israel (see Chapter 4 and our comments on Eph. 2) to mean *sharers* in the covenant with Israel but not citizens in Israel. God must say things according to Hoch's definition of literal or they are taken to mean the opposite of what they say.

Indeed, there are times when the writers in the new dispensational book despair in trying to understand passages,[8] which is understandable given their penchant for demanding that exact words must be used or else the biblical writer is not understood. Another example is 1 Peter 2:6-10 where Peter, using Old Testament words that only spoke of Israel, quotes Hosea that the church is "now God's people" and "now has received mercy," and the church is "a chosen generation, a royal priesthood, *a holy nation*, His own special people." But one of the authors of the new dispensational book concludes that Peter did not mean the church is the true Israel because he did not literally say they were "a *new* Israel" or "a *new* people."[9] Apparently, saying "a holy nation" and all the other expressions is not sufficient, and allegedly Peter did not intend his readers to take the obvious inference that they are now God's Israel. The only thing that counts is saying so specifically or "literally."

In other words, the New Testament cannot interpret Old Testament Israel differently than what these dispensationalists conceive it to be for two reasons: the Old Testament must be understood from its own

---

[6]Ibid., p. 108.

[7]Ibid., p. 113.

[8]Ibid., pp. 111, 242.

[9]Ibid., p. 157.

perspective apart from the New Testament, and the Old Testament patriarchs surely understood that they would have the land in the middle East forever. These two fatal flaws are related, denying that we should understand the Old Testament the way Christ and the Apostles did, as Peter tells us to do in 1 Peter 1:10, 11 and Christ in Luke 24:45ff. In contrast, the literal Old Testament words are not always the ultimate meaning that the divine Author had in mind. The Old Testament *must* be understood from the perspective of the New Testament or we will miss the meaning.

The Old Testament saints had more insight than we sometimes think, for Moses considered the reproaches of *Christ* to be of greater value than all the wealth of Egypt, "for he looked to the reward" (Heb. 11:26). Abraham rejoiced to *Jesus'* day (John 8:56); Paul interpreted the land promises to Abraham to include the world (Rom. 4:13) and apparently so did Christ (Matt. 28:18). The Jerusalem that Abraham and many other Old Testament saints looked for was the "heavenly Jerusalem" (Heb. 12:22), "whose builder and maker is God" (Heb. 11:10) — not a spot in the middle East. And this is taking the New Testament literally! We could compound the obvious.

In spite of the new dispensational book, we conclude that the New Testament writers see the Old Testament as bud and the New Testament as flower, whether the New Testament fulfills the Old Testament directly, typically, analogically, by general sense, or by eschatological Yahweh. Furthermore, as Dr. Johnson pointed out, this *is* the true understanding of the Old Testament. Anything else than the apostles' hermeneutic is based on speculative human reasoning.[10]

---

[10]We understand that these various methods of fulfillment do not exhaust all the possibilities, but our point is that most of the Old Testament prophecies were not fulfilled literally.

Chapter Three

Application of the Apostles' Hermeneutic

Just as the apostles applied Old Testament passages to Christ that one might be enticed to discredit initially, so these same apostles, using the same hermeneutic, applied many Old Testament texts to the New Testament church that originally only referred to Israel. The New Testament authors never contradicted the Old Testament, but saw its true expansion and fulfillment in the New Testament church (bud to flower again); and they defined Israel and church differently than the dispensationalists do. (Dispensationalists prefer to force the New Testament into their Old Testament understanding of Israel rather than allow the New Testament to interpret the Old.) We shall see this concept in Hebrews chapter two, and then survey the New Testament for the same approach.

The author of Hebrews in chapter two is demonstrating the humanity of Christ (vv. 11, 17): He tasted death for all (v. 9), was made perfect through sufferings (v. 10), destroyed the power of Satan and death (vv. 14, 15), is a merciful High Priest who understands and helps His children (vv. 14, 17), and made propitiation for the sins of the people (v. 17).

The first quote in Hebrews two is from Psalm 22:22. The Psalm is by David, containing the introduction (vv. 1-10), lament (vv. 11-21), and trust in God with joy (vv. 22-31). Some understand it to be directly applied to Christ as pure Messianic prophecy. Since, however, David seems to write the Psalm with himself in mind (v. 1 in Hebrew text,

vv. 11-13 in English), it is better to side with Keil and Delitzsch and label it typical.[1] The words transcend David, being elevated to prophecy.

> The same God who communicates His thoughts of redemption to the mind of men, and there causes them to develop into the word of prophetic announcement, has also molded the history itself into a prefiguring representation of the future deliverance; and the evidence for the truth of Christianity which is derived from this factual prophecy is as grand as that derived from the verbal prediction.[2]

The second quote is taken from Isaiah 8:17, 18. It is clear that Isaiah is the one speaking (vv. 11, 16, 19). Even his children had names with prophetic significance: Shearjashub ("Remnant will return"), Mahershalalhashbaz ("Hasten the booty, speed the spoil").[3] Hebrews sees Isaiah as a type of Christ. Observe these parallels between Isaiah and Christ: In Isaiah's time a national hardening was beginning (vv. 14, 15, 17), in Christ's time the hardening was completed (John 12:37-40); Isaiah and his children were a believing remnant (vv. 17, 18), and Christ has a remnant (John 6: 37-40, 44, 45; Matt. 11:25-27; Heb. 2:9f); Isaiah and Christ trusted in God (Heb. 2:13a); and both have children given to them by God (Heb. 2:13b).

Now the point is to emphasize who the people are that Christ came to redeem. In v. 9 He tasted death for "all." But who are the "all"? In v. 10 the "all" are the "many sons," in v. 11 they are "those who are sanctified" and "the brethren," in v. 12 "the church," v. 13 "the children whom God had given" to Christ, v. 16 "the seed of Abraham," and in v. 17 "*the* people." The following points are especially prominent: (1) The "church" in v. 12 is derived from Old Testament Israel in a typological manner and applied to the New Testament reader. Just as Christ tasted death for His Old Testament and New Testament brethren, so they are united in this one church.

(2) The "children given" to Christ in v. 13 no doubt refer to the elect and are synonymous with the church in this context (see also John 6:37-39, 44, 45; 17:1-12). Yet these elect are the Old Testament and New Testament church gathered into one group and called "chil-

---

[1] Keil & Delitzsch, *Old Testament Commentary*, 6 vols (Grand Rapids: Associated Authors & Publishers, 1971), vol.3, pp. 1062-63.

[2] K & D, p. 1063.

[3] F. F. Bruce, *The Epistle to the Hebrews*, NIC Series (Grand Rapids: Eerdmans, 1975), p. 48.

dren." Or, in the words of Ephesians 1:4, 5, all the elect of all ages are identified with Christ, being chosen before the foundation of the world to be in Christ, and were represented by Him when He came. There can be no salvation at any time outside of Jesus the Lord. If salvation is *only* in Christ, then the Old Testament saints are in Christ; and if they are in Christ, they are in the church. Therefore, the "brethren," the "church," and the "children" are one group composed from both Testaments and are given to Christ. We do not see two churches or two groups of children. This is how the Apostles applied Old Testament passages to the church, thereby considering the Old Testament fulfilled.

(3) Who are the "seed of Abraham" if not the church and yet at the same time the Old Testament "brethren"? Does Paul not say that the true seed of Abraham has always been believers in Christ, which seed began at Abraham and continues through today (Gal. 3:29; 4:28; 6:16; Rom. 2:28, 29)?

(4) The reference to "*the* people" in v. 17 is not without tremendous import. The Greek word for people (*laos*) is used in the Septuagint hundreds of times and nearly always in the singular and of Israel. Indeed, "It (*laos*) serves to emphasize the special and privileged religious position of this people as the people of God."[4] How could Hebrews apply this to New Testament believers unless the church is God's Israel? Even though not specifically stated, this is the obvious conclusion.

There are numerous applications of this same hermeneutic throughout the New Testament. A quick survey of the New Testament should prove how satiated the apostles were with seeing the Old Testament passages that spoke of Israel as fulfilled in the church as the new Israel.

Just before the survey, though, I should mention an objection that was common when I was attending Dallas Seminary. Ryrie and others would often say that a figure of speech in a passage does not allow one to spiritualize the whole passage. No one is saying, however, that we should spiritualize passages. The following survey, combined with the previous study of the apostles' hermeneutic, should indicate that we covenant believers are not spiritualizing whole passages. Rather, we are honestly seeking to understand words and concepts as the

---

[4]Gerard Kittel, *Theological Dictionary of the New Testament*, 10 volumes (Grand Rapids: Eerdmans, 1969), 4:32.

apostles intended them to be taken. The puerile comment by J. Vernon McGee on national radio that people are liberal who do not understand the Old Testament prophecies to give ethnic Israel Palestine forever is to besmirch the brethren without understanding them. We could make the same charge because he does not take the apostles' hermeneutic seriously, but we know that he is genuine in his desire to understand Scripture. Keeping in mind the hermeneutic of the Twelve, please peruse the following.

In Ephesians 2 those who were formerly outside Israel (v. 11) are now no longer outside (vv. 13, 19), those once excluded from citizenship in Israel (v. 12) are now *fellow* citizens with *the* saints (the Jews) and members of God's household (not two households).

The church is called Israel (Heb. 2:9-18; Eph. 2:11ff; Gal. 6:16; Rom. 9:6, 24-29) and Israel the church (Matt. 18:17; Acts 7:38; Heb. 2:12).

God has *one* flock composed of Jews and Gentiles (John 10:16; Eph. 2:11ff). God has *one* house with Moses and Christ over the *same* house (Heb. 3:2-6).

The church is heir to the New Covenant (Heb. 8) and to the promises made to Israel, such as: (1) the Holy Spirit (Luke 24:49; Acts 1:4; 2:23, 39); (2) the Messiah (Jer. 33:14-18; Acts 7:17; 13:23, 32; 26:6); (3) justification and eternal life (Eph. 2:11-3:7; Rom. 4:13-20; Heb. 6:15; 9:15; 10:36; 11:13, 39).

God is rebuilding David's tabernacle *now* (Acts 15:15-18), which means the "tabernacle" is the church.

The leaders of Israel and of the church are equated as the *one* bride of Christ (Rev. 21:9, 12, 14), and the analogy of marriage is applied to God and His people in both Testaments (Isa. 54:5; Jer. 3:14; 6:2; 31:32; Hosea 2:19; 2 Cor. 11:2; Eph. 5:23-33). Does Christ have an Old Testament bride and a New Testament bride? Is He a bigamist?

New Testament saints are perfected *concomitantly* with Old Testament saints in *one* body (Heb. 11:39, 40).

James writes to the twelve tribes (1:1), to the synagogue (2:2), and to the church (5:14).

The church is engrafted into the stalk of Israel (Rom. 11).

Leonhard Goppelt, in his excellent book entitled *TYPOS, The Typological Interpretation of the Old Testament in the New*, points out the following factors that indicate Jesus (and the apostles under Him) created a "new people of God and the true Israel":

> The number twelve is clearly an allusion to the twelve tribes of Israel.

This interpretation is confirmed in the New Testament. What Jesus says to Peter in Matthew 16:18 applies to all the twelve. Their names are on the foundation stones of the walls of the new Jerusalem, the perfect church, whose twelve gates bear the names of the twelve tribes of Israel. Therefore, the new Jerusalem represents the twelve new tribes, the new Israel (Rev. 21:12-14; cf. Eph. 2:20).[5]

Goppelt lists other figures used to indicate the new Israel: plantation to indicate God's care of His people (Isa. 5:1ff.; Jer. 2:21; Psalm 80:8ff; Mark 12:1ff; Matt. 21:41), church as a flock (Mark 14:27; Zech. 13:7; Matt. 9:36; 15:24; Isa. 41:14; Dan. 7:27; John 10:1ff), the Passover and the Lord's Supper related as bud to flower (Luke 22:15; Mark 14:17; 1 Cor. 11:23; 5:7; Matt. 26:28).[6]

The true line of Abraham, as was noted earlier, has always been those of faith. Christ deprecated those physically born of Abraham and not spiritually born as having the devil for a father (John 8:37-44), for those who were Israelites *indeed* (John 1:47) would listen to Him (John 8:44-47). In other words, "not all Israel is Israel" (Rom. 9:6ff). The dispensationalists disagree with the Lord and say the one physically born is *indeed* a true Israelite, favored of God, and *automatically* heir to the "promises," which promises include the land. If this were so, then why did the Lord call some Jews "of the devil"? (Notice above how the apostles interpreted the promises: the Holy Spirit, eternal life, adoption, not the land, etc.).

The Southern theologian R. L. Dabney argued this way:[7] It was promised to Abraham that *all* nations would be blessed in Him (Acts 3:23-25). This was only fulfilled as the Gentiles were made members of the Abrahamic covenant (Rom. 4:16, 17). Before the Gentiles were brought in, the blessing was limited to *one* nation — Israel. If the Abrahamic covenant expired before the Gentiles were engrafted, or a parenthesis occurred leaving out the Gentiles, then the promise was never fulfilled. *All* nations were not blessed. Yet the New Testament says the promise was fulfilled. Today the heirs of the promise made to Abraham are not one nation in one geographical location but a spiritual nation from all the nations of the world (1 Peter 2:9, 10). It

[5]Loenhard Goppelt, *Typos, the Typological Interpretation of the Old Testament in the New* (Grand Rapids: Eerdmans, 1982), p. 107.

[6]Goppelt, pp. 106-116.

[7]Robert L. Dabney, *Lectures in Systematic Theology* (Grand Rapids: Zondervan, 1975), pp. 282ff.

is patently inconsistent for dispensationalists to maintain that the church partakes of some of the "spiritual" blessings of Abraham but the physical blessings are yet in the future for the "real" Israel. It was prophesied that the Gentiles would be blessed and be heirs to confirm the promises — all of them — made to the Jews. Paul's statements are clear:

> For I say that Christ has become a servant to the circumcision on behalf of the truth of God *to confirm the promises given to the fathers, and for the Gentiles to glorify God for His mercy*; as it is written, "Therefore I will give praise to Thee among the *Gentiles*, and I will sing to Thy name." And again He says, "Rejoice, O *Gentiles*, with His people." And again, "Praise the Lord all you *Gentiles*, and let all the peoples praise Him." And again Isaiah says, "There shall come the Root of Jesse, and He who arises to rule over the *Gentiles*, in Him shall the *Gentiles* hope" (Rom. 15:8-12).

The Old Testament biblical covenants, all would surely grant, were made with Old Testament Israel down through the centuries. If the Gentiles are heirs to the "covenants of promise" *along with the Jews* (see also Eph. 2:11ff), the conclusion is inescapable that the church is the continuation of God's Israel.

Dispensationalists erect again the dividing wall that Christ abolished in His flesh, namely, the Old Testament ceremonial law that made them distinct, which sacrifices will supposedly be reinstituted in the millennium. But Christ has offered one final sacrifice forever that completely eliminated the Old Testament ceremonial law. The bloody sacraments of the Old Testament (circumcision and Passover) have been replaced by non-bloody ones in the New Testament (baptism and Lord's Supper). To reinstitute bloody sacraments would be an abomination. Furthermore, Christ has now made the two (Jew and Gentile) "into *one new* man," having "reconciled them *both* in one body to God" (Eph. 2:15, 16). Dispensationalists are inconsistent, maintaining from the New Testament that the Gentiles are heirs to Abraham's promise but excluding the Gentiles from the Old Testament Abrahamic promise. It is not possible to have it both ways. Either they must use the apostles' hermeneutic and conclude that we are heirs to the promises and there is no more (what more could one want than Christ?), or else use their Old Testament "literal" hermeneutic and conclude that the Gentiles are not in the covenant (contrary to the New Testament) and not heirs to anything.

Also, dispensationalists try to explain the above survey of passages by showing how the passages can harmonize with their dispensationalism, but this is circular reasoning, trying to harmonize passages with a theology already derived. Instead, they should deduce their theology from the verses themselves. Just as the apostles used Old Testament passages to apply to Christ by literal, typical, analogical and other means, so also they used the same method to say that the church is heir to the promises. A fitting conclusion is by William Hendriksen as quoted by Bruce Waltke:

> The New Testament recognizes only *one* vine, *one* good olive tree, *one* body, *one* elect race, *one* royal priesthood, *one* holy nation, *one* people for God's own possession, *one* bride, *one* holy city, having the names of the apostles written on its foundations and the names of the tribes on its gates.[8]

---

[8]Blaising, *Dispensationalism, Israel and the Church*, p. 354.

Chapter Four

An Exercise in Biblical Hermeneutics

Now that we have examined the dispensational hermeneutic, we must derive a better approach to the interpretation of the Bible. Certainly we must not erect rules of interpretation before we enter the text, mapping out the sea prior to our virgin voyage, such as interpreting "literally." And we have seen that the New Testament writers may set a different course than what we may be tempted to call literal. It would seem, therefore, that we should observe the Scripture's definition of its own terms, and not force our understanding of literal on the text. As S. Lewis Johnson observed, we must sail hermeneutically in the apostles' ship, and not bring our own ship. We must not have a literal or a non-literal hermeneutic. Perhaps a concrete example would help.

In Matthew 24:29 the Lord Jesus says, "But immediately after the tribulation of those days the sun will be darkened, and the moon will not give its light, and the stars will fall from the sky, and the powers of the heavens will be shaken."[1] Dispensationalists usually say that the literal sun must stop giving out light and warmth, and the literal stars must fall for this passage to be fulfilled. However, apart from the fact that for the sun to stop shining would mean a frozen planet and

[1] The Greek word for "stars" does not seem to mean meteors. The Bauer lexicon lists only one time where *aster* may mean meteor and this is figurative (second edition), pp. 117-18.

that most of the stars are millions of times larger than the earth and would immediately annihilate it, we should investigate what the *Bible* means by the terms "sun and moon." These words are used in numerous other texts that could shed light on their meaning.

Matthew 24:29 seems to refer to Isaiah 13:10; 24:23; Ezekiel 32:7. Isaiah 13:1 is the progenitor and the oracle is against Babylon in which God predicts its destruction: "The day of the Lord is coming, cruel, with fury and burning anger, to make the land a desolation; and He will exterminate its sinners from it" (v. 9). Was this fulfilled? Was Babylon destroyed? No one doubts that Babylon was indeed destroyed by the Medo-Persian empire. And even though this prophecy was realized, God says in v. 10: "The stars of heaven and their constellations will not flash forth their light; the sun will be dark when it rises, and the moon will not shed its light." And v. 10 is given as an explanation of why the judgment in v. 9 was sure. Therefore, whatever the sun and moon mean, it has been fulfilled and they have never darkened. J. A. Alexander, in his excellent commentary on Isaiah, observes what the sun and moon motif probably means: "This natural and striking figure for sudden and disastrous change is of frequent occurrence in Scripture (see Isa. 24:23; 34:4; Ez. 32:7, 8; Joel 2:10; 3:15; Amos 8:9; Matt. 24:29)."[2] This explanation is certainly palatable with the context of Isaiah 13, namely, "sudden and disastrous change" and especially is used of fallen leaders.

Similarly, Isaiah 24:23 declares that the "moon will be abashed and the sun ashamed, for the glory of the Lord of hosts will reign on Mount Zion and in Jerusalem, and (His) glory will be before His elders." The Lord seems to be saying that "before the splendour of Jehovah's reign all lesser principalities and powers shall fade away" and that "all inferior luminaries were to be eclipsed."[3] Indeed, the Lord is reigning now from Zion (Psalm 2:7-9; Acts 2:33-36; 1 Cor. 15:23-25) so that all other leaders have fallen. Hence the passage is fully realized.

The same type of language is in the judgment of Edom in Isaiah 34:4, 5: "And all the host of heaven will wear away, and the sky will be rolled up like a scroll; all their hosts will also wither away . . . For My sword is satiated in heaven, it shall descend for judgment upon

---

[2] J. A. Alexander, *The Prophecies of Isaiah* (Grand Rapids: Zondervan, 1974), p. 275.

[3] Alexander, p. 411.

Edom." "Surely, no one will maintain that when the judgment of God came upon Idumea [Edom], the hosts of heaven were literally dissolved and the heavens actually rolled together as a scroll with all the stars falling down like leaves from a vine!"[4] If the heavens were dissolved, then were they recreated for us today? God is emphasizing that the leaders were suddenly put down.

Again in Ezekiel 32:7, 8 God decrees Egypt's judgment: "And when I extinguish you, I will cover the heavens, and darken the stars; I will cover the sun with a cloud, and the moon shall not give its light. All the shining lights in the heavens I will darken over you and will set darkness on your land." Marcellus Kik's comments are to the point:

> Within the context of Ezekiel 32 the judgment against Egypt was personalized in a lamentation for Pharaoh, king of Egypt, who was compared to the young lion and a dragon amidst the nation. Ezekiel prophesied that the king of Babylon would spoil the pomp of Egypt and destroy the inhabitants of that land. Again the vivid imagery of the sun, moon, and stars being darkened is used by the prophet to depict the end of the glory of Egypt.
>
> If the Holy Spirit, speaking through the prophet Ezekiel, uses such figurative language to describe the downfall of Egypt and its Pharaoh, how much more would not such language be used to describe the downfall of the nation of Israel.[5]

Therefore, according to the *Bible's* usage, the literal stars, sun, and moon do not have to be fallen, blotted out, or darkened for Matthew 24 to be fulfilled. Some think that vv. 29-31 were realized at the Ascension. Whether it is accomplished already or not is beyond our scope, but the fact remains that to speak of the destruction of the stars, sun, and moon — according to biblical usage, not man's "literal" understanding — is figurative for God's "sudden and disastrous change," emphasizing the fall of the rulers of the said fallen nations.

Acts 2:20 is another example and refers to Joel 2:10, 31. Acts 2:20 says, "The sun shall be turned into darkness, and the moon into blood." Is this fulfilled? Peter says in v. 16 that "this *is* what was spoken through the prophet, Joel." It is difficult to imagine a more straightforward and candid statement that Joel's prophecy was verily

---

[4]J. Marcellus Kik, *An Eschatology of Victory* (Phillipsburg: Presbyterian and Reformed, 1971), p. 131.

[5]Kik, pp. 131-32.

fulfilled. The copulative "is" certainly states that the Pentecost of Acts two is the prophecy of Joel. And this is indubitably taking Peter literally! Also we know from the Qumran caves that there was a *pesher midrash* style of exposition that used the "this is that" formula to refer to Scripture and its fulfillment.[6] As a matter of fact, the New Testament uses this style of fulfillment frequently, using the Greek words *houtos estin* ["this is"] (Rom. 9:7-9; 10:6-8; Eph. 5:31ff; Gal. 4:22-24; 1 Cor. 10:1-5, 6ff; Acts 2:4; 4:10ff).[7] Even this formula is supported by the usage of Scripture and not by the imagination of the interpreter, and the reader will notice (if he looks up each of these passages) that each of the passages cited above was considered fulfilled by the New Testament authors.

Furthermore, the other events in Acts two were fulfilled: the Spirit poured out (v. 17), sons and daughters prophesying (v. 17), and people saved by calling on the name of the Lord (v. 21). Yet most dispensationalists (because of their concept of literal) maintain that vv. 19, 20 are somehow not fulfilled. But we must ask, Which takes precedence, man's concept of literal or God's fulfillment?

The moderate dispensationalists have now conceded that *most* of this passage has been fulfilled, but they still hold out that not all has been fulfilled since the sun has not literally stopped shining.[8] But this is not to understand the Bible's own use of its terms. Bock even concedes that Jesus is now ruling on David's throne, which is in heaven,[9] but somehow he cannot take the same hermeneutic and see that the darkened sun and moon motif is defined throughout Scripture in a non-literal way of fallen leaders.

Dispensationalists say we are not to "spiritualize" a whole passage if it contains a figure of speech. But do they "literalize" (my word) away a whole passage because a few words do not coincide with their concept of literal? The sword has two edges. How do they relegate half of this passage to the future or for a second "far fulfillment" when the contexts before and after the sun and moon motif indicate fulfillment? From what other texts do they derive their meaning of sun and moon? Again I conclude that Alexander's "sud-

---

[6]I. Howard Marshall, *New Testament Interpretation* (Grand Rapids: Eerdmans, 1979), p. 206.

[7]Marshall, pp. 207-08.

[8]David L. Bock in *Dispensationalism, Israel and the Church*, p. 47ff.

[9]Ibid., p. 50.

den and disastrous change" observation applies, especially to Israel's fallen religious leaders. God suddenly moved from one Israel to another Israel, from Old Testament Israel to New Testament Israel, and the events were cataclysmic in purview. Messiah had tabernacled among men; the devil was thwarted; Jesus was triumphant Lord and Christ, His enthronement firmly authenticated — this was undoubtedly "sudden and disastrous" and final regarding Israel's leaders. God uses the figures that He had always used to indicate this: the sun darkened and the moon turned to blood.

Revelation 6:12, 13 is no different. We have already seen that the stars cannot literally fall to the earth (v. 13) since they are larger than the earth; the sky rolled up (v. 14) was already determined not literal above (Isa. 34:4); every mountain and island moved would cause instant destruction of the earth and is also used in a non-literal way in Scripture (Isa. 54:10; Jer. 4:24; Ez. 38:20; Nahum 1:5; Rev. 16:20).

From consistency of usage we have "tested the mettle" of the Reformed hermeneutic and have not found it wanting. The Reformed hermeneutic is not literal nor spiritual, but surrendered to the usage, regulation, and amelioration of the infallible Word. We are not impervious to but impelled by the hermeneutic of the apostles. We sail in the wake of their example, "taking every thought captive" to their understanding of Scripture.

Israel and the Church: Definitions

Perhaps another example of a biblical hermeneutic would be helpful. At Dallas Theological Seminary we were constantly mimicking the professors who said Israel means Israel, the church means the church, and the two are never "confused" in Scripture. We were inculcated to this distinction, the whole distinction, and nothing but the distinction, so help us dispensationalism. I deemed this an accurate observation at the time. Later I discovered the Israel-church relationship to be a vignette, being difficult to discern when Israel faded into the church, the two forming one picture. Let us see how *Scripture* defines "Israel" and "church."

Israel

In Genesis 32:28 Israel was the personal name of Jacob. By the time we arrive at Exodus, Israel is the name of the Jewish nation (5:1; 12:3, etc.). Then we have the remnant of Israel (Isa. 46:3; Jer. 6:9), which is probably the elect within the nation. Israel meant at least three things within the Old Testament then.

One of the most important passages in the Bible in defining Israel is Romans 9-11, where Paul explains who the true Israel are and how God saves them. All through the chapters Paul uses the word "Israel" in two senses: Physical Israel (9:4, 6b, 27, 31; 10:1, 19, 21; 11:2, 7, 25) and true spiritual Israel (9:6a, 27 [by inference]; 11:26). Also the words "remnant" and "His people" are synonymous to the true elect Israel (9:27; 11:1, 2, 5). Observe the following outline:

I. 9:1-13: The True Israel

II. 9:14-23: How God Saves the True Israel

III. 9:24-29: Gentiles and Jews Part of God's True Israel

IV. 9:30-10:21: Gentiles Accept; Christ Jews Reject Him

V. 11:1-32: If Jews Reject Christ, Has God Forgotten Israel? No.

A. God has not permanently rejected ethnic Israel, vv. 1-10.

B. The salvation of the world will come to pass when God again accepts ethnic Israel, vv. 11-15.

C. The Gentiles are now being grafted into ethnic Israel's olive tree, vv. 16-24.

D. Both the Gentiles and ethnic Israel will be saved, vv. 25-36, though not all of either group.

I. 9:1-13: The True Israel

Paul, in Romans 9:6, states of the promises to the Israelites (vv. 3-5) that they will be realized, "For they are not all Israel who are (descended) from Israel." Here we have Israel of the flesh and Israel of the Spirit, and the true Israel is the remnant, the elect out of physical Israel. Or as Thayer rightly observes of Israel in his lexicon: ". . . not all those that draw their bodily descent from Israel are true Israelites, i.e., are those whom God pronounces to be Israelites and has chosen to salvation, Rom. 9:6" (p. 307). Again, Paul's point is that physical Israel is not the true Israel: "*It is not the children of the flesh who are children of God, but the children of the promise are regarded as seed*" (v. 8).

II. 9:14-23: How God Saves the True Israel

And to emphasize that the choice is God's and not strictly by physical descent from Abraham, Paul cites the Old Testament: "Jacob I loved, but Esau I hated." And this choice was made by God prior to their births. In other words, God's true Israel is the remnant within physical Israel, saved by God's choice: "He has mercy on whom He desires, and He hardens whom He desires" (v. 18).

III. 9:24-29: Both Gentiles and Jews Are Part of God's True Israel

In this paragraph Paul proclaims the Gentiles to be part of true Israel (vv. 24-26), and then the remnant of Israel to be the rest of God's true Israel (vv. 27-29). The Gentiles are demonstrated to be part of God's new Israel when Paul says, "Whom He called . . . from among the Gentiles. As He says also in Hosea, 'I will call those who were not My people, My people'" (vv. 24, 25). But the Hosea passage was addressed to Old Testament Israel, so how could Paul apply this to New Testament Gentiles? Even further, in v. 26 Paul quotes the latter part of Hosea 1:10: "You who are not My people . . . shall be called sons of the living God," applying it to the Gentiles, leaving the reader to remember that Hosea 1:10 begins with: "The number of the sons of *Israel*. . . ." In other words, as precisely and forcefully as Paul can muster, he is stating that the Gentiles compose God's new Israel. Peter, by the way, in 1 Peter 2:9, 10, makes the same application to *Gentiles* from the same verse in Hosea.

Next the Apostle verifies the remnant of Old Testament Israel also to be God's true Israel (vv. 27-29). "Though the remnant of the sons of *Israel* be as the sand of the sea, it is the remnant that will be saved" (v. 27).

IV. 9:30-10:21: Gentiles Accept Christ, Jews Reject Him

The Jews rejected their Messiah, but He was accepted by a *new nation*, the Gentiles (10:16-21). If the Gentiles are a new nation, the inference is that they are God's new Israel.

V. 11:1-32: If the Jews Reject Christ, Has God Forgotten Them? No!

A. God has not permanently rejected ethnic Israel, vv. 1-10. On the contrary, God has an elect remnant within Old Testament Israel as Paul continues:

> In the same way then, there has also come to be at the present time a remnant according to God's gracious choice. But if it is by grace, it is no longer on the basis of works, otherwise grace is no longer grace. . . . What then? That which Israel is seeking for, it has not obtained, but *those who were chosen obtained it, and the rest were hardened* (vv. 5-7).

Indeed, in v. 1 Paul claims to be an Israelite whom God has not rejected. "This makes sense only if, as an Israelite, he is a member of God's people."[10] There is an ethnic Israel, but even these have to be redeemed to become God's people.

---

[10] Gerard Kittel, *Theological Dictionary of the New Testament*, 10 vols. (Grand Rapids: Eerdmans, 1969), 3:386.

B. The salvation of the world will come to pass when God again accepts ethnic Israel, vv. 11-15.

> I say then, they [Jews] did not stumble so as to fall, did they? May it never be! But by their transgression salvation has come to the Gentiles, to make them jealous. . . . But if some of the branches were broken off, and you, being a wild olive, were grafted in *among them* and became partaker *with them* of the rich root of the olive tree (v. 11).

C. The Gentiles are now being grafted into ethnic Israel's olive tree, vv. 16-24. The Gentiles, then, are *now* part of God's Israel. They are grafted in with them, with Old Testament Israel.

D. Both the Gentiles and ethnic Israel will be saved, vv. 25-36, though not all of either group.

> For just as you [Gentiles] once were disobedient to God, but *now* have been shown mercy because of their [Jews] disobedience, so these also *now* have been disobedient, in order that because of the mercy shown to you [Gentiles] they [Jews] also may[11] be shown mercy. For God has shut up all in disobedience that He might show mercy to all [Jews and Gentiles] (vv. 30-32).

Paul has demonstrated from Romans 9-11 that there are two Israels: natural, physical Israel and a true remnant of spiritual Israel. The true Israel is composed of some of the Gentiles and some of ethnic Israel. But even those of ethnic Israel who become the real Israel do so by the new birth — not by physical birth.

One dispensational author challenges, "One can hardly overemphasize the fact that the church is never mentioned per se in this chapter" [Rom. 11].[12] This author concludes that the root and the branches are not the same[13] and that ethnic Israel and the church are still distinct. That the church is not mentioned is an argument from silence. Furthermore, Paul is speaking about Israel and the Gentiles as he did in Ephesians 2 and Galatians. In all three contexts, Paul is speaking about the nature of the church. Furthermore, to say that ethnic Israel and the church are distinct is a truism, for so are blacks and Chinese, neither of whom are changed physically when they are converted. Also, there have been many Reformed theologians who

---

[11]The word *now* is not in the vast majority of manuscripts, though modern translations tend to add the word at this point.

[12]Blaising, *Dispensationalism, Israel and the Church*, p. 228.

[13]Ibid., p. 206.

have held from Romans 11 that there is yet a future for ethnic Israel.[14] This does not make one dispensational. There is also nothing in the context — or anywhere else in the Bible — of a thousand year reign of Christ after His return. This is read into Romans 11. What Paul says is that both Jews and Gentiles are now grafted into the *one* root, making them equal sharers in the *one* covenant, not that Israel will have its own separate covenant later or its own political aspect to the one covenant later.

The book of Galatians is especially powerful. In Galatians 3, for example, the Old Testament words "blessing," "covenant," "promise(s)," and "inheritance" are used to describe and define the salvation that comes to Abraham's seed. And who is Abraham's seed?

> Therefore, be sure that it is those who are of faith who are sons of Abraham. . . . So then, those who are of faith are blessed with Abraham, the believer. . . . And if you belong to Christ, then you are Abraham's seed, *heirs according to promise.* (vv. 7, 9, 29).

The true Israel, according to Paul, is the believer in Jesus, the true seed of Abraham. The true Jew (Rom. 2:28, 29) is the one born of the Spirit — not the one born physically. The descent from Abraham is by faith — *not* by one's body.

Galatians 6:16 is one of the most pungent passages in the Bible on the definition of Israel: "And those who walk by this rule, peace and mercy be upon them, even upon the Israel of God." The dispensationalists attempt to sustain that Paul addresses two peoples here: the Gentiles who walk by this rule, *and* (not "even") the Jews among the Gentiles. I do not think the debate over rendering *kai* "and" or "even" is the determining factor. I might add, though, that many — if not most — of the ablest commentators render it "even." William Hendriksen, in his superb commentary on Galatians adroitly reveals that the context of the epistle determines the following conclusion:

> Now this interpretation tends to make Paul contradict his whole line of reasoning in this epistle. Over against the Judaizers' perversion of the gospel he has emphasized the fact that "the blessing of Abraham" now [!] rests upon all those, and only upon those, "who are of faith" (3:9);

---

[14]See John Murray in his commentary on Romans and Charles Hodge in his *Systematic Theology*. There is even one Reformed man from last century who held not only a future for ethnic Israel but also that it would be in the land: David Brown's work reprinted by Still Waters Revival Books in *Hal Lindsey and The Restoration of the Jews*, p. 65ff. He understood this as happening before the Second Coming and not as separate from but as part of the church.

that all those, and only those, "who belong to Christ are heirs according to promise" (3:29). These are the very people who "walk by the Spirit" (5:16), and "are led by the Spirit" (5:18). Moreover, to make his meaning very clear, the apostle has even called special attention to the fact that God bestows his blessings on all true believers, regardless of nationality, race, social position, or sex: "There can be neither Jew nor Greek; there can be neither slave nor freeman; there can be no male and female; for you are all one in Christ Jesus" (3:28). By means of an allegory (4:21-31) he has re-emphasized this truth. And would he now, at the very close of the letter, undo all this by first of all pronouncing a blessing on "as many as" (or: "all") who walk by the rule of glorying in the cross, be they Jew or Gentile by birth, and then pronouncing a blessing upon those *who do not (or: do not yet) walk by that rule?* [emphasis added] I refuse to accept that explanation. . . . Galatians 6:16 must be interpreted in accordance with *its own specific context and in the light of the entire argument of this particular epistle.* [emphasis his] . . . it is very clear that in his epistles the apostle employs the term *Israel* in more than one sense. In fact, in the small compass of a single verse (Rom. 9:6) he uses it in two different senses. Each passage in which that term occurs must therefore be explained in the light of its context.[15]

The Bauer lexicon agrees, for the authors say of the definition of "Israel": "In a figurative sense of the Christians as the true nation of Israel, in contrast to Israel in the physical sense" (p. 381). They quote Galatians 6:16; 1 Corinthians 10:18; Romans 9:6 for their proof.

Another passage is John 1:47, where Jesus called Nathanael "an Israelite *indeed.*" The word "indeed" is the Greek *alethōs.* Why would the Lord think it necessary to qualify the word "Israelite"? Was not this enough? Apparently not. There were Jews and then there were Jews. As the *Theological Dictionary of the New Testament* puts it: "The term ["indeed" or "true"] shows that he is a member of God's people. But one can be an ostensible member of this people without being a genuine Israelite. This is why we read that he is a 'true Israelite' (see Rom. 9:6; also Rom. 2:28ff.)." The Lord adds of Nathanael, "in whom is no guile." A clause which demonstrates that Jesus' omniscient mind penetrated his heart and pronounced him justified.[16]

The same word (*alethōs*) is used in John 8:31 when the Lord said to those who had superficially "believed" in Him, "If you abide in

---

[15]William Hendriksen, *New Testament Commentary: Galatians* (Grand Rapids: Baker, 1968), pp. 246-47.

[16]Kittel, TDNT, 3:385.

My word, then you are *truly* disciples of Mine; and you shall know the truth, and the truth shall make you free." They were not free, but were slaves to sin (vv. 33, 37, 44). Yet the Lord says they were Abraham's seed. They were the offspring of Abraham physically but not spiritually; for if they had been Abraham's by faith, then they would have loved the Lord Jesus (v. 42). The Lord of glory classed them with the seed of the devil (v. 44).

Nathanael, then, was part of the true Israel, and these artificial "believers" who claimed Abraham were not true Israelites. The word "Israel" must have multiple meanings, therefore, sometimes referring to the ethnic but often referring to the true elect Jew, who is a member of the church (Rom. 2:28, 29). Hence, our Lord Jesus recognized that not all Israel was Israel.

"Ephesians 2:12 is another clear example of the use of Israel for the people of God."[17]

Contrast of the Gentiles

Formerly (v. 12)	Now
Separate from Christ	Brought near by Christ (v. 13)
Not citizens of Israel	Fellow citizens (v. 19)
Strangers to promises	No longer strangers (v. 19)
No hope	Hope (v. 16)
Without God	With God (v. 18)

Results: The New Israel

1. Both groups (Jews and Gentiles) now made into *one* new body (v. 14).

2. The two made into *one* new man (v. 15).

3. Reconciled *both* in *one* body to God (v. 16).

4. Gentiles are *fellow citizens* with the saints (the true Jews), and are of God's *one* household (v. 19).

Who is Israel according to Paul here? Israel existed before (vv. 12, 19) but continues today (vv. 13-21) in a slightly different form: Jews and Gentiles on an equal basis in the same body. But Paul emphasizes the Gentiles are now members of God's true Israel (vv. 12, 19).

To say that the Gentiles are only *sharers* in the covenant with Israel but not *members* of Israel is clearly violated by Paul's arguments and terms. One dispensational author said: "Paul . . . cannot be arguing

---

[17]Kittel, TDNT, 3:387.

for a Gentile incorporation into Israel. . . . Paul never writes of Gentiles as 'in Israel' in any of his letters."[18] Paul, however, uses the same term for *citizen* in verse 12 as he does in verse 19 (with the Greek preposition *sun* added on the front in verse 19 meaning "fellow" citizen), emphasizing that the Gentiles are indeed now members of Israel, not simply sharers in a common covenant. They are grafted into Israel's stock or citizenship so that "Israel" continues in the Gentiles. It is not that "Israel" stops and that they and the Gentiles make up a different covenant, but that together they continue Israel's covenant.

We have seen, therefore, that Israel has several meanings, and that it is not true that Israel and church are never "confused." Israel often means the true elect people of God whether they are in the Old Testament or New Testament, and sometimes is synonymous with church.

Church

Likewise the word "church" has various meanings. It can be used of a gathering of the people, i.e., a secular assembly (Acts 19:32, 39, 40).[19]

The church can be a local body of professors (Rom. 16:1, 5; 1 Cor. 16:19), or the universal body of believers (Eph. 1:22, 23; 5:23-32; Col. 1:18, 24).

As a senior at Dallas Theological Seminary and as a thoroughly convinced dispensationalist, three other students and I went to converse with a professor about the definition of "church." I asked him if to be in Christ was to be in the church and he affirmed this. Next I queried him about Ephesians 1:4: Did not this mean all the elect of all ages were chosen to be in Christ? Again he agreed. My conclusion was that Moses was elect before the foundation of the world and chosen to be in Christ; therefore, he was in the church. Somewhat startled, the professor decided that Ephesians 1:4 did not include all the elect. I still think it does and that Moses, being elect, is in Christ. Paul placed no limits on the elect of v. 4, and if the choice was made prior to the world being created, would not this include all who would ever live on the earth? Interestingly, Galatians 3:17 (Majority text, to which I hold) says that before the law was given God had ratified a promise of salvation *in Christ*, of which promise all the elect partake, including Abraham and New Testament believers (Gal. 3:6-9). And 1

---

[18]Blaising, *Dispensationalism, Israel and the Church*, p. 113.

[19]Kittel, TDNT, 3:505.

Corinthians 1:2 "equates the 'church' and 'those sanctified' *in Christ.*"[20] The church then includes those *in Christ*, whether before or after the Day of Pentecost.

James writes to the twelve *tribes* (1:1), to those who visit the *synagogue* (2:2), and also tells them to call for the elders of the *church* when sick (5:14). Some say James wrote to Jewish Christians. Perhaps they were. But the point is that James has no qualms labeling them tribes, synagogue, and church. To explain this as Jewish Christians is to do two things: to seek to display how Scripture can be explained in light of a system already derived and to admit that the Jews are God's people through the church.

There are three passages where Old Testament Israel is called the church (Matt. 18:17; Acts 7:38; Heb. 2:12). Of course these are explained by dispensationalists to be non-technical uses of the term.

In Matthew 18:16 our Lord quotes Deuteronomy 19:15, requiring at least two witnesses to establish a fact. Then He says if the unrepentant sinner does not listen, tell it to the *church*. The Lord is in Israel speaking to His disciples (18:1), legislating to them the proper procedure for discipline. The procedure was good when He spoke it, and we use it today. If the Lord spoke this to His disciples to use then, while in Old Testament Israel, and yet He refers to the congregation as the church, He must have identified the two.

In Acts 7:38 Stephen, in good Septuagint usage, refers to the Old Testament people as the "church." Or as F. F. Bruce rightly says, "As Moses was with the old church, Christ is with the new, and it is still a pilgrim church. . . ."[21] Moses and Christ are over the same house (Heb. 3:5, 6), and the one house is called the "church" in Acts.

In Hebrews 2 we have already commented that "church" in v. 12 is synonymous to: "sons," "those sanctified," "brethren," "children whom God gave Christ," "seed of Abraham," and "*the* people." I only add one thing: Hebrews 2:12, where the word "church" is used, is a quotation of Psalm 22:22, where David refers to Israel.

One other passage often overlooked is Acts 20:28: "Be on guard . . . for all the flock . . . to shepherd the church of God which He purchased with His own blood." This is a quotation of Psalm 74:1, 2.[22] "Why does thine anger smoke against the sheep of Thy pasture?

---

[20]Kittel, TDNT, 3:507.

[21]F. F. Bruce, *NIC New Testament: Acts* (Grand Rapids: Eerdmans, 1979), p. 152.

[22]Kittel, TDNT, 3:507.

Remember Thy *congregation*, which Thou hast purchased of old, which Thou hast redeemed to be the tribe of Thine inheritance. . . ." (vv. 1b, 2a). The word for "congregation" in the Septuagint is "synagogue," but Paul refers to it as the church. Paul's quote definitely equates the Old Testament "synagogue," "assembly," or Old Testament Israel with the New Testament church.

In Matthew 16:18 the Lord refers to His church as something He will build. First, let me ask why this passage is considered by dispensationalists to be the technical use of church while Matthew 18:17, addressed to the same disciples, is not technical? Second, some say that the church is not in existence yet since the Lord speaks of building His church in the future. This is, however, an invalid inference to make simply from a future tense of a verb. Paul uses the present subjunctive of the same word in a future sense in Romans 15:20: ". . . that I might not build upon another man's foundation." The usage here is to build on an existing structure. And even if the inference were valid, does this preclude that the church would not retroactively include all the Old Testament saints? I think not.

In fact there is an argument that the dispensationalists use to prove that the church did not come into existence until the New Testament period. It was originally formulated by S. Lewis Johnson (though Ryrie got the credit for it), and is this: the church was formed by the baptism of the Holy Spirit (1 Cor. 12:13); this Spirit baptism began at Pentecost (Acts 1:8; 2:1-4; 11:15-17); therefore, the church began at Pentecost. The assumptions, though, are that the baptism was not retroactive and that Old Testament saints were saved apart from union with Christ, for Spirit baptism places one in union with Christ (1 Cor. 12:13). (Mr. Gunn has adequately analyzed the union with Christ issue.) Another assumption is also false, that since it began at Pentecost it was not retroactive. The baptism of the Spirit, like the death of Jesus, was retroactive. How do I know? Two reasons: theologically, from the analogy of faith, we know there is no salvation apart from union with Christ. Therefore, all those who would be saved must have been in union with Him as their covenant Head so that His death was effectual for them. And if they were in union with Him, by definition they were in the church.

Exegetically, Galatians 3:17 says, "The law, which came four hundred and thirty years later, does not invalidate a covenant previously ratified by God *in Christ* so as to nullify the promise." The covenant God made was the promise of salvation in the Messiah, and

Abraham was a partaker of this promise. For Abraham to be a partaker of the promise and not to be in Christ is ludicrous, for Paul says, referring to Jews as well as Gentiles, "you are all one in Christ Jesus" (Gal. 3:28). And the particular Jew Paul is using for his example is Abraham.

A second exegetical argument is found in the New Covenant, which was addressed to Old Testament Israel (Heb. 8:6-12), was effected by the blood of Jesus (Heb. 9:12-14; 10:10-17), and applied to New Testament saints as well (Heb. 10:10-17). Hebrews 10:14 says that "He has perfected for all time those who are sanctified." The word "sanctified" is found twice in Hebrews in this form (present passive participle): here and in 2:11. We have already seen that Hebrews 2:11 defines the sanctified as "many sons," "brethren," "church," "children whom God has given" Jesus, "seed of Abraham," "*the* people." Jesus' blood saved all those who were "sanctified," who were set apart to God, who were the seed of Abraham. How could all these New Testament and Old Testament saints be referred to under the same figures and as mutual members of the same group, be saved by the same death, and yet the New Testament saints be in union with Christ and the Old Testament saints not be in union with Him? Does not Hebrews 11:40 say that both Old Testament and New Testament saints are perfected together?

A third exegetical point is Ephesians 2:11-22, especially vv. 12-18. The passage says that Jesus' death saved the true Israel (Old Testament and New Testament saints) and that as a consequence there is now *one new* body made out of the former two groups. The one new body includes the former Israel (v. 19) who has access by the One Spirit to the Father. And if there is one body and it is new, it must have been formed by the baptism of the Spirit. And this one new body includes the Old Testament saints, for the Gentiles are now members *with them — Old Testament Israel* (v. 19).

Some, however, believe that the New Testament church began at the institution of the Lord's Supper, the new Passover.[23] They argue that just as Old Testament Israel had its inception at the Passover by the blood of the lamb, so New Testament Israel began when the Lord of glory instituted the new Passover in the upper room. The analogy is certainly a strong one and could be correct.

The word "church," then, like "Israel," may mean all the saints

---

[23]Kittel, TDNT, 3:521; Goppelt, pp. 110ff.

of all ages, the true Israel of God, or the elect of God. Finally, we have noted the many parallels between the New Testament "church" and Old Testament "Israel": 1 Peter 2:9: "chosen race," "royal priesthood," "holy nation," "people for possession"; Philippians 3:3: "the circumcision"; 1 Corinthians 10:18: "Israel according to the flesh" and the Spirit; Galatians 3:29: "seed of Abraham"; James 1:1: "the twelve tribes," etc. It is indisputable then that all this evidence leads to the only conclusion possible: that Israel and the church are not two different peoples with different heritages but one and the same people with the same heritage. Or as F. F. Bruce, no mean scholar, so beautifully expressed it:

> In Jesus the promise is confirmed, the covenant is renewed, the prophecies are fulfilled, the law is vindicated, salvation is brought near, sacred history has reached its climax, the perfect sacrifice has been offered and accepted, the great priest over the household of God has taken his seat at God's right hand, the Prophet like Moses has been raised up, the Son of David reigns, the kingdom of God has been inaugurated, the Son of Man has received dominion from the Ancient of Days, the Servant of the Lord, having been smitten to death for his people's transgression and borne the sin of many, has accomplished the divine purpose, has seen light after the travail of his soul and is now exalted and extolled and made very high.[24]

---

[24]Earl D. Radmacher and Robert D. Preus, *Hermeneutics, Inerrancy, and the Bible* (Zondervan: Grand Rapids, 1984), p. 787.

Chapter Five

The Hermeneutic of Christ

Space does not allow the broad development of the Lord's herme-neutic, but one aspect that is crucial to understand the New Testament is the kingdom He established at His first coming.

It is well known that dispensationalists teach that the Lord Jesus offered a millennial kingdom when He came, and that once it was rejected, He withdrew the offer and died on the Cross. They do not teach, though, that if the kingdom had been accepted by the Jews that He would not have gone to the Cross; but that He would have died, been resurrected, and then immediately established the kingdom. However, the question that must be asked: Where do we see the offer of a millennial kingdom?

Many dispensationalists see three forms of the kingdom in the New Testament: the eternal kingdom, the mystery form of the king-dom, and the Messianic kingdom.[1] Christ offered the Messianic, millennial kingdom at His coming which was rejected (climaxed in Matt. 12), then He instituted the mystery form (Matt. 13), which features some principles of God's rule while Christ is in heaven. The eternal kingdom is God's realm of salvation, which is frequently mentioned in the epistles.[2]

By contrast, the majority of commentators see a singularity to the kingdom with a present and future aspect to it (Both Bauer and Thayer lexicons, for example). The future aspect of the kingdom may be held

---

[1] C. C. Ryrie, *Biblical Theology of the New Testament* (Chicago: Moody Press, 1959), p. 72ff.

[2] Ryrie, p. 72ff.

by amillennialists, premillennialists, or postmillennialists, so this is not the point of conflict. The conflict is over the kingdom offered and established in the Gospels, especially in Matthew 1-12, and over the gospel of the kingdom. Thus the kingdom shall be demonstrated to be prophesied in the Old Testament, that it was established at Christ's first coming, that all "three" kingdoms are the same, and that Christ does not establish a new or millennial kingdom when He comes again.

The Kingdom Prophesied in the Old Testament

One is inundated when he considers the many Old Testament passages that predict the coming of the kingdom with the Messiah. One well known passage is Isaiah 9:6, 7:

> For a child will be born to us, a son will be given to us; and the government will rest on His shoulders; and His name will be called Wonderful Counselor, Mighty God, Eternal Father, Prince of Peace. There will be no end to the increase of His government or of peace, on the throne of David and over his kingdom, to establish it and to uphold it with justice and righteousness from then on and forevermore. The zeal of the Lord of Hosts will accomplish this.

Notice that the government rested on Christ *when* He came as a babe — not some time in the future after His coming. Observe that "government" and "kingdom" are used synonymously. And what is the government? It is the realm of the spiritual reign of Christ and of His grace (spiritually, see the names Christ has) but also nature and power (politically, peace will be the mark of His kingdom, see Matthew 28:18, "all power in heaven and on *earth*"). Observe also that the kingdom begins with the birth of the Child, for when He is born the government rests on His shoulders. Luke confirms this when he says: "He will be great, and will be called the Son of the Most High; and the Lord God will give Him the throne of His father David; and He will reign over the house of Jacob forever; and His kingdom will have no end" (1:32, 33). Peter says the same in Acts 2:30-36, namely, that Christ was prophesied by David (Psalm 110:1) to sit on his throne and to rule until all His enemies were a footstool. Therefore, the kingdom Peter mentions began with Christ's birth, was confirmed in His resurrection, continued throughout Acts, and was the same as the kingdom Isaiah and Luke spoke of.

This kingdom is not a literal thousand years, for Isaiah and Luke say that it will last *forever* — slightly longer than a thousand years.

And this kingdom was established when Christ came, as we shall see even more later.

Not only does Isaiah say that Messiah's reign is perpetual but also that it is progressive: "There will be no end to the *increase* of (His) government or of peace." The Hebrew word for increase definitely means that His kingdom will constantly grow from its inception. This one kingdom will continue from Christ's birth and grow quantitatively and qualitatively.

Daniel says the same of Messiah's kingdom: "But the stone that struck the statue became a great mountain and filled the whole earth" (2:35). The stone fills the whole earth, emphasizing the victorious nature of Christ's kingdom. Then Daniel explains:

> And in the days of those kings the God of heaven will set up a kingdom which will never be destroyed, and that kingdom will not be left for another people; it will *crush* and *put an end* to all these [earthly] kingdoms, but it will itself *endure forever*. Inasmuch as you saw that a stone was cut out of the mountain without hands and that it crushed the iron, the bronze, the clay, the silver, and the gold, the great God has made known to the king what will take place in the future. . . . (2:44, 45)

Here again the kingdom is prophesied in the Old Testament. When was it to be established? "In the days of those kings." What kings? Even dispensationalists admit that the kings are the kings of the Roman empire. In this passage Daniel says that there will be four empires or kingdoms until God's kingdom comes: Babylonian, Medo-Persian, Grecian, and Roman. When the last kingdom is on earth, the Roman one, God will set up His everlasting kingdom. And this kingdom of God "will not be left for another people" but it will crush all other kingdoms. God indeed established the kingdom of God when Rome was in power; He sent His only begotten Son.

In a parallel passage in the same book, Daniel (chapter 7) prophesies of the coming kingdom. When was this kingdom established? Daniel says that the Son of Man (Jesus) came to the Ancient of Days (the Father) and received a "kingdom, that all the peoples, nations, and men of every language might serve Him. His dominion is an *everlasting dominion* which will *not pass away*; and His kingdom is one which will not be destroyed" (7:14). Again the victorious nature of this kingdom is obvious. But still the question is when? When did this happen or has it happened at all? In v. 12 Daniel states that the kingdoms of the four beasts, the same four kingdoms he had chronicled in chapter two, will be sovereignly dissolved. In chapter two this happened quite clearly "in the days of those kings" or in the time of Rome, when Messiah was born. Since this passage is parallel, the time of the established kingdom would be the same. Secondly, if the kingdoms of the four beasts were taken from them and Messiah's kingdom took their places, then the inference is that the Messianic kingdom was established when Messiah tabernacled among men.

Other Old Testament prophecies of the kingdom are: Isaiah 11:1-10; 16:5; 42:1-9; Micah 5:2-5a; Zechariah 9:9, 10; Psalm 2; 110:1; 22:25-31, etc. This does not nearly exhaust the list. It should be noted that if these prophecies were fulfilled when Christ came the first time, then there is no parenthesis, for what happened in the New Testament was exactly what God had foretold. He did not set aside Israel; He is fulfilling the promises to Israel.

No Millennium When Jesus Returns

There are many New Testament passages that indicate that there is no millennium to come. For instance, the Scriptures that say there is to be one — not two — resurrection deny a thousand years between two so-called resurrections: John 5:29; Matthew 25:46; Acts 24:15. But there is one passage that is singularly pungent in disaffirming that a kingdom is to be established when He comes again, and that is 1 Corinthians 15:23-26:

> But each in his own order: Christ the first fruits, after that those who are Christ's *at His coming, then (comes) the end, when He* delivers up the kingdom to the God and Father, *when* He has abolished all rule and all authority and power. For He must reign until He has put all His enemies under His feet. The last enemy that will be abolished is death.

First we must consider these: the word for "coming" is used consistently in the New Testament for the Second Coming of Jesus to the earth. Secondly, "at His coming" is synonymous to "the end." Or, as A.T. Robertson says, we should supply "at His coming" after "then comes the end," making the sense: "Then comes the end at His coming."[3] The word "then" (*eita*) is certainly temporal and not logical because of the temporal context. The Bauer lexicon agrees.[4]

But what has "ended" at the Second Coming? Paul tells us: the

---

[3]A. T. Robertson, *Word Pictures, 6 vols.* (Nashville: Broadman, 1931), vol. 4, p. 191.

[4]Bauer Lexicon, second edition, p. 233.

kingdom has ended. Observe the words emphasized in the above quote. By the time the Second Coming invades the earth two things have happened (both followed by "when," *hotan* in Greek): (1) He has abolished all rule, (2) and He delivers to the Father a conquered kingdom. How do we know it is a victorious kingdom? Paul says so: "For He must reign until He has put all His enemies under His feet." Therefore, when the Lord of Glory returns, He gives to the Father a kingdom subdued to the glory of the Father. He does not establish a new kingdom. He does not return to a defeated kingdom to erect a victorious realm by cataclysm. He fulfills the Old Testament promises that His domain would endure forever and would crush all other kingdoms. All Scripture at this point will have been fulfilled. There is no parenthesis, no returning to the old economy of the Old Testament, no rebuilding of Judaism or the temple, just judgment and eternity. The kingdom then will enter its eternal state and will be absolute perfection with no curse, not even on creation (Rom. 8:18-22), with no possibility of further rebellion, for the Lord's victorious work is perfect. Satan will not ruin Christ's kingdom as the dispensationalists teach. When the Lord returns, He will offer to God a conquered kingdom, with the wicked judged and cast into hell forever (Matt. 25; 2 Thess. 1; John 5:29).

Christ Established His One Kingdom

The dispensationalists make a strong distinction between the Messianic political kingdom and the kingdom of God. Supposedly, the Lord offered the political kingdom when He came the first time, and when the Jews disdained it He began proffering the kingdom of God or the spiritual kingdom. However, we shall see that what the Lord offered was one kingdom that had both political and soteriological import.

From a lexicon. Thayer says of the kingdom that:

> . . . Jesus employed the phrase "kingdom of God" or "of heaven" to indicate that perfect order of things which he was about to establish, in which all those of every nation who should believe in him were to be gathered together into one society, dedicated and intimately united to God, and made partakers of eternal salvation.[5]

---

[5] John Henry Thayer, *A Greek English Lexicon of the New Testament* (London: T. & T. Clark, 1901), p. 97.

Thayer knows nothing of any separate political kingdom.

From John the Baptist. The kingdom John proclaimed "at hand" was one of repentance for forgiveness of sins, and he promulgated this right from the dawn of Christ's ministry (Matt. 3:1-12). He did not wait for a separate political kingdom to be announced first. At the genesis of his ministry, John said Jesus was God's lamb who would take away sin (John 1:29).

The proclamation of John from Isaiah 40:3 (quoted in Matt. 3:3; John 1:23) speaks of making the paths straight, a declaration that is addressed not only for the individual but also for the nations (see Isa. 40:1, 2, 15, 17). "Making the paths straight" and the desert motif speak of a moral return to God's law.[6] Nothing is said of a separate political kingdom.

From Christ. In Mark 1:14, 15 with v. 1, Jesus preached the gospel of God or the kingdom of God. Is not this gospel of God salvation, when the word gospel throughout the New Testament always denotes the good news about Christ the Savior? The gospel and the kingdom are synonymous here, indicating that early in Jesus' ministry, indeed at the beginning of His ministry, He preached one thing: the gospel or the kingdom. Observe, too, that the requirement for entering this kingdom, whether at the beginning of His ministry or at the end, is not physical birth into the Jewish nation but conversion: one must be righteous (Matt. 5:20), repent (Matt. 3:2; 4:17), be converted (Matt. 18:3; Mark 10:14, 15; Luke 18:16, 17), hard for the rich to enter (Matt. 19:23-25; Luke 18:24-30), be born again (John 3:3-5). Thus His kingdom is a present reality that concerns a right relationship with God.

Christ stated on numerous occasions that the purpose for His first coming was to save His people from their sins, *not* to establish an immediately full-blown kingdom that would instantaneously crush all the enemies of the Jews (Matt. 1:21; 9:13; 11:25-30; 16:21; 17:22, 23; 18:11; 20:18, 19, 28; 26:27, 28; Mark 1:1, 14, 15; 8:31; 9:12, 31; 10:33, 34, 45; 14:24, 25; Luke 1:68; 2:38; 4:18, 19; 5:32; 9:22, 44; 18:31-34; 19:10; John 1:29; 2:19-22; 3:16; 4:42; 5:38-47; 6:14, 29, 38-40; 10:11, 15-27, 28; 11:25-27, 51, 52; 12:27, 46). An offer of an earthly kingdom that would establish His immediate reign in Jerusalem is not stated nor insinuated anywhere in the Gospels. He repeat-

---

[6]E. J. Young, *The Book of Isaiah, 3 vols.* (Grand Rapids: Eerdmans, 1972), vol. 3, p. 28ff.

edly divulges that he came to bring salvation to His people, and that *then* He — through His people — would bring in a kingdom (Dan. 7:18, 22, 27; Matt. 13:31-33; 1 Cor. 15:21-28; 1 John 5:4; Rev. 2:26, 27; 5:10; 12:10).

Notice these examples of His stated purpose: (1) He came to preach the kingdom of God (Luke 4:43), which is salvation as the parallel in Mark 1:1, 14, 15, 35-39 makes clear. (2) In John 13:3 Jesus came from God and was returning to Him with no indication of an immediate earthly Jewish-only kingdom in between. In Mark 10:45 Jesus declares He came to die and not to be served by man. If He presented Himself as the immediate political king of the earth, then He would have come to be served. (3) In Luke 24:25-27 Jesus says the Old Testament declared that Christ should suffer and *then* enter His glory. No separate political kingdom is present. Similarly, In Luke 24:44-47 the Lord proclaims that the Old Testament predicted that Christ should suffer, rise, and that repentance should be preached to all nations, with no intimation of an earthly realm ruled from Jerusalem at His first coming. Apparently, Jesus perceived that the kingdom would be established at His first coming, that it would be primarily soteriological, and that it would gradually overcome all earthly kingdoms by His sovereign power through His people.

The Lord states that His casting out demons is evidence that the kingdom of God had established a "beachhead" of light in the darkness (Matt. 12:28; Luke 11:20). This miracle, which had been performed early and late in His ministry, demonstrated that this same kingdom had been manifested all along.

Jesus also said that the kingdom was in them (or in their midst) in Luke 17:20, 21, that it was *not* going to come with great signs and wonders, as the Jews and dispensationalists imagine.

From the Elect Who Were Waiting for Him. Those who were the elect were looking for a Messiah who would save them from their sins — not for a Jewish only political kingdom. They understood though that the one kingdom would have political overtones and that it would eventually overthrow all other kingdoms in fulfillment of Daniel the prophet. In John chapter one Peter and Nathanael looked to Jesus as the sacrificial Lamb, Simeon declared that baby Jesus was salvation for Israel and for the *Gentiles* (Luke 2:28-32), and Anna thanked God for Christ who was Jerusalem's redemption (Luke 2:38). It was announced to Joseph that Mary's baby was God in the flesh who would save His people from their sins (Matt. 1:19-23). Where is the mention of a Jewish political kingdom? (See chapter 19 for my extended note on this under Old Testament Salvation.)

From the Historical Setting. Thayer's lexicon comments: "The Jews were expecting a kingdom of the greatest felicity, which God through the Messiah would set up, raising the dead to life again and renovation of earth and heaven; and that in this kingdom they would bear sway forever over all the nations of the world."[7] Some Jews, it is true, did want this kind of kingdom, but the true Jews of the New Testament, that is the elect Jews, looked for a different Messiah, as we have already seen. Some, however, were confused and even tried to compel Jesus to be their political King (John 6:15). They gladly rejoiced when He came to Jerusalem at His triumphal entry. If Jesus had presented a Jewish political kingdom that was precisely what the Jews were anticipating, why did they crucify Him? Why was this kingdom rejected? Could it be that the Jews finally realized that His kingdom was not going to displace their political enemies immediately, and so they killed Him? Of course they did not want to lose their own power with the people either.

Even further, the Jews accused Christ of sedition and political upheaval before Pilate (Luke 23:1, 2). They said that Jesus was offering Himself as a political King. But Pilate recognized that though Jesus claimed to be a King, it was not a political kingdom He retained and acquitted Him of the charge (John 18:33-38). The phrase "King of the Jews" or "King of Israel," by the way, is a term of absolute deity — not so much a term of political rule (see John 1:49 with Isa. 6:5; 33:22; 43:15; 44:6). Yet dispensationalists want to sustain the charge of insurrection made by the Jews and to maintain that Christ did come as a Jewish political King. Who is right? Jesus and Pilate or the Jews and the dispensationalists?

From the Kingdom of God and the Kingdom of Heaven. It was popular at one time for dispensationalists to maintain a distinction between these two phrases, especially since kingdom of heaven is used only in Matthew, the Jewish Gospel. They maintained that kingdom of heaven was the earthly kingdom and kingdom of God the sphere of eternal salvation. Though this distinction is not held by many dispensationalists today, it may prove profitable to demonstrate that such a distinction is impossible, since many laymen still espouse the distinction. It may also prove helpful to show that "the gospel of the

---

[7]Thayer, p. 97.

kingdom" is not an earthly kingdom but simply the gospel of salvation.

The Jewish idiom used "heavens" (plural) as equivalent to the divine name (see Luke 15:18).[8] The Jews used the divine names as little as possible to avoid blasphemy; and since Matthew wrote to Jews, it is not surprising that only he used kingdom of heaven (about 33 times). The other Gospels, writing to Gentiles who would not understand the idiom, used kingdom of God. Therefore, since "heavens" is an idiom for God, there can be no distinction between the two phrases.

The parallel passages between the Gospels demonstrate that the two phrases are synonymous (Matt. 4:17 with Mark 1:14, 15; Matt. 4:23 with Luke 4:43; Matt. 10:6, 7 with Luke 9:2; Matt. 5:3 with Mark 13:10). While Matthew uses "kingdom of heaven," the other Gospels, commenting on the same events, use "kingdom of God."

Matthew himself uses the phrases interchangeably (6:33; 19:23, 24; 21:31, 43 with 22:2). Notice especially Matthew 19:23-25 where Jesus uses the two synonymously and says that entrance into the kingdom is salvation. Early in His ministry the Lord legislated that entrance into this kingdom of God is by the new birth (John 3:3-8), which must be a kingdom of spiritual salvation.

The requirement for entering the kingdom of heaven and the kingdom of God is the same: a right relationship with God (Matt. 18:3; Mark 10:14, 15; Luke 18:16, 17; John 3:3-8). Thus the two must be identical.

Someone may object: "Is not the mystery form of the kingdom of heaven different from the kingdom of God, containing both saved and lost (Matt. 13:41, 47-50), while the kingdom of God admits only those born again?" Though Matthew 13 speaks of professors (not possessors) as *in* the kingdom of heaven, they are not really *of* the kingdom of God (Mark 10:14, 15). The sphere of profession is often characterized by salvation or covenantal terms (John 8:30, 31, 44; 15:2, 6; Gal. 5:4; Heb. 6:4-6; 10:29; 2 Peter 2:20-22) when those referred to are actually lost. So Matthew does here. It seems doubtful, in light of the synonymous way the two phrases are constantly used, that Matthew intended a distinction.

From the Gospel of the Kingdom. Is this phrase the good news

---

[8]George E. Ladd, *Theology of the New Testament* (Grand Rapids: Eerdmans, 1975), p. 64; Kittel, *Theological Dictionary of the New Testament*, 1:582.

of an earthly kingdom or of salvation from sin with political over-tones? Is this the millennium that is meant, the alleged literal thousand year reign of Christ on the earth? It is used three times and only in Matthew (4:23; 9:35; 24:14), and the dispensationalists interpret this as the "gospel" of an earthly kingdom.[9]

I have studied every occurrence of the word "gospel" in the New Testament (both the noun and the verb), and I found only one place where "gospel" did not refer to the Good News about Christ (1 Thess. 3:6). And this passage speaks of the "good news of your faith," an indirect reference to Christ, for the faith spoken of is in Christ. It would be most unusual for a word to refer to Christ's person and work 124 times but 3 times to an earthly kingdom.[10]

The genitive construction also supports the meaning of "gospel of the kingdom" as the "gospel about Christ," for consider the following words that often follow "gospel": the gospel *of God* (Mark 1:14), gospel *of the grace of God* (Acts 20:24), gospel *of peace* (Eph. 6:15), gospel *of the glory of Christ* (2 Cor. 4:4), the gospel *of Christ* (Gal. 1:7), the gospel *of the uncircumcision* (Gal. 2:7), gospel *of salvation* (Eph. 1:13), gospel *of our Lord* (2 Thess. 1:8), gospel *of Jesus Christ* (Mark 1:1), and so forth. Thus why should one try to affirm that the gospel *of the kingdom* is unique and about an earthly millennium, especially with only three occurrences. Observe too that all the above phrases refer to the Lord Jesus, implying strongly that the "gospel of the kingdom" is about Him, too.

The parallels from the other Gospels to Matthew's three uses of "gospel of the kingdom" argue for it to be the Good News about Jesus. The parallel to Matthew 4:23 is Mark 1:14, 15 where Mark discourses on the "gospel of God" and on repentance and faith in the gospel. The gospel, repentance, and faith are all about Jesus (Mark 1:1).

The parallel to Matthew 24:14 is Mark 13:10 which says, "and the gospel must first be preached to all the nations." What Matthew calls "the gospel of the kingdom" Mark terms simply the "gospel." Who could read an earthly kingdom into Mark's account?

John 4:35-38 is parallel to Matthew 9:35. In John the harvest is said to be fruit for eternal life, which is very clear.

The conclusion is no different within Matthew itself. It would be

---

[9]J. Dwight Pentecost, *Things To Come* (Grand Rapids: Dunham Pub., 1966), pp. 465, 469, 472.

[10]Bauer lexicon, second edition, p. 317ff.

subjective to assign arbitrarily a meaning to "gospel of the kingdom" and then interpret the context from the assumed meaning. Each context must be examined independently to discern the meaning of the phrase.

In Matthew 4:23 the gospel of the kingdom is the same as John the Baptist's kingdom and is entered by repentance. No earthly Jewish political kingdom is mentioned. Also in v. 24 the result of Jesus' preaching is stated thusly: "And the news about *Him* went out . . . ." In chapter four, then, the gospel of the kingdom concerns repentance and Christ.

Matthew 9:35 is the same. The gospel of the kingdom is described as healing diseases and as a harvest. This Lord of the harvest motif is often correctly used by missionaries in exhorting others to engage in evangelism. The preceding context speaks of Christ forgiving sins (9:1-6) and coming to earth to call sinners to repentance (9:12, 13). In the following context Jesus sent out the twelve to heal the sick and raise the dead. But those to whom they went are termed the *lost sheep* of Israel. "Lost" is a word used numerous times of perishing or being unsaved (Matt. 5:29; 15:24; 18:14; Luke 15:4, 7, 8, 10, 24, 32; John 18:9; 1 Cor. 1:18; 2 Cor. 2:15; 4:3; 2 Thess. 2:10, etc.). The "sheep" most likely refer to the elect of God (see John 10:3-30). We have, therefore, the kingdom of forgiveness but no special kingdom for the Jews in the sense of an immediate political kingdom.

Matthew 19:28 is not the political Jewish millennium when Matthew speaks of the "regeneration." Luke uses the word "kingdom" in lieu of "regeneration" (Luke 22:29). Thus we know that the Lord is speaking of a kingdom. But what kind of kingdom? In both passages the Lord speaks of the twelve disciples "judging the twelve tribes of Israel" as they sit on the thrones prepared for them by Christ. We have seen that the kingdom is already here by virtue of Christ's birth, death, and resurrection. Furthermore, the saints are already reigning with Christ today (1 Peter 2:5-9; Rev. 1:5, 6; 3:21; 12:11, 12), and Revelation 2:26, 27 is especially clear: "And he who overcomes, and he who keeps My deeds until the end, to him I will give authority over the nations; and he shall rule them with a rod of iron, as the vessels of the potter are broken to pieces, as I also have received authority from My Father." Paul states that the Corinthians were already reigning as kings (1 Cor. 4:8). Saints rule today by their faith (1 John 5:4), and Revelation 12:11 is an example of reigning by faith: "And they overcame him because of the blood of the Lamb and because of the word of their testimony. . . ." By contrast the dispensational view of the kingdom causes Christians to cower down at the first inkling of any little resistance they encounter instead of conquering the enemies of God by faith in Jesus' name. We are reigning with Jesus now, and are called to overthrow the enemies of God — not to run from them!

Matthew 8:10-12 speaks of many from the East and West sitting down with Abraham, Isaac, and Jacob. This is a strong covenantal passage, for we see the Gentiles (those from the East and West) being blessed through the promises to Abraham. There is one kingdom with both Jews and Gentiles sharing it. The figure of "reclining at table" does not necessarily indicate a literal eating, but, according to Scriptural usage (not according to what man may consider literal), it implies a close fellowship (Psalm 23:5; Prov. 9:1-5; Isa. 25:6; Matt. 22:1ff; 26:29; Mark 14:25; Luke 14:15; Rev. 3:20; 19:9, 17). Even if the eating is literal, it could easily take place in the eternal state, as Jesus ate after He was glorified.

The only conclusion we can reach is that the kingdom of God and the kingdom of heaven are synonymous. Matthew uses "heaven" as an idiom for God, the parallels between the Gospels as well as the context within each Gospel, and the word "gospel" with the genitive all sketch a crystalline picture that the two are the same and that the kingdom spoken of is the ever present reign of Christ through His people, conquering a little at a time until the end, which is the return of Christ.

Chapter Six

A Distinguishable Economy?

In *Walvoord: A Tribute* two chapters are devoted to defining dispensationalism, one by Stanley D. Toussaint and the other by Elliott E. Johnson, both currently professors at Dallas Theological Seminary. Both define a dispensation as ". . . a distinguishable economy in the out-working of God's purpose."[1] Both rely heavily on the use of the word *oikonomia* as used in Ephesians and Colossians to defend this idea. This Greek word means "dispensation" or "stewardship."

Dr. Toussaint finds two such dispensations — the present one and a future one — in Ephesians 3:2 and Colossians 1:25, 26.[2] Both passages, however, speak of a "stewardship" God gave to Paul to preach the gospel to the Gentiles:

> If indeed you have heard of the *stewardship* of God's grace which was given to me for you.

> Of this church I was made a minister according to the *stewardship* from God bestowed on me for your benefit, that I might fully carry out the preaching of the word of God, that is, the mystery which has been hidden from the past ages and generations; but has now been manifested to His saints. . . .

Dr. Toussaint is incorrect; there is obviously no future age referred

---

[1] Donald K. Campbell, *Walvoord: A Tribute* (Chicago: Moody Press, 1982), pp. 82, 245.

[2] Campbell, p. 83.

to in these verses, and the "stewardship" Paul received was a commission to preach the gospel to the Gentiles, which expired when he expired. Of course the gospel is still preached to Gentiles long after Paul's death, and in this sense his ministry continues. But if this is a "dispensation" and it began with Paul's ministry, then it began in Acts 13 with Paul's first missionary journey — not in Acts 2 on the day of Pentecost.

Furthermore, I have no problem seeing six of their seven "dispensations" (I cannot see a 1000 year reign of Christ from Jerusalem). Truly there are changes in the Bible, the most dramatic being the fall of man into sin and the coming of Messiah. What is incomprehensible is how they exclude virtually all former revelation from each succeeding "dispensation,"[3] or as other dispensationalists maintain, some "dispensations" contain former ones while other "dispensations" exclude the former ones.[4]

The dispensationalists are guilty of equivocating on the term "dispensation," using the word that Scripture uses but defining it not simply as a stewardship but as a time period with a test that ends in failure.[5] This subtle error may be seen in the "dispensation of promise." For example, where is the test and failure of Abraham in the so-called dispensation of promise? Abraham passed his "test" beautifully in Genesis 22 when he was willing to offer Isaac to God.

And where is the *one* test of Israel "under law"? They had many tests and failures, and when the ultimate "David" came, the Messiah of the law, He fulfilled the law for the true Israel. He elevated "Israel" to the greatest success possible and now rules for "Israel" until all His enemies are under His feet. Is this failure? It is impossible that God the Messiah should fail either personally or through His people. It was only the rejected part of national Israel that failed — they went to hell. The elect were victorious (Rom. 11:1-10). Many verses indicate that this "dispensation" will not end in failure (Dan. 7:18, 22, 27; Matt. 22:44; Rom. 16:20; 8:37; 1 Cor. 15:22-26; 6:2; Acts 2:34, 35; 1 John 2:13; 4:4; 5:4; Heb. 10:12-14; Rev. 2:26, 27; 12:10, 11). These verses definitively state that victory belongs to Christ through His people in this age.

Marsden is insightful about the ages or dispensations:

---

[3]Ryrie, class notes.

[4]Campbell, p. 84.

[5]Campbell, p. 83.

Marxism in fact has some formal similarities to the nearly contemporary development of dispensationalism. History is divided into distinct periods, each dominated by a prevailing principle or characteristic. Each age ends in failure, conflict, judgment on those who rule, and the violent introduction of a wholly new era.[6]

Since both Marxism and dispensationalism developed during the same time period, could it be that the philosophical milieu served to give rise to both? I am not saying dispensationalists are Marxists, only that maybe their system is more a product of the times than they think.

But someone is bound to object by referring to the passages that ostensibly speak of things getting worse "in the last days." First Timothy 4:1-3 and 2 Timothy 3:1-5 speak of apostasy "in the last days," which phrase is virtually technical for the "last days" of the old covenant as consummated in A. D. 70 when Jerusalem was destroyed (Isa. 2:2; Micah 4:1; Dan. 2:28 with v. 45; Joel 2:28 with Acts 2:17; Heb. 1:1, 2; 1 Peter 1:20, cf. also 1 John 2:18; James 5:3 seems to refer to this age but see vv. 7, 8: the commentators are divided on James here). "Last days" does not refer, therefore, to the few years just prior to the Second Coming of Christ. These parallel passages of Paul to Timothy speak of wolves among the flock, similar to Acts 20:28-30; 2 Corinthians 11:3, 4, 13-15; 2 Peter 2:1-22. A warning against false people does not mean that all of Christendom will apostatize, for God says, even in the midst of such apostasy, He knows how to deliver His people (2 Peter 2:7-9). There is no indication in Scripture that the exalted Lord is so incompetent that most of His people depart from Him and that He must come bodily to "bail them out." Rather He conquers His enemies through His people by His grace. Why do some people think that He is more powerful when He is bodily on earth than when He is exalted and enthroned in heaven? In addition, the Lord is omnipresent so that He is personally present with His people.

Having said all this we must recognize that there may be an apostasy that develops just prior to the Second Coming (2 Thess. 2:1-12), but this does not involve the elect (2 Thess. 2:13-15), nor is it stated how many will follow the Man of sin. This is left for other passages, and we know that the elect cannot be led astray (Matt. 24:24; Jude 24, 25; 1 Thess. 3:13; 1 Cor. 2:15; 1 John 3:9; Phil. 1:6; 2:12, 13). We also know that the number saved no man is able to count,

---

[6]George M. Marsden, *Fundamentalism and American Culture* (New York: Oxford, 1982), p. 64.

being saved from every nation and tribe (Rev. 5:11; 7:9), and that the number saved is more than the number lost. Or as Paul stated it: "More are the children of the desolate than of the one who has a husband" (Gal. 4:27). More are the children of Sarah (Isa. 54:1) than of Hagar, more are of the Jerusalem from above than of the literal Jerusalem, more are the elect than the non-elect.[7]

What neither Toussaint nor Elliott Johnson establish is the precise test and failure of each "dispensation," nor *how* one can discern that previous revelation continues into the next dispensation, stops, or only partly enters the new dispensation. This lack is insuperable.

When I was a dispensationalist, we always harped about the perfect way we orchestrated Scripture into a beautiful symphony, with each dissected segment playing its role with perfect harmony, with this part "for today," the adjacent part "not for today," and the next contiguous passage again "for today" — all within a few verses. As the instruments fade in and out in an orchestra, so passages — the same passages — can do the same. For example, Ryrie states that the Sermon on the Mount is not for this dispensation by strict interpretation but can be for today by application.[8]

We who write this book have not systematically developed the continuity of Scripture in a separate chapter though we have done so sporadically in our arguments. I recommend, though, Pierre CH. Marcel's book, *Baptism: Sacrament of the Covenant of Grace*, from Mack Publishing Co. A summary of my view is this: there is one Savior and one people united with Him in one theological covenant (Eph. 1:4; Gal. 3:17 [majority text]; Heb. 13:20), with the promises of Messiah and His people beginning in Genesis 3:15 and growing in number and specificity, progressively revealed in the biblical covenants (Abrahamic, Davidic, New) until He comes in the New Testament. Then all the promises are fulfilled and inherited. The changes or so-called dispensations are accounted for by the progress of revelation. However, since there is one people of God and one Messiah, we do not hack the Bible into segments that are "for today" and "not for today." We see all Scripture as inspired by God and profitable for our lives (2 Tim. 3:15-17).

Then how do we understand the passages that say we are not under

---

[7] See B.B. Warfield's excellent study: "Are There Few that be Saved?" in *Biblical and Theological Studies*, pp. 334ff.

[8] C. C. Ryrie, *Dispensationalism Today* (Chicago: Moody Press, 1969), pp. 107ff.

law? We are not under the ceremonial law (Heb. 8:1-9; Gal. 3:15-29), nor under the moral law (whether Old Testament Ten Commandments or New Testament Sermon on the Mount or Eph. 6) in the sense of earning our justification by personal obedience (Gal. 2:16; 4:21; Rom. 3:9 with vv. 19, 20) nor in the sense of deriving power from it to live the Christian life (Rom. 6:14; 7:4-6), but we are under the moral law as our guide to pleasing God and as His right of dominion over us (James 2:8-12; Rom. 13:8-10). How else are we to harmonize statements that we are not under the law but we are obligated to obey the law or reap what we sow (Gal. 6:7)? Why does Paul say we are to obey all that is in the Old Testament (1 Cor. 10:6, 11; Rom. 15:4; 2 Tim. 3:16, 17) if we are not under the law in any sense? Indeed, it is this moral law that is inscribed *permanently* in our hearts, insuring its continuity (2 Cor. 3:1-3; Heb. 8:10).[9]

And is the New Testament law or moral code a contradiction to the Old Testament moral code? It cannot be a contradiction if God has not changed; and if He is immutable, the New Testament law is simply a restatement of the same Old Testament law. To say, as dispensationalists do, that we are not under Old Testament law but under New Testament law is to posit two kinds of law for one immutable God. There is one law and one Lawgiver (James 4:11, 12). The same Ten Commandments that judged Israel judge us (Rom. 13:8-10; James 2:8-13). To posit two law systems is incipient idolatry, for two conflicting systems of morality imply two gods with differing moralities. If the two law systems are the same, then why the fuss that we are not under Old Testament moral law? If the New Testament law is only a "higher" law — which I dispute — then we simply have a grander restatement of the same law, which we are under. And who could improve on God's Old Testament laws on adultery, theft, sodomy, blasphemy, and so on? What law would we use to replace His, and who would want to meet Him in the judgment having developed a "better" law system? Whose law would prevail then?

---

[9] For the most comprehensive study of the law see Greg Bahnsen's book: *Theonomy In Christian Ethics* (Nutley: Craig Press, 1977), 600+ pages.

Chapter Seven

Theological Tendencies

The reader is encouraged to read R. L. Dabney's chapters "Theology of the Plymouth Brethren" in his book, *Discussions, vol. 1*, pp. 169-228 for an excellent discussion of dispensational theology. His insights were made one hundred years ago and are still pertinent.

The following are tendencies that either accompany dispensationalism or are inherent to it. As you read over these errors, you may find yourself asking why they fall prey to so many blunders. George Santayana (1863-1952) once said, "Those who cannot remember the past are condemned to fulfill it." Likewise dispensationalists, generally speaking, not being able to find identity in the history of the church, have separated themselves from the mainstream of church history and, being ignorant of the ancient errors, are repeating them. For instant confirmation of this, just read Dabney's work mentioned above, for the errors he enumerates a hundred years ago are still being made today. Just read Zane Hodges book, *The Siege of the Gospel*, in which he says one can be a Christian and an unbeliever simultaneously. Several years ago I talked to one well known professor at Dallas Theological Seminary who had never read the Westminster Confession (and this is not an exception). When I asked him to read it, he said it would not be profitable, for he would disagree with its eschatology.[1] There is a tendency in dispensationalism to neglect works that have an eschatology contrary to their scheme, believing all truth is

---

[1] Craig Blaising in *Dispensationalism, Israel and the Church* incorrectly states that the "*Westminster Confession* states that the chief end of man is 'to glorify God and enjoy him forever'" (p. 27). As any small Reformed child would know, this is question 1 in the *Shorter Catechism*, not the *Confession*.

contained among themselves.

Some of the errors Dabney mentions are: denunciatory spirit toward brethren who disagree with them;[2] definition of saving faith as being mental assent (pp. 172ff.; 214ff.); assurance of salvation as mental assent and having nothing to do with fruit in one's life (pp. 173ff.); justification not based on the active obedience of Christ to God's law but only on His Cross-work (p. 187); sanctification an optional work of grace that begins when and if the saint obeys some command, sometimes called the victorious life (pp. 190ff.); regeneration as the adding of something new but not the changing of the person himself (p. 191) resulting in two natures (p. 193); "literal" hermeneutic (p. 192); no Christian Sabbath (p. 199); the discovery of God's will by prayer or by some mystical feeling of the heart (p. 201); premillennialism (p. 209); and pietistic retreat from involvement in the world because things will only get worse with Christ coming soon to "bail out the church." None of these errors has been corrected.

Repentance and Faith[3]

Rejecting moral law, especially Old Testament moral law, results in a number of consequences. They tend to reject the idea that Christ is ruling now by His law (or any law for that matter) as King of kings, relegating this to a future millennium. This in turn leads them to reject His Lordship in salvation, and maintain that one can have faith without works (the carnal Christian idea). There is a domino effect: rejecting the absoluteness of God's moral law as infallibly binding on all men at all times means Christ is not Lord now (He has no means of exercising dominion except by brute power) and also results in the lordship of Christ as optional in salvation; no lordship results in no repentance and no repentance means "saving faith" is mental assent. To cover up for those easy decisions their theology gives birth to, they brought forth the "carnal Christian" idea, which says that most Christians are living a life of disobedience to God and His Word. This is no doubt one of the most pernicious blunders within dispensationalism, for many in their churches are dying and going to hell, with the

---

[2] I think few dispensationalists would want to claim Peter Ruckman, but his extremely vitriolic spirit towards others is an example of this attitude.

[3] I have a very detailed discussion of repentance and faith in my new book, *Lordship Salvation: The Only Kind There Is*. It may be purchased from the publisher in the front of this book.

blessing of their leaders.

Not all dispensationalists hold to such error. Professor Marc T. Mueller at Talbot Theological Seminary has written a fine paper against the no repentance, no lordship view. Dr. Ryrie and Zane Hodges of Dallas Theological Seminary, however, are two of the most ardent defenders of the carnal Christian, no lordship idea. They completely misunderstand the nature of saving faith, which necessarily has works or else it is dead (James 2:14-28; 1 John 2:3, 4; Eph. 2:10; Titus 1:16). The works, of course, are not the grounds of our acceptance with God; they are the necessary evidence, without which no one will see the Lord (Heb. 12:14). Apparently Hodges is oblivious to this distinction between the ground of our acceptance (the blood of Christ), the means (faith), and the effect of acceptance (works). As one reads Hodges's book *The Hungry Inherit*, it is palpable that Mr. Hodges does not have an inkling of the nature of saving faith. His view of saving faith is the same as that among the Plymouth Brethren of Dabney's day, ". . . that false and soul-destroying Pelagian view of faith advanced by the followers of Alexander Campbell.[4] He [Campbell and the dispensationalists of his day] describes faith and unbelief as two antithetic states of *opinion*. . . ." Or faith is a ". . . mere matter of natural knowledge" or "a *means of* regeneration."[5] With the inordinate emphasis that dispensationalists place on eschatology, they tend to be sloppy in other areas of theology, from Dabney's day to ours.

There is a difference between Ryrie and Hodges that should be noted. Ryrie seems to live with a contradiction, believing that no one will be saved without works[6] but also denying the Lordship of Christ in salvation.[7] Hodges, on the other hand, solves the logical problem by denying *any* necessity for works in the Christian's life. At least Ryrie is more biblical. It may be that Ryrie does not want to make lordship a condition for *becoming* a Christian while lordship is necessary sooner or later once one has become a Christian, which is still unbiblical (Luke 14:25-35) but more forgivable than Hodges's ranker antinomianism.

---

[4]Campbellites are the modern day Churches of Christ.

[5]R. L. Dabney, *Discussions*, vol. 1 (Harrisonburg: Sprinkle Pub., 1982), pp. 185, 186.

[6]C. C. Ryrie, *Ryrie Study Bible*, note on James 2:24.

[7]C. C. Ryrie, *Balancing The Christian Life* (Chicago: Moody Press, 1971), p. 169ff.

And how do I know that Mr. Hodges holds to these same Pelagian views? Notice what he says on the nature of saving faith:

> It must be emphasized that there is no call here [woman at the well] for surrender, submission, acknowledgement of Christ's Lordship, or anything else of this kind. A gift is being offered to one totally unworthy of God's favor. And to get it, the woman is required *to make no spiritual commitment whatsoever* [emphasis added]. She is merely invited to ask.[8]

Is not this the mental assent Dabney spoke of? Is it not clear that Hodges has no idea of the nature of saving faith? He assumes that the faith spoken of in the John four text involves the mind but not the will and affections. He does not allow the possibility that Scripture may elsewhere define faith as necessarily involving the will (1 John 2:3, 4) and affections (1Cor. 16:22). Do all passages have to say *everything* about faith? With the dispensational hermeneutic of pitting one passage against another, of dividing Scripture into convenient parts with some parts not for today, he builds his whole concept of saving faith from a few passages. How does he handle the passages that contradict his thesis? He explains them in light of his already developed theory. In other words, in lieu of taking *all* of Scripture *before* deriving his view of faith, he takes a few verses that ostensibly support his position, and then he explains the other verses from this "derived" position. The same hermeneutic of polarizing the Bible is used by dispensationalists in their eschatology, taking a few Old Testament passages to establish their system ["unconditional" covenant with Abraham] and then explaining the rest of the Bible from this "derived" position.

As an oddity of this polarized hermeneutic, Mr. Hodges also says that the Jews in Palestine during the time of the apostles had to be water baptized to be saved.[9] Why does he say this? Because Acts 2:38 and Acts 22:16 seem to promote this at first glance, and no other passage can be considered, for this would violate the hermeneutic of "taking each passage as it stands." Dispensationalists tend to have distinction without unity, pitting passage against passage, finding the analogy of faith hermeneutic useless. Interestingly, though, when one points out that saints must endure to the end to be saved (Matt. 24:13), then they use the analogy of faith to say that this passage contradicts other verses, or that this passage is for the "kingdom," not for us today.

---

[8]Zane Hodges, *The Gospel Under Siege* (Redencion Viva, Box 141167, Dallas, TX 75214), p. 14.

[9]Hodges, p. 101ff.

Truly the words of the Puritan divine John Flavel are apropos at this point:

> Christ is offered to us in the gospel entirely and undividedly, as clothed with all his offices, priestly, prophetical, and regal; as Christ Jesus the Lord, Acts 16:31, and so the true believer receives him; the *hypocrite*, like the *harlot*, is for dividing, but the sincere believer finds the need he hath of every office of Christ, and knows not how to want any thing that is in him.

> His ignorance makes him necessary and desirable to him as a *prophet*: His guilt makes him necessary as a *priest*: His strong and powerful lusts and corruptions make him necessary as a *king*: and in truth, he sees not anything in Christ he can spare; he needs all that is in Christ, and admires infinite wisdom in nothing more than the investing Christ with all these offices, which are so suited to the poor sinner's wants and miseries. Look, as the three offices are undivided in Christ, so they are in the believer's acceptance; and before this trial no hypocrite can stand; for all hypocrites reject and quarrel with something in Christ; they like his pardon better than his government. They call him, indeed, Lord and Master, but it is an empty title they bestow upon him; for let them ask their own hearts if Christ be Lord over their *thoughts*, as well as *words*; over their *secret* as well as *open* actions; over their *darling* lusts, as well as others; let them ask, who will appear to be Lord and Master over them, when Christ and the world come into competition? When the pleasure of sin shall stand upon one side, and sufferings to death, and deepest points of self-denial upon the other side? *Surely it is the greatest affront that can be offered to the divine wisdom and goodness, to separate in our acceptance, what is so united in Christ, for our salvation and happiness.* As without one of these offices, the work of our salvation could not be completed, so without acceptance of Christ in them all, our union with him by faith cannot be completed.

> The gospel offer of Christ includes all his offices, and gospel faith just so receives him; to submit to him, as well as to be redeemed by him; to imitate him in the holiness of his life, as well as to reap the purchases and fruits of his death. It must be an entire receiving of the Lord Jesus Christ.[10]

Mr. Hodges's definition of grace is no better: "The bestowal of a superlatively valuable gift as an act of unconditional generosity was precisely the kind of action most likely to *woo* [emphasis added] her from her former ways. It is more likely by far to have accomplished

---

[10]John Flavel, *The Works of John Flavel, Six Volumes* (London: Banner of Truth Trust, reprint), vol. 2, pp. 110-11.

this result than any legalistic undertaking into which she might have entered."[11] Notice the word "woo." All Jesus can do is hope to "persuade" the woman at the well from her unbelief; His grace is resistible and impotent. She has the final say and the innate ability to believe. This concept of "grace" is the moral influence view, the legalistic (to use his word) idea that man merits God's grace by his moral ability to cooperate with God. Has he not read in the Scriptures that God irresistibly opens the hearts of men to enable them to believe (Acts 13:48; 16:14; John 6:44, 45; Rom. 9:16, 18; 11:7; Phil. 1:29) and that the natural man *cannot* understand or believe (John 6:44; 1 Cor. 2:14; Rom. 8:5-8)? Most dispensationalists agree with Hodges's semi-Pelagianism.

Again I quote from Mr. Hodges: "It is He who decides to regenerate. We simply open ourselves to that action with the receptivity of a believing heart."[12] Observe that the word "simply" shows how easy this autosoterism is, how easy it is to open one's own heart, how easy it is to lift up oneself by his boot straps, how easy it is to open our *totally* depraved hearts. Such semi-Pelagianism is also reflected in the doctrinal statement of Dallas Theological Seminary: "We believe that the new birth of the believer comes only through faith in Christ. . . ." (Article VII). But how does one get faith in Christ? Where in the "goodness" of man's totally depraved heart does this faith arise? Faith is the effect of the new birth, not the cause, as John the Apostle points out. In 1 John 2:29; 3:9; 4:7 the effect of regeneration is living righteously and loving God and the brethren while in 5:1, 4 the effect is faith. The effect is seen by the relationship of the perfect tense — new birth — to the present tense — practicing righteousness, loving God, overcoming, and faith. Just as we would not say we are born again by works in 2:29; 3:9; 4:7, so we would not maintain we are born again by faith in 5:1, 4. The Greek construction is the same.

James two legislates that faith without works is dead. Hodges agrees but says the person is still saved.[13] A Christian, he maintains, is not necessarily a present believer but one who has believed once in the past. What incredible antinomianism! And he accuses those who reject his position of being of the devil.[14] Of course such a position

---

[11]Hodges, p. 15.

[12]Hodges, p. 21.

[13]Hodges, pp. 20, 33.

[14]Hodges, p. 6.

places a wide temporal gap between justification (being accepted by God as His child) and sanctification (being made into the moral image of Christ), making sanctification a subsequent and optional work of grace to justification.

Likewise Ryrie, in *Balancing the Christian Life*, devotes a whole chapter to "prove" that a "Christian" can have Jesus as His justifier while rejecting Him as his sanctifier. And like Hodges, he strongly implies that J. I. Packer, A. W. Pink, and John R. W. Stott are preachers of another gospel[15] because they believe in Lordship salvation. Again it is obvious that Ryrie does not understand the nature of saving faith. For if faith necessarily contains works (Eph. 2:10), then one cannot believe without surrendering to Christ; and if there is a false faith (Matt. 7:15-23; 13:18-23), then there must be some way to discriminate between the genuine and the counterfeit. Faith is like a bulb from which the flower blooms. The life and works are inseparable from the bulb and contained in the bulb, necessarily growing and blooming into a flower to the glory of its Maker.

And how does Mr. Hodges understand Galatians 5:21 and 1 Corinthians 6:9, 10 that say that those who practice unrighteousness will not inherit the kingdom of God? His reply is that *inheriting* is not the same as *entering*[16] but *inheriting* refers to obtaining a reward by works![17] Yet we run into such passages as "it is through many tribulations that we *enter* the kingdom of God" (Acts 14:22). Paul preached *about* the kingdom of God (Acts 19:8) and *just* the kingdom of God (Acts 20:25; 28:23, 31) with no hint that such a distinction between *entering* and *inheriting* was ever in his mind. Also Paul speaks of "inheriting" the kingdom of God in 1 Corinthians 15:50 as the same as "entering" it, of no immoral person "inheriting" the kingdom in Ephesians 5:5, and then he adds in v. 6: "Let no one deceive you with empty words, for because of these things *the wrath of God* comes upon *the sons of disobedience.*" Does Mr. Hodges also maintain that there is a wrath of God on true believers and that they are called "sons of disobedience"? In short we are *transferred* into the kingdom of Christ (Col. 1:13), *called* into this kingdom (1 Thess. 2:12), *considered worthy* of the kingdom (2 Thess. 1:5), *enter* the

---

[15]Ryrie, *Balancing the Christian Life*, pp. 169-70. This whole chapter argues against lordship.

[16]Hodges, p. 115.

[17]Hodges, p. 116.

kingdom (Acts 14:22), and *inherit* the kingdom (1 Cor. 6:9, 10; Gal. 5:21; Eph. 5:5), with little or no distinction between the expressions.

In 1 John when John says no murderer has eternal life (3:15), the key word, according to Hodges, is *abiding*. One may *have* eternal life without having eternal life *abiding* in him.[18] When John legislates that one's character reveals whether he belongs to Satan or Christ (3:10), John supposedly meant that this is the way one reveals his true spiritual father. In other words, if he chooses to live correctly, then it may be discerned by his character that his father is God. But we should not conclude from this, Hodges asserts, that one's character is *always* meant to be a sure sign of his paternal relationship.[19] It can be if the Christian so chooses, but may not be if he chooses to live ungodly. The surest answer to such casuistry is to quote the passage:

> Little children, let no one deceive you; the one who practices righteousness is righteous, just as He is righteous; the one who practices sin is of the devil; for the devil has sinned from the beginning. The Son of God appeared for this purpose, that He might destroy the works of the devil. No one who is born of God practices sin, because His seed abides in him; and he cannot (practice) sin, because he is born of God. *By this the children of God and the children of the devil are obvious*: anyone who does not practice righteousness is not of God, nor the one who does not love his brother (3:7-10).

Is not John clear? "*Anyone* who does not practice righteousness is not of God"! We know from the analogy of faith that John is not presenting sinless perfection because he says in 1:7-2:2 that Christians do sin; but he is telling us that sin *cannot* be master over the believer anymore (see Rom. 6:14), for Christ came to destroy the devil's works, not to give believers the option to promote them.

In addition, Mr. Hodges perused the whole book of 1 John in his book but never mentioned this passage:

> By this we know that we have come to know Him, if we keep His commandments. The one who says, "I have come to know Him," and does not keep His commandments is a liar, and the truth is not in him (2:3, 4).

Mr. Hodges and dispensationalists in general have another domino in their chain reaction, which is perfectionism, the idea that sanctification is by one's works, which has two corollaries: either a "victori-

---

[18]Hodges, p. 64.

[19]Hodges, p. 62.

ous" life or a sinless life. Not many dispensationalists believe in absolute perfection in this life, but Mr. Hodges has a strange twist: "The point unmistakably is: if you abide in a sinless Person, you do not sin."[20] Apparently, one can be sinless if he abides in Christ. Now according to Hodges and most dispensationalists, some Christians abide in Christ and some do not. There is a distinction (the great disparity hermeneutic again) between those who are "positionally" in Christ and those who "practically" abide in Christ. Such specious reasoning is easily toppled by John 6:55; 15:6; 1 John 3:14; 4:12-16, in which we see that all Christians abide in Christ, and Christ in them. There is mutual abiding of Christ in them and they in Him or no abiding at all.

The other corollary is the "victorious life." If we simply "*let* God" sanctify us enough, we will live on a higher plane than other Christians and not be "carnal" but "victorious." (See Warfield's critique of *He That Is Spiritual* in Appendix 1 for further discussion of this.)

This works theology stems from an errant view of regeneration, a view that says that the new birth only adds a "new nature" alongside the old nature, so that now the Christian must cast the deciding vote as to whether he will, at any given moment, function through the "new" or "old" nature. If the Christian functions through the new nature, he is "victorious." And the old nature cannot be improved nor the new nature lessened. This alleged switching back and forth between these two "natures" is dangerous, for it tends to promote the carnal Christian theory with its corollary of "victorious" living, or absolute perfectionism. It is not by accident that most of the perfectionistic and victorious life groups, such as Holiness and Pentecostal people, are also dispensational.

Thomas Constable, a current professor at Dallas Theological Seminary, promotes the same doctrine as Hodges. On the one hand he says faith "is an act of the whole man: intellect, emotion, and will."[21] This much is good. Then he denies that repentance involves anything but a change of mind.[22] He says that some believe repentance is a separate act that must precede faith. Who the some are who maintain such a monstrosity he does not say, but it is not from the Reformed. We hold that repentance and faith are inseparably bound together.

---

[20]Hodges, p. 60.

[21]Donald K. Campbell, *Walvoord: A Tribute* (Chicago: Moody Press, 1982), p. 206.

[22]Campbell, p. 207.

Dr. Constable maintains that one can have repentance without faith but not faith without repentance.[23] Ostensibly the latter half of this sounds good. But remember, for our professor repentance is only a mental activity — not an activity of the will and affections: "Repentance means to change one's mind; it does not mean to change one's life (though that should follow changing one's mind)."[24] And whoever thought differently about repentance, that it is a change of mind that results in a change of life? Apparently for him repentance may not result in a change of life; it "should" but not necessarily. Then how does he explain all those passages that demonstrate that repentance *necessarily* results in a change of life and involves the will as well as the mind? His answer is: "In those passages repentance is viewed not as an act separate from believing but as the process involved in transferring one's trust to Christ."[25] How — in the name of all that is sensible — can one transfer his trust to Christ without an act of the will? And that repentance does involve the will is abundantly clear: ". . . that they should repent and turn to God, *performing deeds appropriate to repentance*" (Acts 26:20).[26] John the Baptist refused to baptize those who had not first brought forth fruit in keeping with their profession of repentance (Matt. 3:7-10). Of course this passage is before Pentecost, but unless the dispensationalists believe in two ways of salvation, the verses must stand in all their strength. And we have already seen that faith has the same works (James 2:14-26; 1 John 2:3, 4). What these dispensationalists do not realize is that the nature of faith or repentance necessarily entails works. Neither the works nor the faith saves — only Jesus does. The Christian's confidence is never in his works but only in Christ. But a lack of works indicates a non-genuine faith (Titus 1:16). Faith is the only instrument of justification, but it is never alone. And Scripture has no problem in commanding a sinner to turn from his sins in order to be saved (Acts 3:19, 26; 26:18-20; Luke 24:47).

One good illustration is physical birth. How many works does a

---

[23]Campbell, p. 208.

[24]Campbell, p. 207.

[25]Campbell, pp. 207-08.

[26]I have written a book on the lordship issue, especially concentrating on regeneration, faith/repentance, justification/sanctification, and assurance. The reader may order the book from the same publisher at the front of this book and ask for *Lordship Salvation: The Only Kind There Is*, by Curtis I. Crenshaw.

child do for his parents before he is conceived? None. Why? He has no life. Once the child is born he manifests his life by years of works. The commands he obeys from his father do not produce life in him but only manifest the life. If the child is stillborn, however, and consequently never works, never moves, never blinks, and never breathes, we would rightly conclude that he had no life. The same is true of faith and works; one cannot believe or obey until the life is given. Even faith is an obedience to God (John 3:36; 1 Peter 2:7, 8) that manifests the life of the new birth (1 John 5:1). To say one can have faith or repentance without works is to promote a faith of mental assent. The demons have this. It is quite impossible to believe the gospel message without bowing to Christ as Lord, for the faith that saves is a working faith.

Observe how lucid and balanced the Westminster Confession is concerning sanctification, faith, works, and sin in the life of a believer:

CONCERNING SANCTIFICATION: They, who are at once effectually called, and regenerated, having a new heart, and a new spirit created in them, are further sanctified, really and personally [Ed: not "positionally"], through the virtue of Christ's death and resurrection, by His Word and Spirit dwelling in them: the dominion of the whole body is destroyed, and the several lusts thereof are more and more weakened and mortified ["old nature" or indwelling sin is destroyed]; and they more and more quickened and strengthened in all saving graces, to the practice of true holiness, without which no man shall see the Lord (Chapter 13).

CONCERNING SAVING FAITH: But the principal acts of saving faith are accepting, receiving, and resting upon Christ alone for justification, sanctification, and eternal life. . . . (Chapter 14).

CONCERNING GOOD WORKS: These good works, done in obedience to God's commandments, are the fruits and evidences of a true and lively faith. . . . Their [saints] ability to do good works is not at all of themselves, but wholly from the Spirit of Christ [works stem from grace, not the reverse]. And that they may be enabled thereunto, beside the graces they have already received, there is required an actual influence [not moral influence as the Pelagians teach, for observe the rest of the words] of the same Holy Spirit, to work in them to will, and to do, of His good pleasure: yet are they not hereupon to grow negligent, as if they were not bound to perform any duty unless upon a special motion of the Spirit; but they ought to be diligent in stirring up the grace of God that is in them. . . . We cannot by our best works merit pardon of sin . . . nor satisfy the debt of our former sins, but when we have done all we can, we have done but our duty, and are unprofitable servants: and because, as they [works] are good, they proceed from His Spirit; and as they are wrought by us, they are defiled, and mixed with so much weakness and imperfection [no work is ever perfect in this life; so much for sinlessly abiding in Christ], that they cannot endure the severity of God's judgment (Chapter 16).

CONCERNING PERSEVERANCE: They, whom God hath accepted in His Beloved, effectually called, and sanctified by His Spirit, can neither totally nor finally fall away from the state of grace, but shall certainly persevere therein to the end [not sin all they want], and be eternally saved. This perseverance of the saints depends not upon their own free will, but upon the immutability of the decree of election, flowing from the free and unchangeable love of God the Father; upon the efficacy of the merit and intercession of Jesus Christ, the abiding of the Spirit, and of the seed of God within them, and the nature of the covenant of grace: from all which ariseth also the certainty and infallibility thereof. Nevertheless, they may, through the temptations of Satan and of the world, the prevalence of corruption remaining in them, and the neglect of the means of their preservation, fall into grievous sins; and, *for a time* [not indefinitely], continue therein: whereby they incur God's displeasure, and grieve His Holy Spirit, come to be deprived of some measure of their graces and comforts, have their hearts hardened, and their consciences wounded; hurt and scandalize others, and bring temporal judgments upon themselves (Chapter 17).

My heart was greatly refreshed when I first read these gems; I felt like I had had a second conversion. At last I was out of the bondage of sanctification by works. Warfield's book entitled *Perfectionism* had also helped tremendously.

Ryrie's chapter on sanctification in the *Festschrift*, *Walvoord: A Tribute* indicates the same confusion over the Reformed view of sanctification. He says that Dallas Theological Seminary's view of progressive sanctification is the same as the Reformed, differing only in emphasis. However, why did Warfield critique Chafer's book, *He That Is Spiritual*, if there is no difference, and why does Ryrie say in this chapter that the Reformed emphasize the sovereignty of God too much and that they tend to make sanctification automatic?[27] Has he not read the above Confession where works and human co-operation are made the necessary result of God's grace, that divine activity engenders human activity and not the reverse?[28] The bottom line is, Who controls the process in the growth of sanctification, God or man? Ryrie and the dispensationalists in general want the individual Chris-

---

[27]Campbell, p. 198.

[28]Campbell, p. 199.

tian to be "boss," and the Reformed, reflecting the Bible, say that God is in control (Phil. 2:12, 13; 1 John 3:9), that the statements of fact in Romans 6:1-10 necessarily produce the response of Romans 6:11-13. The Reformed do not maintain that the response of Romans 6:11-13 makes the facts of Romans 6:1-10 true. The "is," in other words, gives rise to the "ought," for Paul only gives a command after he shows us that the grace of God will enable us to perform the "ought." It would be bondage and works for Paul to teach that our obedience merits God's grace, and that our effort brings the "position" to bear in our lives. The Reformed believe that grace produces obedience and the dispensationalists believe that obedience merits grace.

Nor is it true that Warfield and John Murray held to differing views on this as Ryrie would lead us to believe,[29] for both men held to the same Confession of faith. Nor is it even close to true that Murray held to "an initial act of dedication" that was like Chafer's. Murray does mention an act of dedication in his commentary on Romans, but that this is not the "initial act" that begins sanctification as Chafer taught is clear from his comments in *Redemption Accomplished and Applied*, for he begins sanctification in regeneration,[30] logically prior to faith.

Ryrie is also wrong in saying that the Reformed hold to the same teaching on positional sanctification as the typical dispensationalist, for again Murray says:

> We must appreciate this teaching of Scripture. Every one called effectually by God and regenerated by the Spirit has secured the victory in the terms of Romans 6:14; 1 John 3:9; 5:4, 18. And this victory is actual or it is nothing. *It is a reflection upon and a deflection from the pervasive New Testament witness to speak of it as merely potential or positional.* It is actual and practical as much as anything comprised in the application of redemption is actual and practical.[31]

For Ryrie positional sanctification means only possibility but for the Reformed it is actual, effecting the life of the believer. For Ryrie one makes his position true by obedience, but for the Reformed the position causes our obedience. And this is the heart of the matter: Does the imperative (obedience) *optionally* make the indicative true (position), or does the indicative *necessarily* give rise to the imperative?

---

[29]Campbell, p. 195.

[30]John Murray, *Redemption Accomplished and Applied* (Grand Rapids: Eerdmans, 1973), p. 141.

[31]Murray, p. 142.

Philippians 2:12, 13 demands the latter.

Marsden describes this teaching as common among dispensation-alists around the turn of the century, especially with Moody and with the Keswick movement of Moody's day, the two being essentially the same:

> The rest of Keswick teaching follows from these concepts of sin and counteracting grace. There are two stages of Christian experience: that of the "carnal Christian," and that of the "spiritual." To move from the lower to the higher state takes a definite act of faith or "consecration," the prerequisite to being filled with the Spirit. This consecration means an "absolute surrender," almost always described by the Biblical term "yielding." Self is dethroned, God is enthroned. This sanctification is a process, but one that begins with a distinct crisis experience.[32]

This faulty view of faith and sanctification is one of the most serious errors in dispensationalism, for it condemns many to hell who think they are believers and are "just" carnal. They have no fruit in their lives, but they are told not to worry: they do not have to evidence any salvation. A former pastor of mine counselled a lady and told her she was carnal but saved. She had no fruit. Later by her own admission she realized she was lost. She was challenged out of her superficial "faith" when she attended a church that preached holiness. If she had stayed in her old church (humanly speaking), she would have died and gone to hell. But in essence she was told that she could have had the best of both worlds, heaven later and her sin for a season now. Indeed, many will profess to know Jesus at the judgment, but He will tell them to depart: "You will know them by their fruits," and "I never knew you, depart from Me, *you who practice lawlessness*" (Matt. 7:16, 23). The consequences are eternal.

Dispensationalists must turn from this low view of God's holiness and of His law, and command all men everywhere to repent (Acts 17:30), which means that sinners must turn from their sins (Acts 3:29, 26), bringing forth the fruit of works as evidence of their (Acts 20:21) repentance (Acts 26:18, 20). Commanding people to turn from their sins is to recognize biblical faith, a faith that works. All people must believe and repent (Mark 1:14, 15; Acts 20:21; 2 Tim. 2:25; 2 Cor. 7:8-10; Rom. 2:4). One cannot have true faith without having repentance; the two necessarily go together.

---

[32] George M. Marsden, *Fundamentalism and American Culture* (New York: Oxford, 1982), p. 80.

Pietism

Another tendency of dispensationalism, almost as bad as the one above, is preoccupation with the insignificant with the attending retreat into pietism. Pietism is the idea that the political world is somehow evil and to be retreated from, that the individual Christian and his private spiritual life are the only concerns. If I may quote two scholars: "At its worst the pietistic tendency can lead to inordinate subjectivism and emotionalism . . . ."[33] Again, "Some say it [pietism] was essentially a revival of medieval monastic and mystical piety. . . ."[34] The words "subjectivism" and "monastic" as used by these scholars confirms the basic idea that pietists retreat from society. It is a retreat into passive do-nothing-but-wait-for-the-rapture syndrome. It may be recognized by such statements as, "The Christian should not be in politics." Why not? Who should be there? The devil's children? Pietistic people promote the idea (however unconsciously) that there are some areas over which Satan is lord, and Jesus and His children dare not challenge him for fear of defeat.

In his chapter David K. Lowery develops this pietism,[35] (see heading "Who Rules the World" below), and he says: ". . . . righteousness is fundamentally inward rather than external. . . ."[36] In this age the Lord's kingdom allegedly has nothing to do with the nations and with political forces. One can practice righteousness between his ears, but he should not think that he can or should do so any other place. Christians must not be the salt and light. Christians may have internal success, but externally they will only experience defeat: "That kingdom [the Lord's] exists alongside the kingdoms of earth and suffers tribulation at those kingdoms' hands."[37]

This pietistic retreat comes not only from their pessimistic eschatology but also from three other sources: (1) Manichaeism, (2) denial of the present Lordship of Christ, and (3) denying the relevance of the Old Testament with a corresponding move to a more "private" Christianity. (1) Manichaeism is the teaching that matter and externals

---

[33]Walter A. Elwell, Editor, *Evangelical Dictionary of Theology*, (Grand Rapids: Baker Book House, 1984), p. 858.

[34]J. D. Douglas, *The New International Dictionary of the Christian Church* (Grand Rapids: Zondervan, 1974), p. 780.

[35]Craig Blaising, *Dispensationalism, Israel and the Church*, chapter 7.

[36]Ibid., p. 246.

[37]Ibid., p. 64.

are evil and the spiritual good. Consequently they go to Bible studies since this is inward, spiritual and therefore good; but they leave politics alone. If one were trained for the ministry and then worked at a book company, this would be terrible, for the ministry is spiritual and the book company second rate.

Along with Manichaeism is narcissism; everything must be for me and my growth. Little or nothing is presented for our culture or for others. No Mother Teresa can come out of this.[38]

(2) Also they relegate the rulership of Christ to the so-called millennium or thousand year reign of Christ on earth. Since Christ is not reigning now, the Christian has everything to fear and could not possibly conquer Satan in his own territory. But consider this verse: "When He had disarmed the rulers and authorities, He made a public display of them, having triumphed over them through it (the cross)" (Col. 2:15), or "He must reign until He has put all His enemies under His feet" (1 Cor. 15:25), and "The Lord said to my Lord, 'Sit at my right hand, until I make thine enemies a footstool for thy feet.' Therefore let all the house of Israel know *for certain* that God has made Him both Lord and Christ" (Acts 2:34, 35). Does this sound like defeat? I thought we were to subdue our enemies under our feet (Rom. 16:20). In regard to abortion God says:

> Deliver those who are being taken away to death; and those who are staggering to slaughter, O hold them back. If you say, "See, we did not know this," Does He not consider it who weighs the hearts? And does He not know it who keeps your soul? *And will He not render to man according to his work*? (Prov. 24:11, 12)

Does this sound like God will overlook the sin of omission, of not speaking out? Consider again what the Holy One of Israel commands:

> But if the watchman sees the sword coming and does not blow the trumpet, and the people are not warned, and a sword comes and takes a person from them, he is taken away in his iniquity; but his blood I will require from the watchman's hand. (Ez. 33:6)

Does this not sound like God will require us to stand against the tide, and not run to the nearest church to hide and pray for the rapture?

(3) Marsden points out that dispensationalism brought in a "more private view of Christianity" (p. 88). He elaborates on this by saying

---

[38]One must read Philip Lee's *Against the Protestant Gnostics* (Oxford University Press) for a brilliant examination of gnosticism in Protestantism, especially in dispensationalism.

that the departure from the Old Testament ethic, with its strong legislations for society, has lead the dispensationalists and the fundamentalists into a retreat from society. Since God allegedly only works in individual conversion, and since Satan ostensibly rules this world and its governments, Christians should avoid all political involvement. God only works with individuals; He cannot work with a covenanted group, whether that group is a local church or a nation. God cannot operate through the legislation of a nation to sanctify the nation (pp. 86-88). Since the Old Testament concerned itself primarily with these things, who needs it? God will again deal with the Israel of the Old Testament sometime in the future, so these laws are not for us today. Meanwhile we must preach the gospel for conversion, as nothing else will change society. By contrast just look at Deuteronomy 8 and 28 for chapters that refute the idea that God is not concerned with national sanctification as well as personal sanctification.

Marsden documents two famous dispensationalists, James M. Gray and Arno C. Gaebelein, saying that Christians should stay out of social areas, that the gospel is the only way to change society.[39] These dispensational men said this in 1916 - 1919. Have dispensationalists changed? Ryrie in *You Mean the Bible Teaches That*, says that the "Christian's primary responsibilities are evangelism and godly living. Through witnessing he changes men; through righteous living he affects society. . . ."[40] The implication is that we should not be too concerned about the evils of society directly, only indirectly.

Of course the Scripture is replete with instructions to nations. God commands that the nation which obeys Him will be blessed and the one that does not will be cursed (Deut. 8, 28); that the individual has the responsibility to warn the nation of God's temporal judgment (Ez. 33: 1-9), to pray for it (Psalm 85:1-7; 1 Tim. 2:1, 2), to teach the nations the laws of Christ (Matt. 28:19, 20), to influence it all he can (Prov. 14:34); and that the citizens of a nation are accountable for the sins of the leaders and of the sins of the nation as a whole (2 Sam. 24:10-17; 1 Chron. 21:1-8; Joshua 7:1, 11-26).

There is a national sanctification. When the nation through its leaders honors God's laws, God honors the nation. How else are we to understand Deuteronomy 28 where God promises blessings, economic, military, and social ones, to the nation that obeys His laws?

---

[39]Marsden, pp. 154-156.

[40]Ryrie, p. 22.

How else can we take Proverbs 14:34 that says that righteousness exalts a nation? Is the righteousness conversion or national obedience? The context is obedience. And how does a king give stability to a land by justice (Prov. 29:4) if the justice is not based on God's law, indeed, obedience to God's law?

And gaze on this verse: "Where there is no vision [revelation], the people are unrestrained, but happy is he who *keeps the law*" (Prov. 29:18). The word for "vision" is consistently used in the Old Testament for supernatural revelation from God, so that the people or nation who keep God's law are blessed. The people are *restrained* by revelation from God, which is national sanctification. Gary North has well observed this inherent contradiction in dispensationalism:

> Why is it that Satan's earthly followers, who violate God's principles for successful living, supposedly will remain in control of the world until the Rapture? Are we supposed to believe that Satan's principles produce personal failure but cultural success, while biblical principles produce personal success but cultural failure? Does this make sense to you? It doesn't to me.[41]

Humanistic

A third tendency in dispensationalism, since it discards most of the Old Testament law and biblical law as irrelevant, is to look to humanism for answers in many areas. For example, we were taught at Dallas Theological Seminary that the Bible is not a textbook on counselling, and therefore we needed Freud, Rogers, Mowrer, Narramore and other humanists for our counselling techniques and messages. Or, they give equal weight to the secular techniques and to the Bible, attempting to mix the oil and the water. In a practice counselling session at Seminary one professor mandated me not to use Scripture initially but to reflect back to the counselee what he was saying and see if he could discover his own problem. I could not (and still do not) understand why I should play a "cat and mouse" game with one who was hurting and needed an answer from God. Do our medical doctors let their patients discover what is wrong with themselves? Jay Adams was quite refreshing when he came to the seminary and spoke on counselling, both its message and its methods. He is Reformed, of course.

Likewise we were told that the Bible was not a textbook on

---

[41] "Christian Reconstruction," July/August, 1985, box 8000, Tyler, Tx. 75711

economics so we had to be trained by secular men if we wanted to enter that field. Gary North, Tom Rose, and others have certainly proved the futility of such a statement, as they have derived a whole economic philosophy and laws of money from the Bible. They observed that God has ordained silver and gold for money and not worthless paper, that fiat money is both theft and inflationary, and many other insights that we should be imitating to protect ourselves before God judges the whole economy.

And since the Bible was not a manual on politics, we should not judge the government or worry about it. The government is allegedly autonomous, creating its own laws and morality with God's blessing, indicating separation of church and state, or better, separation of state and God. Then along came R. J. Rushdoony with the *Institutes of Biblical Law*, demonstrating how wonderful God's laws are for society, especially when compared to men's fickle and tyrannical laws. He, armed with God's law, vitiated the "morality" of man. We either have autonomy (self law) or Theonomy (God's law), the two being mutually exclusive, with only God's law being immutable and crushing all other laws into the dust. Rebellion against the Almighty's morality is like being trapped in quicksand: the more a supercilious nation rebels against God's precepts, the deeper it sinks into the quagmire of its own self-destruction. Indeed, the nation's rebellion is the fuel for the fire of its own judgment. Its "self government" is the whetstone against which God sharpens the sword of His almighty wrath. As a guillotine blade is suspended over a bare neck with a small cord supporting it, so every man-made law "snaps a thread" of the cord, tempting God to "cut the cord" and chop the nation's head off.

But the Adams, Norths, and Rushdoonys use all the Bible, in obedience to Romans 15:4; 1 Corinthians 9:8-10; 10:6, 11; 2 Timothy 3:15-17. Why do the dispensationalists seldom — if ever — write in the areas of counselling with the Bible, or of economics, politics, etc.? I'm convinced that the main reason is that they have a weak view of biblical inspiration. I'm not saying that they do not believe in verbal, plenary infallibility — I learned this view from them and count it one of the blessings I gained from them. But what they affirm with their lips they deny with their lives. How? In two ways: (1) practically they deny the wonderful relevance of the Old Testament for today, (2) and they would seldom — if ever — take an inference from Scripture or follow an example from the Bible.

(1) I never could decipher the dispensational method of applying

the Old Testament to today. I recall asking one professor how we are to utilize it, and he said we should take the principles of the Old Testament as long as it did not contradict the New Testament. I asked him how we derive a principle from Proverbs 3:5, 6, where God says to trust Him in all circumstances. This did not look like a principle but a divine command. He said we should take the Old Testament as it stands when it speaks of God. I asked where we find this hermeneutic in the New Testament, for our hermeneutic was supposed to come from the New Testament. He did not know.

Another professor said only take the Old Testament when it is repeated in the New Testament. Another said none of it was applicable. It is not my purpose to give a defense of using the Old Testament for today, only let me ask, Were the Old Testament laws good for Israel? Were they arbitrary morals God used for a while and then discarded? Were they not a revelation of God's own holy and immutable character? If they were good laws for Israel, why wouldn't they be good for us? Who could improve on God's laws regarding adultery, murder, rape, etc. I am speaking of the moral laws, of course, as the ceremonial law found its eternal location in the death and resurrection of Christ. What laws would we use to replace these moral laws? Man's laws? Whose morality is better? God's or man's?

(2) We use not only the Bible but also its implications, for this is the teaching of the Bible, too. We were taught at Seminary that we should seldom take an inference from the biblical text. If God wanted us to know something, He would tell us outright. If God does not specifically command something, we felt no obligation to obey. For example, the fact that God indicts Israel for having silver diluted with dross leads North to conclude that we should use it for money and must not dilute it through printing more and more paper into existence (Isa. 1:22).[42] Paul took the inference from the unmuzzled ox that ministers should be paid (1 Cor. 9:8-10). If one says, "Yes, but their writings are inspired and they were directed by God," our reply is, "The Reformed use the apostles' hermeneutic; whose hermeneutic does the objector use? Who gave the objector this hermeneutic? Was it derived from a 'sound philosophy of language,' from man, or from the Scriptures?"

R. L. Dabney quotes the Westminster Confession of Faith: "There is not an intelligent protestant in the world, who does not hold that

---

[42]North stated this to me in private conversation.

what follows from the express Word, 'by good and necessary inference,' is binding, as well as the Word itself."[43] Of course we understand that Dabney means a *valid* ("necessary") inference according
to the canons of logic, not arbitrary ones that the reader wishes to
make. One cannot violate the rules of logic in taking invalid inferences
and maintain this is what the Bible says. The Lord Jesus took a valid
inference from the present tense of "I *am* the God of Abraham" to
prove the resurrection. Furthermore, nowhere does the Bible explicitly
state that "there is one God eternally existing in three equal persons,
the same in substance, equal in power and glory," but we would rightly
regard as heretical anyone who denied this valid inference and summary of biblical truth.

Another aspect of no inference is that for dispensationalists truths
in Scripture are like isolated beads spilled on the floor, unstrung,
independent of one another, without reference by inference to other
doctrines. Their truncated hermeneutic leads them to consider the part
without the whole, one passage without the rest of the Bible. This is
why they can say that parts of the New Testament are for today, but
the rest of the Bible is for "Israel" or irrelevant, that justification exists
without sanctification and election without reprobation; that atonement is substitutionary but Christ substituted for those who do not go
free, and so on. Though the latest book by dispensationalists, *Dispensationalism, Israel and the Church*, now disavows the literal hermeneutic, the isolation method of interpreting passages without the
analogy of faith and of pitting one passage against another, of considering doctrines independent of other truths, is still very much part of
the system. By contrast, since God is one, His Word is one so that each
part of the Bible *necessarily* implies all the rest. The whole leads to
the parts, and the parts to the whole. We must give equal weight to the
whole and the parts in our hermeneutic.

But dispensationalists isolate one passage and force other passages
into their assumed interpretation of the one passage. Instead of interpreting a passage in light of the whole, they interpret the passage as
if the whole did not exist.[44] For example, Zane Hodges sees nothing
but faith mentioned for the gift of eternal life in the Gospel of John
which means that repentance and turning from one's sins have no part

---

[43] R. L. Dabney, *Systematic Theology*, p. 786.

[44] It would be ok to interpret the part in light of the whole and the whole in light of
the part.

in one's conversion, and the rest of the Bible is made to conform to this horrible interpretation. Rather, if Hodges had considered the conceptual parallels to repentance in John[45] (the whole), he would not have misunderstood John (the part). I am firmly convinced that this hermeneutic is still with them and that it is the reason they cannot (or will not) see that the Old Testament saints had faith in the coming Messiah (they object that this would be reading the New Testament back into the Old and each Testament must stand on its own), that the Old Testament saints were regenerated and permanently indwelt by the Holy Spirit or both, that the Old Testament saints were in union with Jesus, that the church is the continuation of Israel, for the promises to Israel were not merely physical and concerning the land, and so forth.

When Paul says the Galatians are the "Israel of God" (Gal. 6:16), dispensationalists must find a distinction that makes the passage say that Paul means only the Jewish Christians. This is allegedly taking the Old Testament literally, but it is certainly not taking the New Testament literally nor considering the whole Bible before drawing conclusions.

The more they move away from this isolation hermeneutic the more unity they see in the Bible. In their latest book on dispensationalism, we see that the Ten Commandments and "[their] exposition in the Pentateuch and later Old Testament literature" can be seen by one dispensationalist as eternally binding;[46] Jesus is now reigning on David's throne;[47] the Sermon on the Mount is for today after all;[48] and so on. Since dispensationalism is obviously in a state of flux, being unable to find itself theologically, we are hopeful that many more will leave the system altogether.

From these two problems — no Old Testament for today and no inference — we can see that though they give lip service to the inspiration of all Scripture, only part of Scripture has *authority* over

---

[45] See my book *Lordship Salvation: The Only Kind There Is*, which may be ordered from the publisher in the front.

[46] My former Hebrew professor, Kenneth L. Barker in *Dispensationalism, Israel and the Church*, p. 297. Is he a theonomic dispensationalist? This would indeed be a strange hybrid.

[47] Darrell Bock in Ibid., p. 49. The former generation of dispensationalists would never have said this.

[48] John A. Martin in Ibid., chapter 8.

them. What they give with their left hand, they take back with the right hand. The Bible is *necessary* for them but not *sufficient* for *all* of life, so that politics, education, counseling (etc.) must be supplemented from humanism. In other words, Jesus is King over some of life and humanism over the balance.

As a consequence of rejecting Old Testament morality and refusing to take inferences, they confidently state that the Bible says nothing of politics, economics, education, and so on. The Bible is only a book for "practical" matters such as family living, preaching, worship, and other such things. Dispensationalists tend, therefore, to be impotent in their culture.

Arminianism

Arminianism, or the doctrine of human sovereignty as expressed in free will, often accompanies dispensationalism. "Free will" refers to the innate ability to obey God's commands. It is undeniable that the Pentecostals, Churches of God, charismatic groups, independent Bible churches, fundamental Baptists, and many others, are both Arminian and dispensational. Along with this Arminianism is an incipient rationalism (irrationalism!), a tendency to deny systematic theology, or to deny a logical system. For example, when the Dallas Theological Seminary professors are pushed on the doctrine of passive regeneration, they retreat into the "antinomy" solution (both regeneration and faith cause one another, they maintain). They tend to be contradictory, espousing unconditional election but denying reprobation; adducing substitutionary atonement, saying Christ died for all without exception, but denying that all are saved; believing in irresistible grace for justification and denying the same for sanctification; claiming to hold to the unity of the Bible and using only Acts through Revelation for today.

In the new book, *Dispensationalism, Israel and the Church*, the same Arminianism prevails. We repeatedly read of God's grace being "provided,"[49] that saints "can" have God's grace,[50] and that redemption is "made possible."[51] Potential words are all they can muster since they do not believe in effectual grace.

---

[49] Blaising, *Dispensationalism, Israel and the Church*, pp. 90, 97, 120, 121, etc.

[50] Ibid., pp. 231, 232.

[51] Ibid., p. 243.

Subjective Individualism

Dan Morse (in a paper to me privately) has rightly observed that there are three positions on the church and the individual: (1) insisting on one's individual rights (Baptists, dispensationalists, etc.), (2) always yielding to the rights of the ruling person (Roman Catholic), (3) and responsible communion (Episcopal, Presbyterian). The second position has unity without diversity. The individual has virtually no place in the church. The first has diversity but no unity, the individual reigning supreme. Only the last position maintains both unity and diversity in balance. This biblical position is found in 1 Corinthians 12, for example, where we see that each individual has at least one gift to use for the good of the body. There is such corporate unity to God's church that "if one member suffers, all the members suffer with it" (v. 26). Yet each individual is to use his gift for the edification of the whole body (1 Cor. 14:3-5, 12, 19, 23, 26) — not just for personal benefit.

However, in baptist theology in general and in dispensational theology in particular, the individual receives all the emphasis. This is true because they see no covenantal unity to God's people in Scripture; they only see distinctions. This individualism can be seen in their emphasis on individual response to the gospel, in which most of them preach that each person must "do something" to indicate his "decision," such as "going forward" in a meeting, raising the hand, signing a pledge card, or whatever. All evangelistic effort is aimed at motivating the will of the individual to "decide for Christ," with the idea that each one's will is sovereign. Each one has "free will." With true American democratic spirit the individual or the minority rules supreme — even over God's will. For God may wish to save a certain individual but the individual will not let Him.

One can clearly see the anarchy that ensues in church discipline. If each one is sovereign, then no one can judge another. In my 31 years in dispensationalism I never saw any church discipline. If the individual was upset with the church, he left and went to another church, with neither the individual nor the church caring about the problems involved.

This individualism may be seen again in their view of sanctification in which they know nothing of corporate sanctification. There is only personal conformity to Christ; the church collectively is not considered.

But Paul considered it. The whole church grows together (Eph.

2:19-22); each individual contributes to the growth of the whole body (Eph. 4:16); the Old Testament and New Testament saints made perfect together (Heb. 11:40); the gifts each one has are for the good of the body (1 Cor. 12:12-31); the church is collectively the temple of God (1 Cor. 3:16; 2 Cor. 6:16); we are members of one body and individually members of one another (Rom. 12:4, 5); the whole body grows together by Christ's power (Col. 2:19). By contrast, dispensationalists tend to be very lax in church attendance. Why? They view sanctification or growth as individual, having little to do with the group at church. A typical example is what a friend said to me about going to church: "I already know what they will say. I've already learned this. I don't need to go." The assumptions are several: (1) To grow I must learn something new; (2) growth is only a mental activity and not encouragement and exhortation from the brethren; (3) my presence will make no difference; (4) if I can't learn something new I will not go (this is selfish); (5) I do not contribute by being there, (6) sanctification is only individual, and so forth. None of these assumptions is true according to Paul above. There is a sanctifying effect just by one's presence, and unbelievers are convicted of their sins by the presence of all even if only one person speaks (1 Cor. 14:24). Christ is present in His church, and where He is, the individual must be.

Worship in dispensational churches is all but non-existent, for the individual needs knowledge so teaching is the emphasis of the Sunday morning services. The focus is on man, the individual, and his needs — which can be met at home with a good book — rather than on the Triune God, His glory, attributes, and praise to Him. Corporate worship, corporate praise, corporate confession of sin, corporate reading of His Word, are virtually gone.[52] The sacraments receive little if any emphasis.[53] There was no course offered at Dallas Theological Seminary on worship when I was there, and I cannot remember a single discussion on worship by students or professors in four years. At one dispensational church I attended, the pastor used a chalk board and overhead projector as in a classroom for the morning "worship." If one were interested in the particular discussion, he came; otherwise he stayed home and no one questioned his "sovereign" right to neglect

---

[52]In R. B. Thieme's church in Houston, gnosticism has reached its logical conclusion as knowledge only is emphasized and every service is Thieme teaching to get "doctrine in the frontal lobe."

[53]In some hyper-dispensational churches, they are not practiced at all since they are for "Israel."

church.

Even further, too often people view sanctification as mere activities, such as Bible study, prayer, memorizing verses, going to church, most of which can be done by the individual at home. However, these things are a means to an end and not the end itself, for the goal of all activities such as these is obedience to the law of God or the Word of God. I know a man who does not use his time wisely in studying Scripture as he should, but he has an impeccable memory, "being not a forgetful hearer but a doer of the word." His life radiates obedience to Christ. Truly he has a practical grasp of sanctification.

Consistent with individualism but not consistent with the Bible, dispensationalists tend to preach the love of God to the virtual exclusion of the wrath of God.[54]

Who Rules the World?

If Christ will rule the world during the millennium, then who is ruling the world now? The tendency in dispensationalism is to say that Satan is ruling the world now. For example, Norman Geisler quotes Lewis Chafer approvingly in Bibliotheca Sacra (third quarter, 1985): ". . . the governments of this world system (Matt. 4:8-9) are under Satan's authority." Dr. Geisler said this in response to others who say that the nations are under Christ and His law. Or again, Tommy Ice favorably quotes Clough, another dispensationalist: ". . . all-pervading domain of Satan over both the social order and its physical environment" (Bibliotheca Sacra, 1988, third quarter). How anyone could read the Bible and believe that Satan is the kings of kings and lord of lords is beyond me. But this errant stance causes them to have little faith either in the conversion of the masses or the sanctification of nations.

The possibility of Christ ruling now seems to be a major threat to Geisler, for he rightly perceives that if all of God's Word is for today, and especially if the nations are under His law, then there would be no need for a future literal thousand years reign of Christ on the earth since He would be reigning now. Notice the extreme to which Geisler goes to avoid the rulership of Christ through His law:

> Premillenarians do not believe the millennium will come about by any political process continuous with the present. They insist rather on a divine, cataclysmic, and supernatural inauguration of the reign of Christ

---

[54]Marsden, p. 35.

on earth. *This relieves premillennialists of any divine duty to Christianize the world.* Their duty is to be salt, light, and to do good to all men. . . . They can be content with a democracy or any government which allows freedom to preach the gospel. . . . *And their obligation is to promote a good and just government (1 Tim. 2:1-4), not necessarily a uniquely Christian one.*

Premillenarians need not work for Christian civil laws but only for fair ones.

The Ten Commandments are a case in point. Postmillennial theonomy, and its stepchild biblionomy, demands that the Ten Commandments are the basis for civil law. *This, however, is impossible if true freedom of religion is to be allowed.* For the first commandment(s) demands allegiance to a monotheistic God as opposed to all false gods or idols. If the civil law of the United States followed the Ten Commandments, then there would be no freedom of religion for polytheists, Taoists, Hindus, Buddhists, secular humanists, or atheists. So making the Bible the basis for civil law is a contradiction to freedom of religion such as exists in the United States today. *But if the Bible is not the basis for civil law, then what is?*

But nowhere in the Bible is God's judgment of the nations based on His special written revelation (the Bible). Rather it is always based on general principles of goodness and justice known to all men by general revelation (cf. Amos 1; Obad. 1; Jonah 3:8-10; Nahum 2) [emphasis added].[55]

These statements are the most incredible and blatantly false that we have read in years. We have several responses. First, if the nations are not under the law of God, then the gospel cannot be preached to them, for the gospel necessitates that we demonstrate that they have broken God's written revelation: "For by the law is the knowledge of sin" (Rom. 3:20).

Second, the assumption to these statements is that man's laws produce freedom while God's laws produce bondage. Now it is true that God's law produces bondage in the sense that it shows us how far short we fall from His standard. But God's law also produces freedom, for obedience to the "no adultery" commandment means we are not as likely to get AIDS as violators. Man says not to obey and God says to obey. Which command brings greater freedom? Freedom is to be enslaved to Christ, which means that by His Spirit we are enabled to be enslaved to His law. How could one be enslaved to Christ and

---

[55]*Bibliotheca Sacra*, third quarter, 1985, pp. 256-257, 261.

despise His law, which is a revelation of His holy character? Mr. Geisler assumes that there are neutral commands, that some areas of life must not be under the dominion of King Jesus but that the government has God's blessings to create its own moral laws.

Third, has he not read in Leviticus?

> Do not defile yourselves with any of these things; for by all these [i.e., adultery, homosexuality, killing children, etc.] the nations are defiled, which I am casting out before you. For the land is defiled; therefore I visit the punishment of its iniquity upon it, and the land vomits out its inhabitants. You shall therefore keep My statutes and My judgments, and shall not commit any of these abominations, either any of your own nation or any stranger who dwells among with you. (For all these abominations the men of the land have done, who were before you, and thus the land is defiled) (18:24-27).

These verses demonstrate that the Canaanites were disobedient to God's Bible, His statutes and commandments, and that *it was for this reason* that He was judging them. Notice also that the law applied to the stranger, to the one who was not part of Israel. In other words, God's law is universal, for His law is a revelation of His own holy character, which cannot change. Perhaps the reader would like to look up these passages: Leviticus 20:22-24 and the first half of Isaiah. These do not exhaust the list of verses that contradict Mr. Geisler's statement that "nowhere in the Bible is God's judgment of the nations based on His special revelation" (the Bible).

We have already seen that Ice and Geisler believe that Satan is lord of the world, and the latest defense of dispensationalism is no different. Though David L. Bock sees Jesus as ruling in a limited sense on David's throne, yet we are not to conclude that this means Jesus' present reign has any political implications: ". . . the current kingdom lacks political, nationalistic elements."[56] It will only be when Jesus is physically present in Jerusalem that His full power and especially His political authority over the nations will be realized. Somehow His physical presence is more potent than His omnipresence. Apparently Satan rules the political arena.[57] There are allegedly two stages to His rule, Christ ruling only spiritually now (Satan ruling politically) and later Christ and the saints ruling spiritually and politically.[58] This

---

[56]Blaising, *Dispensationalism, Israel and the Church*, p. 53.

[57]Ibid., pp. 64-66; see also pp. **53ff**, 66, 94, **225**.

[58]Ibid., pp. 61-64.

leaves us with gnostic dualism, Satan ruling the outward, physical, political world and Jesus ruling the inward, spiritual world of His people. Of course according to dispensationalists, Satan wins, at least in this age.

However, not only was Jesus Lord because He was (is) God but also because He was Messiah. In Isaiah. 9:6, 7 we read that He would be governor (political) from His birth and that His kingdom would continually increase from the time of His birth:

> For unto us a Child is born, unto us a Son is given; and the government will be upon His shoulder. And His name will be called Wonderful Counselor, Mighty God, Everlasting Father, Prince of Peace. Of the increase of His government and peace there will be no end, upon the throne of David and over His kingdom, to order it and establish it with judgment and justice from that time forward, even forever. The zeal of the Lord of hosts will perform this.

Again of Christ we read: "Then to Him [Messiah] was given dominion and glory and a kingdom, that all peoples, nations, and languages should serve Him. His dominion is an everlasting dominion, which shall not pass away, and His kingdom the one which shall not be destroyed" (Dan. 7:14). This was given to Christ by the Father at His Ascension.

If the Lord is to spread His gospel throughout the world, it is necessary for Him to have the authority to do so. In other words, if nations had authority over Him or if Satan had the political authority, then either the gospel could not be preached in a nation whose leaders outlawed the gospel or the Lord would be in rebellion. Yet the Lord Himself said after His resurrection, "All authority has been given to Me in heaven and *on earth*" (Matt. 28:18), which includes the authority over the nations to preach the gospel: "Go therefore and make disciples of all the *nations.*"

By virtue of His resurrection, Jesus was enthroned as both Lord and Messiah (Acts 2:36). He is not waiting for some future date to *become* Lord of lords; He is *now*. Indeed, "He must reign till He has put all enemies under His feet" (1 Cor. 15:25), and at the end of this current reign He will deliver to the Father a conquered kingdom (1 Cor. 15:24). He is political King as well as King of the church. All nations are accountable to Him — now. Though His dominion is now, He has not yet finished conquering (Heb. 2:7-9).

The Lord is ruler over creation as well as the church, which includes the whole world and its political power:

He is the image of the invisible God, the firstborn[59] over all creation. For by Him all things were created that are in heaven and that are on earth, visible and invisible, whether thrones or dominions or principalities or powers. All things were created through Him and for Him (Col. 1:15, 16).

He is stated to be Lord over Satan and all his hosts: "He must reign till He has put all enemies under His feet" (1 Cor. 15:25). "Having disarmed principalities and powers, He made a public spectacle of them, triumphing over them in it" (Col. 2:15). "For this purpose the Son of God was manifested, that He might destroy the works of the devil" (1 John 3:8). "Inasmuch then as the children have partaken of flesh and blood, He Himself likewise shared in the same, that through death He might destroy him who had the power of death, that is, the devil, and release those who through fear of death were all their lifetime subject to bondage" (Heb. 2:14, 15).

If Christ had spiritual power without political authority, we would have gnosticism, the idea that Jesus conquered spiritually but not physically, that His laws were only for the hearts of His people and not for all people outwardly. We would have a Platonic dualism between nature and grace. For Christ to revert back to the land of Israel in the so-called millennium would be to retreat to shadows, to have only the land of Palestine when He now has the world.

Even the saints are ruling politically. In typology we have Joshua conquering the land of Canaan under the Angel of the Lord, who was the preincarnate Jesus. Now we have the new Joshua, the resurrected Jesus, proclaiming that He has all authority *on earth*, and *therefore* (Matt. 28:19) His followers must conquer the *nations* with the gospel (Matt. 28:18-20). And we saints partake of the benefits now and are conquering now:

And the God of peace will crush Satan *under your feet shortly*. The grace of our Lord Jesus Christ be with you. Amen (Rom. 16:20).

For whatever is born of God overcomes the world. And this is the victory that has overcome the world — our faith. Who is he who overcomes the world, but he who believes that Jesus is the Son of God? (1 John 5:4, 5).

And he who overcomes, and keeps My works until the end, to him I will give power over the nations — "He shall rule them with a rod of iron; as the potter's vessels shall be broken to pieces" — as I also have

---

[59]"Firstborn" here means preeminent and sovereign; see Lightfoot on Colossians.

received from My Father; and I will give him the morning star (Rev.
2:26-28).

The last quote is from Psalm 2 in which it is said that Jesus rules the
nations with a rod of iron, but since His saints are in union with Him,
so do they! And if Christ has already conquered the world, the land
promise must be extended to include the whole world, not just the land
of Palestine. And do we not read in the New Testament that the land
promise to Abraham now includes the world? "For the promise that
he would be the heir *of the world* was not to Abraham or to his seed
through the law, but through the righteousness of faith" (Rom. 4:13).
Now the meek, the true seed of Abraham, shall inherit the earth (Matt.
5:5). Even Abraham understood that the literal land in the East was
not what God had in mind ultimately:

> By faith Abraham obeyed when he was called to go out to the place
> which he would afterward receive as an inheritance. And he went out,
> not knowing where he was going. By faith he sojourned in the land of
> promise as in a foreign country, dwelling in tents with Isaac and Jacob,
> the heirs with him of the same promise; *for he waited for the city which
> has foundations, whose builder and maker is God* (Heb. 11:8-10).

This is the New Testament's understanding of the land, and it is to be
taken literally! The Lord Himself proclaimed that worship in Jerusalem would cease (John 4:21), indicating that it would be world wide.[60]

The dispensationalists, however, promote Satan as lord who is
ruling the earth, who sits as the prince of the nations, who has the
authority to rule the hearts and lives of men. Chafer boldly proclaims:
". . . Satan . . . is *now* in authority over the unregenerate world, and
the unsaved are unconsciously organized and federated under his
leading" [emphasis added]. He goes on to say that Satan has authority
over the world as a whole, that Satan's offer of the world to Jesus was
valid, and that "the whole world lies in the evil one" (1 John 5:19).[61]
That John did not mean that Satan is king of kings is obvious in that
"whole world" did not mean the elect are in Satan and also because
Christ and Christians rule the world, the former by virtue of His death
and resurrection (Col. 2:14ff; see also 1 John 3:8; Rev. 1:5) and the
latter by faith in Jesus (1 John 5:4, 5; Rev. 2:26-28). Revelation 1:5,
6 summarizes this for Him and us: "From Jesus Christ, the faithful
witness, the firstborn from the dead, and *the ruler over the kings of*

---

[60]This is from my editor, Teresa Johnson.

[61]Lewis Sperry Chafer, *Satan* (Chicago: Moody Press, 1919), p. 52ff.

the earth. To Him who loved us and washed us from our sins in His own blood, and *has made us kings* and priests to His God and Father, to Him be glory and dominion forever and ever. Amen.''[62]

But consider what else the Bible says: "The kingdoms of this world *have become* the kingdoms of our Lord and of His Christ, and He shall reign forever and ever!" (Rev. 11:15). The Apostle John did not say the nations would some day be His, but that they "have become" His, and he said this before Revelation 20.[63] We read in Psalm 2 that the Father says to the Son: "Ask of Me, and I will give You the nations for Your inheritance, and the ends of the earth for Your possession. You shall break them with a rod of iron; You shall dash them in pieces like a potter's vessel'" (vv. 8, 9), which is quoted five times in the New Testament (Acts 4:25; 8:33; Heb. 1:5; 5:5; Rev. 2:27), emphasizing its present fulfillment. Rev. Alexander McLeod (1774-1833) cites several other passages demonstrating that Jesus is presently political Lord over the nations as well as spiritual Lord over the church:[64]

> Jesus spoke these words, lifted up His eyes to heaven, and said: "Father, the hour has come. Glorify Your Son, that Your Son also may glorify You, as You have given Him authority over all flesh. . . ." (John 17:1, 2).

> The Lord is at Your right hand; He shall execute kings in the day of His wrath. He shall judge among the nations, He shall fill the places with dead bodies, He shall execute the heads of many countries (Ps. 110:5, 6. This Messianic Psalm is quoted more than any other Old Testament passage in the New Testament).

> And what is the exceeding greatness of His power toward us who believe, according to the working of His mighty power which He worked in Christ when He raised Him from the dead and seated [Him] at His right hand in the heavenly places, far above all principality and power and might and dominion, and every name that is named, *not only in this age* but also in that which is to come (Eph. 1:19-21).

> Therefore God also has highly exalted Him and given Him the name which is above every name, that at the name of Jesus every knee

---

[62]Dispensationalists consider the book of Revelation to be in the future, but they also consider chapter 1, from where these verses are taken, to be past.

[63]Premillennialists believe that Revelation 20 is when Jesus becomes Lord of the world.

[64]Alexander McLeod, *Messiah: Governor of the Nations of the Earth* (Elwood Park, NJ: Reformed Presbyterian Press, 1803, 1992).

should bow, of those in heaven, and of those on earth, and of those under the earth, and that every tongue should confess that Jesus Christ is Lord, to the glory of God the Father (Phil. 2:9-11).

When did God give Jesus this exalted Name and dominion? It was both before the resurrection (John 17:1, 2) and after the resurrection (Matt. 28:18-20), indicating that He always has had this dominion but also received it in renewed form at His Ascension.

Someone may object that the Lord said that His kingdom was "not *of* this world" (John 18:36). He did not mean that His kingdom would have nothing to do with this world but that His kingdom did not *originate* from this world and was not of the moral character of this world.[65]

The expression that Satan is the "god of this world" does not mean he is lord of lords, but that he is the god of this world in the sense that *many worship him* — not that he is almighty. His work is primarily in blinding the minds of people to the gospel (2 Cor. 4:4; John 12:31, 14:30; 16:11; Eph. 2:2; 1 John 5:19), but even that blindness is stripped away when the mighty grace of Jesus brings one to belief in Himself (Matt. 11:27; Acts 13:48; 16:14; Phil. 1:29).

Furthermore, that Satan is called by the Lord Jesus "the ruler of this world" (John 14:30) does not mean that there is not a Ruler above him, Who is Ruler of the universe and the Ruler of all rulers. Because there is a governor of Tennessee, do we conclude that there is not also a President of the United States who has greater authority than the governor? Besides, the Lord also stated: "*Now* is the judgment of this world; *now* the ruler of this world will be cast out" (John 12:31). What else does the expression "Lord of lords" mean except that Jesus is the *ultimate* Ruler? And was it not true when Jesus commanded Satan to leave Him in Matthew 4:10, 11 that Satan did so without a word? Did not the demons obey the Lord every time He commanded them without hesitation?

The major passage for dispensationalists is in Luke 4:6: "And the

---

[65]Study John's technical use of the prepositions *of* and *in*, (Greek is εκ, εν.) which has been noticed by more than one grammarian, (Nigel Turner, *A Grammar of New Testament Greek* [Edinburgh: T. & T. Clark, 1963], vol. 3, pp. 260-263; Vol. 4, p. 76; Maximillan Zerwick, *Biblical Greek* [Rome: Biblical Institute Press, 1963], #134-5; Nigel Turner, *Grammatical Insights Into the New Testament* [Edinburgh: T. & T. Clark, 1965], p. 120; A. T. Robertson, *Word Pictures in the New Testament* [Nashville: Broadman Press, 1932], vol. 5, p. 57). For example, we are to be spatially *in* the world (John 17:11, 15) but not morally *of* the world (John 17:14, 16; 1 John 4:5).

devil said to Him, 'All this authority I will give You, and their glory; for this has been delivered to me, and I give it to whomever I wish'" (Luke 4:6). Our first response must be that *Satan is a liar* (John 8:44). Some say that Satan is telling the truth since Jesus did not rebuke him. But it is an argument from silence that leads dispensationalists to the deafening conclusion that Satan was for once telling the truth. Even if the Lord had not answered the devil, the inference is not valid. In the most elementary logic class, one learns that he can conclude anything or nothing from what is *not* stated. But the Lord did answer Satan: "Get behind Me, Satan! For it is written, 'You shall worship the Lord your God, and Him only you shall serve'" (v. 8). The Lord answered the real point behind Satan's pseudo-offer: worship reveals Who the real God is, and we are to worship the Triune God only. If the Lord had said the kingdoms did not belong to Satan, He would not have been confronting the point of the offer. Observe also that Satan instantly obeyed the Lord when He commanded him to leave, which showed Who was really in authority.

Secondly, *God the Father made the same offer to Christ.* Psalm 2 is a Messianic Psalm, using the name "Messiah" in verse two (sometimes translated "anointed") and the word "Son" in verse twelve. In verse seven the Son quotes the Father: "I will declare the decree: The Lord has said to Me, 'You are My Son, today I have begotten You.'" This verse is quoted several times in the New Testament of the resurrection of Jesus. The Father raised Him from the dead, and, to the consternation of the nations (vv. 1-3), He made Jesus King of kings. In other words, even though the nations did not want Him ruling over them, and even though they sought to cast off His "bonds" (vv. 1-3; bonds=His law, see Jer. 2:20; 5:5), the Father laughed and made Him King over them anyway. In light of this, the Father says to His only Son: "Ask of Me, and I will give You the nations for Your inheritance, and the ends of the earth for Your possession" (v. 8).

Now who has made the genuine offer of the world to Jesus, God or Satan? Who is the liar, God the Father or the devil? Who really owns the world and could offer it to Jesus, the Father or Satan? In the verses that follow the Father's offer, it is obvious that the Son did ask and the Father gave Him the nations, for He shall rule them with a rod of iron (v. 9), and the rulers must repent (vv. 10, 11) or perish under the Son's wrath (v. 12). The Lord Jesus emphatically stated, "All authority has been given to Me in heaven and *on earth*" at the resurrection (Matt. 28:18; see also Dan. 7:14). (Most commentators agree with this interpretation.[66])

There are many other tendencies of dispensationalism than the ones we've mentioned in this chapter, but these are sufficient to see that the system is inherently bad.

---

[66]See William Hendriksen, *New Testament Commentary: Luke* (Grand Rapids: Baker Book House, 1978), p. 236; Norval Geldenhuys, *Commentary of the Gospel of Luke* (Grand Rapids: Wm. B. Eerdmans Pub. Co., p. 1975), p. 160; I. Howard Marshall, *The Gospel of Luke: A Commentary of the Greek Text* (Grand Rapids: Wm. B. Eerdmans Pub. Co., 1978), p. 172; Frederick Louis Godet, *Commentary on the Gospel of Luke* (Grand Rapids: Zondervan Pub. House, 1887), p. 214ff.

Chapter Eight

Antinomianism
in
Dispensationalism

We have already looked at the dispensational view of lordship salvation in the previous chapter, but we shall consider in more detail their antinomianism. Antinomianism has many facets,[1] but we shall consider that which is inherent in antinomianism: a denial that works have any *necessary* place in salvation. Antinomianism can appear anywhere. It appears in some Primitive Baptists who believe in "time salvation," that those regenerated may not have faith and works at all. This is hyper-Calvinism at its worst. But antinomianism especially appears in dispensationalism. Why?

Historically, the founder of Dallas Theological Seminary, Lewis Sperry Chafer, studied at Oberlin, the school founded by the virtually pure Pelagians, Asa Mahan and Charles Finney. Chafer had no formal theological training, being a musician. And though he did not pursue theology at Oberlin, the Pelagian assumption of human autonomy was undoubtedly absorbed by Chafer from the school. One who is not aware of this assumption tends to develop his theology around it, and

---

[1] See *The New Schaff-Herzog Encyclopedia of Religious Knowledge* (Grand Rapids: Baker Book House, 1977), 1:196ff; Cotton Mather, *The Great Works of Christ in America* (Edinburgh: The Banner of Truth Trust, 1702, 1979), 2:508ff; Edwin H. Palmer, *The Encyclopedia of Christianity* (Wilmington: National Foundation for Christian Foundation, 1964), 1:270ff; John Calvin, *Treatises Against the Anabaptists and the Against the Libertines* (Grand Rapids: Baker Book House, 1982), p. 159ff.

it controls every doctrine he believes. Indeed, in a sense there is no heresy except Pelagianism, for every false doctrine can be traced to it. There is not a cult in existence that denies "free will," with the possible exception of Islam, though if they really received the revelation of God through Scripture instead of trying to manufacture their own based on human sovereignty, they would be orthodox. I have read all seven volumes of Chafer's theology, and he did not understand Pelagianism. This confusion continues in his legacy, especially among those directly influenced by him, saying that in the converted there will be some change, somehow, but man is in charge.[2]

The root of all legalistic and license heresies is Pelagianism, the idea that man is good, that man has the ability to please God either without His grace or by using His grace at man's initiative. It is this latter concept that is especially prominent at Dallas Theological Seminary: that God is always waiting for the sinner to do something so that one uses God's grace for his own benefit. Unfortunately, Dallas Theological Seminary has infected much of the evangelical community in America with this errant teaching. In the new book on dispensationalism, one author even says the law has the power to sanctify,[3] which is directly contradictory to Paul (Rom. 6:14; 8:3, 4). This semi-Pelagianism is both legalistic and given to license.

It is legal in that God is seen as always waiting to grant the sinner some favor, thus the only hindrance is the will of man. All man has to do is. . . . The answer varies with the form of antinomianism involved, but at Dallas Theological Seminary and in dispensationalism in general the answer is faith, so that faith obligates God and becomes a work: hence legalism. This sovereignty of man is carried over into the whole of salvation so that once one has *allowed* God to justify him, he can allow or disallow God to sanctify him: hence license. Just as justification was up to man, so sanctification is too. The irony is that what are seemingly opposites, legalism and license, are actually Siamese twins, born of the same hideous parents, the old idol "free will" and human goodness. That man is seen to be good is obvious in that any time he chooses he can improve the grace already *available* to him and get himself saved. Others who had the same opportunity did not improve their grace, making the difference in the sinner, not

---

[2]Charles Ryrie, *So Great Salvation* (Victor Books, 1989), pp. 46-47; Roy Zuck, *Kindred Spirit*, published by DTS, Summer 1989, p. 5.

[3]Blaising, *Dispensationalism, Israel and the Church*, p. 262.

in God's grace. In other words, if each sinner has equal opportunity to avail himself of God's grace, the one who does is better than the one who does not. To the degree that man is able to please God, to that degree he is good, whether the goodness extends to his whole being, with him earning his "salvation" by works (Pelagianism), or extends partially, with him earning it by faith (semi-Pelagianism).

Some dispensationalists, like John F. MacArthur, Jr., and the Master's seminary, reject semi-Pelagianism, and for this we are grateful. But there is still an antinomianism inherent in dispensationalism, waiting to manifest itself. Why do dispensationalists tend to reject works of any kind as necessary in salvation, even as the fruit? There are theological reasons inherent in dispensationalism that give the answer: They (1) place a wall between law and grace, (2) deny that Old Testament saints were justified by faith in Jesus, (3) maintain that Jesus is not ruling now, and (4) assert that the Old Testament biblical covenants were only unconditional. These four seemingly unrelated beliefs are actually related, all in some way disconnecting good works as the *necessary* product of grace.

(1) The Old Testament was supposedly a time of law and the New Testament a time of grace, which places a wall between law and grace. Even though the neo-dispensationalists place both law and grace in each time period, there is still a mental wall between the concepts. They do not see that the law is about righteousness and the gospel is about righteousness, implying one another, as Paul teaches in Romans 3:20ff; 6:14; Galatians 3:24, and so on. The law demands righteousness and the gospel gives it, enabling us by the Spirit to produce holiness or the righteousness of the law in our lives (Rom. 3:31; 8:4). But according to dispensationalism, one need not turn from sin (law) to be justified (grace), for law and grace have nothing to do with one another. If one need not turn from his sins to be justified, he has made the law irrelevant, which carries over into sanctification, making obedience optional. The wall between law and grace is also between justification (grace) and sanctification (law).

If the moral laws of the Old Testament are not for today, as dispensationalists say, we have a dichotomy between the moral precepts for Israel and the precepts for the church. This means that God's laws are not unified, that God has one moral code for one period of time and another code for a different period, which implies that God's laws are arbitrary. If they are arbitrary, God having changed His mind about moral law for today as opposed to the Old Testament, then all morality would seem to be legitimate (or illegitimate). This would also imply that there can be many lawgivers or gods, each with his own sphere of authority. Thus there is one way of salvation and moral code for Israel and another for the church. This dichotomy further implies that God's truth is not one, that "truths" can exist in isolation from one another, which would imply that God is not one. *It cannot be stated too strongly that seeing parts of the Bible as isolated from one another is a major, inherent weakness of dispensationalism*, implying all that we have just stated.

Daniel P. Fuller is very astute in his analysis of dispensationalism and of the relationship between law and grace, but he does not understand the Reformed position, which he castigates for having a law-grace dichotomy.[4] The Reformed have a dichotomy, but it is not absolute as is the dispensationalists, believing rather that the connection between law and grace is righteousness: the gospel is about righteousness, and the law is righteous. The law is God's commandments and shows us what God requires but is unable to produce the requisite righteousness; the gospel gives legal righteousness in justification as a free gift, and consequently sanctifying righteousness is produced in us by the Spirit, enabling us to perform the law, though not perfectly in this life. Thus law and grace are connected by righteousness. The law leads to the gospel, and then the gospel in turn back to the law. The law reveals God's righteousness (1 Peter 1:13-16), and the gospel gives it to the believer. The Reformed do not believe that keeping the law brings sanctification but that sanctification enables the believer to keep the law. Because dispensationalism separates the two absolutely, one can have grace without law-keeping. Berkhof says in refutation of Fuller's understanding of the Reformed:

> The law seeks to awaken in the heart of man contrition on account of sin, while the gospel aims at the awakening of saving faith in Jesus Christ. The work of the law is in a sense preparatory to that of the gospel. It deepens the consciousness of sin and thus makes the sinner aware of the need of redemption. *Both are subservient to the same end,* and both are indispensable parts of the means of grace. This truth has not always been sufficiently recognized. The condemning aspect of the law has sometimes been stressed at the expense of its character as a part of the means of grace. Ever since the days of Marcion there have always been some who saw only contrast between law and the gospel and proceeded

---

[4]See the extended discussion of these things in Daniel P. Fuller, *Gospel & Law: Contrast or Continuum?* (Grand Rapids: Wm. B. Eerdmans Pub. Co., 1980).

on the assumption that the one excluded the other. . . . They lost sight of the fact that Paul also says that the law served as a tutor to lead men to Christ (Gal. 3:24), and that the Epistle to the Hebrews represents the law, not as standing in antithetical relation to the gospel, but rather as the gospel in its preliminary and imperfect state [emphasis added].[5]

The law leads us to Christ, and Christ leads us to the law. One cannot have the righteousness of Christ and reject the righteousness of the law, for they imply one another. Christ in His life was obedient to the law, and this obedience is imputed to us.[6] In being conformed to the moral image of Christ, believers are being made holy, like the law. Perfect holiness entails perfect law-keeping. The law is not a legal requirement to merit salvation or the power for sanctification but the path over which sanctification leads us. In the gospel, the law is written on our hearts (2 Cor. 3), and the Spirit enables us to obey the law (Rom. 8:3, 4).

Dispensationalists also deny the active obedience of Christ, saying that only what He did on the Cross was vicarious and atoning.[7] Consistent with this, they say that when one is justified he only receives cancellation of guilt and judgment and not also the active obedience of Christ, which leads them to conclude that the Christian does not have to obey the law since this is not an issue in Christ's work. Again there is a wall between law and grace, and just as Jesus did not have to satisfy the positive demands of the law for His people, neither do we have to obey as the necessary evidence of our faith.

(2) Dallas Theological Seminary's doctrinal statement reads: "We believe that it was historically impossible that they [Old Testament

---

[5]Berkhof, *Systematic Theology*, p. 612.

[6]See Hebrews 2:10 ("in bringing many sons to glory, to make the author of their salvation perfect through sufferings") where the participle "bringing" is simultaneous with "to perfect" so that as Christ was being perfected He was at the same time bringing many sons to glory. In other words, as He obeyed, He was bringing. See A. A. Hodge, *The Atonement*, p. 253. His being perfected was counting for the "many sons." The perfecting was not His being made personally righteous as if the sinless Son of God had personal sin, but the completion of a life of perfect obedience. His perfect obedience to the law is imputed to us, not His attribute of righteousness. Christ obeyed for His people as He owed no obedience to the law for Himself. See also Romans 5:12ff; Philippians 2:7-8.

[7]We recognize that the Lord's whole life of obedience was both active and passive, but the emphasis of His work on the Cross was passive. For validation of the typical dispensational view on this, see Robert P. Lightner, professor of systematic theology at Dallas Theological Seminary, *The Death Christ Died* (Des Plaines, IL: Regular Baptist Press, 1967), p. 19ff.

saints] should have had as the conscious object of their faith the incarnate, crucified Son, the Lamb of God." The doctrinal statement elaborates that the Old Testament saints did not understand the types and sacrifices and that their faith was manifested in other ways, making reference to Hebrews 11 as proof of this. Thus Abraham was justified because he believed he would have a large family,[8] making the content of his faith having nothing to do with his sin and repentance, even though Scripture indicates the opposite when he offered up Isaac, and Jesus said he rejoiced to see His day (John 8:56). Likewise, many of the other Old Testament saints. That this is a false view should be obvious (John 1:41, 46; 3:3-4, 10; 4:25; 5:39; 8:56; Luke 2:25-26, 38; 24:25-27, 44-47; Acts 10:43; Rom. 1:1-3; 4:1-4; 9:33; Gal. 3:8-10, 26, 29; 1 Cor. 10:2-4; Eph. 2:12; Heb. 11:24-26; 1 Peter 1:11; Ps. 2; Job 16:19; 19:25, etc. See my section in chapter 19 for Jesus allegedly not being the object of faith.).[9]

Dispensationalists are constantly changing, but Chafer held that Israel was earthly and the church heavenly, that Israel was saved by her works and the church by Christ.[10] Keeping with this defective view of Old Testament faith, they have Old Testament Israel married to Yahweh and the New Testament church married to Christ, making God a bigamist. The newer dispensationalists say that Israel and the church will eventually be merged, but nevertheless they are two separate entities until some time in eternity.

Dispensationalists despise the charge of two ways of salvation (election, union with Christ, regeneration, justification, sanctification, glorification), but when they still maintain that Old Testament saints had a different content to faith than New Testament saints, eliminating sin and Jesus from the Old Testament saints, that they either were not regenerated or were not permanently indwelt by the Holy Spirit, this

---

[8]See Allen P. Ross's chapter in John S. Feinberg, *Continuity and Discontinuity* (Westchester, IL: Crossway Books, 1988), p. 169ff.

[9]Though their faith was not as developed as ours, there still was a core truth of Messiah and His death and resurrection for their sins. How else could we explain Isaiah 53, Hebrews 11:26, 40, etc? If one tries to use the New Testament to understand the Old Testament saints' faith, dispensationalists respond that we are reading the New Testament back into the Old, to which we say, so what? Again their disparity hermeneutic leads them astray in pitting one passage (New Testament) against another (Old Testament).

[10]Chafer stated in his theology: "Men [in the Old Testament] were therefore just because of their own works for God, whereas New Testament justification is God's work for man in answer to faith." *Systematic Theology*, 7:219.

is two ways.[11] Sin is eliminated from the content of faith of Old
Testament saints by saying that they did not believe the gospel but
believed the revelation God gave them. In other words, Abraham was
justified because he believed he would have a large family ("your seed
shall number as the stars"), which had nothing to do with personal
need of forgiveness of his sins.[12] (See my section in chapter 19 for
Jesus allegedly not being the object of faith.) The Reformed maintain
that the content of faith has always had a common kernel but expanded
as time went on, while dispensationalists say the content was completely different.

As we alluded earlier, dispensationalists find themselves on the
horns of a very sharp dilemma: If the Old Testament saints were saved
in the same way as New Testament ones, then they were regenerated,
believed in the coming Messiah, had the Holy Spirit permanently, are
in union with Christ as their Head, and do works by God's grace.
Therefore, we must ask, What possible difference could there be
between Israel and the church? But if the Old Testament saints were
not regenerated, did not believe in Jesus, did not have the Holy Spirit,
or were not in union with Christ, then we necessarily have different
ways of salvation.

The moderate dispensationalists say Israel will have a political
aspect to her salvation in the millennium that the church will not have,
which means Israel's salvation has broader implications than the
church's. This in turn is two concepts of salvation. Furthermore, if
Israel has one law and the church another, then the fruit of salvation
is different: Israel being obedient to a different law than the church.
Since both are allegedly being conformed to the image of Christ,
which law-character of His are they being conformed to, the Old
Testament or the New Testament one?

As a side comment, I should observe that dispensationalists say
Old Testament saints were not permanently indwelt by the Holy
Spirit.[13] If this is so, then how did they live a life for God, by raw will
power? If this is their answer, then we have pure Pelagianism, the
doctrine of pleasing God by human effort. They sometimes argue from

[11]See Ross in Feinberg, p. 161ff.

[12]Blaising, *Dispensationalism, Israel and the Church*, p. 247.

[13]The "moderate" dispensationalists still hold that Old Testament saints were not
permanently indwelt: Blaising, *Dispensationalism, Israel and the Church*, p. 78ff,
82, 86ff.

John 14:17, the Spirit "abides *with* you and will be *in* you." They draw the conclusion from the prepositions and the future tense that the Spirit was not *in* the twelve disciples then — only *with* them. The Spirit would be *in* them sometime in the future. Since the twelve were still "under law," they draw the further conclusion that no Old Testament saint was permanently indwelt by the Holy Spirit.

In answer to this, notice first that there is a textual problem so the text may be saying the Spirit "is" (present tense) *in* them now. However, the evidence seems to be on the side of the future tense. Secondly, observe that just because John says the Spirit is "with" them does not mean He is not now indwelling them. It is very risky to build a whole theology on such a tenuous inference. Furthermore, John loves to use variation of style to say the same thing, probably more than any other New Testament author. In v. 16, for example, John says the Spirit is *with* (*meta*) them, in v. 17 he says He is *beside* (*para*) them, and in v. 17 that He will be *in* (*en*) them. Second John 2 uses similar terms: "because the truth abides *in* (*en*) us and will be *with* (*meta*) us forever." Observe that John varies the prepositions and the tenses from present to future, just as he did in his Gospel. He is not denying that the truth was with them at the time he wrote but only emphasizing the certainty of the truth remaining with them forever. The best conclusion, then, is that John is simply varying his style in John 14:17 and saying in effect: "The Spirit is with you now and will continue to be with (or in) you forever." John has no intention of saying that they are not indwelt now.

Also, we know John taught that Old Testament saints were indeed permanently indwelt by the Spirit. For the Lord Jesus in John 3 deprecated Nicodemus, an Old Testament saint, for not knowing about the new birth, being surprised that this teacher of Israel did not know these things. This amazement shows that the Lord believed that Old Testament saints should experience the new birth, and how could one be born of the Spirit and not have the Holy Spirit? The same apostle in 1 John 3:9 implies that the new birth involves the permanent indwelling of the Spirit when he says, "Everyone who has been born of God does not practice sin, because His seed [the Spirit] abides in him." The "seed" could not be the Word of God, for the Pharisees had the Scriptures and still lived in sin. Nor could "seed" be the gospel, for the gospel is death apart from the working of the Spirit (2 Cor. 2:15, 16; 1 Cor. 1:18 with 2:14). And John said in his Gospel that being born again was by the Holy Spirit (3:1-8).

The statement by David in Psalm 51:11 where he prayed that God would not take His Spirit from him is covenantal, revealing that David feared for his salvation.[14] If God's Spirit were taken from him, it would indicate that he had never truly been regenerated (see 1 John 2:19). This is what happened to Saul in 1 Samuel 16:14 when the Spirit left him and an evil spirit came on him. Perseverance of the saints is an Old Testament doctrine as well as a New Testament one. Thus, asking for the Holy Spirit is asking for persevering grace (Luke 11:13). We see the Holy Spirit removed from those in the New Testament who had not persevered in the covenant:

> For it is impossible for those who were once enlightened, and have tasted the heavenly gift, and have become partakers of the Holy Spirit, and have tasted the good word of God and the powers of the age to come, if they fall away, to renew them again to repentance, since they crucify again for themselves the Son of God, and put [Him] to an open shame (Heb. 6:4-6).

Those who were partakers of the Holy Spirit and fell away were never truly converted though they were covenant members, and the Spirit was removed from them. Likewise in Hebrews 10:26 some in the covenant continued to sin willfully after receiving the knowledge of the truth, consequently "there no longer remains a sacrifice for sins." God's Spirit will not always strive with men, and even the Pharisees, covenant members while Jesus was physically present, were told that if they refused the working of the Holy Spirit that they had committed the unpardonable sin (Matt. 12:36ff).

(3) Dispensationalists postpone Jesus' reign to the so-called millennium, denying His regal realm now and giving it to Satan. If "Satan is alive and well on planet earth" in the sense that he rules the world, then antinomianism is established. How? Allegedly, obedience to God's laws does not bring success in the earth as Satan overrules God's children, and disobedience does not necessarily bring God's curse. Indeed, it is Satan and his seed that will conquer the earth by their wickedness and disobedience, not Jesus and His seed through the gospel and obedience (contrary to Gen. 3:15; Rom. 16:20; 1 Cor. 15:22-26), further indicating that God's laws are irrelevant. In other words, the more antinomian Satan and his people become, the more success they will have in spreading wickedness and Satan's kingdom in the world, hastening the end of the world, rather than the biblical

---

[14]See Paul's covenantal fear in 1 Corinthians 9:27.

truth that disobedience reaps judgment, shrinking Satan's kingdom. Similarly, when carried over into salvation, the Christian who is antinomian, giving ultimate allegiance to Satan, will still go to heaven. Therefore, we have the incredible conclusion that wickedness is "blessed" and nothing is accomplished by obedience.[15] The truth, however, is that Christ rules the world providentially by sovereign power but especially by His moral law, and those who obey are blessed and those who disobey are cursed. This is Jesus' world, not Satan's, and the terms are His.[16]

(4) The Old Testament covenants were supposedly unconditional promises to Abraham and David that they would have the land of Palestine forever. It made no difference what Abraham and David did or if they had faith; the land was theirs forever.[17] This same idea is transferred to salvation so once one enters the covenant, it does not matter what one does — the covenant is unconditional.

Dispensationalists have never understood the Reformed and biblical idea that the covenants are both unconditional and conditional, depending on the point of view. From God's view, He knows His own, and it is certain they will arrive safely home (unconditional). From man's view, the promise is to those who persevere (conditional). God gives to His elect what He requires: the ability to persevere in faith and holiness. Likewise justification, sanctification, and glorification are conditioned on a faith that perseveres, and Jesus gives faith to His elect and the Holy Spirit to enable them to persevere.[18] The very warnings in Scripture are used to keep the elect on the path of holiness and to cause the reprobate to manifest themselves. The law becomes a blessing to the elect as they love it and keep it (imperfectly) by the Spirit while the same law is a curse to the reprobate who hate it and crash on it, making havoc of their lives. Yet both could be in the covenant as historically manifested.

A Bible college professor once lamented that the brightest students

---

[15] Even in the so-called millennial reign, Jesus will not be successful, for there will be a Satan led rebellion.

[16] For more on Jesus ruling and not Satan, covering the passages pertinent to the issue, see my book, *Man as God: The Word of Faith Movement*, chapter 10, which may be ordered from the publisher in the front of this book.

[17] "Forever" is usually interpreted as 1000 years in the so-called millennium.

[18] We do not deny that justification is legal, once for all, and not improvable but only emphasize that the kind of faith that justifies is one that perseveres.

of the dispensational college were abandoning dispensationalism for the Reformed faith, especially when they abandoned the dispensational concept of law and grace and of Pelagianism. The answer to his puzzle is obvious: Once one sees that salvation is all of grace (no Pelagianism), that in "the volume of the Book" it is written of Jesus so that all saving faith is in Him, that law and grace imply one another, that there is only one way to be justified, then the logical conclusion is that Jesus is the Head of His *one* people as their legal representative. Hence there are not two brides or two peoples of God, and the Bible is seen as a book of unity rather than diversity.

Chapter Nine

Dispensationalism: Defining the Basic System

Part of our local church's antiquated cooling system is a water tower that uses a float mechanism to regulate the water level. This exposed float presents an inviting diversion for children who pass by. A few of the men in the church have commented for several years that we need to install a protective screen over the float, but no one has taken the initiative to repair it. This year someone broke off the float, and I had to go to the hardware store to get a new one. Near the plumbing supplies stood Rommy, a good Christian friend and the leader of an influential community Bible study. Rommy and his family had left a theologically liberal church a few years back and had joined a newly forming dispensational Bible church. I had had opportunities to explain to Rommy why I had come to disagree with dispensationalism but had had little success. I remember well the time Rommy had looked me straight in the eye and had said with deliberate seriousness, "Grover, I am a dispensationalist."

I greeted Rommy; and he looked up from the faucet parts. Immediately he thanked me for the copy of my little self-published book on dispensationalism that I had mailed him. And then Rommy made another statement that burned itself indelibly into my mind: "Grover, I want you to know that after reading your book, I am never again going to call myself a dispensationalist." The Lord had established the work of my hand beyond my expectations; I was grateful.

I wondered what in the little book had been used of God to help effect this dramatic reversal. Was it the exegesis of some verse? Was it the logical force of some theological argument? Rommy soon answered my question. It was the list of the seven dispensational teachings, that which I also find most objectionable. Rommy told me repeatedly that he did not espouse any of those teachings.

I do not believe that Rommy's situation is unusual. Today there are many Bible believing Christians who have to some degree been influenced in their understanding of prophecy and the church by dispensationalism. And yet many, if not most, of these do not have a clear understanding of dispensationalism as it has been classically defined by writers such as Dr. C. I. Scofield and Dr. Lewis Sperry Chafer. They have not consistently thought through dispensationalism as a system, and have not become familiar with its controlling presuppositions. They are mostly unaware of the theological and exegetical conclusions to which this system logically leads. My conviction is that many people who are now favorably disposed toward dispensationalism would not be if they were better informed concerning the dispensational system.

A person's theological system is his understanding of what the overall teachings of Scripture are and how they interrelate. A verse of Scripture taken alone can often have more than one meaning. One important characteristic of the correct meaning of any verse is that it must harmonize with the overall teaching of Scripture, which is summarized in the theological system. The interpreter's job is, on the one hand, to interpret Scripture with the help of his theological system, and, on the other hand, to constantly evaluate and adjust his system in the light of Scripture. The interpreter must always seek to confirm that his theological system is indeed consistent with all the teachings of Scripture and also logically consistent within itself. This is a lifelong process. Really, it is a lives long process since the interpreter always builds on the work of previous exegetes and since the job is never finished.

The first step in arguing against the dispensational system is to define and document what I mean by the "dispensational system." Dispensationalism is the reigning system in many Christian circles today, and the task of proclaiming that "the king is naked" is never pleasant or popular. Before I assume this unpopular task, I want to make sure that people understand what I mean by "dispensationalism." In this chapter I will be discussing the recent development of dispensational theology, the fundamental Christian teaching which dispensationalism contradicts, and the three foundational presuppositions of dispensationalism.

Recent Development of Dispensationalism

The dispensationalists themselves have said that their system, which first began to be taught in the early nineteenth century, is a rediscovery of truths lost since the early days of Christianity. When I was a student at Dallas Theological Seminary, Alan Boyd, an unusually gifted student, studied in the original Greek the early church writings to the death of Justin Martyr to gather evidence that dispensationalism was indeed the system of early Christianity. Specifically, he was historically evaluating (in a master's thesis) Dr. Charles C. Ryrie's claim: "Premillennialism is the historic faith of the Church."[1] Mr. Boyd's conclusion was that Dr. Ryrie's statement was invalid.[2] He further noted that "based on classroom and private discussion," Dr. Ryrie had "clarified his position on these matters."[3] Mr. Boyd found the prophetic "beliefs of the period studied" to be "generally inimical to those of the modern system."[4] He concluded that there is no evidence that several of the church fathers who are routinely claimed by dispensationalists as fellow premillennialists were even premillennial, much less dispensational, and that the premillennialists in the early church "were a rather limited number."[5] He concluded that those church fathers who were premillennial, such as Papias and Justin Martyr, had little in common with modern day dispensationalists.[6] Mr. Boyd, as a dispensationalist, explained his findings as an example of the rapid loss of New Testament truth in the early church.[7] In other words, there is no extant concrete evidence that dispensationalism or anything significantly resembling it was ever taught in the

---

[1] Charles Caldwell Ryrie, *The Basis of the Premillennial Faith* (Neptune, N.J.: Loizeaux Brothers, 1953), page 17, compare page 33.

[2] Alan Patrick Boyd, "A Dispensational Premillennial Analysis of the Eschatology of the Post-Apostolic Fathers (until the Death of Justin Martyr)" (Th. M. thesis, Dallas Theological Seminary, 1977), page 89.

[3] Ibid., unnumbered preface.

[4] Ibid., pages 90-91.

[5] Ibid., page 92, footnote 1.

[6] Ibid., page 89.

[7] Ibid., page 91, footnote 2.

church any time until the nineteenth century.[8]

Dispensationalists like to compare themselves with covenant theologians because they can claim that covenant theology is almost as recent a theological innovation as dispensationalism.[9] They appear to be referring to covenant theology as a highly structured system that involves the doctrine of the covenant of works, which explains in covenantal terms God's relationship with Adam in the garden of Eden. Covenant theology so defined is, like dispensationalism, a recent development in the history of doctrine,[10] but I personally do not believe this is a valid comparison. Dispensationalism is a system that offered a new and totally different paradigm for understanding the church and prophecy. The covenant of works is a minor doctrine that built on a previously accepted foundation and that is not universally accepted among opponents of dispensationalism. My purpose is to contrast dispensationalism, not with the covenant of works or with a highly structured covenant theology, but with the general teaching that God has one plan of salvation through the ages that has resulted in one salvifically united people of God. This teaching that there has always been one plan of salvation and one people of God has, in general, been the historic position of the church, and is specifically the position found in Reformed theology. Though this theology has recognized administrative changes throughout redemptive history, it has also maintained only one people of God.

Dispensationalism Contradicts Basic Unity

God's plan of salvation as administered through the ages has found its unity in Christ, the one Mediator between God and man and the one who is the same yesterday, today and forever. God's eternal covenant of grace from eternity past to eternity future has always been based on the historical work of the incarnate Christ, whether that work was historically future or past. And God's covenant of grace has always been administered through faith in Christ, whether Christ was the one to come or the one who has come. This position finds eloquent expression in the words of the great Reformer, John Calvin:

---

[8] See Long Footnotes, p. 114.

[9] Charles Caldwell Ryrie, *Dispensationalism Today* (Chicago: Moody Press, 1965), pages 178-183.

[10] See Long Footnote, p. 114.

... since God cannot without the Mediator be propitious toward the human race, under the law Christ was always set before the holy fathers as the end to which they should direct their faith.[11]

... apart from Christ the saving knowledge of God does not stand. From the beginning of the world he had consequently been set before all the elect that they should look unto him and put their trust in him.[12]

... all men adopted by God into the company of his people since the beginning of the world were covenanted to him by the same law and by the bond of the same doctrine as obtains among us. ... [the patriarchs] participated in the same inheritance and hoped for a common salvation with us by the grace of the same Mediator. ... God's people have never had any other rule of reverence and piety.[13]

The covenant made with all the patriarchs is so much like ours in substance and reality that the two are actually one and the same. Yet they differ in the mode of dispensation.[14]

The Lord held to this orderly plan in administering the covenant of his mercy: as the day of full revelation approached with the passing of time, the more he increased each day the brightness of its manifestation. Accordingly, at the beginning when the first promise of salvation was given to Adam, it glowed like a feeble spark. Then, as it was added to, the light grew in fullness, breaking forth increasingly and shedding its radiance more widely. At last — when all the clouds were dispersed — Christ, the Sun of Righteousness, fully illumined the whole earth.[15]

The Reformed faith holds that the Bible contains a unified progression of revelation in which God has one people who form the universal church. While acknowledging that God's final purpose in every detail of history is His own glory, the Reformed faith teaches that God's plan to save a people through the death of Christ forms the unifying purpose that runs like a scarlet thread throughout redemptive history from Genesis to Revelation, tying it all together. There is an essential unity to God's people throughout the ages and a continuity

---

[11]John T. McNeill, editor and Ford Lewis Battles, translator, *The Library of Christian Classics, Volume XX: Calvin: Institutes of the Christian Religion* (Philadelphia: The Westminster Press, 1960), pages 344-345 (II.VI.2.).

[12]Ibid., page 347 (II.VI.4.).

[13]Ibid., pages 428-429 (II.X.1.).

[14]Ibid., page 429 (II.X.2.).

[15]Ibid., page 446 (II.X.20.).

in God's program throughout the Bible.

This teaching on the unity of God's people and the continuity of God's program is the fundamental teaching with which dispensationalists disagree. Dispensationalists hold Biblical revelation to be an interrupted progression in which God has two peoples: the earthly seed, Israel, and the heavenly seed, the church. Dispensationalists tend, in various degrees, to deny that redemption through Christ is the unifying purpose in Scripture and to deny the continuity of God's plan of salvation in the Old and New Testaments. This two-people view of redemptive history can also lead to strong dichotomies between law and grace, between conditional and unconditional covenants, between earthly and heavenly purposes, and between Jewish and Christian end-time prophetic events. As Dr. John F. Walvoord explains, dispensationalism "maintains sharply the distinctions between law and grace, between Israel and the church, between earthly and heavenly, and between prophecies being fulfilled and those which will be fulfilled in the millennium."[16]

Three Presuppositions of Dispensationalism

(1) Literalism

When one examines in more detail the basics of the dispensational system, one finds three bedrock concepts. The first of these is a literal and Jewish understanding of Old Testament prophecy and the Messianic kingdom with the result that these require a future fulfillment in terms of a resurrected Old Testament order with certain enhancements and variations. The dispensationalist argues that the nature of the kingdom announced by John the Baptist and offered by Jesus Christ should be understood in terms of the popular Jewish understanding of the kingdom at that time, and that the Jews at that time were expecting a literal restoration of Davidic political rule.[17] Similarly, the dispensationalist views the Messianic kingdom as a glorified extension of the Mosaic ceremonial law[18] and the Davidic political kingdom.

---

[16]John F. Walvoord, *The Millennial Kingdom* (Grand Rapids: Zondervan Publishing House, 1959), page 224.

[17]J. Dwight Pentecost, *Things to Come, A Study in Biblical Eschatology* (Grand Rapids: Zondervan Publishing House, 1958), pages 446-447; John F. Walvoord, *The Millennial Kingdom*, page 213; Paul Lee Tan, *The Interpretation of Prophecy* (Rockville, Maryland: Assurance Publishers, 1974), pages 300-301.

[18]See Long Footnotes, p. 114.

In reality there is no strong evidence of a unified Jewish view of the kingdom at the time of Christ. The Jewish understanding of the Messiah and the coming kingdom was varied.[19] What we do know is that among the various understandings of the Messianic kingdom at the time of Christ, there was a national and political hope that expected the earthly restoration of an idealized Davidic kingdom with deliverance from national enemies and the exaltation of national Israel. The disciples at times gave possible evidence of being influenced by such a view of the kingdom (Matthew 20:21; Acts 1:6). The dispensationalist assumes that this national, Jewish understanding of the kingdom was the correct view.

The dispensationalist defends his view of the Messianic kingdom by a literal interpretation of Old Testament prophecy. An easy way to explain the dispensational system of interpretation (i.e., hermeneutic) is to illustrate it with a description of the millennial situation expected by respected dispensational authorities based on their interpretation of prophecy. Dispensationalists are expecting literal and cataclysmic topographical changes in the land of Palestine. The Mount of Olives will be split in two to form a new valley running east and west. Mount Zion will be elevated above all the surrounding hills and the rest of Palestine will be transformed from a mountainous terrain to a great fertile plain.[20] There will be an earthly Jerusalem from which Jesus will exercise his earthly Davidic rule and a heavenly Jerusalem hovering over Palestine from which Christ will co-reign with the church. The heavenly city will have a foundation 1500 miles square and will be either a cube, a pyramid, or a sphere that is 1500 miles high.[21] The land in general and the temple area will be enlarged. The land will be redistributed to the twelve Jewish tribes, and the temple described in Ezekiel's temple vision will be built. The Old Testament priestly and levitical orders will be reestablished under the sons of Zadok, and the offering of bloody sacrifices will be reinstituted. From the temple a small flow of water will come forth whose volume will progressively increase with distance from the temple, becoming a

---

[19] See Long Footnotes, p. 115.

[20] John F. Walvoord, *The Millennial Kingdom*, pages 320-321. J. Dwight Pentecost, *Things to Come*, pages 509-510; Charles Caldwell Ryrie, *The Basis of the Premillennial Faith*, pages 147-148.

[21] J. Dwight Pentecost, *Things to Come*, pages 578, 580; John F. Walvoord, *The Millennial Kingdom*, pages 327-328, 334. Walvoord, *The Church In Prophecy* (Grand Rapids: Zondervan, 1964), page 162.

mighty river within a little over a mile from the temple. The river will flow south through Jerusalem and divide to flow west into the Mediterranean Sea and east into the Dead Sea, the Dead Sea being transformed into a fresh water body full of fish and surrounded by vegetation.[22] Jerusalem will be the center of a world government system, national Israel will be exalted, and the Gentile nations will be subordinated as Israel's servants.[23] This is the millennial situation as described by Dr. John F. Walvoord and Dr. J. Dwight Pentecost, who are influential and respected dispensational authorities.

(2) Parenthesis Theory

The interpretation of prophecy with the degree of literalism necessary to produce the above view of the Messianic kingdom is the first foundation stone of dispensationalism. The second foundation stone is the parenthesis theory. According to this theory, the church age is an unforeseen parenthesis or interjection in the Jewish program prophesied by the Old Testament prophets. If the Jews had not rejected Jesus, the Jewish kingdom age would have begun at Christ's first coming. But since the Jews did reject Christ, the prophetic program was supposedly interrupted, and the church age, totally unforeseen by the Old Testament prophets, was interjected. The kingdom program is to resume in the future in the tribulation and millennium after the church age. According to dispensationalism, no Old Testament prophecy can refer directly to the parenthetical church age. These prophecies must be fulfilled literally in the context of a recontinued Old Testament Jewish economy. This parenthesis theory is the logical implication of the dispensational literal hermeneutic. If the dispensational interpretation of the Old Testament prophets is correct, these prophecies are not pointing to the church age and there must be a future Jewish age if these prophecies are going to be fulfilled.

This parenthesis doctrine is dogmatically asserted by Dr. Lewis Sperry Chafer, the founder and first president of Dallas Theological Seminary, in the following statement about the beginning of the church age:

> Up to that time Judaism had not only occupied the field, but had been engendered, promoted and blessed of God. It was God's will for his

---

[22]John F. Walvoord, *The Millennial Kingdom*, pages 309-315, 320; J. Dwight Pentecost, *Things to Come*, pages 509-511.

[23]J. Dwight Pentecost, *Things to Come*, pages 495-507; John F. Walvoord, *The Millennial Kingdom*, pages 299-304.

people in the world. The beneficiaries of Judaism were as entrenched in their religious position and convictions and as much sustained by divine sanctions as are the most orthodox believers today. The new divine program had intentionally been unrevealed before its inauguration. It came, therefore, not only with great suddenness, but wholly without Old Testament revelation. The case would be nearly parallel if a new and unpredicted project were to be forced in at this time to supersede Christianity. The unyielding prejudice and violent resistance which arose in the Jewish mind was in direct ratio to the sincerity with which the individual Jew cherished his agelong privileges. Added to all this and calculated to make the new divine enterprise many-fold more difficult was its bold announcement that the despised Gentiles would be placed on equal footing with the Jew. . . .

. . . In fact, the new, hitherto unrevealed purpose of God in the out-calling of a heavenly people from the Jews and Gentiles is so divergent with respect to the divine purpose toward Israel, which purpose preceded it and will yet follow it, that the term *parenthetical,* commonly employed to describe the new age-purpose, is inaccurate. A parenthetical portion sustains some direct or indirect relation to that which goes before or that which follows; but the present age is not thus related and therefore is more precisely termed an *intercalation.* The appropriateness of this word will be seen in the fact that, as an interpolation is formed by inserting a word or phrase into a context, so an intercalation is formed by introducing a day or a period of time into the calendar. The present age of the Church is an intercalation into the revealed calendar or program of God as that program was foreseen by the prophets of old. Such, indeed, is the precise character of the present age.[24]

Dr. Charles C. Ryrie, a more recent dispensationalist, has said:

The Church is not fulfilling in any sense the promises to Israel. . . . The church age is not seen in God's program for Israel. It is an intercalation. . . . The Church is a mystery in the sense that it was completely unrevealed in the Old Testament and now revealed in the New Testament.[25]

This parenthesis view can also be vividly seen in the dispensational interpretation of Daniel's seventy weeks prophecy. According to the dispensationalists, the church age is a prophetically unforeseen parenthesis between the sixty-ninth and the seventieth week of Daniel's seventy weeks (Daniel 9:20-27). The seventieth week is

---

[24]Lewis Sperry Chafer, *Systematic Theology, 8 vols.* (Dallas: Dallas Seminary Press, 1948), 4:40-41.

[25]Charles Caldwell Ryrie, *The Basis of the Premillennial Faith*, page 136.

identified with a future seven year tribulation period that precedes the millennium and during which God's program for Israel will be resumed.

(3) Israel Versus the Church

The third foundation stone of the dispensational system is the dichotomy between Old Testament Israel and the New Testament church. According to dispensationalism, the Old Testament saints are not in the church universal, which is the Body of Christ and the Bride of Christ. The New Testament church is God's heavenly people while Old Testament and millennial Israel is God's earthly people. According to Dr. C. I. Scofield and Dr. Lewis Sperry Chafer, leading dispensationalists in an earlier generation, the earthly seed Israel is to spend eternity on the new earth, and the heavenly seed, the church, is to spend eternity in heaven. In other words, the dichotomy between Israel and the church even lasts throughout eternity.

More recent dispensationalists have put the saints of all ages together on the new earth in eternity but maintain their dichotomy throughout eternity by eternally excluding Old Testament saints, tribulation saints, and millennial saints from the Body and Bride of Christ. This dispensational teaching on the dichotomy between Israel and the church is found in the following quotations:

> Israel's distinction, glory and destiny will always be earthly. They will also be a spiritual people, Jehovah's possession. There is no division, however, between the saved Jew and the saved Gentile of this dispensation, both being in the church. But after the church is complete, at the end of this dispensation, there will of necessity be a division. The "holy Jerusalem" of Revelation 21 is the "bride, the Lamb's wife," for whom is the "new heaven," while the "new earth" will be for Israel, the tabernacle of God is to be with them, and "God himself shall be with them, and be their God." The distinctive New Testament spiritual and heavenly blessings are for the Church; those blessings of and on the earth, for Israel.[26]

> Judaism is not the bud which has blossomed into Christianity. These systems do have features which are common to both — God, holiness, Satan, man, sin, redemption, human responsibility, and the issues of eternity — yet they introduce differences so vast that they cannot coalesce. Each sets up its ground of relationship between God and man — the Jew by physical birth, the Christian by spiritual birth; each provides its instructions on the life of its adherents — the law for Israel, the

---

[26]C. I. Scofield with Ella E. Pohle, compiler, *Dr. C. I. Scofield's Question Box* (Chicago: Moody Press, 1917), page 70.

teachings of grace for the Church; each has its sphere of existence — Israel in the earth for all ages to come, the Church in heaven. To the end that the Church might be called out from both Jews and Gentiles, a peculiar, unrelated age has been thrust into the one consistent ongoing of the divine program for the earth. It is this sense that Judaism, which is the abiding portion of the nation Israel, has ceased. With the completion and departure of the Church from earth, Judaism will be again the embodiment of all the divine purpose in the world.[27]

The fact that revelation concerning both Israel and the Church includes truth about God, holiness, sin and redemption by blood, does not eliminate a far greater body of truth in which it is disclosed that Israelites become such by natural birth while Christians become such by a spiritual birth; that Israelites were appointed to live and serve under a meritorious, legal system, while Christians live and serve under a gracious system; that Israelites, as a nation, have their citizenship now and their future destiny centered only in the earth, reaching on to the new earth which is yet to be, while Christians have their citizenship and future destiny centered only in heaven, extending on into the new heavens that are yet to be . . .[28]

That God is continuing His work of redemption in calling out a people for His name in the Church the body of Christ we gladly affirm, but we also insist that this Body of Christ is distinct from any previous body of redeemed people in its nature, characteristics, time, and promises.[29]

. . .the Church in a technical sense is strictly limited to those who have accepted Christ in this age. Therefore, the Church is a distinct body of saints in this age.[30]

The marriage of the Lamb is an event which evidently involves only Christ and the Church. . . . While it would be impossible to eliminate [Old Testament saints and tribulation saints] from the place of observers, they cannot be in the position of participants in the event itself.[31]

Reformed theology disagrees with all three of these dispensational

---

[27]Lewis Sperry Chafer, *Systematic Theology*, 4:248-249

[28]Ibid., 4:30.

[29]Charles Caldwell Ryrie, *Dispensationalism Today*, page 144.

[30]Charles Caldwell Ryrie, *The Basis of the Premillennial Faith*, page 138.

[31]J. Dwight Pentecost, *Things to Come*, page 227. "From these Scriptures the evidence is conclusive that the Church is the Bride of Christ and that Israel will have her place of honor in the kingdom as companions of the Bride," Lewis Sperry Chafer, *Systematic Theology*, 4:133.

foundation stones. According to Reformed theology the people of God from all ages will be members of the Body and Bride of Christ and will enjoy eternity together on the new earth. Old Testament Israel is seen as organically related to the New Testament church as childhood is related to adulthood in the life of a man (Galatians 4:1-7). Many of the Old Testament prophecies about Israel — even Old Testament prophecies that refer to ceremonial law, the tribes, the ancient enemies of Israel — are seen as being fulfilled in and through the church in this age. Obviously there is a clear and dramatic contrast between the Reformed and the dispensational understandings of the church and prophecy. My thesis is that the Reformed understanding of prophecy and the church is Biblically sound and the dispensational understanding is an artificial imposition on the Scripture.

Long Footnotes:

[8]". . . until brought to the fore through the writings and preaching and teaching of a distinguished ex-clergyman, Mr. J. N. Darby, in the early part of the last century, it is scarcely to be found in a single book or sermon through a period of sixteen hundred years! If any doubt this statement, let them search, as the writer has in a measure done, the remarks of the so-called Fathers, both pre- and post-Nicene; the theological treatises of the scholastic divines; Roman Catholic writers of all shades of thought; the literature of the Reformation; the sermons and expositions of the Puritans; the general theological works of the day." Harry A. Ironside, *The Mysteries of God* (New York: Loizeaux Brothers, 1908), pages 50-51. Quoted in Daniel Payton Fuller, "The Hermeneutics of Dispensationalism" (dissertation, Northern Baptist Theological Seminary, 1957), page 29.

[10]"It is difficult to discover the genealogy of the doctrine of the Covenant of Works which appeared in fully developed form in the last decade of the 16th century." John Murray, *Collected Writings of John Murray: Volume Four: Studies in Theology, Reviews* (The Banner of Truth Trust, 1982), page 219.

[18] Dr. J. Dwight Pentecost objects to the association of the dispensational millennium with the Mosaic system: "The kingdom expectation is based on the Abrahamic covenant, the Davidic covenant, and the Palestinic covenant, but is no way based on the Mosaic covenant. It is insisted that the covenants will be fulfilled in the kingdom age. This does not, however, link the Mosaic covenant with the kingdom necessarily. It is therefore fallacious to reason that because one believes in the fulfillment of the determinative covenants he must also believe in the restora-

tion of the Mosaic order, which was a conditional covenant, non-determinative and non-eschatological in intent, but given rather to govern the life of the people in their relation to God in the old economy. One great stumbling block that hinders the acceptance of literal sacrifices in the millennium is removed by observing that, while there are many similarities between the Aaronic and millennial systems, there are also many differences between them that make it impossible that they should be equated."

Dr. Pentecost, however, goes on to argue: "It can thus be seen that the form of worship in the millennium will bear a strong similarity to the old Aaronic order. The very fact that God has instituted an order strangely like the old Aaronic order is one of the best arguments that the millennium is not being fulfilled in the church, composed of Gentiles and Jew, in the present age." J. Dwight Pentecost, *Things to Come*, pages 518-519.

[19] "As to the contents of the future expectation thus indicated, there was a great diversity of conceptions. For a knowledge of what was actually believed in some circles prior to and at the time of the birth of Christ, the pseudoepigraphic and apocryphal writings of the period are especially important. But they are far from unanimous in their eschatological outlook. It is, consequently, very difficult to state accurately what the future outlook of the Jews actually was at the beginning of the Christian era. Alongside of utterances that start from the prophecies of the restoration of the people of Israel and of the house of David, other writings lay more emphasis on the supernatural-transcendent character of the great time of salvation." Herman Ridderbos, *The Coming of the Kingdom* (Philadelphia: The Presbyterian and Reformed Publishing Company, 1962), page 10.

Chapter Ten

Dispensationalism: Israel and the Church

The consistent dispensationalist is a theologian in the grip of an idea — the idea that there is a strong dichotomy between Israel and the church. This idea is a relatively modern theory in the history of doctrine that was initially developed and popularized by J. N. Darby (1800-1882), the father of dispensational thought. During a period of convalescence in 1827, Darby meditated on the fact that the true Christian through the baptizing work of the Spirit is in union with Christ and therefore is seated with Christ in the heavenlies (Ephesians 2:4-7). With this in mind, Darby read in Isaiah 32:15-20 about a prophesied outpouring of the Spirit on Israel that would bring earthly blessings on the people of God. Darby took this Scriptural data and concluded that the passages implied a strong contrast between earthly blessings prophesied for Israel and heavenly blessings promised to the Christian in the New Testament. From this Darby developed his theory that God has two peoples, an earthly people and a heavenly people.[1]

In 1840 Darby gave the following summary of his new ideas on prophecy:

> Prophecy applies itself properly to the earth; its object is not heaven. It was about things that were to happen on the earth; and the not seeing this has misled the Church. We have thought that we ourselves had

[1] Daniel Fuller, "The Hermeneutics of Dispensationalism" (dissertation, Northern Baptist Theological Seminary, 1957), pages 38-41.

within us the accomplishments of these earthly blessings, whereas we are called to heavenly blessings. The privilege of the Church is to have its portion in the heavenly places; and later blessings will be shed forth on the earthly people. The Church is something altogether apart — a kind of heavenly economy, during the rejection of the earthly people, who are put aside on account of their sins, and driven out among the nations, out of the midst of which nations God chooses a people for the enjoyment of heavenly glory with Jesus Himself. The Lord, having been rejected by the Jewish people, is become wholly a heavenly person. This is the doctrine which we find peculiarly in the apostle Paul. It is no longer the Messiah for the Jews, but a Christ exalted, glorified; and it is for want of taking hold of this exhilarating truth, that the Church has become so weak.[2]

This summary statement demonstrates that Darby had come to interpret Scripture in terms of the dispensational dichotomy and parenthesis theories. He had come to view the Jews as the earthly people of God with an earthly purpose, destiny and hope, the Christians as the heavenly people of God with a heavenly purpose, destiny and hope, and the church age as the heavenly parenthesis in the earthly program.

Reformed theology, of course, strongly disagrees with this radical dichotomy between Israel and the church. Reformed theologians do recognize Biblical distinctions between Old Testament Israel and the New Testament church but not a strong dichotomy. The Biblical distinctions between Old Testament Israel and the New Testament church involve an organic progression analogous to the development of a child into an adult (Galatians 4:3-4). The organic development brought about during the time of the New Testament includes the unprecedentedly clear revelation through the Incarnate Word and His apostles, the historical accomplishment of the prophesied Messianic atonement, the outpouring of the Spirit in unprecedented fullness, the cessation of the burdensome Mosaic ceremonial laws, and the universalization of the kingdom previously limited to the Jewish nation. In the midst of these developmental changes, there was also a strong continuity with the Old Testament program. Although God often treated Old Testament Israel in terms of earthly institutions and promises, these were pictures of the same heavenly realities later

---

[2]Ibid., page 45; quoting from J. N. Darby, "The Hopes of the Church of God," *Collected Writings* (William Kelly, editor; 35 volumes; second edition; London: G. Morrish, n.d.), 2:571-572.

spoken of in the New Testament. And although the New Testament often speaks in terms of heavenly and spiritual realities, the Christian is still in the world and has been given the earthly task of being the light of the world, the salt of the earth, and the discipler of the nations.

Ephesians 2:12-21

Here are two antithetical systems in regard to the relationship between Israel and the church. A New Testament passage that speaks to this issue is Ephesians 2:12-21, a passage in which the Apostle Paul contrasts the covenant status of Gentiles under the old covenant with that of Gentile Christians under the new covenant. In this passage Paul first reminds the Ephesian Christians of their former spiritual poverty before they believed in Christ in the new covenant age. As "Gentiles in the flesh," they were uncircumcised and were therefore formerly without the sign and seal of God's covenant (verse 11). Then in verse 12 Paul summarizes what had once been the Gentile covenant status: "at that time ye were without Christ, being aliens from the commonwealth of Israel, and strangers from the covenants of promise, having no hope, and without God in the world."

As the uncircumcised, they had been "aliens from the commonwealth of Israel" (verse 12). Outward membership in God's covenant community does not guarantee inward membership and salvation, but it is important. Outward membership in Old Testament Israel had not been without its advantages:

> What advantage then hath the Jew? Or what profit is there in circumcision? Much every way: chiefly, because that unto them were committed the oracles of God (Romans 3:1-2).

> . . . Israelites; to whom pertaineth the adoption, and the glory, and the covenants, and the giving of the law, and the service of God, and the promises; whose are the fathers, and of whom concerning the flesh Christ came, who is over all, God blessed forever. Amen (Romans 9:4-5).

> . . . salvation is of the Jews (John 4:22).

The "Gentiles in the flesh" under the old covenant had been without these advantages because of their alienation from Israel. The word translated "being aliens" is a strong term used at times to speak of estrangement from God due to moral abominations (Ezekiel 14:5, 7-8 LXX; Hosea 9:10 LXX). After the formation of the nations at the tower of Babel, God had chosen one man, Abraham, to father the one nation, Israel, through which He would exclusively administer His covenants until the universalism of the new covenant age when His people would be from every tribe, nation and tongue. God had "suffered all nations to walk in their own ways" during the era of Jewish particularism (Acts 14:16). He allowed them to remain in their bondage to demonic paganism and therefore in alienation from Himself and His people.

The Gentiles in the flesh, as "aliens from the commonwealth of Israel," had been, most significantly, "without Christ." Under the old covenant the Jews, of course, had not known the historically manifested Jesus of Nazareth, but they had known the Messiah yet to come through the "covenants of promise" (verse 12). Paul, in a sermon addressed to physical Jews, stated that ". . . the promise which was made unto the fathers, God hath fulfilled the same unto us their children, in that he hath raised up Jesus again. . . ." (Acts 13:32b-33a). The uncircumcised Gentile relationship to these promises had been that of the "stranger," a general term for the foreigner or alien who was without the rights associated with citizenship in the covenant community.

Paul then contrasts this former position of spiritual poverty with the covenant status of believing Gentiles in this age. Contrary to their former status, they are now "no more strangers and foreigners, but fellow-citizens with the saints, and of the household of God" (verse 19). The Greek word translated "foreigners" is used in the Greek translation of the Old Testament to refer to the resident aliens who lived in Israel and had certain legal rights but who were not citizens in Israel and could not partake of the Passover (Exodus 12:45 LXX). This word literally means "the one beside the *house*," and Paul states that to be no longer a foreigner is to be "of the *house*hold of God." The word house is a symbolic expression for membership in God's people under both the old and the new covenants (Numbers 12:7; 1 Timothy 3:15; Hebrews 3:5-6).

The Gentiles in Christ are also now "fellow-citizens with the saints." In the Greek the word translated "fellow-citizen" in verse 19 is closely related to the word in verse 12 translated "commonwealth" in the King James Version. In the New International Version this word from verse 12 is translated "citizenship," a translation which better shows the close affinity of this word with the one translated "fellow-citizen." The Gentile in the flesh had been alienated "from the commonwealth of Israel," but the Gentile Christian is now a "fellow-citizen with the saints." The "saints" are God's holy people, the people of the covenant. The Christian, a citizen of the heavenly Jerusalem (Galatians 4:26; Philippians 3:20; Revelation 3:12), is a fellow-citizen with the saints of all ages (Hebrews 12:22-23).

In verse 13 the Gentile Christians at Ephesus are referred to as "ye who sometimes were far off." Then in verse 17 the apostle says, "And (Christ) came and preached peace to you which were afar off, and to them that were nigh." As we have seen from verse 13, those who are referred to as "afar off" are the pagan Gentiles who had lived as "aliens from the commonwealth of Israel." Who then are those referred to as "them that were nigh"? Many believe that this term has reference to the Jews at Ephesus who had heard the Gospel message.[3] The Jew as a member of God's covenant people was already provisionally near to the Gospel since the Gospel was the fulfillment of the covenants of promise that had been made with Old Testament Israel. Peter had told the Jews at Pentecost that the New Covenant promise of the Spirit in a sense belonged to them (Acts 2:39). Of course if the Jew persisted in rejecting the Messiah, he was cut off from the true covenant people; but the Gospel was offered to the Jew first and then to the Gentile (Romans 1:16).

In verse 13 of Ephesians 2, Paul says, "But now in Christ Jesus ye who sometimes were afar off are made nigh by the blood of Christ." We have seen that the terms "near" and "far" refer to the respective relationships of the Jew and the pagan Gentile to the Old Testament covenants of promise at the time of the transition between the old and new covenants when the new covenant Gospel was first being offered. Then in verse 13 Paul is teaching that the pagan Gentile who believed in Christ was no longer "afar off" but "near"; he had been made an heir in new covenant fullness of those Old Testament covenants of promise that formerly had belonged exclusively to Old Testament Israel.

This passage is not teaching that the Gentile Christian has become a member of Old Testament Israel. Instead, it teaches that the Gentile believer has become a member of the church of Messianic fullness, which Paul calls "the new man" (verse 15). The importance of this passage is that it stresses the newness of the church and then emphasizes the continuity of the church with God's previous covenant program. The answer to Gentile alienation from Israel and her covenants is membership in the new man, which makes one a fellow-citi-

---

[3]See end of chapter, Long Footnote, p. 131.

zen with God's covenant people and a member of God's house. These terms, as we have seen, have roots in the Old Testament, and this passage fits in well with the Reformed teaching that the New Testament church is Old Testament Israel come to new covenant maturity.

The dispensational interpretation of this Ephesian passage places all the emphasis on the teaching that the New Testament church is a "new man."[4] True, there is a significant newness to the New Testament church, but that does not nullify the equally valid teaching in Ephesians 2 that the New Testament church has a strong relationship of organic continuity with Old Testament Israel. Is the newness of the new covenant church the newness of maturity in a context of organic continuity with the past? Or is the newness of the new covenant church best explained by the rigid dispensational dichotomy and parenthesis theories? For the dispensationalist to assume automatically and dogmatically that the "new man" has no organic continuity with the Old Testament covenant people is to commit the logical fallacy of begging the question.

Under the Mosaic covenant only practicing Jews were members of God's covenant people. In this age of the new covenant, however, believing Jews and Gentiles together are full members of God's holy people (Galatians 3:28; Ephesians 2:14), and unbelieving individual Jews and Gentiles together are outside the camp of covenant blessings. There are two ways this equalization of spiritual status between Jew and Gentile could have been effected. (1) In line with the dispensational dichotomy and parenthesis theories, the Old Testament covenants could have parenthetically become inoperative. Dr. Lewis Sperry Chafer comments, ". . . the Jew has been removed from the place of special privilege which was his in the past age and leveled to the same standing as the Gentile . . . ."[5] And similarly John F. Walvoord sets forth, "In the present age, Israel has been set aside, her promises held in abeyance, with no progress in the fulfillment of her program."[6]

(2) Or, in line with the Reformed teaching that the church age is an exalted continuation of the Old Testament covenant program, believing Gentiles could have been elevated to the privileged position

---

[4] John F. Walvoord, *The Millennial Kingdom* (Grand Rapids: Zondervan Publishing House, 1959), page 165.

[5] See Long Footnotes, p. 131.

[6] See end of chapter, Long Footnote, p. 131.

of spiritual Israel by being made full heirs of the Old Testament covenants in new covenant fullness. Believing Jews would have remained in spiritual Israel during the transition between the old and new covenants, and unbelieving Jews would have been cut off from the covenant people in judgment (Romans 11:20). To be cut off from the church in judgment was to be reduced in the eyes of the covenant people to the religious status of a pagan (Matthew 18:17). Ephesians 2 supports this second suggestion through its teaching that believing Gentiles today participate in the covenants of promise that formerly had been limited to the commonwealth of Israel.

Another relevant passage is Romans 11 in which Paul discusses the status of Jews in the church age. The olive tree of Romans 11 represents the privileged position of blessing that belonged to Old Testament Israel (compare Jeremiah 11:16; Hosea 14:6). It is an olive tree whose roots are firmly established in the Old Testament covenants made with the Jewish patriarchs. How should we expect Paul to use the olive tree figure if he really were a dispensationalist? Since, according to dispensationalism, all the Jews in this parenthetical age are cut off from their Old Testament privileges, we should expect Paul to teach that *all* the branches on the olive tree of Israel were broken off at the beginning of the church age. Like the clock of the Jewish prophetic program that supposedly stopped ticking at the beginning of the church age, the old Jewish olive tree would have to stand dormant during the church age until that future tribulation period and millennium when God again resumes the Jewish prophetic program. It could be compared to the Jewish train that is waiting on the side track until the church train bypasses on the track of history, to use another illustration popular with dispensationalists. Also, since God's program for the church is allegedly distinct from God's program for Israel, we should expect Paul to teach that a new olive tree representing the church was divinely planted at the beginning of the church age. And all the believing Jews who were broken off from the olive tree of dormant Israel and all the believing Gentiles who were formerly in the wild olive tree of paganism are in this age grafted into the new olive tree of church blessings. But this, of course, is not what Paul teaches. Instead, Paul teaches that only unbelieving Jews were broken off from the olive tree of Israel. Jews who accepted Christ remained where they always had been — in the olive tree of Israel! And believing Gentiles were grafted into the same olive tree of Israel! This explanation from Romans 11 of the status of Jews in the church age strongly implies — indeed demands! — that the church is spiritual Israel in this new covenant age!

Another passage that presents the cogent continuity between Israel and the church is Hebrews 3:5-6. This passage refers to both Old Testament Israel and the New Testament church as God's one house (singular, not houses), which demonstrates their unity as the one people of God. The verses build on Numbers 12:7, where the term "God's house" definitely refers to Israel.[7] Furthermore, we see the organic progression between the testaments in that both Moses and Christ are administrators of the *same* house. Only now the administration has passed solely to Christ!

Revelation 21

Another passage that speaks of the relationship between Old Testament Israel and the New Testament church is Revelation 21. The passage reveals that the New Jerusalem is symbolic for the saints of all the ages. The city's twelve foundation stones, having the names of the twelve apostles inscribed on them, represent the New Testament saints. And the city's twelve gates, having the names of the twelve tribes of Israel on them, represent the Old Testament saints (Revelation 21:12, 14). The New Jerusalem, a city whose citizenship includes the saints of all the ages, is also called the Bride of Christ (Revelation 21:2, 9-10). The Bride of Christ is elsewhere defined as the church universal, the Body of Christ (Ephesians 5:22-33). This means that both Old Testament Israel and the New Testament church are together in the one Body of Christ and together in this *one* city!

Hebrews 11 and 12

The conclusion that Old Testament saints are included in the New Jerusalem is further confirmed by Hebrews 11 and 12. Hebrews 11 sets forth examples of faith in the lives of Old Testament saints and concludes concerning their status of salvation:

> And these all, having obtained a good report through faith, received not the promise: God having provided some better thing for us, that they without us should not be made perfect.

In Hebrews 12:22-24 the inhabitants of the New Jerusalem are

---

[7]Compare Exodus 16:31; 2 Samuel 1:12; Jeremiah 31:31; Matthew 10:6; 15:24; Acts 2:36.

described as follows:

> But you have come unto mount Sion, and unto the city of the living God, the heavenly Jerusalem, and to an innumerable company of angels, to the general assembly and church of the firstborn, which are written in heaven, and to God the Judge of all, and to the spirits of just men made perfect, and to Jesus the mediator of the new covenant, and to the blood of sprinkling, that speaketh better things than that of Abel.

A comparison of the above verses can leave little doubt that both Old Testament and New Testament saints are citizens of the heavenly city. Hebrews 12:22-23 teaches that "the spirits of just men made perfect" are included among the New Jerusalem inhabitants, and Hebrews 11:39-40 gives evidence that this designation is inclusive of the Old Testament saints.

Dr. J. Dwight Pentecost attempts to disarm the implications of the above reference to the New Jerusalem being the Bride of Christ. He argues that though the New Jerusalem does contain all the saints of all the ages, the city takes its "chief characterization" from the New Testament church, which alone is the Bride of Christ.[8]

Dr. C. I. Scofield has a different explanation:

> The "Lamb's wife" here [Revelation 19:7] is the "bride" (Rev. 21.9), the Church, identified with the "heavenly Jerusalem" (Heb. 12.22, 23), and to be distinguished from Israel, the adulterous and repudiated "wife" of Jehovah, yet to be restored (Isa. 54.1-10; Hosea 2.1-17), who is identified with the earth (Hosea. 2.23). A forgiven and restored *wife* could not be called either a *virgin* (2 Cor. 11.2, 3), or a *bride*.[9]

Dr. Lewis Sperry Chafer falls in line with Dr. Pentecost:

> It is named for the Bride of Christ and probably because she has some superior right to it; yet other peoples and beings enter her gates.[10]

And Dr. John F. Walvoord is not substantially different:

> The New Jerusalem is given detailed revelation and is described in general "as a bride adorned for her husband" (Revelation 21:2). The figure of marriage is used for the church, for Israel, and here for the city in which the saints of all ages will dwell. The fact that the marriage figure is used

---

[8]J. Dwight Pentecost, *Things to Come* (Grand Rapids: Zondervan Publishing House, 1958), page 576; compare page 227.

[9]C. I. Scofield, editor, *The Scofield Reference Bible* (New York: Oxford University Press, 1909), page 1348 (note on Revelation 19:7).

[10]Lewis Sperry Chafer, *Systematic Theology*, 5:367.

for more than one entity in Scripture should not be considered confusing, nor should the city be identified specifically with the church. It is rather that the New Jerusalem has all the beauty and freshness of a bride adorned for her husband.[11]

Pentecost, Scofield, Chafer, and Walvoord concede the force of the passage by their futile attempt to harmonize the passage with their system, which is "found wanting." They admit that other saints in addition to the church reside in the New Jerusalem, but then they try to explain away the Bible's reference to the city as the Bride of Christ.

Matthew 21:43

Another significant passage that speaks to this issue is Matthew 21:43, a statement which Christ made to the Jewish leaders near the end of His earthly ministry: "Therefore say I unto you, the kingdom of God shall be taken from you, and given to a nation bringing forth the fruit thereof." The question this statement raises is, "Who is this nation that was given the kingdom of God?" The obvious answer is the church, which is elsewhere designated a nation (1 Peter 2:9). If the church was given the kingdom program that God had first administered through Old Testament Israel and had previously rooted in the Old Testament covenants, then there is a strong continuity from Israel to the church. If the church assumes the Old Testament kingdom program begun with Old Testament Israel, then the church truly is the Israel of the new covenant.

A common dispensational answer to the above question is that the kingdom will be given "to the nation Israel when she shall turn to the Lord and be saved before entering the millennial kingdom."[12] This means that the whole church age must intervene between the first clause of the verse in which the kingdom is taken away from physical Israel and the second clause in which the kingdom is given to another nation! Some dispensationalists do admit that this verse is teaching that the kingdom in some sense has been transferred in this age from Old Testament Israel to the New Testament church or to the believing Gentiles of this age.[13] Those who make this admission must define

---

[11]Dr. John F. Walvoord, *The Church in Prophecy* (Grand Rapids: Zondervan Publishing House, 1964), page 161.

[12]Charles Caldwell Ryrie, *The Basis of the Premillennial Faith*, page 71.

[13]C. C. Ryrie, *Ryrie Study Bible: The New Testament*, note on Matthew 21:43; J. Dwight Pentecost, *Things to Come*, pages 465-466.

away through qualifications the significance and meaning of this transfer if they are to maintain their dichotomy between Israel and the church. Whenever dispensationalists admit that the kingdom is related to the church, they usually interpret it as either the kingdom in mystery form of Matthew 13 or as God's non-theocratic rule of providence.

Messianic Shepherd

Additional insight into the transition of the kingdom from Old Testament Israel to the New Testament church can be found in the Biblical teaching on the Messianic Good Shepherd. The Messianic Good Shepherd was to do two things: dispossess the "bad shepherd" leaders of Israel and to judge between members of the flock of Israel (Ezekiel 34:7-31). Jesus Christ took the kingdom away from the leaders of Israel who had opposed Him and gave the kingdom to the "poor of the flock" (Zechariah 11:7, 11), the righteous remnant within the nation who were His disciples. In Luke 12:32 Jesus said to His disciples: "Fear not, little flock; for it is your Father's good pleasure to give you the kingdom." His disciples were the true sheep in Israel, for the true sheep within the flock of Israel were those who recognized the Messianic Shepherd, listened to His teachings, and obediently followed Him (John 10:14, 27). Those Jews who rejected Christ did not believe because they were not true sheep (John 10:26).

Jesus also taught that He had sheep outside the fold of His Jewish disciples (John 10:16). Jesus was speaking of the Gentiles who would later believe and be incorporated into His church. Though these had not yet believed, Christ spoke of them as those chosen and predestined before the foundation of the world to be His. Christ said that these Gentile sheep were outside His present fold of disciples and that He would lead them into His one flock.[14] The word translated "fold" in John 10:16 literally refers to a walled court (compare John 10:1) and brings to mind a picture of Israel walled off from the Gentile nations by her ceremonial laws. Jesus was to lead these Gentile sheep into His one flock, "for He is our peace, who hath made both one, and hath broken down the middle wall of partition between us" (Ephesians 2:14). The new covenant people of God are one flock with no distinction between Jew and Gentile.

The use of the flock metaphor in John 10 demonstrates the

---

[14]This distinction between the flock and the fold in John 10:16 is not made clear in the King James Version where both Greek words are translated "fold."

relationship of continuity between old covenant Israel and the new covenant church. Both old covenant Israel and the new covenant church are identified as God's flock.[15] *Christ's sheep are those for whom He savingly died (John 10:11) and to whom He has given eternal life (John 10:28). Since salvation is found in Christ alone, God's true sheep are the saints of all ages.*

These gems about the Good Shepherd teach that Jesus took the kingdom away from the leaders and members of old covenant Israel who rejected Him, gave this kingdom to the righteous remnant within the nation who received Him in faith, and then added to this one flock the believing Gentiles. This message given under the figure of the one flock is similar to the message that Paul teaches in Romans 11 under the figure of the one olive tree. Both John 10 and Romans 11 teach the essential unity of the people of God through the ages as *one* flock and *one* olive tree and illustrate the organic progression and the developmental continuity in the transition between the old and new covenants.

Church Has Jewish Names

Another group of passages that are relevant to our discussion of continuity are those that give the church a Jewish name. The most commonly discussed of these is Galatians 6:16, where Paul refers to the church as the "Israel of God." Dispensationalists argue that Paul was referring exclusively to the Jews in the early church and not to the church as a whole.[16] But one must remember that a major theme in Galatians is that the Jews have no special privileges over the Gentiles in this age (Galatians 3:28). Christ has broken down the religious dividing wall between Jew and Gentile in the Christian church (Ephesians 2:14). Paul would have destroyed his own argument if he would have given the Jews in the church a special status or recognition by referring to them exclusively as the Israel of God. He would have succumbed to the Judaizers by giving them a valid reason for arguing that Gentile Christians could improve their covenant status by becoming Jewish proselytes as well as Christians. According to dispensationalists, believing Jews and Gentiles in the church are heirs

---

[15]Israel: Psalm 74:1; 78:52; 79:13; 95:7; 100:3; Isaiah 40:11; 63:11; Jeremiah 13:17; 23:1; 50:6; Ezekiel 34:31; Micah 7:14; Zechariah 10:3; 13:7; Matthew 10:6; 15:24. Church: Acts 20:28-29; 1 Peter 2:25; 5:2-3.

[16]See end of chapter, Long Footnote, p. 132.

together of spiritual promises, but Jews, believing and unbelieving, are exclusive heirs of national promises.[17] Since Paul taught that there is no Jew or Gentile in Christ (Galatians 3:28), he must have been referring to the whole church when he spoke of the Israel of God in Galatians 6:16. If this interpretation is correct, then this verse would best be translated: "Peace and mercy to all who follow this rule, *even* to the Israel of God," as in the New International Version. Then the true Israel of God in this age would be defined as all those who walk by the rule of not boasting except in the cross of Christ.

Elsewhere the church is called the "diaspora," a technical term for Jews living in Gentile nations (1 Peter 1:1; James 1:1); the twelve tribes (James 1:1; Revelation 7:4; Luke 22:30); a chosen race, a royal priesthood, a holy nation, a people for God's own possession (1 Peter 2:9-10; Revelation 1:6; Titus 2:14; compare Exodus 19:6; Deuteronomy 7:6); Jews who are Jews inwardly (Romans 2:28-29); the circumcision (Philippians 3:3; compare Colossians 2:11, Romans 2:29); comers unto Mount Zion (Hebrews 12:22); citizens of the heavenly Jerusalem (Galatians 4:26); children of promise like Isaac (Galatians 4:28); Abraham's seed and heirs according to the promise of Abraham (Galatians 3:29).

Dispensationalists typically argue that these Jewish names given to the church refer only to believing Jews in the church. There are some cases where the New Testament does make a limited reference to believing Jews, as in Romans 9:6: "For they are not all Israel, which are of Israel." That verse is contrasting believing Jews and unbelieving Jews. There are, however, many other cases where Paul is clearly referring to the whole church when he uses a Jewish title. For example, Paul defined the circumcision as those "which worship God in the spirit, and rejoice in Christ Jesus, and have no confidence in the flesh" (Philippians 3:3). "The circumcision" is a title for Israel (Ephesians 2:11), and this description of the true circumcision in this age is inclusive of all true believers, both Jew and Gentile. All Christians are spiritually circumcised (Colossians 2:11-12), and "*he is a Jew*, which is one inwardly; and circumcision is that of the heart" (Romans 2:29).

It is also relevant that in Revelation 2:9 and 3:9 Jesus called the Jews who were persecuting the churches at Smyrna and Philadelphia those "which say they are Jews, and are not" and "the synagogue of Satan." These verses clearly show that those ethnic Jews who rejected

---

[17] John F. Walvoord, *The Millennial Kingdom*, page 169.

Christ were no longer considered a part of the true Israel. Paul said in Romans 2:28: "For he is not a Jew, which is one outwardly; neither is that circumcision, which is outward in the flesh." He went on to proclaim that the true Jew has been circumcised in heart.

Even the Greek word translated "church" in the New Testament (*ekklesia*) demonstrates the strong continuity between Old Testament Israel and the New Testament church:

> Thus the gathering of Israel at Sinai was not a mere congregation or assembling of the people to each other, but a meeting with God; and this fact is very remarkably indicated in the Septuagint Greek. In the description of the Sinai scene, given in Deut. iv, in that version, the tenth verse stands thus: "The day that thou stoodest before the Lord thy God in Horeb (*te hemera tes ekklesias*), *in the day of the assembly*, when the Lord said to me (*ekklesiason pros me*), *assemble to me* the people." Previous to that occasion the word "*ekklesia*" is not found in the Greek Scriptures. That day was, by Moses, habitually designated "the day of the ekklesia — the *assembly*" (Deut. ix,10; x,4; xviii,16), and the reason of the designation is thus, by the Greek translators, stamped upon the face of that version. It was so called because the people on that day met with God, in compliance with the command (ekklesiason), " *Assemble to me* the people." In accordance with the special meaning to which the word was thus appropriated it is used throughout Scripture. In the Old Testament and Apocrypha it occurs nearly one hundred times, and a careful examination fails to discover an instance in which it is used otherwise than to designate Israel in their sacred character as the covenant people of God. In that sense it passed into the New Testament. In one place it is exceptionally used by the town clerk of the Greek city of Ephesus, and by Luke, after him, in its classic meaning, to designate an assembly of the freemen of the city (Acts xix,39, 41). But everywhere else it is thus applied (1) to Israel in the wilderness (Acts vii,38), and at the temple (Heb. ii,12); (2) to the religious assemblies of the Jews during the time of Christ's ministry (Matt. xviii,17), and ever afterwards in the Acts, Epistles, and Revelation, to the New Testament Church. According, therefore, to the uniform usage of the Scriptures, the word is appropriated to designate an assembly with God, and, in a secondary sense, the people as related to such assembly. Such is the designation given to Israel as the people of God by covenant and fellowship, among whom he held the communion of mutual converse, he with them in the words of his testimony and the communications of his grace, and they with him in all things in which they called upon him (Deut. iv,7. Compare Matt. xviii,20; Acts x,33). In the assembly of Israel, the church of the apostles finds an origin in no wise unworthy of her own lofty character and

office.[18]

The relationship between Old Testament Israel and the New Testament church is not one of strong dichotomy but one of organic, developmental continuity. If the Bible presents any group as being in a dichotomous relationship with spiritual Israel, it is not the New Testament church but New Testament Phariseeism, which developed into what is today called normative Judaism. The New Testament age differs from the Old Testament period in its non-bloody rituals and its greater spiritual fullness, but the saints of both ages constitute the one people of God who are together the Body and Bride of Christ.

LONG FOOTNOTES

[3]"In Eph. 2:13 Gentile Christians are reminded of God's gift that those who were once far from God, . . ., have been brought near to Him by Christ and become His children. In Eph. 2:17, which sets Is. 57:19 in the context of salvation history . . ., the Gentiles are told that to them, who are far from God . . ., Christ brought peace and salvation no less than to the Jews, so that the distant and the near, Gentile and Jewish Christians, experience as the great mystery of God through Christ their union into the new people of God." Gerhard Kittel, editor; Geoffrey W. Bromily, editor and translator, *Theological Dictionary of the New Testament* (Grand Rapids: Wm. B. Eerdmans Publishing Company, 1967), 4:374.

See also Lewis Sperry Chafer, *Systematic Theology, 8 vols.* (Dallas: Dallas Seminary Press, 1948), 4:74; John Eadie, *Commentary on the Epistle to the Ephesians* (reprint: Minneapolis: James and Klock Christian Publishing Co., 1977; original: Edinburgh: T. and T. Clark, 1883), pages 169-170; William Hendriksen, *New Testament Commentary: Exposition on Ephesians* (Grand Rapids: Baker Book House, 1967, pages 213-214; T.K. Abbott, *The International Critical Commentary: A Critical and Exegetical Commentary on the Epistles to the Ephesians and to the Colossians* (Edinburgh: T. & T. Clerk, 1897), page 60.

[5]Lewis Sperry Chafer, *Systematic Theology*, 4:248. "The Gentile was not elevated to the level of Jewish privilege; but the Jew was lowered to the level of the hopeless Gentile, from which position either Jew or Gentile might be saved through grace alone into a heavenly position and glory," Ibid., 4:75.

[6]John F. Walvoord, *The Millennial Kingdom*, page 136. Yet on page 165, Dr. Walvoord argues that "Israel is not reduced to the bankruptcy

---

[18]unknown, *Baptism and Bible History*, pp. 51, 52.

of Gentiles — to become 'strangers from the covenants of promise' . . . ."
Dr. Walvoord's point may be that although unbelieving individual Jews
are not heirs of spiritual blessings, all Jews, believing and unbelieving,
remain heirs of the national promises, in dispensational theory (page
169). On page 136, he says, "Promises may be delayed in fulfillment but
not cancelled."

[16]Charles Caldwell Ryrie, *Dispensationalism Today*, pages 139-140.
According to Dr. J. Dwight Pentecost, there is no spiritual Israel in this
age: "There is a distinction between the true church and true or spiritual
Israel. Prior to Pentecost there were saved individuals, but there was no
church, and they were a part of spiritual Israel, not the church. After the
day of Pentecost and until the rapture we find the church which is His
body, but no spiritual Israel. After the rapture we find no church, but a
true or spiritual Israel again. These distinctions must be kept clearly in
mind." J. Dwight Pentecost, *Things to Come*, page 199.

Dr. Pentecost defines Jewish Christians as those "who would be a
part of spiritual Israel" (Ibid, page 89). I assume him to mean that Jewish
Christians are those Jews who, because of their faith, would be a part of
spiritual Israel if this were not the parenthetical church age.

Chapter Eleven

Dispensationalism: The Parenthesis Theory and the Church in Prophecy

The most basic disagreement between dispensationalism and Reformed theology centers around the relationship between the New Testament church and Old Testament Israel. According to dispensationalism, the church age is a parenthesis in the Jewish kingdom program prophesied in the Old Testament. According to Reformed theology, the church is spiritual Israel come to maturity and is the fulfillment of many prophecies concerning Israel in the Old Testament.

Which of these two opposing views of the relationship between Israel and the church is correct? From the nature of the question one should expect to find some clues to the correct answer by studying the New Testament's use of Old Testament prophecy. If the New Testament ever quotes any Old Testament prophecy as referring directly to the New Testament church, then a basic element of the dispensational system is thereby discredited. Unfortunately for the dispensationalists, there are such quotations in the New Testament.

Joel 2:28

Probably the best known such Old Testament prophecy is Joel 2:28. The dispensationalists claim that the Old Testament prophets were completely ignorant of the coming church age. They supposedly had been led by God to believe that the coming of the Messiah would be followed by the Jewish millennium, not by a church age. Also, the prophecy of Joel was addressed to Israel and the children of Zion (Joel 2:23, 27), not to the church. Since "Israel" means "Israel," and since "church" means "church," a prophecy about Israel can have no direct relationship to the church, so reason the dispensationalists. Now comes the test: What does the New Testament have to say about the fulfillment of Joel 2:28?

We find Joel 2:28 quoted by Simon Peter in Acts 2:16-17 on Pentecost, the birthday of the New Testament church! The Holy Spirit was poured out on the church in unprecedented fullness, and Peter explained this phenomenon by saying, "This is that which was spoken by the prophet Joel," and then by quoting Joel 2:28-32! If words are to be taken in their normal and literal sense, it is hard to imagine how one could communicate more clearly that an event was a fulfillment of prophecy than with the words "this is that."

The Bible also indicates that Joel 2 continues to be fulfilled throughout this age. In his Pentecost sermon Peter indicated that the gift of the Spirit as promised in prophecy was also for "all that are afar off, even as many as the Lord our God shall call" (Acts 2:39), a reference to pagan Gentiles who would believe. The blessings of the Pentecost outpouring were extended to believing uncircumcised Gentiles in Acts 10. Now that the blessings of the new covenant have been ushered in and extended to all nations, the Holy Spirit is poured out in fulfillment of Joel 2 every time a person is regenerated (Titus 3:5-6).

Consistent dispensationalists, because of their presupposed theological system, have difficulty with such an understanding of Joel 2. They cannot even admit that Pentecost, where Peter said "this is that," was an outpouring of the Spirit foreseen by the prophet Joel. Dispensationalists believe that Joel's prophesied outpouring will occur in their yet future Jewish tribulation period and millennium, in an age in which there is no baptizing work of the Holy Spirit.[1] There is a note

---

[1] J. Dwight Pentecost, *Things to Come* (Grand Rapids: Zondervan Publishing House, 1958), pages 271, 486; Charles Caldwell Ryrie, *The Ryrie Study Bible: The New Testament* (Chicago: Moody Press, 1976), pages 208-209 (note on Acts 2:16-21); John B. Graber, "Ultra-Dispensationalism" (dissertation, Dallas Theological

of irony here. The Pentecost outpouring is identified as the baptism of the Holy Spirit (Acts 1:5; 10:44-48; 11:15-18), that divine work that puts one into the Body of Christ, the church universal (1 Corinthians 12:13). Yet dispensationalists say that the true outpouring, the one foreseen by the prophet, will occur in an age in which there is no baptizing work of the Holy Spirit, in their earthly millennial program.

How do dispensationalists circumnavigate Peter's words at Pentecost? The following quotation from Merrill F. Unger is typical:

> Peter's phraseology "this is that" means nothing more than "this is [an illustration of that] which was spoken by the prophet Joel" (Acts 2:16). In the reference there is not the slightest hint at a continued fulfillment during the church age or a coming fulfillment toward the end of the church age. The reference is solely in an illustrative sense to Jewish listeners at Pentecost. Fulfillment of Joel's prophecy is still future and awaits Christ's second coming in glory and a copious spiritual outpouring ushering in kingdom blessing (cf. Zech. 12:10-13:1; Acts 1:6, 7).[2]

And another dispensational writer tries to explain away the clear meaning of Peter's words:

> Peter says that the events of Acts 2 are *what* Joel spoke of but not necessarily the fulfillment of what Joel spoke of![3]

The same writer proceeds to speak of the Pentecostal event as containing "a breakthrough" and "a specimen" of the kingdom age prophesied by Joel. Dispensationalists interpret Peter's words "this is that" in a less than literal manner so they can interpret Joel's prophecy with a dispensationally strict literality.

The ultra-dispensationalists are more consistent at this point. They believe that Joel's prophecy did have a direct fulfillment on Pentecost.[4] They adduce three peoples of God: Old Testament Israel, the early Jewish Petrine church, and the later Pauline "Body of Christ" Christian church. Since ultra-dispensationalists associate Pentecost exclusively with the early Jewish church and not with the Christian

---

Seminary, 1949), pages 88-89.

[2]Merrill F. Unger, *New Testament Teaching on Tongues* (Grand Rapids: Kregel Publications, 1971), page 26.

[3]Joseph Dillow, *Speaking in Tongues: Seven Crucial Questions* (Grand Rapids: Zondervan Publishing House, 1975), page 105. See also Paul Lee Tan, *The Interpretation of Prophecy* (Rockville, Maryland: Assurance Publishers, 1974), pages 183-185.

[4]John B. Graber, "Ultra-Dispensationalism," page 85.

church, they can allow a fulfillment of Jewish prophecy in Acts and still consistently maintain the dichotomy between Israel and the Christian church. Just as dispensationalists believe the Sermon on the Mount to be Jewish truth not directly related to the church, so some ultra-dispensationalists believe the book of Acts and all the New Testament epistles written during that time period to be Jewish truth not directly related to the Christian church.

Dispensationalists argue for their futuristic view of Joel's prophecy from the prophecy's mention of cataclysmic events in the heavens. They ask when in the church age was the sun turned to darkness and when did the moon become blood. In the Old Testament, however, similar language was used to describe the national disasters prophesied for Babylon (Isaiah 13:10), Egypt (Ezekiel 32:7-8), Edom, and the Gentile nations in general (Isaiah 34:4-5). Historical accounts of the fall of ancient political empires may be boring to us, but there was nothing boring about the prophecies of such events for the ancient Jews. The prophesied fall of these powerful, antagonistic pagan powers were events poetically comparable to the fall of stars and the darkening of the sun. For the ancient people who were exposed to the splendor and glory of ancient Babylon, the fall of that city would have seemed about as likely as the fall of the heavenly bodies that ruled the sky. The Bible speaks of the sun and moon as rulers over the heavenly realm (Genesis 1:16) whose continuing rule is a metaphor for permanency (Jeremiah 31:35-36).

Others view such language as a literal description of the second coming of Christ and believe that the prophets spoke of these ancient national judgments in terms of the final judgment or in conjunction with a description of the final judgment. What is certain is that Biblical prophetic language sometimes associates cataclysmic events in the heavens with the fall of supposedly infallible and everlasting political systems. First century Judea was no mighty political power but it was God's chosen nation and regarded by first century Jews as under God's protection. Its fall and destruction was unthinkable.

I believe Joel used this language associated with cataclysmic national judgments to refer to the general principle that God pours out His wrath on His enemies as well as His Spirit on His people. Throughout the new covenant era the conquering Messiah leads the horsemen of the Apocalypse in judgment against those nations that reject Him (Revelation 6).

This general principle about the outpouring of God's wrath had a special application in God's judgment on the apostate Jewish nation in 70 A.D. (compare 1 Thessalonians 2:14-16). At the time of Jesus' crucifixion, there were literal signs and wonders in heaven and on earth — the darkening of the sun, the quaking of the earth, the rending of the rocks, the opening of graves (Matthew 27:45-54). Some who observed these extraordinary events were filled with fear and smote their breasts (Matthew 27:54; Luke 23:48), indications that they may have recognized these events as warnings of a coming divine judgment. Peter in his Pentecostal sermon exhorted his Jewish listeners to "be saved from this perverse generation!" (Acts 2:40). This exhortation had reference to salvation from this coming national judgment which Jesus had prophesied; history testifies that the Jewish church was delivered from that catastrophe. Also, when Jesus prophesied this national judgment, He used apocalyptic language similar to that found in Joel 2 (Matthew 24:29; Luke 21:11, 25). This interpretation of Joel 2 finds further support in John the Baptist's statement that the Messiah would baptize not only with the Holy Spirit but also with the fire of judgment (Matthew 3:10-12; compare Malachi 3:1-2; 4:5-6).

The prophecy in Joel as quoted by Peter also spoke about "*wonders* in heaven above, and *signs* in the earth beneath; blood, fire and vapor of smoke" (Acts 2:19). In Jewish literature the phrase "signs and wonders" is almost always associated with Moses and the deliverance of Israel from Egypt through mighty acts of God.[5] The last words of the Five Books of Moses are:

> And there arose not a prophet since in Israel like unto Moses, whom the Lord knew face to face. In all *the signs and wonders* which the Lord sent him to do in the land of Egypt, to Pharoah, and to all his servants, and to all his land, and in all that mighty hand, and in all the great terror which Moses showed in the sight of all Israel. Deuteronomy 34:10-12. (compare Acts 7:36).

Joel's mention of "blood, fire and vapor of smoke" pointed to the Nile being turned to blood, to the plague of outpoured hail and fire, and to the fire and smoke on Mount Sinai. Also, his mention of the darkened sun suggested another of the ten plagues on Egypt. The age of the Messiah was to include new wonders like those associated with the exodus from Egypt (Micah 7:15). Peter proclaimed that Jesus was

---

[5] Gerhard Friedrich, editor; Geoffrey W. Bromiley, editor, *Theological Dictionary of the New Testament*, 10 vols. (Grand Rapids: Wm. B. Eerdmans Publishing Company, 1971), 7:216, 221.

"a man approved of God among you by miracles and wonders and signs" (Acts 2:22). Indeed Jesus was the prophesied Messianic prophet like unto Moses (Deuteronomy 18:18; Acts 3:22). The apostles (as well as those supernaturally gifted by the apostles through the laying on of hands) continued to perform Messianic signs and wonders (Acts 2:43; 4:30; 5:12; 6:8; 8:13; 14:3; 15:12) as evidences of their genuine apostleship (2 Corinthians 12:12). The mention of signs and wonders in Joel's prophecy is no basis for teaching that it has yet to find a direct fulfillment.

Lastly, dispensationalists sometimes argue that only their system can adequately explain the cessation of the gift of prophecy after the age of the apostles. Dispensationalists argue that if the kingdom period prophesied in Joel 2 is the church age, then this age should be an age of continuing prophecy and miracles in the daily lives of believers.[6] There is a note of historical irony here. Dispensationalists argue that only their system can adequately counter charismatic claims that the revelatory gifts of tongues and prophecy should be normative experiences throughout the church age. And yet many Pentecostals who were exposed to the dispensational system through the Keswick movement readily accepted the dispensational system as compatible with their own.[7]

Joel prophesied the Messianic age of the Spirit in which all the people of God would receive the Spirit and spiritual gifts in new covenant fullness. In the Old Testament the gift of prophecy was associated with the coming of the Spirit in power on a person (Numbers 11:25, 29; 1 Samuel 10:10; 19:20). Joel's prophecy described the new covenant age of spiritual fullness in terms of prophesying, dreaming dreams and seeing visions, all of which the Old Testament associated with the prophetic office (Numbers 12:6). Joel's message was of a coming age in which all God's people would receive the Spirit with a fullness and power that was then associated with the prophetic office. And indeed in this age the least in the kingdom is greater than the greatest of the old covenant prophets (Luke 7:28). I see no need to interpret Joel's prophecy to mean that the whole new covenant age is to be characterized by literal dreams, visions and prophecies. It was so in time past when God spoke in these divers manners through the prophets (Hebrew 1:1). Joel, ministering "in time past," simply spoke

---

[6]Joseph Dillow, *Speaking in Tongues: Seven Crucial Questions*, page 101.

[7]See end of chapter, Long Footnote, p. 147.

of the then unknown future in terms of the working of the Spirit in his day.

There was a more "literal" fulfillment of Joel's prophecy during the days of the apostles and the New Testament prophets. This was the period during which the New Testament canon was not completed, the apostles were still performing signs and wonders as proofs of apostleship, the extraordinary revelatory gifts of the Spirit were common among the people of God, the Jewish age had not yet ended through the destruction of the temple, and the church was adjusting to the differences between the old and new covenants. This apostolic period was foundational and not normative for the new covenant age (Ephesians 2:20). Through the inscripturating of the apostolic revelations and the completing of the New Testament canon, the faith was once for all delivered to the saints (Jude 3). Now, through this completed and all sufficient revelation, all the people of God have access to a greater prophetic revelation than was ever granted to any prophets of old. With the written Word and the illuminating work of the Spirit, the people of God are now no longer dependent on the prophetic elite for divine teaching (1 John 2:27). This is the age in which all God's people know the Lord — from the least to the greatest (Jeremiah 31:34).[8] God's perfect revelation through Jesus Christ has been committed to Scripture. Many prophets and righteous men longed to see what we now behold through the completed Bible but did not.

I see a parallel between the difficulties the modern day dispensationalist has in accepting a direct fulfillment of Joel 2 and the difficulties that some early Jewish Christians had in affirming a fulfillment of Joel 2 among the uncircumcised Gentiles. To prepare Peter, the Jew, for this event, God gave him a special instructive vision (Acts 10:9-16). And in Acts 10:44-45, we read of the total surprise experienced by some of the Jewish students of prophecy in the early church when Joel 2 found its first fulfillment among believing uncircumcised Gentiles at the house of Cornelius:

> While Peter yet spake these words, the Holy Ghost fell on all them which heard the word. And they of the circumcision which believed were astonished, as many as came with Peter, because that on the Gentiles also was poured out the gift of the Holy Ghost. The Holy Spirit was poured out on the believing uncircumcised Gentiles even as He had been

---

[8]See Long Footnotes, p. 148.

poured out on believing Jews at Pentecost (Acts 10:47; 11:15).

Joel 2 had specifically prophesied that the Spirit would be poured out on "all flesh" but these early Jewish Christians had apparently assumed that this universal term referred strictly to the Spirit being given without reference to sex, age or economic status within Israel. This new covenant outpouring on uncircumcised Gentiles did not fit their preconceived understanding of the prophet's message. The issue of the spiritual equality of uncircumcised Gentile believers within new covenant Israel continued to plague the early church and was not officially settled until the Jerusalem council in Acts 15.

Acts 15

At the Jerusalem council there was additional New Testament revelation on the fulfillment of an Old Testament prophecy. This Old Testament prophecy is quoted in Acts 15:13-17 in James' speech:

> And after they had held their peace, James answered, saying, Men and brethren, hearken unto me: Simeon hath declared how God at the first did visit the Gentiles, to take out of them a people for His name. And to this agree the words of the prophets; as it is written, After this I will return, and will build again the tabernacle of David, which is fallen down; and I will build again the ruins thereof, and I will set it up: that the residue of men shall seek after the Lord, and all the Gentiles, upon whom My name is called, saith the Lord, who doeth all these things.

The issue before the council was the status of Gentile Christians in the church age. Some Jewish Christians were contending that it was necessary for all Gentile Christians to be circumcised and to be required to observe all the Old Testament ceremonial laws. In other words, some Jewish Christians wanted all the Gentile converts to become Jewish proselytes, to become members of Israel in the Old Testament sense. At the Jerusalem council Peter argued that in the church age neither Jew nor Gentile had to bear the yoke of observing the ceremonial law in order to receive the full covenantal status of a true Jew. Peter emphasized that God had given the Holy Spirit at Cornelius' house just as freely to uncircumcised Gentile believers as He had given Him to Jewish believers. Paul and Barnabas then related "what miracles and wonders God had wrought among the Gentiles by them." Then James made his climactic speech in which he pointed out that the words of the prophets agreed with what Peter had said about God taking "out of (the Gentiles) a people for His name." Here we have the words of the Jewish prophets, who were supposedly ignorant of the church age, agreeing with and confirming an event in the church age. James then paraphrased Amos 9:11-12. The context of Amos reveals that sometime after the destruction of northern Israel by Assyria, God would again return to Israel in a visitation of blessing to rebuild and to restore the Davidic kingdom so that "all the Gentiles, upon whom (God's) name is called," "might seek after the Lord." James viewed this Old Testament prophecy about Gentiles being included in the covenantal program as fulfilled. How? By the inclusion of uncircumcised Gentile believers in the New Testament church!

The dispensationalists beg to differ. I believe the following fairly represents the dispensational interpretation of Amos 9 found in the *Scofield Reference Bible* at Acts 15:15-17:[9]

> After God has taken out a people for His name from among the Gentiles to form the church (which Simeon related would occur first before the second advent), the second advent of Christ will occur and Christ will reestablish the Davidic rule over Israel in order that Israelites may seek after the Lord and also in order that all the millennial Gentiles may do the same.

The dispensationalists stress the words "after" and "first" in James' speech. They teach that James addressed the issue of Gentile equality in the church by pointing out that the newly inaugurated and parenthetical period of Gentile blessing must come *first* and the prophesied period of Jewish blessing must come *afterwards*. The dispensationalists interpret this as prophetic evidence that there was to be a time of Gentile blessing and that God's special millennial program for Israel had not been abandoned.[10]

There are several inaccuracies that make their exegesis unacceptable.[11] First, the phrase "after this" in Amos does not refer to "after God has taken out a people for His name from among the Gentiles to form the church," an interpretation that puts the time reference after the entire church age in a Jewish millennium. Nor does "after this" relate chronologically to James' previous statement about Peter's

---

[9] See end of chapter, Long Footnote, p. 148.

[10] John F. Walvoord, *The Millennial Kingdom*, pages 205-206; C. C. Ryrie, *The Ryrie Study Bible: The New Testament,* page 236 (note on Acts 15:15-17).

[11] See also William E. Bell, Jr., "A Critical Evaluation of the Pre-tribulation Rapture Doctrine in Christian Eschatology" (dissertation, School of Education of New York University, 1967), pages 197-203.

testimony concerning the calling of the Gentile Cornelius (Acts 15:14). "After this" must be related chronologically to the context in Amos. The prophecy of Amos was directed primarily against the northern kingdom of Israel, and the context of Amos 9 refers to the scattering of the northern kingdom of Israel, which was fulfilled by the Assyrians under Sargon in 722 B.C. (Amos 9:9-10). Therefore, the phrase "after this," which is James' paraphrase of Amos' phrase "in that day" (compare Joel 2:28 and Acts 2:17), refers to the time of the establishment of the New Testament church, which was the prophesied spiritual renewal in Israel *after* the prophesied scattering in Amos.

If dispensationalists interpret "after this" to mean after the church age, then they contradict the dispensational parenthesis theory. The church age, according to dispensationalists, was not foreseen in any Old Testament prophecy. If Amos knew about the church age as a period of Gentile opportunity before the Jewish millennium, then the parenthesis theory is wrong. If Amos did not know about the coming church age, then "after this" could not mean after the church age. Either way the dispensationalists have encountered their coup de grace.

Dr. John F. Walvoord seems to interpret "after this" to mean "after the times of the Gentiles." The times of the Gentiles in dispensational interpretation is that period from the Babylonian captivity to the end of Daniel's seventy weeks during which Jerusalem is under Gentile political rule.[12] The church age is a parenthetical interruption in the times of the Gentiles. Dr. Walvoord identifies the "this" of "after this" with "the period of Gentile opportunity" and "the Gentile period." He further argues that James quotes Amos' prophecy to demonstrate that the restoration of the Davidic kingdom would occur *after* the Gentile period.[13] In another book Dr. Walvoord comments:

> It was difficult for the Jews to understand that for the time being the Gentiles should have a place of equality with Israel, in view of the many prophecies in the Old Testament which anticipated Israel's pre-eminence and glory....
>
> ... it seems that "after these things I will return" refers to the return of Christ after the period of Gentile prominence which began in 606 B.C.

---

[12] J. Dwight Pentecost, *Things To Come*, pages 314-316; C. I. Scofield, editor, *The Scofield Reference Bible*, page 1345 (note on Revelation 16:19).

[13] John F. Walvoord, *The Millennial Kingdom*, page 205.

and is destined to continue until the second coming. It is after these things — i.e., judgment on Israel, their scattering, and discipline — that Christ will return and build again the tabernacle or tent of David. . . .

. . . The divine order therefore is judgment on Israel and blessing upon Gentile first, to be followed by judgment on Gentile and blessing on Israel. This is not only the order of the Old Testament, but it is the order of this portion in Acts . . . .[14]

If Dr. Walvoord is saying that "after this" means "after the times of the Gentiles," then that interpretation does not contradict the dispensational parenthesis theory. That interpretation, however, does take away any relevance the Amos passage would have had to the controversy over the spiritual equality of Gentiles in the church age. All the passage would have said is that after the time of Gentile political rule over Jerusalem, the Davidic political kingdom will be restored. Amos' prophecy would have said nothing about the church age and nothing about spiritual equality for Gentiles. There is no spiritual equality for Gentiles during the "times of the Gentiles" except during the parenthetical and unrevealed church age, of which Amos would have been totally unaware. Is Dr. Walvoord saying that James' argument was that just as there is to be no Jewish *political* superiority until after the times of the Gentiles, so by analogy the Jew is to have no *spiritual* superiority over the Gentiles until after the times of the Gentiles? This, however, would not be a valid argument. The Jews will have spiritual superiority over the Gentiles in the last seven years of the times of the Gentiles, according to dispensationalism. During the future seven year tribulation period, which is after the parenthetical church age and is the last of Daniel's seventy weeks, the Old Testament economy will be restored.

A second inaccuracy in the dispensational exegesis of Acts 15 is the word "first" in the sentence "Simeon hath declared how God at the *first* did visit the Gentiles to take out of them a people for His name." It does not mean first in sequence before a Jewish millennium. James is referring to Peter's testimony about the introduction of the Gospel into the house of Cornelius (Acts 15:7-9; Acts 10), where the Gospel was introduced to uncircumcised Gentiles for the first time. The Cornelius experience was first in sequence before the miracles done by Paul and Barnabas among the Gentiles.

Third, the clause "I will return" does not refer to the second

---

[14]John F. Walvoord, *Israel In Prophecy*, pages 91-93.

advent. This clause is not found in the Amos passage, and some commentators suggest that it may be based on Jeremiah 12:15 where the return is a return of favor and a divine visitation of blessing. The Hebrew of Jeremiah 12:15 literally says "I will return and have compassion," and the New International Version translates this as "I will again have compassion." The same Greek word translated "return" in Acts 15 is found in the LXX translation of Genesis 18:10 & 14. There the Angel of the Lord promised to return to Abraham and bless him with a son through Sarah. This was fulfilled through a visitation of blessing recorded in Genesis 21:1-2, not through a literal bodily return. The concept of a visitation of blessing is not uncommon in the Old Testament.[15]

Fourth, the phrase "the residue of men" does not refer to Israel. There is no reference to Israel in this quotation from Amos 9, yet the *Scofield Reference Bible* specifically identifies the phrase "the residue of men" with "Israelites." This phrase is the Septuagint translation of the original Hebrew "the remnant of Edom." One can view this as a paraphrase that interpretatively viewed Edom as symbolic for all the Gentile enemies of Israel (compare Isaiah 34:1-5). Or the explanation may be that the early Hebrew text did not have the vowel points and the Hebrew words for Edom and mankind (i.e., *adam*) without the vowel pointing are almost identical. Regardless of the correct explanation for the paraphrase, this passage specifically states that the house of David would be reestablished in order that Gentiles might seek the Lord. The passage from Amos points to the Messianic age as a time of special spiritual blessings on Gentiles, and James used this teaching as an argument for recognizing and accepting God's spiritual blessings on the Gentiles in the church age. The dispensational position is that the Messianic age spoken of in Amos is not the church age but a yet future Jewish millennium and that James quoted Amos to prove that the time of special Jewish blessing follows the time of Gentile blessing. The Amos passage, however, presents the Messianic age as a period of Gentile spiritual blessings, not as an age of Jewish blessing following an age of Gentile blessing.

Fifth, the dispensational interpretation fails to see the identification between "*the heathen*, which are *called by My name*" in Amos 9:12 (Acts 15:17) and Cornelius' household where "God at the first did visit *the Gentiles*, to take out of them *a people for His name*" (Acts

---

[15] See Long Footnotes, p. 148.

15:14). In the dispensational interpretation, the first phrase refers to millennial Gentiles and the second phrase refers to church age Gentiles. Even in this passage dispensationalists attempt to promote distinctions and ignore unity or sameness of expression!!

The basis of the dispensational interpretation of Acts 15 which I have just critiqued has been the alleged *contrast* between a Gentile church age and a Jewish millennium. Some dispensationalists have adopted a completely different interpretation of Acts 15 based on the alleged *harmony* between the church age and the dispensational millennium. For example, dispensationalist Charles L. Feinberg says:

> It was left to James to make the concluding remarks. He pointed to the testimony of Peter, which showed conclusively that God was visiting the Gentiles "to take out of them a people for his name." Then followed his statement as to the harmonization of that with the return of the Lord and the setting up of the Davidic kingdom with the conversion of those in Israel and the Gentiles also.[16]

I view the church age as the fulfillment of Amos 9 and Dr. Feinberg does not. Instead he sees Amos 9 as referring to the dispensational millennium and relates it to the church age as a "harmonization." But what is harmonious between the dispensational millennium and the church age spiritual equality of believing Jews and Gentiles? According to Dr. J. Dwight Pentecost, Israel in the millennium "will be exalted above the Gentiles," "the Gentiles will be Israel's servants," and "the distinction of Israel from the Gentiles will again be resumed."[17] According to Dr. Feinberg, "The nations in the kingdom will recognize the favored condition of Israel . . ." and ". . . Israel will also rule over the nations under the direct command of the King."[18] According to Dr. John F. Walvoord: "In contrast to the present church age in which Jew and Gentile are on an equal plane of privilege, the millennium is clearly a period of time in which Israel is in prominence and blessing."[19] If the dispensational interpretation of the millennial situation is correct, then the party of the circumcision who wanted Gentiles admitted into the church as they had been admitted into the

---

[16]Charles L. Feinberg, *Millennialism: The Two Major Views*, Third and enlarged edition (Chicago: Moody Press, 1936), page 154. See also Paul Lee Tan, *The Interpretation of Prophecy*, pages 128-130.

[17]J. Dwight Pentecost, *Things to Come*, pp. 507-08, 519-20

[18]Charles L. Feinberg, *Millennialism: The Two Major Views*, p. 186.

[19]John F. Walvoord, *Millennial Kingdom*, pp. 302-03

synagogue (i.e. as circumcised proselytes) could have made better use of this passage than did James.[20] They could have argued that the prophesied inferior status of spiritually blessed millennial Gentiles is evidence for a similarly inferior status for church age Gentiles.

Scofield describes this passage in Acts 15 as "dispensationally . . . the most important passage in the New Testament."[21] He was perhaps correct, but not in the sense that he intended. The correct interpretation of this passage demonstrates that, contrary to dispensational claims, a prophecy about Israel and the Jewish Davidic covenant is here declared to be fulfilled in and through the Christian church in the church age.

Acts 13

I would like to discuss the New Testament's use of one last Old Testament prophecy. We read in Acts 13 that Paul spoke to the synagogue at Pisidian Antioch about Jesus of Nazareth as the fulfillment of Messianic prophecy. Acts 13:44-48 records what happened on the following Sabbath:

> And the next sabbath day came almost the whole city together to hear the word of God. But when the Jews saw the multitudes, they were filled with envy, and spake against those things which were spoken by Paul, contradicting and blaspheming. Then Paul and Barnabas waxed bold, and said, It is necessary that the word of God should first have been spoken to you: but seeing ye put it from you, and judge yourselves unworthy of everlasting life, lo, we turn to the Gentiles. For so hath the Lord commanded us, saying, I have set thee to be a light of the Gentiles, that thou shouldest be for salvation unto the ends of the earth. And when the Gentiles heard this, they were glad, and glorified the word of the Lord: and as many as were ordained to eternal life believed.

Here we observe Paul quoting Isaiah 49:6, one of the many Old Testament prophecies about the spiritual blessings that were to come on the Gentiles in the age of the Messiah.[22] If the dispensationalist is

---

[20]Daniel P. Fuller, "The Hermeneutics of Dispensationalism" (dissertation, Northern Baptist Theological Seminary, 1957), page 347, footnote 18.

[21]C. I. Scofield, editor, *The Scofield Reference Bible*, page 1169 (note on Acts 15:13).

[22]Psalm 22:27-30; 68:29-31; 72:8-11, 17; Isaiah 2:2-5; 11:9-10; 19:24-30; 42:1-4; 45:14; 49:6-7, 22-23; 52:10; 54:1-3; 60:3ff; 65:1; 66:19; Jeremiah 16:19; Amos 9:11-12; Zechariah 2:3-13; 8:20-24; Malachi 1:11.

to hold to his parenthesis theory with strict consistency, he would directly relate these prophecies about the nations to millennial Gentiles and relate these prophecies to the church age only indirectly. Also, some of these prophecies spoke about the coming spiritual blessings on the Gentiles in terms of the Old Testament system of worship. For example, Malachi 1:11 says:

> For from the rising of the sun even unto the going down of the same my name shall be great among the Gentiles; and in every place incense shall be offered unto my name, and a pure offering; for my name shall be great among the heathen, saith the Lord of hosts.

For the consistent dispensationalist, these prophecies have no direct reference to the church age. Therefore, Dr. J. Dwight Pentecost is only being consistent when he uses Isaiah 49:6 as a proof text for the statement: "the fact of Gentiles' participation in the millennium is promised in the prophetic Scriptures."[23] Paul, however, believed that he was an agent in fulfilling this prophecy!

The Old Testament prophets spoke about the coming day when Israel would enlarge her tent to include the Gentiles (Isaiah 54:2). All three of the Old Testament prophecies that we have examined in this chapter have pointed to this theme of the day when God's covenantal blessing would be on all flesh and not just on physical Israel. In all three cases we have seen that dispensationalists refer these prophecies to a future Jewish millennium, and the New Testament refers these prophecies to the present church age. The New Testament's use of Old Testament prophecy contradicts the dispensational parenthesis theory.

LONG FOOTNOTES

[7] "Dispensationalism, which fit so well with the Pentecostal and holiness ideas of the 'Age of the Spirit,' easily gained acceptance in the new Pentecostal movement, even though Scofield-type dispensationalists maintained that tongues ceased with the apostles." George M. Marsden, *Fundamentalism and American Culture: The Shaping of Twentieth-Century Evangelicalism: 1870-1925* (New York/Oxford: Oxford University Press, 1980), page 94.

"The Keswick movement, as we shall see, was absolutely crucial to the development of Pentecostalism. . . . that wing of the Pentecostal movement which had earlier connections with Wesleyanism became

[23]J. Dwight Pentecost, *Things To Come*, page 508.

Pentecostal by accepting Keswick (i.e. Calvinist) teachings on dispensationalism, premillennialism and the Baptism of the Holy Spirit." Robert
Mapes Anderson, *Vision of the Disinherited: The Making of American
Pentecostalism* (New York/Oxford: Oxford University Press, 1979), page
43.

[8]"The correct understanding of the words results from a right
perception of the contrast involved, viz. that under the old covenant the
knowledge of the Lord was connected with the mediation of priests and
prophets." C. F. Keil and F. Delitzsch, *Commentary on the Old Testament in Ten Volumes: Volume VIII: Jeremiah, Lamentations* (Grand
Rapids: William B. Eerdmans Publishing Company, 1973), 2:40.

[9] C. I. Scofield, editor, *The Scofield Reference Bible* (New York:
Oxford University Press, 1909), pages 1169-1170 (note on Acts 15:13);
see also Charles Caldwell Ryrie, *The Basis of the Premillennial Faith*
(Neptune, N.J.: Loizeaux Brothers, 1953), pages 102-103; J. Dwight
Pentecost, *Things to Come*, page 133; John F. Walvoord, *The Millennial
Kingdom* (Grand Rapids: Zondervan Publishing House, 1959), pages
204-207; John F. Walvoord, *Israel in Prophecy* (Grand Rapids: Zonder-
van Publishing House, 1962), pages 91-93; Charles Caldwell Ryrie, *The
Ryrie Study Bible: The New Testament*, page 236 (note on Acts 15:15-
17).

[15]"*paqad*": Genesis 21:1; 50:24-25; Exodus 13:19; Ruth 1:6; Psalm
65:9; Jeremiah 15:15; 29:10; 32:5; "*shub*": Genesis18:10, 14; 2 Chronicles
30:6; Psalm 6:4; 80:14; 90:13; Isaiah 63:17; Jeremiah 12:15; Zechariah
1:3; Malachi 3:7.

Chapter Twelve

Dispensationalism: The New Covenant (Part One)

Before discussing the new covenant, I would like to review the basic distinction between dispensationalism and Reformed theology. This distinction revolves around the concepts of *unity* in reference to God's people and *continuity* in reference to God's program. First, according to Reformed theology, the people of God in all ages are in union with Christ and are therefore united together in the universal church, which is the Body and Bride of Christ. By contrast dispensationalists view only those who are saved between the Pentecost of Acts 2 and the end time rapture as in the universal church. In other words, Mary, the mother of Jesus, will be in the Bride of Christ, but Joseph her husband who died before Pentecost will only be a guest at the wedding of the Lamb. Also, John the Apostle will be in the Body of Christ in eternity, but not John the Baptist. Even further the Old Testament saints who died before Acts 2 are not to be made perfect together with the New Testament saints (compare Hebrews 11:39-40), but instead are to remain spiritually inferior throughout eternity, never being in the Body and Bride of Christ.

Second, according to Reformed theology, the New Testament church is a continuation of the Old Testament program and is directly rooted in the Old Testament covenants. The dispensationalist though says the New Testament church is a parenthesis in the program begun in the Old Testament, not a continuation. They continue the Old Testament program in a future Jewish millennium that is a glorified extension of the Davidic national kingdom and the Mosaic ceremonial laws.

I shall proceed with the examination of the dispensational teaching on the new covenant. Since those twenty-seven books of Scripture that were written after the life of Jesus are named the New Testament or covenant, one would expect that all Christians would uncompromisingly acknowledge the Christian nature of the new covenant. Such an acknowledgment, however, is not easy or simple for the consistent dispensationalist. When the dispensationalist attempts to warp Scripture to fit his system, the Biblical data on the new covenant is among the most unyielding and uncooperative. For instance, Dr. Ryrie makes this admission:

> Although the new covenant is one of the major covenants of Scripture, a clear statement of its meaning and of its relationship to the [dispensational] premillennial system is needed. Even among [dispensational] premillennialists there seems to be a lack of knowledge concerning this covenant.[1]

> [Dispensational] premillennialists are divided into three groups as far as their interpretation of the new covenant is concerned. This does not evince weakness, for not one of the views contradicts the system.[2]

The classic passage on the new covenant is Jeremiah 31. Please take notice: Jeremiah is an Old Testament prophecy, and dispensationalists teach that no Old Testament prophecy can refer directly to the New Testament church. Dispensationalists interpret Jeremiah 30 and 31 as referring to their futuristic tribulation period, which is to occur after the rapture of the church, and to their Judaistic millennium.[3] The "time of Jacob's trouble" (Jeremiah 30:7) is identified with the seven-year tribulation period, and the new covenant of Jeremiah 31 is viewed as a millennial blessing on Israel. Dr. Pentecost is typical:

---

[1]Charles Caldwell Ryrie, *The Basis of the Premillennial Faith* (Neptune, N.J.: Loizeaux Brothers, 1953), page 105.

[2]Ibid., pages 106-107.

[3]See end of chapter, Long Footnotes, p. 158.

This covenant *must follow the return of Christ* at the second advent.[4]

This covenant will be realized in the millennial age.[5]

Regardless of the relationship of the church to the new covenant as explained in these three views, there is one general point of agreement: the new covenant of Jeremiah 31:31-34 must and can be fulfilled only by the nation Israel and not by the Church.[6]

Walvoord is no different:

... the [dispensational] premillennial position is that the new covenant is with Israel and the fulfillment in the millennial kingdom after the Second Coming of Christ.[7]

The [dispensational] premillennial view, though varying in detail, insists that the new covenant as revealed in the Old Testament concerns Israel and requires fulfillment in the millennial kingdom.[8]

Even Dr. Ryrie agrees: "... it can be shown that the period of the new covenant is millennial."[9] Observe that Jeremiah's new covenant prophecy is to be made "with the house of Israel and with the house of Judah" (Jeremiah 31:31), but dispensationalists teach their strong dichotomy between Israel and the church. In other words, what has a prophecy for Israel to do with the church in a direct and primary sense? Nothing, says the consistent dispensationalist. For him the new covenant of Jeremiah 31 must be for the Jewish millennium and not for the church age. For the new covenant to be fulfilled in and by the church would be to abrogate the new covenant with Israel and to alter its most essential meaning and intention.[10] The significance of this point is emphasized by Dr. Pentecost: "If the church fulfills this covenant, she may also fulfill the other covenants made with Israel and there is no need for an earthly millennium."[11] Ryrie is more emphatic: "If the church is fulfilling Israel's promises as contained in the new covenant

---

[4]Pentecost, *Things to Come*, page 120.

[5]Ibid., page 121.

[6]Ibid., page 124.

[7]Walvoord, *The Millennial Kingdom*, page 209.

[8]Ibid., page 210.

[9]Ryrie, *The Basis of the Premillennial Faith*, page 111.

[10]Ibid., pages 105-106.

[11]Pentecost, *Things to Come*, page 116.

or anywhere in the Scriptures, then [dispensational] premillennialism is condemned."[12]

We have seen that dispensationalists interpret the Old Testament data regarding the new covenant to refer solely to the nation Israel in a future millennium. When one comes to the New Testament data on the new covenant, this dispensational theory encounters some insuperable complications. In Hebrews 8:6-13, for example, the inspired Book hailed Christ "the mediator of a better covenant, which was established on better promises" and then quoted extensively from the Jeremiah new covenant prophecy.

In Hebrews 10:14-18 the inspired writer quoted from the Jeremiah new covenant prophecy in an argument for the discontinuation of animal sacrifices. This indeed is ironic, for the dispensationalist refers this prophecy to a Jewish millennium in which animal sacrifices are renewed!

In Hebrews 12:22-24 several Old Testament concepts, like Mount Zion, Jerusalem, the blood of Abel, and the new covenant, are applied directly to the Christian. In 2 Corinthians 3 Paul called himself and Timothy "ministers of the new covenant." As if to remove any doubt about which new covenant he had in mind, Paul in verse 3 mentions the Jeremiah new covenant concept of writing on human hearts (Jeremiah 31:33). When Christ inaugurated the Lord's Supper, He said, "This cup is the new covenant in My blood, which is shed for you" (Luke 22:20). What did the Jewish disciples associate with this statement? Undoubtedly they related it to Jeremiah 31. What other new covenant did they know?!

Surely you can see that the consistent dispensationalist has a difficult problem with the new covenant! They believe the new covenant of Jeremiah 31 is for Israel in a Jewish millennium, not for the New Testament church now. Dispensationalists are divided among three suggested solutions to this serious problem in their system.

First Explanation: Two New Covenants

I shall begin by examining the theory most consistent with dispensational assumptions, the theory of Drs. Lewis Sperry Chafer and John F. Walvoord, the first two presidents of Dallas Theological Seminary (and only presidents so far). This theory is that there are two new covenants in Scripture, one for Israel and one for the church. If a new

---

[12]See end of chapter, Long Footnotes, p. 158.

covenant passage refers to "Israel," then what is meant is the Jewish new covenant of the Jewish millennium. If a new covenant passage relates to the New Testament church, then the verses are referring to the Christian new covenant of the so-called church age. The following quotations by Drs. Chafer, Walvoord, and Pentecost respectively explain the two covenant view:

> There remains to be recognized a heavenly covenant for the heavenly people, which is also styled like the preceding one for Israel, a "new covenant." It is made in the blood of Christ (cf. Mark 14:24) and continues in effect throughout this age, where as the new covenant made with Israel happens to be future in its application. To suppose that these two covenants — one for Israel and one for the Church — are the same is to assume that there is a latitude of common interest between God's purpose for Israel and His purpose for the Church.[13]

> [Dispensational] premillenarians are in agreement that the new covenant with Israel awaits its complete fulfillment in the millennial kingdom. However, there exists some difference of opinion how the new covenant relates to the present interadvent age. . . .

> The point of view that holds to two covenants in the present age has certain advantages. It provides a sensible reason for establishing the Lord's supper for believers in this age in commemoration of the blood of the covenant. The language of 1 Corinthians 11:25 seems to require it: "This cup is the new covenant in My blood: this do, as often as ye drink it, in remembrance of Me." It hardly seems reasonable to expect Christians to distinguish between the cup and the new covenant when these appear to be identified in this passage. In 2 Corinthians 3:6, Paul speaking of himself states: "Our sufficiency is of God: who also made us sufficient as ministers of a new covenant." It would be difficult to adjust the ministry of Paul as a minister of the new covenant if, in fact, there is no new covenant for the present age.[14]

This view holds that there are two new covenants presented in the New Testament; the first with Israel in reaffirmation of the covenant promised in Jeremiah 31 and the second made with the church in this age. This view, essentially, would divide the references to the new covenant in the New Testament into two groups. The references in the gospels and in Hebrews 8:6; 9:15; 10:29; and 13:20 would refer to the new covenant with the church, Hebrews 8:7-13 and 10:16 would refer to the new

---

[13]Lewis Sperry Chafer, *Systematic Theology, 8 volumes* (Dallas: Dallas Seminary Press, 1948), 7:98.

[14]Walvoord, *The Millennial Kingdom*, pages 218-219.

covenant with Israel, and Hebrews 12:24 would refer, perhaps, to both, emphasizing the fact of the mediation accomplished and the covenant program established without designating the recipients.[15]

This theory is a pristine application of the dispensational dichotomy between Israel and the church, but it requires "swallowing a camel" and "straining a gnat" exegesis to reconcile it with the Scriptural data. A closer examination of the New Testament passages on the new covenant will naturally show the artificial nature of this two-covenant theory.

Some of New Testament data on the new covenant not only relates a new covenant to the church but also clearly relates the Jewish Jeremiah 31 new covenant to the church. One such passage is Hebrews 8:

> 6. But now hath He obtained a more excellent ministry, by how much also He is the mediator of a better covenant, which was established on better promises.
>
> 7. For if that first covenant had been faultless, then should no place have been sought for the second.
>
> 8. For finding fault with them, He saith, Behold, the days come, saith the Lord, when I will make a new covenant with the house of Israel and with the house of Judah. . . .
>
> 13. In that He saith, A new covenant, He hath made the first old. Now that which decayeth and waxeth old is ready to vanish away.

According to the two-covenant interpretation, the "better covenant" of verse 6 is the church new covenant but the "new covenant" of verses 7-13 is the Jewish new covenant for the millennium. Proponents of this view emphasize that the text never specifically equates the "better covenant" of verse six with the "new covenant" of verses 7-13. This is supposed to be a strong argument from silence. They argue that the writer of Hebrews quoted the Jeremiah new covenant passage to prove that the Mosaic covenant was temporary but that he did not intend to leave the impression that the "better covenant" of verse 6 is the new covenant mentioned in the quotation from Jeremiah.[16]

According to the dispensational understanding of prophecy, the

---

[15]Pentecost, *Things to Come*, page 124. Also, compare Walvoord, *The Millennial Kingdom*, page 214.

[16]Walvoord, *The Millennial Kingdom*, pages 216-217.

church age is an unforeseen parenthesis in the prophetic program between the sixty-ninth and seventieth of the seventy weeks of Daniel 9. Therefore it would have been impossible for Jeremiah to have foreseen the church new covenant. The new covenant prophesied by Jeremiah must take effect in the millennium after the future seventieth week (i.e., the tribulation), not in the unforeseen church age between weeks sixty-nine and seventy.

The two-covenant theory dispensationalists are correct that the author of Hebrews would not have taught a church fulfillment for Jeremiah's new covenant prophecy if he had been a consistent dispensationalist. If, however, the author of Hebrews had held to the two-covenant theory, he could have avoided any confusion by calling the Mosaic covenant the first covenant, the church new covenant the second covenant, and the Jewish millennial new covenant the third covenant. Instead the author of Hebrews 8:7 termed the Mosaic covenant the first covenant and the Jewish new covenant the second covenant. Assuming the author of Hebrews was a two-covenant theory dispensationalist, we could speculate that he did not count the church new covenant in his calculations, even though he had mentioned it as the "better covenant" of verse 6.

The new covenant of Jeremiah 31 is also quoted in Hebrews 10:14-18:

> For by one offering (God) hath perfected for ever them that are sanctified. Whereof the Holy Ghost also is a witness to us: for after that He had said before, This is the covenant that I will make with them after those days, saith the Lord; I will put My laws into their hearts, and in their minds will I write them; And their sins and iniquities will I remember no more. Now where remission of these is, there is no more offering for sin.

Here the author of Hebrews is quoting the Jeremiah 31 new covenant prophecy as the climax of his argument for the discontinuance of the Levitical sacrifices in the church age and as a divine witness to us (i.e. to Christians, not to millennial Jews). The two-covenant theory dispensationalists relate the above passage not to the church new covenant but to the Jewish millennial new covenant that will be in effect when the Levitical sacrificial system will be reinstituted. Dr. Walvoord explains that "the new covenant with Israel not only anticipated the abrogation of the law but also the end of Mosaic sacrifices as a basis for forgiveness." Is he saying that the Old Testament Levitical sacrifices were a basis for forgiveness but that the millennial Levitical sacrifices will not be a basis for forgiveness? If so then in what sense were the Old Testament sacrifices a basis for forgiveness? The blood of bulls and goats never took away sins (Hebrews 10:4). Dr. Walvoord himself, in defending millennial sacrifices, proceeds to say, "The millennial sacrifices are no more expiatory than were the Mosaic sacrifices which preceded the cross."[17]

Another relevant passage in Hebrews is 12:22-24:

> But ye are come unto mount Sion, and unto the city of the living God, the heavenly Jerusalem, and to an innumerable company of angels, To the general assembly and church of the firstborn, which are written in heaven, and to God the Judge of all, and to the spirits of just men made perfect, And to Jesus the mediator of the new covenant, and to the blood of sprinkling, that speaketh better things than that of Able.

This passage is full of references to the Old Testament: Mount Zion, the sprinkled blood of sacrifice, the blood of Abel and the new covenant. Are we to say that in this context the author of Hebrews was not referring to the new covenant spoken of in the Old Testament? Yet these new covenant verses also are addressed to the Christian and applied to the Christian! Dr. Walvoord stresses that the word translated "new" in this passage is "nea," a Greek word meaning "recent." Therefore, he says, "Reference is apparently to the covenant with the church and not to Israel's new covenant."[18]

> [Ed. note: On the contrary, the classical distinction between the two words for "new" (kainos, neos) is not upheld in Koine Greek; the two terms are identical. Just compare Ephesians 4:24 with Colossians 3:10 where "new man" occurs in both passages synonymously and both words for "new" are used. Also, all other occurrences of "new covenant" use kainos; only here "neos." Virtually no modern linguistic commentator agrees with Walvoord. See Philip Edgcumbe Hughes's excellent commentary on Hebrews published by Eerdmans, p. 551, note 162. This note is by Curtis Crenshaw.]

Dr. Walvoord is correct in arguing that the new covenant of Hebrews 12:24 applies to the Christian but wrong in arguing that this is not the same new covenant spoken of in Jeremiah 31.

Bernard Ramm has said that the interpretation of the book of Hebrews, which does not apply the new covenant to the church, but instead applies it to a Judaistic future, is an "oddity in the history of

---

[17]Ibid., pages 217, 312.

[18]Ibid., page 218.

the exegesis of this book."[19] Elsewhere he has said:

> The New Covenant is one of several items discussed in Hebrews all of
> which are realized in the Church and the present age. That Christ is our
> Moses, our Aaron, our Sacrifice, the strict literalists readily admit. To
> isolate the New Covenant and forward it to the millennium is to disrupt
> the entire structure of Hebrews.[20]

There are New Testament passages outside of the book of Hebrews that also show the error of the two-covenant theory. For example, in 2 Corinthians 3:6 the apostle Paul called himself and Timothy "ministers of the new testament [i.e. covenant]." In this passage Paul makes reference to the Jeremiah 31 concept of writing on human hearts (Jeremiah 31:33). In 2 Corinthians 3:3 Paul spoke of the Corinthian Christians as being human letters, "written not with ink, but with the Spirit of the living God; not in tables of stone, but in fleshly tables of the heart." Paul then contrasted his ministry of the new covenant with the old Mosaic ministration that was "written and engraven in stones" (verse 7). This is an application of not just any new covenant but *the* Jeremiah 31 new covenant to the church and the church age!

Christ also proclaimed a new covenant when He instituted the Lord's Supper: "This is My blood of the new testament [i.e. covenant], which is shed for many" (Mark 14:24). Moses also had spoken of the "blood of the covenant" at the inauguration of the old covenant (Exodus 24:8). Surely the disciples would have recognized that Christ was instituting a second covenant to replace the Mosaic covenant, whose many types He was fulfilling. Did Christ fulfill two new covenants in the upper room? Even Dr. J. Dwight Pentecost has to admit the force of the new covenant in the upper room:

> In its historical setting, the disciples who heard the Lord refer to the new
> covenant in the upper room the night before His death would certainly
> have understood Him to be referring to the new covenant of Jeremiah
> 31. . . . Since the disciples would certainly have understood any reference
> to the new covenant on that occasion as a reference to Israel's anticipated
> covenant of Jeremiah, it seems that the Lord must have been stating that

---

[19]Bernard Ramm, "Christ and Aaron," Eternity, 13:18, May 1962. Quoted in Bell, "A Critical Evaluation of the Pretribulation Rapture Doctrine in Christian Eschatology," page 182.

[20]Bernard Ramm, *Protestant Biblical Interpretation: A Textbook of Hermeneutics* (Grand Rapids: Baker Book House, 1970), page 264.

that very covenant was being instituted with His death . . . .[21]

This close association of the Lord's Supper to Jeremiah's new covenant with Israel may explain why E. W. Bullinger, the father of ultra-dispensationalism, taught that the Lord's Supper is a Jewish ordinance that has no place in the Christian church.[22]

The two-covenant theory, the most consistent theory dispensationally, is the most difficult to defend Scripturally. Therefore, it has not received widespread acceptance among dispensationalists. For example, the popular dispensational writer Harry Ironside has said:

> It were folly to speak of a *new* covenant with the Church, when no former covenant has been made with us. In the case of Israel and Judah it is different. They entered into the covenant of works at Sinai.[23]

John F. McGahey in his doctor's dissertation at Dallas Theological Seminary came to a similar conclusion:

> Consequently, it has been established that there is no warrant in Scripture for maintaining that there are two new covenants. It has been evident from this study that the theory of the two new covenants was born of controversy rather than strong exegesis. For it appears that it was manufactured to avoid the assumed conclusion that to relate the church to Israel's new covenant necessitated that church fulfilling the promises given to Israel under that covenant.[24]

LONG FOOTNOTES

[3] H. A. Ironside, *Notes on the Prophecy and Lamentations of Jeremiah "The Weeping Prophet"* (Neptune, N.J.: Loizeaux Brothers, 1906), pages 146-166; Charles Caldwell Ryrie, *The Basis of the Premillennial Faith*, pages 108-114; John F. Walvoord, *The Millennial Kingdom* (Grand Rapids: Zondervan Publishing House, 1959), pages 481, 183-184, 210-211, 258-259; J. Dwight Pentecost, *Things to Come* (Grand Rapids: Zondervan Publishing House, 1958), pages 120-121.

[12] Charles Caldwell Ryrie, "The Relationship of the New Covenant

---

[21]Pentecost, *Things to Come*, page 126.

[22]See end of chapter, Long Footnote, p. 159.

[23]Ironside, *Notes on the Prophecy and Lamentations of Jeremiah "The Weeping Prophet,"* page 163.

[24]John F. McGahey, "An Exposition of the New Covenant" (dissertation, Dallas Theological Seminary, 1957), page 262. Quoted in Bell, "A Critical Evaluation of the Pretribulation Rapture Doctrine in Christian Eschatology," page 189.

to Premillennialism" (unpublished Master's thesis, Dallas Theological Seminary, 1947), page 31. Quoted in William Everett Bell, Jr., "A Critical Evaluation of the Pretribulation Rapture Doctrine in Christian Eschatology" (dissertation, School of Education of New York University, 1967), pages 178-179. In Dr. Ryrie's book, *The Basis of the Premillennial Faith*, the word "condemned" is changed to "weakened."

[22] John B. Graber, "Ultra-Dispensationalism" (dissertation, Dallas Theological Seminary, 1949), pages 36-37. Mr. Graber defines an ultra-dispensationalist as "any student of Scripture who places two dispensations between Pentecost and the end of the church age" (page 6). These two dispensations involve "the Pentecostal apostolic church of the book of Acts and the mystery Pauline church of the prison epistles" (page 6). According to Mr. Graber, dispensationalists and ultra-dispensationalists use the same hermeneutic but differ only in the interpretation of certain passages. For example, ultra-dispensationalists believe that Joel 2:28-32 was fulfilled at Pentecost and dispensationalists do not. Since Joel 2 is a prophecy about Israel and since Joel 2 was fulfilled at Pentecost, the ultra-dispensationalist does not believe that the church age began at Pentecost because of the dispensational dichotomy between Israel and the church (pages 88-89). In its extreme form, ultra-dispensationalism teaches that the church was not formed until after Acts 28. This means that the only Scriptures directly relevant to the church are those Pauline epistles written after Acts 28 (page 32). Mr. Graber makes the following statements:

". . . it is admitted by both premillennialists and amillennialists that the root of their difference lies in the method of Biblical interpretation. Such, however, is not the case in the systems of dispensationalism and ultra-dispensationalism. In the final analysis, the validity of ultra-dispensationalism must be examined on the basis of its exegesis of various passages of Scripture upon which the system claims to rest" (page 1).

"The distinction between dispensationalism and ultra-dispensationalism is not one of kind but one of degree" (page 7).

Chapter Thirteen

Dispensationalism: The New Covenant (Part Two)

One of the greatest challenges before anyone who calls himself a dispensationalist is explaining how the new covenant, which Jeremiah said would be made with Israel and Judah, is related to the Christian church today. In the previous chapter, we examined the dispensational answer to this challenge that is most consistent with the dispensational system and found it wanting. In this chapter we will examine the other two dispensational attempts to meet this challenge.

Second Explanation: Church Related Only to the Blood of the New Covenant

A second dispensational theory on the relationship of the new covenant to the Christian is the one advanced by John Nelson Darby, the father of dispensational thought. Darby taught that the Christian is not directly related to any new covenant but is related only to the *blood* of the new covenant. [This is similar to the view espoused by the moderate dispensationalists who say the church partakes of the spiritual blessings but not the political blessings.] This theory emphasizes that the blood of Christ is not only the gracious ground for the new covenant to be made with Israel but also the source of all spiritual benefits and blessings, both heavenly and earthly.[1] Since there is no Christian new covenant, every mention of a new covenant in both the Old and New Testaments must always be a reference to a Jewish millennial covenant to which the church is not directly related. The Christian is directly related to "the annexed circumstances of the covenant,"[2] to "the essential privileges of the new covenant,"[3] to the "benefit" of the covenant, and to "the Mediator of the covenant,"[4] but not to the covenant itself. Darby expressed his theory in the following:

> This covenant of the letter is made with Israel, not with us; but we get the benefit of it.[5]

> The gospel is not a covenant, but the revelation of the salvation of God. It proclaims the great salvation. We enjoy indeed all the essential privileges of the new covenant, its foundation being laid on God's part in the blood of Christ, but we do so in spirit, not according to the letter.

> The new covenant will be established formally with Israel in the millennium.[6]

This theory is defined and defended in greater detail by dispensationalists Harry Ironside and E. Schuyler English in the following quotes:

> It is important to notice that while the *blessings* of the new covenant are ours, yet it is never said to be made with the Church. . . . The Mediator of that covenant is the Lord Jesus Christ. The blood of the new covenant is that which he shed for our sins. Therefore believers now rejoice in the distinctive blessings it insures; but it is with the earthly, not with the

---

[1]John F. Walvoord, *The Millennial Kingdom* (Grand Rapids: Zondervan Publishing House, 1959), pages 210, 218; J. Dwight Pentecost, *Things to Come* (Grand Rapids: Zondervan Publishing Company, 1958), pages 121-122.

[2]J. Dwight Pentecost, *Things to Come*, page 122.

[3]William Everett Bell, Jr., "A Critical Evaluation of the Pre-tribulation Rapture Doctrine in Christian Eschatology" (dissertation, School of Education of New York University, 1967), page 210; John F. Walvoord, *The Millennial Kingdom*, page 210; J. Dwight Pentecost, *Things to Come*, page 122.

[4]J. Dwight Pentecost, *Things to Come*, page 121.

[5]Ibid., page 121.

[6]William Everett Bell, Jr., "A Critical Evaluation of the Pre-tribulation Rapture Doctrine in Christian Eschatology" (dissertation, School of Education of New York University, 1967), page 210; John F. Walvoord, *The Millennial Kingdom*, page 210; J. Dwight Pentecost, *Things to Come*, page 122.

heavenly, people that the covenant itself is to be made.[7]

> . . . surely the grace of God has embraced the Church within the benefits of the new covenant. When our Lord took the cup, on the night in which He was betrayed, He said: "This is My cup of the new testament (covenant) in My blood" (1 Cor. 11:25). The cup was taken by Him for all His own through faith — His Church, His Body, His Bride.
>
> Nevertheless, fundamentally the Gentiles are not a covenant-people, neither is the Church made up of a covenant-people. . . . The Church, then, is not *under* the new covenant; the Church is, however, a beneficiary of the new covenant in its heavenly, spiritual and eternal operation. The Church, now on earth, is at the same time seated together "in the heavenlies in Christ Jesus" (Eph. 2:6) because of the blood of the new covenant, shed by the Mediator of the new covenant, for us.
>
> But now, since it is Israel which is God's covenant people, . . . we must discover the primary facts and functions of the new covenant established for them.[8]

We must analyze the work of Christ in terms of Darby's theory on the new covenant. Jesus Christ at His first coming came to be the mediator of an earthly, nationalistic and Jewish new covenant that is totally unrelated to church age Christianity. He offered to Israel a theocratic political kingdom based on this Jewish new covenant, and He shed His blood to establish this Jewish new covenant. When the Jewish nation rejected the Christ, the offer was withdrawn and the theocratic kingdom was postponed. In this parenthetical age of postponement, God began an entirely new and unprophesied work in the calling of a heavenly people, the Christian church. Although the blood of Christ was shed for the establishment of the earthly people's national new covenant, there was enough efficacy in the Messianic sacrifice for individual salvation and heavenly blessings in the church age. Christ had assumed the office of mediator to mediate the Jewish covenant, but in this parenthetical age, His mediatorial office is available for the spiritual benefit of Christians even though they are totally unrelated to the covenant of which He is mediator.

Now that we grasp Darby's theory, we must appraise it. Darby's theory makes God's entire program for the church seem incidental and

---

[7] H. A. Ironside, *Notes on the Prophecy and Lamentations of Jeremiah "The Weeping Prophet"* (Neptune, N.J.: Loizeaux Brothers, 1906), page 163.

[8] E. Schuyler English, *Studies in the Epistle to the Hebrews* (Travelers Rest, S. C.: Southern Bible House, 1955), pages 226-227.

secondary to God's program for Israel but at the same time Darby greatly limits Israel's eternal inheritance. This is true of dispensationalism in general, but it is especially true of Darby's theory on the new covenant. This theory is that Christian salvation in the church age is an unprophesied benefit of the atoning work of Christ. The atonement's prophesied purpose was the establishment of the Jewish new covenant and kingdom, to which the Christian is unrelated. And yet those saints who are under this new covenant and who inherit this kingdom will be, throughout eternity, inferior in status to the Body of Christ church saints! The Christian will remain throughout eternity a stranger to the new covenant, having only the secondary blessings of the blood of this covenant, and yet his spiritual position will be as high above Israel's as the heavens are above the earth, and Israel will be the main heir of the New Covenant!

Furthermore, the New Testament gives no support to Darby's suggestion that the Christian is related to the basis and benefits of the new covenant but not to the new covenant itself. In contrast Paul taught that Christians before conversion from paganism were "strangers from the covenants of promise" but "now in Christ Jesus ye who sometimes were far off have been made nigh by the blood of Christ" and "are no more strangers" (Ephesians 2:12-13, 19). To be brought nigh by the blood of the covenant is to be no longer a stranger to the covenant. And if no longer a stranger, then Christians today are members of the very covenants made with Israel! Also, Paul considered himself to be a minister not only of the blood of the covenant but of the Jeremiah 31 new covenant itself (2 Corinthians 3:6). And the sacramental statement of Christ: "This cup *is* the new testament (i.e., covenant) in My blood" (1 Corinthians 11:25) makes little sense if the new covenant itself is not directly related to the church in this age. The writer of Hebrews taught that Christ is today "the mediator of a better covenant" (Hebrews 8:6). Is the Christian related to the mediator of this better covenant but not to the better covenant itself? Bernard Ramm has appropriately noticed: "To say that we are under the benefits of the Covenant without actually being under the covenant is to clandestinely admit what is boldly denied."[9]

Many dispensationalists have recognized the validity of these criticisms and have rejected Darby's explanation of the church's

---

[9] Bernard Ramm, *Protestant Biblical Interpretation: A Textbook of Hermeneutics* (Grand Rapids: Baker Book House, 1970), page 264.

relationship to the new covenant. For example, Dr. John F. Walvoord has said: "Most [dispensational] premillenarians (Darby excepted) would agree that *a* new covenant has been provided for the church, but not *the* new covenant for Israel."[10]

Third Explanation: New Covenant Primarily for Israel, Secondarily for the Church

The third dispensational theory on the church's relationship to the new covenant of Jeremiah 31 is the theory advanced by Dr. C. I. Scofield in the *Scofield Reference Bible*. According to Dr. Charles C. Ryrie, this is the theory most widely accepted among dispensationalists.[11] In his reference Bible notes, Scofield simply applies the new covenant both to the church and to Israel with no explanation about how this is accomplished, as evidenced by the following quotations: "The New Covenant . . . secures the perpetuity, future conversion, and blessing of Israel . . . ."[12] "The New Covenant rests upon the sacrifice of Christ, and secures the eternal blessedness, under the Abrahamic Covenant (Gal. 3:13-29), of all who believe."[13]

Later dispensationalists have elaborated on Scofield's theory, such as Dr. J. Dwight Pentecost:

> . . . according to this view, there is one new covenant with a two-fold application; one to Israel in the future and one to the church now.[14]

> This view places the church under the new covenant, and views the relationship as a partial fulfillment of the covenant.[15]

> Scofield agrees with Darby fully that the covenant was primarily for Israel and will be fulfilled by them. Any application of it to the church, as the Scofield position holds, does not nullify the primary application to Israel.[16]

---

[10]John F. Walvoord, *The Millennial Kingdom*, page 214.

[11]Charles Caldwell Ryrie, *The Basis of the Premillennial Faith* (Neptune, N.J.: Loizeaux Brothers, 1953), page 107.

[12]C. I. Scofield, editor, *The Scofield Reference Bible* (New York: Oxford University Press, 1909), page 1297, note 1 on Hebrews 8:8.

[13]Ibid., page 1298, note 2 on Hebrews 8:8.

[14]J. Dwight Pentecost, *Things to Come*, page 123.

[15]Ibid., page 124.

[16]Ibid., page 124.

Dr. Pentecost in his writing on Scofield's new covenant theory quotes another writer who says that the new covenant is not *made* with the Christian but is *ministered* to the Christian. Dr. John F. Walvoord has the following comments on Scofield's theory:

> The [dispensational] premillennial view popularized by the *Scofield Reference Bible* regards the new covenant as having a twofold application, first to Israel fulfilled in the millennium, and, second, to the church in the present age.[17]

> . . . Scofield . . . regards the new covenant with Israel as having an oblique reference to the believers of this age, though concerned primarily with Israel.[18]

Dr. Charles C. Ryrie understands Scofield similarly:

> This interpretation holds that the one new covenant has two aspects, one which applies to Israel, and one which applies to the church. These have been called the realistic and spiritual aspects of the covenant, but both aspects comprise essentially one covenant based on the sacrifice of the Lord Jesus Christ.[19]

W. H. Griffith Thomas has expounded this dispensational theory as follows:

> It will be observed that the covenant is said to be made "with the house of Israel and with the house of Judah," that is, with the whole Jewish nation. There is no doubt that this is the primary designation and purpose of the covenant. The promise of Israel's restoration is clear, together with the specification of benefits. Jeremiah's words are: "Lo the days are coming," and it is well known that the New Testament antitype of the Old Testament types is not the Christian Church but the Kingdom which is still future. . . . But we Christians have the spiritual reality of this covenant, which, while made with Israel, is for our benefit as well, through grace, and so we distinguish between the primary interpretation to Israel and the secondary (spiritual) application to the Church today. We now enjoy in the power of the Holy Spirit all the blessings of the new covenant, and yet there will be still further and fuller manifestations in the future for Israel, according to God's promise (Rom. 11:25-32).[20]

---

[17] John F. Walvoord, *The Millennial Kingdom*, page 210.

[18] Ibid., page 218.

[19] Charles Caldwell Ryrie, *The Basis of the Premillennial Faith*, page 210.

[20] W. H. Griffith Thomas, *Hebrews: A Devotional Study* (Grand Rapids: Wm. B. Eerdmans Publishing Company, 1961), pages 106-107.

The problem with the Scofield theory is that it violates both (1) the dispensational dichotomy between Israel and the church and (2) the dispensational literal hermeneutic (i.e., theory of interpretation). (1) Scofield's theory violates the dispensational dichotomy in that it allows the church to partially fulfill a prophecy made for Israel and to partially be under a covenant belonging to Israel. If the church can fulfill this Jewish prophecy and be under this Jewish covenant, then why not others? This theory in effect says that the church can be partially identified with Israel. Dispensationalists have acknowledged this weakness in Scofield's theory. For example, Dr. J. Dwight Pentecost in his discussion of Scofield's theory notes: "The church, however, can not be placed under Israel's covenant."[21] Dr. Ryrie has also noted this weakness in the Scofield theory:

> If the Church is fulfilling Israel's promises as contained in the new covenant or anywhere else in Scripture, then [dispensational] premillennialism is weakened. One might well ask why there are not two aspects to one new covenant. This may be the case, and it is the position held by many [dispensational] premillennialists, but we agree that the amillennialist has every right to say of this view that it is "a practical admission that the new covenant is fulfilled in and to the Church."[22]

Elsewhere Dr. Ryrie attacks non-dispensationalism:

> . . . the amillennialist's hermeneutics allow him to blur completely the meanings of the two words [Israel and the Church] in the New Testament so that the Church takes over the fulfillment of the promises to Israel. In that view true Israel is the Church. The covenant premillennialist goes halfway. The Church and Israel are somewhat blended, though not amalgamated. The dispensationalist studies the words in the New Testament, finds that they are kept distinct, and therefore concludes that when the Church was introduced, God did not abrogate His promises to Israel nor enmesh them into the Church. This is why the dispensationalist recognizes two purposes of God and insists in maintaining the distinction between Israel and the Church.[23]

These dispensational criticisms against covenant premillennialism could just as well have been applied to Scofield's theory on the new covenant. Scofield's theory blends Israel and the church and

---

[21] J. Dwight Pentecost, *Things to Come*, page 124.

[22] Charles Caldwell Ryrie, *The Basis of the Premillennial Faith*, page 118.

[23] Charles Caldwell Ryrie, *Dispensationalism Today* (Chicago: Moody Press, 1965), pages 95-96.

enmeshes promises made to Israel into the church.

(2) Scofield's theory also contradicts the dispensational herme-neutic. The cardinal rule of the dispensational hermeneutic is never to spiritualize or allegorize. Dr. Walvoord explicates spiritualizing:

> Spiritualization of the . . . word Israel would involve in Webster's definition of spiritualization: "to take in a spiritual sense, — opposed to literalize." In other words, if Israel should mean something else than Israel, e.g., the church in the New Testament composed largely of Gentiles, this would be spiritualization.[24]

Similarly Dr. J. Dwight Pentecost disapproves of the allegorical method: "Allegorism is the method of interpreting a literary text that regards the literal sense as the vehicle for a secondary, more spiritual and more profound sense."[25]

In the Scofield theory the new covenant for Israel has a primary reference to Israel and an oblique reference to the church. The new covenant has a realistic and a spiritual aspect, an earthly and a heavenly application, a primary interpretation and a secondary spiri-tual interpretation. In this theory the new covenant with Israel can mean something else than the new covenant with literal, national, earthly Israel. The very criticism of "spiritualizing" and "allegoriz-ing" that the dispensationalists so freely cast at Reformed theologians can also be cast back — the sword has two edges.

This survey of the three dispensational theories on the new cove-nant reveals that dispensationalists are strikingly divided, effectually confused, and unable to reconcile the New Testament data of the new covenant with their presuppositions. Dr. William Everett Bell, Jr. has well described this division among dispensationalists over the new covenant and its symptomatic significance:

> Since the two-covenant view, although it is consistent dispensation-alism, has not found wide acceptance among dispensationalists because of its obvious exegetical failings, leading dispensationalists are found to be seriously at odds over the problem. All are agreed that the church must not fulfill any of Israel's promises, but the method of preserving the dichotomy with regard to the new covenant is elusive.
>
> On the one hand, some recognize the exegetical casuistry involved in trying to retain the blessings of the covenant apart from any vital relationship to the covenant, and thus posit a second covenant. On the

---

[24] John F. Walvoord, *The Millennial Kingdom*, page 64.

[25] J. Dwight Pentecost, *Things to Come*, page 4.

other hand, others recognize the exegetical impossibility of a second covenant and prefer to ignore the casuistry. In either case, the position is basically untenable and points up rather dramatically the hermeneutical dilemma of dispensationalism in attempting to reconcile scripture to a basic presupposition.[26]

The New Testament data on the new covenant fits well with Reformed theology. No bending is necessary; no artificial exegesis is required; no hair splitting distinctions are needed, no double talk necessary (New Covenant *ministered* to the Christian but *made* with Israel). Since the New Testament church is the continuation of the Old Testament kingdom program and is spiritual Israel in this age and the fulfillment of many Old Testament prophecies, there is no problem in directly relating the Jeremiah 31 new covenant to the church in this age as is done by the New Testament writers. The new covenant relates directly to physical Israel only insofar as Jews accept Christ and are regrafted back into the olive tree of spiritual Israel, which is the church (Romans 11:26-27).[27]

---

[26] William Everett Bell, Jr., "A Critical Evaluation of the Pre-tribulation Rapture Doctrine in Christian Eschatology," page 190.

[27] Iain H. Murray, *The Puritan Hope: A Study in Revival and the Interpretation of Prophecy* (Carlisle, Penn.: The Banner of Truth Trust, 1971), pages 72-74; John Murray, *The Epistle to the Romans* (Grand Rapids: Wm. B. Eerdmans Pub. Co., 1968), 2:91-103.

Chapter Fourteen

Dispensationalism: How They Argue Their Case

In the previous chapters we have examined several passages whose teachings, on the positive side, give strong testimony to the correctness of Reformed theology; and, on the negative side, greatly contradict the dispensational assumptions. I became aware of these Biblical arguments only a few years ago when I was painfully leaving the dispensational system while a student at Dallas Theological Seminary, the Mecca of dispensational thought. Dallas was then the home of such well-known dispensational writers as Drs. Charles C. Ryrie, J. Dwight Pentecost, and John F. Walvoord. Its legacy from the past includes Drs. Lewis Sperry Chafer and Merrill F. Unger. One of its graduates is the well-known Hal Lindsey, the great popularizer of dispensationalism in this generation. So, not only have I been enlightened to the arguments for Reformed theology, I have also been exposed to the Biblical arguments for dispensationalism as expounded by some of its leading proponents. Now that I have grazed from both pastures, I have found the "theological grass" to be much greener on the Reformed side. Yet, I still remember that at one time my thinking was dominated and controlled by the dispensational arguments, and I can sympathetically understand how a sincere Christian can be led astray into the dispensational system. Therefore, I want to examine the main arguments used by the dispensationalists to defend their theorized dichotomy between Israel and the New Testament church.

Baptism of the Holy Spirit

As I analyze my former devotion to the dispensational system, I believe that the dispensational argument that held me most powerfully was the one predicated on the baptism of the Holy Spirit.[1] The argument is this: It is the baptism of the Holy Spirit that puts one into the Body of Christ, which is the church universal (1 Corinthians 12:13); there was no baptism of the Holy Spirit before Acts 2 (Matthew 3:11; Acts 1:5; 11:15-16); therefore, none of God's people who died before Acts 2 can be in the church universal; consequently, there is an absolute dichotomy between Old Testament Israel and the church. This is a subtle argument that can appear, on the surface, to be an irrefutable deduction from Scriptural data. The apparent strength of this argument, however, is illusionary. Its forcefulness is imaginary, popping like a soap bubble when one examines the unstated and hidden assumptions at the core. We will examine these assumptions in the penetrating light of Scripture.

First, this dispensational argument assumes that at glorification the Old Testament saints will not be made perfect together with the New Testament saints. It assumes that those advances in spiritual benefits that were historically realized at the inauguration of the New Testament era cannot be applied in glorification to those who died before the New Testament era began in fullness at Acts 2. This assumption contradicts the teaching of Scripture. No one's salvation, whether Old Testament saint or New Testament saint, is made perfect or complete during this life. This completion of the application of salvation occurs at glorification when the Lord returns. The Scriptures clearly teach in Hebrews 11:39-40 that the Old Testament saints will be made perfect together with, not apart from, the New Testament saints. Why? Because God has provided better benefits for saints in this age of spiritual fullness. Both Old Testament saints and New Testament saints will receive the full benefits of the Trinity's salvific work at glorification, and that includes the post-Pentecost baptism of the Spirit for the Old Testament saints. This conclusion is further validated by Revelation 21, where the Old Testament saints will be included in the Bride of Christ, which is the church universal.

Second, this argument assumes that the baptism of the Spirit at Pentecost was totally different in nature from the Spirit's Old Testa-

---

[1] Charles Caldwell Ryrie, *Dispensationalism Today* (Chicago: Moody Press, 1965), pages 136-137.

ment ministry of salvation. The Spirit's new covenant ministry can be both significantly superior to and significantly continuous with His old covenant ministry. Was not the Spirit renewing, sustaining, illuminating and giving the people of God gifts before Pentecost? Was not this work in both ages based on the person, work and covenant headship of Christ? Before Pentecost the saving work of the Spirit was based on Messianic promises, and after Pentecost, the saving work of the Spirit is based on historically realized Messianic accomplishments. The Spirit's present ministry is superior to His old covenant ministry because it no longer relates to the Christ to come but to the Christ who has come and been glorified and who now reigns in power (John 7:39). Just because the Spirit was poured out in unprecedented fullness on and after the Pentecost of Acts 2, does not entail that the Spirit had not been previously uniting the people of God into covenant union with the Christ who was yet to come.

Third, this dispensational argument assumes that salvation was possible in the Old Testament apart from the union with Christ effected by the Spirit. This would mean that Old Testament salvation could not have embraced those spiritual benefits received from union with Christ, which union is effected by the Spirit. This would even include regeneration (2 Corinthians 5:17; Ephesians 2:5, 10),[2] justification or freedom from divine condemnation (Romans 8:1), sanctification or freedom from sin's dominion (Romans 6:1-4), and a place in the resurrection of the righteous under the covenant headship of Christ (1 Corinthians 15:22)! Union with Christ must have been possible in the Old Testament to some degree through the work of the Spirit, or there could have been no salvation. Of course, the Old Testament saint did not live in the age of spiritual fullness ushered in by the Son's redemptive work, but neither was the Old Testament an age in which all the main effects of the Son's work were totally absent. God applied the Son's work to Old Testament believers to some degree even before that work was historically accomplished. There was a relative difference of degree in Old Testament spirituality, not an absolute difference of kind.

I should mention that some dispensational writers consistently accept that their system implies that Old Testament salvation must have been accomplished apart from union with Christ. (A "salvation" apart from union with Christ is another way to be saved.) For example,

---

[2]See end of chapter, Long Footnote, p. 180.

Dr. Charles C. Ryrie has said that "those who died before Christ's first advent" are not among the "dead in Christ."[3] Likewise Dr. Lewis Sperry Chafer stated that Old Testament saints were not "in the new federal Headship of the resurrected Christ"; that their lives were not "hid with Christ in God";[4] that "the Old Testament saints were not part of the New Creation in Christ";[5] that other than Christ needing to be raised from the dead to sit on David's throne, "the nation Israel sustains no relation to the resurrection of Christ";[6] and that "there is no kind of a position in Christ in any teaching of the law or of the kingdom."[7] Can you believe it? Salvation outside Christ!

Fourth, this dispensational argument fails to recognize the close relationship between spiritual baptism and spiritual circumcision (Colossians 2:11-12). There definitely was spiritual circumcision in the Old Testament. This was an Old Testament ministry of the Spirit that differed from New Testament spiritual baptism only in degree. If New Testament baptism takes the place of Old Testament circumcision, as the Lord's Supper is substituted for Passover, then New Testament baptism only continues what the Old Testament began.

Fifth, the New Testament speaks of salvation in Christ as a participation in the Old Testament covenants of promise (Ephesians 2:12-13). This would indeed be ironic if Old Testament salvation were accomplished apart from union with Christ.

The Church a Mystery

There is another dispensational argument for their dichotomy between Israel and the church. This argument is based on the New Testament's reference to the church age as a mystery.[8] In Scripture a mystery is a previously unknown secret that God has newly revealed. Dispensationalists argue that the church age was a mystery in Old Testament times in an absolute sense. Since the church age was unknown in the Old Testament, then no Old Testament prophecy could refer to the church age. This means that all Old Testament

---

[3]See end of chapter, Long Footnote, p. 180.

[4]Lewis Sperry Chafer, *Systematic Theology*, 4:181.

[5]Ibid., 4:63.

[6]Ibid., 1:xvi-xvii.

[7]Ibid., 4:98.

[8]See end of chapter, Long Footnote, p. 181.

prophecies about a coming age had to refer to the dispensational Jewish millennium, not to the church age. Then the church age is truly an unforeseen parenthesis in God's program for Israel. The Reformed answer to this argument is that the church was a mystery in a relative sense. This answer is based on Ephesians 3:3-6: ". . . the mystery . . ., which in other ages was not made known unto the sons of men, *as* it is now revealed unto (God's) holy apostles and prophets by the Spirit." The "as" is comparative indicating that the church age was relatively unknown in the Old Testament, not absolutely unknown. Certain characteristics of the church age that are referred to as a mystery (Ephesians 3:6) are elsewhere shown to be predicted in Old Testament prophecy (Romans 15:7-13), which proves the mystery to be relative, not absolute.

Chuch in the Future

Another dispensational argument is based on Christ's statement, "I will build My church" (Matthew 16:18). The dispensationalists argue that if the church were being built when Christ spoke, then it could not have existed in Old Testament times. Dr. Lewis Sperry Chafer has argued:

> When the stress falls on the word "will," the prophetic aspect is introduced and the reader is reminded that the Church did not exist at the moment Christ was speaking, but was to be realized in the future. This is a difficult aspect of truth for those who contend that the Church has existed throughout the period covered by the Old Testament, or any part of it.[9]

The answer to this argument is simple. The New Testament church at the time of Christ's earthly ministry was both old and new. It was old in that having a church or a called out people was rooted in the Old Testament. It was new in that God's people reached a new maturity because of the historical work of the Son. The Old Testament church was in the infancy of ceremonial shadows and a nationally confined kingdom; the New Testament church was in the maturity of spiritual realities and a universalized kingdom. In the Old Testament Moses served the church as a servant; in the New Testament Christ was faithful over the church as a Son (Hebrews 3:5-8). The newness in Matthew 16 is not an absolute newness as if God had never had a

---

[9]Lewis Sperry Chafer, *Systematic Theology, 8 vols.* (Dallas: Dallas Seminary Press, 1948), 4:43.

church or called out people. The newness is the newness of God's people belonging to the Christ in a new and intimate way. Christ was referring to the mature church of Messianic realities as opposed to the immature church of Messianic prefigurations. Christ was saying that He would build His new covenant church not from scratch but out of the material of the old covenant church, replacing the typological shadows with spiritual substance, excluding the Jews who would not accept Him, and expanding the Jewish tent to include the Gentiles (Isaiah 54:1-3).

On the side, when the Greek word translated "church" is applied to Old Testament Israel in Scripture (Acts 7:38), dispensationalists say that the word is being used in a non-theological sense, as it is used in Acts 19:32 to refer to a secular assembly.[10] Whenever the word "Israel" is used to refer to the New Testament church (Galatians 6:16), dispensationalists say that it refers strictly to the physical Jews in the church.

A similar argument to the one based on Matthew 16:18 is grounded on Ephesians 2:20, where the apostles and prophets are said to be the foundation of the church. If the church is described as a temple founded on the New Testament apostles and on Christ, argues the dispensationalist, then it cannot have an Old Testament foundation. I have heard that some Reformed interpreters try to answer this argument by pointing out that Ephesians 2:20 also teaches that the church is founded on Old Testament prophets as well as New Testament apostles, but I consider that to be an inadequate argument. The prophets in Ephesians 2:20 are New Testament prophets (compare Ephesians 3:5, especially the word *now*; Ephesians 4:11). One should acknowledge that Ephesians 2:20 is referring to the church in its New Testament manifestation, to the church in its Messianic maturity, and not to the church in its broader sense. The passage that discusses the church in its broader sense with the use of an architectural figure is Revelation 21:9-14. The word "church" as used in the New Testament can refer broadly to the elect of all ages or it can refer narrowly to the assembly of Old Testament Israel, to the covenant community in its New Testament manifestations, or to a local New Testament congregation. In Ephesians 2:20 the word "church" is not even used directly. The reference is to the "new man" (Ephesians 2:15), which refers to

---

[10]Charles Caldwell Ryrie, *The Basis of the Premillennial Faith*, page 137; C. I. Scofield, editor, *The Scofield Reference Bible* (New York: Oxford University Press, 1909), page 1021 (note on Matthew 16:18).

the church in its New Testament form.

If one examines the church as the community with God's promise of salvation, its foundation ultimately refers back to the Trinitarian covenant of redemption in eternity past and historically refers to the promise of the Seed Redeemer given to Adam and Eve after the fall. If one examines the church as a covenant community with a system of sacramental administration, its foundation is the Abrahamic and Mosaic covenants. If one examines the church as the covenant community of Messianic fullness, then its foundation is the historical work of Christ and the New Testament apostles and prophets. Ephesians 2:20 is a discussion of the church strictly in its New Testament form, but Ephesians 2:12-19 also stresses the strong continuity of the New Testament church with Old Testament Israel and with the Old Testament covenants. The Reformed theologian acknowledges both the newness of the New Testament church and its continuity with the Old Testament covenant community. The dispensationalist radicalizes the former and denies the latter. Also, the Reformed theologian recognizes that the word "church" at times refers to the elect of all the ages (Ephesians 5:25) and to the assembly of Old Testament Israel (Acts 7:38), usages which dispensationalists have to deny.

Jew, Gentile, Church

I will interact with one more argument that the dispensationalists use. They assert that since the New Testament continues to distinguish between physical Israelites, physical Gentiles and the Christian church (1 Corinthians 10:32), then one cannot identify Israel and the church. Are not Israel and the church kept separate in Scripture?[11] This argument rests on a restricted understanding of the term "Israel."

Though the physical Jew may have a sense of racial identity, membership in Israel has never been strictly a racial matter but instead primarily a matter of covenant relationship. Israel was the name of the Old Testament covenant community that was distinguished from the nations by the covenant of circumcision. Physical descent and blood lines were emphasized because the Messiah was to be a literal descendant of both Abraham and David, but Gentiles could join Israel through the proselyte laws. In the genealogy of David, we find Tamar

---

[11]John F. Walvoord, *The Millennial Kingdom*, page 164; J. Dwight Pentecost, *Things to Come*, page 88; Charles Caldwell Ryrie, *Dispensationalism Today*, page 138.

the Canaanite, Rahab the harlot from Jericho, and Ruth the Moabitess; all Gentiles. All of Abraham's servants were circumcised into Israel in Genesis 17. When Abraham delivered Lot, his household servants included 318 men trained for warfare (Genesis 14:14). The total number of servants and their families was undoubtedly a larger number, and all the males were circumcised. When Jacob went to Egypt, his physical descendants numbered seventy, but his household was so large that they were given the entire land of Goshen in which to live. A mixed multitude came out of Egypt with the physical descendants of Abraham (Exodus 12:38). Many of the mighty men of David's army were of foreign extraction (1 Chronicles 11:26-47), the best known being Uriah the Hittite. Gentiles throughout the ancient world became Jews in the days of Queen Esther (Esther 8:17). During the intertestamental Maccabean era, many Edomites, descendants of Esau, became Jews.[12] In the eighth century A.D., long after the great divorce between Christianity and Judaism, the Gentile Khazars of eastern Europe converted to Judaism. And thousands of professed Christians are converting to Judaism each year in our own day. To be a Jew is to be covenanted into the Jewish people by circumcision just as to be a Christian is to be covenanted into the Christian people by baptism.

Also, members of Israel under the old covenant could be excommunicated from the covenant community for certain high handed sins. One could be a member of Israel by racial descent without being a member of Israel as a citizen or church member. Furthermore, when much of Israel lapsed into idolatry, the prophets spoke of the remnant within the nation who were Jews inwardly as well as outwardly. This concept of being a true inward Jew was stressed by John the Baptist (Matthew 3:9), Jesus (John 8:37, 39), and Paul (Romans 2:28-29; 9:6). One could be a member of Israel physically, nationally, culturally, and religiously without being a member of Israel spiritually.

In this age of the new covenant, the physical Jew must follow the example of Zacchaeus and believe in Christ to be a true son of Abraham (Luke 19:9). To covenant into ethnic Israel by circumcision is to covenant into a people who reject Jesus of Nazareth. In this age many Gentiles have followed the example of the Roman centurion of great faith and have come from east and west to sit down with Abraham, Isaac and Jacob in the kingdom of heaven (Matthew 8:11).

---

[12]Josephus, *Antiquities of the Jews*, XIII, ix, 1.

In the New Testament one can be a physical Jew and not be a spiritual Jew (Revelation 2:9; 3:9), and one could be a physical Gentile and be a spiritual seed of Abraham (Galatians 3:29; Romans 4:11). All Christians are inward Jews, just as Paul teaches that "he is a Jew, which is one inwardly" (Romans 2:28).

Although both Christianity and Judaism have roots in the Old Testament religion, only Christianity is the seed according to promise like Isaac (Galatians 4:21-31) and the true heir of the Old Testament covenants. Paul compares unbelieving ethnic Israel to Ishmael, the one who was a physical descendant of Abraham but who was cast out of the covenant community. As long as ethnic Israel remains in spiritual hardness and blindness through her rejection of God's Messiah, she remains cut off from spiritual Israel and from the sap of God's saving grace (Romans 11:23; compare Matthew 8:12), and is an enemy of God concerning the gospel (Romans 11:28). For a season in the days of transition between the old and new covenants, the status of the unbelieving Jews as members of the covenant community with a special interest in God's promises was honored (Acts 2:39; 3:25); but those who hardened their hearts were eventually pruned off the tree of the true Israel (Romans 11:20).

The use of the word "Israel" in reference to physical Jews or to ethnic Israel or to the religious heirs of the Pharisees does not imply that the church is not spiritual Israel, the true Israel of God (Galatians 6:16) and the true heir of the Old Testament covenants. This may violate the dispensationalists' concept of literal but not God's.

"But," asks the dispensationalist, "What about Romans 11:29: 'For the gifts and calling of God are without repentance'?" This verse is teaching that there is a sense in which ethnic Israel remains beloved of God because of the special role of her fathers in redemptive history and because of her national election under the old covenant (Romans 9:1-5). This is not to say that ethnic Israel has its own prophetic future apart from the Christian church. This is to say that because of God's respect for ethnic Israel's former participation in the covenant promises, ethnic Israel's apostasy from spiritual Israel will never be full or final. Many Jews have been cut off from the olive tree of spiritual Israel, but there will always be an elect remnant within ethnic Israel who are Jews inwardly as well as outwardly and members of the true Israel of God, which is the Christian church (Romans 11:1-7). And ethnic Israel will one day experience a spiritual fullness that will be in direct contrast to the hardness, blindness and stumbling of her national rejection of Jesus (Romans 11:12, 15, 26-29). God continues to have a place for ethnic Israel in His prophetic plans in spite of her national stumbling but that future is not divorced from the Christian church. And that future will be realized in and through the Christian church when the cast off natural branches are grafted back into the olive tree through faith in Christ (Romans 11:23). At that point all Israel will be saved and will experience the blessings of the new covenant (Romans 11:26-27).[13]

In summary we see that dispensationalism overstresses the differences of kind between the Old and New Testaments to the point of neglecting their organic relationship of developmental continuity. Old Testament Israel was the church in infancy; Acts 2 was the church's Bar Mitzvah; the New Testament church is Israel come to maturity. The New Testament church is organically related to Old Testament Israel like a man's adulthood is organically related to that same man's childhood (Galatians 4:1-7). In such a relationship, there is both newness and continuity.

LONG FOOTNOTES

[2] Jesus' discourse with Nicodemus in John 3 is a classic passage on regeneration. Since that passage was spoken under the old covenant dispensation, dispensationalists tend to acknowledge that there was regeneration under the old covenant economy. Dr. John F. Walvoord says, on the same page, both that people could be born again under the old covenant and that Old Testament saints were not in Christ. The difficulty with this teaching is that the New Testament associates regeneration with union with Christ. John F. Walvoord, *The Holy Spirit at Work Today* (Chicago: Moody Press, 1973), page 21; compare J. Dwight Pentecost, *Things to Come, A Study in Biblical Eschatology* (Grand Rapids: Zondervan Publishing House, 1958), page 271; contrast with Lewis Sperry Chafer, *Systematic Theology, 8 vols.* (Dallas: Dallas Seminary Press, 1948), 4:16.

[3] Charles Caldwell Ryrie, *Dispensationalism Today*, page 136; compare John F. Walvoord, *The Millennial Kingdom* (Grand Rapids: Zondervan Publishing House, 1959), page 280.

Darby, William Kelly, A. C. Gaebelein, C. I. Scofield and others have held that the "dead in Christ" of 1 Thessalonians 4:16 includes the Old Testament saints. The most obvious difficulty with this position is the difficulty in putting the Old Testament saints "in Christ" as Paul used

[13]See end of chapter, Long Footnote, p. 181.

that term and keeping them out of the Body of Christ. Many dispensationalists today limit the "dead in Christ" to church saints, and William Everett Bell, Jr. explains the history of this doctrinal evolution: "In 1937, in his *The Approaching Advent of Christ*, Alexander Reese launched a vitriolic attack on Pretribulationism. The major thrust of his argument lay in the identification of the resurrection of the righteous dead with the time of Christ's second coming. He then demonstrated conclusively from scripture that the resurrection of Old Testament saints was to follow the tribulation period; therefore the second coming of Christ must follow the tribulation period also. The force of his argument was felt keenly by pretribulationalists, but an ingenious solution was devised to get around the problem. Pretribulationists simply conceded Reese's point that the Old Testament saints would be resurrected after the tribulation, but they maintained that the New Testament church saints would still be resurrected at the rapture before the tribulation." William Everett Bell, Jr., "A Critical Evaluation of the Pre-tribulation Rapture Doctrine in Christian Eschatology" (dissertation, School of Education of New York University, 1967), pages 15-16.

[8] John F. Walvoord, *The Millennial Kingdom*, pages 232-237; Charles Caldwell Ryrie, *Dispensationalism Today*, page 134, footnote 4. On page 201 of *Dispensationalism Today*, Dr. Ryrie quotes a dispensational writer who comments as follows on Ephesians 3:5: "The 'as it has now been revealed' may indeed suggest that this mystery had been hinted at in the Old Testament, but under veiled forms or types, and only now was properly revealed." On page 134, footnote 4, Dr. Ryrie gives the normal dispensational interpretation on this point when he denies that : ". . . the 'as' clause of Ephesians 3:5 might imply a partial revelation in the Old Testament . . ." Elsewhere, Dr. Ryrie says, "The Church is a mystery in the sense that it was completely unrevealed in the Old Testament and now revealed in the New Testament." Charles Caldwell Ryrie, *The Basis of the Premillennial Faith* (Neptune, N.J.: Loizeaux Brothers, 1953), page 136.

[13] For a defense of this view of "all Israel shall be saved," see Iain H. Murray, *The Puritan Hope: A Study in Revival and the Interpretation of Prophecy* (Carlisle, Penn.: The Banner of Truth Trust, 1971), pages 72-74; John Murray, *The Epistle to the Romans* (Grand Rapids: Wm. B. Eerdmans Publishing Company, 1968), 2:91-103. For a defense of the view that "all Israel" refers to the believing remnant within ethnic Israel throughout the ages, see William Hendriksen, *Israel in Prophecy* (Grand Rapids: Baker Book House, 1968), pages 35-52, and Curtis Crenshaw in this book.

Chapter Fifteen

Dispensationalism: Consistent Literalism

I believe that if one were to ask the knowledgeable dispensationalist to specify the fundamental element in his system, he would probably say *consistent literalism* or some equivalent expression. The dispensationalist believes that consistent literalism is the basic key to the correct interpretation of Scripture and the only sure hedge against liberalism. The dispensationalist's main criticism of the Reformed theologian is that he "spiritualizes" or "allegorizes," which is to say that he is not consistently literal.

This dispensational criticism is most often directed against the Reformed theologian who directly applies Old Testament prophecies that speak of Israel and the Messianic age to the New Testament church. Many dispensationalists also regard the Reformed theologian as an incipient liberal because they believe that it is only the Reformed theologian's inconsistency to apply his non-literal hermeneutic (i.e., system of interpretation) throughout his system of theology that saves him from liberalism.[1] Furthermore, the Reformed theologian's tendency to "spiritualize" Jewish prophecies by applying them directly to the church differs only in degree from the liberal who spiritualizes the creation account or the virgin birth by saying that these are myths, reasons the dispensationalist. The dispensationalist is emotionally committed to his literal hermeneutic and believes that he alone has the

---

[1] See end of chapter, Long Footnote, p. 192.

moral courage and integrity necessary to accept what Scripture "literally" teaches.

Dr. Charles C. Ryrie explains the dispensational emphasis on consistently literal interpretation as follows:

> The distinction between Israel and the Church is born out of a system of hermeneutics which is usually called literal interpretation. . . . The word "literal" is perhaps not as good as either the word "normal" or "plain," but in any case it is interpretation that does not spiritualize or allegorize as nondispensational interpretation does. . . . Consistently literal or plain interpretation is indicative of a dispensational approach to the interpretation of Scripture. And it is this very consistency — the strength of dispensational interpretation — that irks the nondispensationalist and becomes the object of his ridicule.[2]

> If plain or normal interpretation is the only valid hermeneutical principle, and if it is consistently applied, it will cause one to be a dispensationalist. As basic as one believes normal interpretation to be, to that extent he will of necessity become a dispensationalist.[3]

Dr. Walvoord captures the spirit of dispensational literalism in his dramatic statements:

> History is history, not allegory. Facts are facts. Prophesied future events are just what they are prophesied. Israel means Israel, earth means earth, heaven means heaven.[4]

> *A literal promise spiritualized is exegetical fraud.*[5]

The importance of *consistent* literalism to the dispensationalist cannot be overstated. Dispensationalists incessantly adduce that consistent literalism is their first principle and that the dichotomy and parenthesis theories logically follow from the application of this first principle to the study of Scripture. I believe that the reverse is the truth: dispensational interpretation uses the degree of literalism necessary to interpret prophecy in terms of the dispensational dichotomy and parenthesis assumptions. One example of this is that differing degrees of figurativeness and literality can be found in dispensational interpretations.

---

[2]Charles Caldwell Ryrie, *Dispensationalism Today* (Chicago: Moody Press, 1965), pages 45-46.

[3]Ibid., page 91.

[4]John F. Walvoord, *The Millennial Kingdom*, pages 129-130.

[5]Ibid., page 200.

Problem of Family and Tribe

Certain passages dramatically demonstrate the difficulty in trying to interpret prophecy with so-called consistent literalism. One such class of passages is that class which dispensationalists apply to their Jewish millennium and which refer to some ancient enemies of Old Testament Israel, which long ago passed out of existence, such as the Ammonites (Isaiah 11:14; Daniel 11:41), the Assyrians (Micah 5:5; Isaiah 19:23-25), the Edomites (Isaiah 11:14; 63:1-6; Joel 3:19; Amos 9:11-12; Daniel 11:41), the Egyptians (Zechariah 14:16-19; Isaiah 19:23-25), and the Moabites (Isaiah 11:14; Daniel 11:41).[6] Dr. William Everett Bell has observed:

> One wonders if "Israel means Israel," why Assyria does not mean Assyria and Egypt mean Egypt. The answer, obviously, is that plain common sense militates against any interpretation that sees a necessary revival of ancient peoples who passed off the scene of history thousands of years ago. No Christian would deny that God could once again bring together an Assyrian empire or a Philistine nation if He chose to do so, but few expositors, dispensationalists included, look for such an occurrence.[7]

Still another problem exists for the theory of "consistent" literalism. Dispensationalists argue that there is a future generation of Jews who will fulfill the Old Testament prophecies about a Messianic age, but some of these prophecies specifically mention the existence of ancient family and tribal relationships. For example, Zechariah chapters 9-12 are usually considered by dispensationalists to be a passage especially supportive of their system. Zechariah 12:11-14, however, specifically speaks of the separate and distinct existence of the families of David, Nathan, Levi and Shimei. Other passages about the Messianic age speak of the distinct existence of the tribe of Levi (Isaiah 66:21; Malachi 3:3), and some even speak of the continued existence of the sons of Zadok within the tribe of Levi (Ezekiel 44:15; 48:11). Other prophetic passages speak of all the separate and distinct twelve tribes of Israel (Ezekiel 48; Revelation 7). These tribal and family relationships, however, have long been lost. God has not been pleased to preserve these genealogical distinctions past the time of the

---

[6]Compare John F. Walvoord, *The Nations in Prophecy* (Grand Rapids: Zondervan Publishing House, 1967) pages 160-169.

[7]William Everett Bell, Jr., "A Critical Evaluation of the Pre-tribulation Rapture Doctrine in Christian Eschatology" (dissertation, School of Education of New York University, 1967), pages 85-86.

New Testament. Once tribal and family relationships are lost, they cannot be restored except by resurrecting the family and tribal heads and starting over again. Because of such considerations, Patrick Fairbairn has insightfully observed:

> So long as any prophecies were depending for their fulfillment on the separate existence of tribes and families in Israel, the distinction betwixt them was preserved; and so, also, were the genealogical records, which were needed to attest the fulfillment. These prophecies terminated in the Son of Mary, the branch of the house of David, and the lion of the tribe of Judah; but with him this, and all other old things, ceased — a new era, independent of such outward and formal differences, began. Hence, we find the apostle discharging all from giving heed to endless genealogies, as no longer of any avail in the church of God; and the providence of God shortly after sealed the word by scattering their genealogies to the winds, and fusing together in one undistinguishable, inextricable mass, the surviving remnants of the Jewish family. Now, prophecy is not to be verified by halves; it is either wholly true, in the sense in which it ought to be understood, or it is a failure. And since God's providence has rendered the fulfillment of the parts referred to manifestly impossible on the literal principle of interpretation, it affords conclusive evidence, that on this principle such prophecies are misread. In what it calls men to believe, it does violence to their reason; and it commits the word of God to expectations, which never can be properly realized.[8]

Problem of Ezekiel

The passage most commonly mentioned that presents great difficulty to dispensational literalism is Ezekiel's temple vision (Ezekiel 40-48). The dispensationalists are looking for a reinstitution of bloody animal sacrifices in a millennial temple built in accordance with the description found in this passage.[9] Dispensationalists are careful to qualify that these sacrifices are merely memorials of Christ's death and will be the millennial equivalent of the Lord's Supper. The problem with this is that Ezekiel's vision refers to these sacrifices as literally making atonement (Ezekiel 45:15, 17, 20; Hebrew: "kaphar," atone). Of course, a dispensationalist can go to the book of Hebrews

---

[8]Patrick Fairbairn, *Prophecy Viewed in Respect to Its Distinct Nature, Its Special Function, and Proper Interpretation* (Grand Rapids: Baker Book House, 1967), pages 276-277.

[9]J. Dwight Pentecost, *Things to Come, A Study in Biblical Eschatology* (Grand Rapids: Zondervan Publishing House, 1958), page 519.

to prove that animal sacrifices in the Old Testament never literally atoned for sin (Hebrews 10:4). When the Reformed theologian, however, goes to Hebrews to prove that animal sacrifices were rescinded forever [no memorial sacrifice] by Christ's once for all offering (Hebrews 10:10-18), then that is "theological interpretation" and "reading the New Testament back into the Old Testament" — two practices which dispensationalists routinely criticize.

Problem of Ancient Weapons

Another problem area for strict literalism is the prophecies that dispensationalists interpret as end-time events and also refer to ancient weapons systems. For example, Ezekiel 38-39 is a passage that dispensationalists interpret as referring to an end-time invasion of Israel by a Russian army. And yet the prophecy speaks of this army as equipped with primitive weapons: "shields and bucklers, . . . bows and arrows, and . . . handstaves, and . . . spears" (Ezekiel 39:9). These weapons are largely made of wood as evidenced by their being burned as firewood. Dr. John F. Walvoord suggests the following explanation:

> Modern missile warfare will have developed in that day to the point where missiles will seek out any considerable amount of metal. Under those circumstances, it would be necessary to abandon the large use of metal weapons and substitute wood such as is indicated in the primitive weapons. Whatever the explanation, the most sensible interpretation is that the passage refers to actual weapons pressed into use because of the particular circumstances of that day.[10]

For the sake of argument, let us assume that the dispensationalist is correct in referring this prophecy to a specific futuristic end-time event as opposed to a preterite or axiomatic interpretation. Given that assumption, to teach that the prophet was simply speaking of warfare in terms familiar to ancient Israel would be to compromise the dispensational literal hermeneutic. If the prophet could have prophesied a war with modern weapons in terms of the primitive weapons with which ancient Israel was familiar, then the prophet could also have prophesied the church age in terms of the Old Testament religious system with which ancient Israel was familiar. If the dispensationalist does not interpret the wooden weapons of Ezekiel 39 literally,

---

[10]John F. Walvoord, *The Nations in Prophecy*, page 116. Quoted in Paul Lee Tan, *The Interpretation of Prophecy*, page 224.

then he has little reason to criticize the Reformed interpreter when he "spiritualizes" Ezekiel's temple vision as a prophecy of the church age in terms of the Old Testament religious system.

Not all dispensational interpreters guard the literal hermeneutic as carefully as does Dr. Walvoord. The popular dispensational writer Hal Lindsey, a graduate of the seminary where Dr. Walvoord is president, is not quite as "literal" as Walvoord in his hermeneutical approach to the book of Revelation:

> Some writers have chosen to interpret each symbol quite literally. For example, a locust with the face of a man, the teeth of a lion, a breastplate of iron, a tail that can sting, and wings that made the sound of many chariots would have to be specially created by God to look just like that description.

> I personally tend to think that God might utilize in his judgments some modern devices which the Apostle John was at a loss for words to describe nineteen centuries ago! In the case just mentioned, the locust might symbolize an advanced kind of helicopter.[11]

Mr. Lindsey later suggests that the composite locust creatures of the Apocalypse might be Cobra helicopters that spray nerve gas from their tails.[12] And yet, interpreters such as Mr. Lindsey also complain strongly against the Reformed teaching that the Old Testament prophets spoke of the coming church age in terms of the Old Testment religious economy with which the people of God were familiar!

Problem of the New Jerusalem

Another passage where dispensationalists generally insist on strict literality is the description of the New Jerusalem in Revelation 21. The new Jerusalem vision of Revelation 21, if interpreted with strict literality, predicts the coming to earth of a city whose length, width and height are each 12,000 stadia (i.e., about 1,500 miles). Stop to visualize a city fifteen hundred miles long, wide and tall resting on planet earth! Such a metropolitan mass would put a definite wobble in this planet's orbital spin! Of course, God could do such a feat and overcome any such difficulties, but is it not more likely that these outrageous dimensions were used intentionally to prevent an overly

---

[11]Hal Lindsey, *There's a New World Coming: "A Prophetic Odyssey"* (Irvine, California: Harvest House Publishers, 1973), page 16.

[12]Ibid., pages 138-139.

literal interpretation? Also, the use of the highly symbolic number 12,000 would seem enough to indicate that this city, which elsewhere is said to be the Bride of Christ (Revelation 21:9-10), is a symbol for the full number of the people of God of all the ages. The number twelve is associated with the twelve tribes of Israel and the twelve apostles (Revelation 21:12, 14) and therefore with the covenant people of both ages. The numbers ten and thousand are associated with fullness or completion. Why the insistence on a literal city with such outrageous and disproportionate dimensions relative to planet earth?

The dispensationalist Dr. Paul Lee Tan explains that Biblical prophecy should be interpreted literally whenever this is possible or plausible. As an example, he mentions the pearls that are to serve as gates in the extraordinarily large city described in Revelation 21.[13] Of course, it is possible for God to create such extraordinary pearls. And it is possible for the omnipotent God to recreate many elements of the Old Testament world and to cataclysmically rearrange the earth's topography in order to allow for a very literal fulfillment of Messianic prophecies. The question, however, is not whether or not such fulfillments are theoretically possible. The issue is what God was intending to communicate by the language used in Biblical prophecy.

Dispensationalists sometimes do lay aside this insistence on "literality if possible." For example, in Psalm 22, it was prophesied that the Messiah would be surrounded by "bulls of Bashan." Most interpreters take this prophecy to refer to those people who persecuted our Lord at His passion. One must admit, however, that this interpretation is not a "literal if possible" interpretation of the passage. And yet, I am aware of no dispensationalist who insists in the name of literalism that our Lord at His Second Coming must suffer again under the threats of literal bulls from literal Bashan in order to fulfill all prophecy literally. These same interpreters, however, argue that Christ will not begin His prophesied Messianic reign until He is ruling from a literal Mount Zion in literal Palestine (Psalm 2:6) even though the New Testament teaches that Christ obtained His Messianic throne at His ascension into heaven (Revelation 12:5; 2:26-27; compare Psalm 2:9) and that Mount Zion and Jerusalem in this age are heavenly realities (Hebrews 12:22).

The editors of the *New Scofield Reference Bible* have made a significant admission regarding literalism and the interpretation of

---

[13]Paul Lee Tan, *The Interpretation of Prophecy*, pages 157-160.

Old Testament prophecy. They have acknowledged that the animal sacrifices in Ezekiel's temple vision do not need to be interpreted literally but may be validly regarded as a general prophecy of future worship in terms of the Old Testament economy with which the original recipients of the prophecy were familiar.[14] If this principle can be applied here, then why not elsewhere in other prophecies of the Messianic age? If this principle applies to the sacrifices in Ezekiel's temple vision, then why not also to the entire temple setting? Once this principle is acknowledged in regard to one element of Old Testament worship in a Messianic prophecy, it is arbitrary to deny it in regard to other elements of Old Testament worship and other Messianic prophecies. The more this principle is applied in dispensational interpretation of prophecy, the less Judaistic will be the dispensational millennium and the closer dispensational interpretation will come to traditional Reformed prophetic interpretation and to Scripture. Therefore, the dispensational system determines his hermemeutic — not the reverse!

I opened this chapter with some criticisms that dispensationalists have of the Reformed hermeneutic. Now I shall close by answering these criticisms. First, consistent literalism is not the final key to proper Biblical interpretation. It is too subjective and rationalistic. One man's consistency is another man's absurdity. Consistent literalism means that the interpreter must ultimately look to his own personal sense of literary usage to determine the degree of literalism and figurativeness in prophecy, a point Mr. Crenshaw has made quite well.

The proper hermeneutic involves a study of how Scripture interprets other Scripture as a guide to what is Scripturally normal language. If Matthew's interpretation of prophecy seems abnormal to us, then we should adjust our understanding of what normal language is.

The proper hermeneutic involves a willingness to interpret difficult passages of Scripture in the light of the teaching of clearer passages of Scripture and with a sensitivity to literary genre. One should not build a theological system on possible interpretations of poetic or apocalyptic passages when those interpretations require one to twist the clear meaning of straightforward didactic passages. For example, the clear teaching of the New Testament on the finished sacrifice of Christ should guide one in interpreting the animal sacri-

---

[14]C. I. Scofield, editor, *The New Scofield Reference Bible* (New York: Oxford University Press, 1967), page 888.

fices in Ezekiel's vision.

The proper hermeneutic involves a prayerful dependence on the Holy Spirit, who sanctifies in truth. The interpreter should not be a rationalist who puts his ultimate trust in his own personal sense of language. The interpreter's personal sense of language is reliable only to the extent that it has been sanctified by the Spirit in truth. The interpreter should humbly acknowledge that his ultimate dependence is on the Spirit's illumination for spiritual discernment and for deliverance from sinful biases and blindnesses. Interpretation of Scripture is a moral endeavor as well as an intellectual endeavor. We are dependent on the Spirit to help us to understand Scripture as God meant it to be understood.

Second, strict literalism is not the final hedge against liberalism. Both liberals and cultists defend their distorted theologies both by literalizing Scripture and by allegorizing Scripture. For example, Armstrongism literalizes the eternal throne in the Davidic covenant and insists on a fulfillment involving a literal, physical throne. The true hedge against doctrinal distortion is not literalizing. The true hedge is a real submission to the illumination of the Holy Spirit and to the teachings of Scripture. Only here in this double combination of Word and Spirit does one find truth safely hedged against error.

What is truly objective interpretation? The ultimate objectivity is found in the divine subjectivity as expressed in the "thus saith the Lord" of the written Word. And for us to have reliable access to this ultimate objectivity, we are ultimately dependent on the Spirit's work in giving us the subjective ability to understand God's Word. In the last analysis, truth and understanding are gifts from God. But for the grace of God, I, too, would be blinded to God's clear revelation and I would be enslaved by cultic error. As is true with many issues, in the end we come to the apparent antinomy between human responsibility and divine sovereignty. I am morally responsible for seeing and obeying the clear message of Scripture. Apart from Christ, I can do nothing and am spiritually blind and dead. When I do understand and obey God's message, it is an unmerited gift from God. And yet my natural inability and my total dependence on God does not relieve me of my responsibility to use all my God given facilities in an effort to understand His Word. And if I am right and my dispensational friends are wrong in understanding prophecy, I have no basis for boasting. "For what do I have that I did not receive?" "Every good and perfect gift is from above."

LONG FOOTNOTES

[1] "The amillennial method of interpreting Scripture is correctly defined as the spiritualizing method. It is clear, however, that conservative amillennialists limit the use of this method, and in fact adopt the literal method of interpreting most of the Scriptures. . . . "The modern liberal scholar, who is also an amillenarian, feels free to use the spiritualizing method rather freely in areas other than prophecy whenever it suits his fancy, and being bound by no law of infallible inspiration need not be concerned if the result is not consistent. The spiritualizing method once admitted is not easy to regulate and tends to destroy the literal method. While the amillennial use of the literal method is general among conservatives, among liberal groups it has less standing and use." John F. Walvoord, *The Millennial Kingdom* (Grand Rapids: Zondervan Publishing House, 1959), pages 62-63. See also Paul Lee Tan, *The Interpretation of Prophecy* (Rockville, Maryland: Assurance Publishers, 1974), pages 275-277.

Chapter Sixteen

Dispensationalism: Interpreting the Prophets

Interpreting Biblical prophecy is not exactly like reading the morning newspaper. To read Biblical prophecy is to encounter statements about mighty bulls of Bashan, strange composite beasts, armies of locusts, and cataclysmic events in the heavens and on earth. One does not often encounter language like that even in the more extravagant tabloids. Interpreting this sort of language is a challenge, especially since we are no longer surrounded by the cultural and linguistic context in which Biblical prophecy was originally given. Interpreting prophecy, however, is a challenge that every Christian should accept. "*All* Scripture is profitable for doctrine and instruction," not just the easier to understand portions of Scripture.

The dispensationalist and the Reformed interpreter have disagreements about how the language of prophecy should be interpreted. It would be impractical to go through all the prophecies of Scripture in this chapter and to explain the differences between dispensational and Reformed approaches to interpretation. A more practical approach would be to examine some of the general issues in the interpretation of prophecy to illustrate the differences between dispensational and Reformed prophetic interpretation.

"Normal" Interpretation

A primary criticism that dispensationalists have of the Reformed interpretation of prophecy is that the Reformed interpreter treats prophecy with a different hermeneutic (i.e., system of interpretation) than he uses with the rest of Scripture. According to Dr. Walvoord, the non-dispensational interpreter "uses two methods of interpretation, the spiritualizing method for prophecy and the literal method for other Scriptures."[1] According to Dr. Charles C. Ryrie:

> What, then, is the difference between the dispensationalists' use of this hermeneutical principle [literalism] and the nondispensationalists'? The difference lies in the fact that the dispensationalist claims to use the normal principle of interpretation *consistently* in *all* his study of the Bible. He further claims that the nondispensationalist does not use the principle everywhere. He admits that the nondispensationalist is a literalist in much of his interpretation of the Scriptures, but charges him with allegorizing or spiritualizing when it comes to the interpretation of prophecy.[2]

> In other words, the nondispensationalist position is simply that the literal principle is sufficient except for the interpretation of prophecy. In this area, the spiritualizing principle must be introduced.[3]

The issue is the question of what was "normal" language when God spoke about the future. Should we expect God to have spoken through the prophets about the future with the same language that He used when He chronicled the history of the covenant people? Or should we expect a literary difference between Genesis and Zechariah, between 1 Samuel and Daniel, between the Acts of the Apostles and the Apocalypse of John? Is the only literary difference between history and predictive prophecy that one looks at the past and the other at the future? Should we interpret predictive prophecy as if it were prewritten history or futuristic newspaper reporting? According to Reformed interpreters, there is a literary difference between historical chronicles and prophetic visions. Many Old Testament prophecies were given in dreams, visions, and dark sayings (Numbers 12:6-8) in which one should expect to find more figurative speech than in historical accounts or didactic literature. One should not interpret the prophets as if their message is in the simple literary form of prewritten history.

---

[1] John F. Walvoord, *The Millennial Kingdom* (Grand Rapids: Zondervan Publishing House, 1959), page 63.

[2] Charles Caldwell Ryrie, *Dispensationalism Today* (Chicago: Moody Press, 1965), page 89.

[3] Ibid., page 91.

One of the greatest contrasts between the Reformed and dispensational understanding of "normal" language in the prophets revolves around the question of whether the prophets ever spoke of the future in terms of the past. The Reformed position is that God through the Old Testament prophets revealed selected truths about the coming church age without revealing exhaustively the church age. There were certain mysteries about the church age that were not revealed until New Testament times, such as the believing Gentiles becoming equal members of the people of God under the new covenant without submitting to the Mosaic ceremonial laws as Jewish proselytes. In the Old Testament prophets God revealed these selected truths about the church age in the descriptive context of the Old Testament religious and political economy with which the prophets and their listeners were familiar. God prophetically spoke of the unknown future in terms of then known and understood realities. God, in the prophets, predicted certain essentials of the church age in terms of the concrete details of the Old Testament world even though some of these details would terminate in the coming age. For example, God, in the prophets, revealed that in the Messianic age many Gentiles would worship and serve the God of Abraham along with Israel, but, as mentioned above, with no hint that the ceremonial dividing wall between Jew and Gentile would be torn down. According to the Reformed interpreter, this was God's *normal* way of revealing selected truths about the future. According to the dispensationalist, this would have been a deceptive way for God to have spoken about the future:

> New revelation cannot mean contradictory revelation. Later revelation on a subject does not make the earlier revelation mean something different. It may add to it or even supersede it, but it does not contradict it. A word or concept cannot mean one thing in the Old Testament and take on opposite meaning in the New Testament. If this were so, then the Bible would be filled with contradictions, and God would have to be conceived as deceiving the Old Testament prophets when He revealed to them a nationalistic kingdom, since He would have known all the time that He would completely reverse the concept in later revelation.[4]

> It is almost standard among detractors of the literal method to explain prophecy in terms of "Jewish coloration," "historical and contemporary garb," "Israelitish form," and "Old Testament outer covering." By these slogans, interpreters mean that the words or forms of prophecy are

---

[4]Ibid., pages 94-95.

colored and influenced by the prophet's contemporary backgrounds, and should therefore not be interpreted literally. . . . God allegedly manipulates things before the prophets so that spiritual, heavenly ideas appear in earthly, comprehensible garb.[5]

It is incredible that God should in the most important matters, affecting the interests and the happiness of man and nearly touching his own veracity, clothe them in words, which, *if not true* in their obvious and common sense, *would deceive* the pious and God-fearing of many ages.[6]

The practical result of this understanding of "normal" language in prophecy is the dispensational position that no Old Testament prophecy can refer directly to the church age. For example, since the prophecies about Gentiles worshiping the God of Abraham in the Messianic age are generally given in the descriptive context of the Old Testament religious and political economy, these prophecies must be fulfilled in the coming Jewish age when this religious and political context will be literally reestablished. For these prophecies to be fulfilled in the church age apart from a nationalistic Jewish kingdom would be a divine deception, according to the dispensationalists. The church age, therefore, must be viewed as a totally unrevealed parenthesis in the Jewish program prophesied in the prophets. It is instructive to contrast this view of the church age and the Old Testament prophets with that of the apostle Paul:

Having therefore obtained help of God, I continue unto this day, witnessing both to small and great, saying none other things than those which the prophets and Moses did say should come: that Christ should suffer and that He should rise from the dead, and should shew light unto the people, and *to the Gentiles* (Acts 26:22-23).

In the last chapter we quoted Malachi 1:11 where God prophesied a coming age in which God's name would be great among the Gentile nations. The prophet spoke of the coming day when the God of Abraham would be universally worshiped in terms of the universal offering of incense and pure offerings. The Reformed interpreter sees a direct fulfillment of this prophecy in the church age in which Christians from many nations throughout the world worship the God of Israel. According to this interpretation, Malachi spoke about the

---

[5]Paul Lee Tan, *The Interpretation of Prophecy* (Rockville, Maryland: Assurance Publishers, 1974), pages 217, 218.

[6]George N.H. Peters, *The Theocratic Kingdom* (3 vols.; Grand Rapids: Kregal Press, 1952), 1.315; quoted in Paul Lee Tan, *The Interpretation of Prophecy*, page 222.

coming church age in terms of the Old Testament worship system. To the Reformed interpreter such usage of language in prophecy is both normal and non-deceptive. The dispensationalist insists that this prophecy can be directly fulfilled only in a coming Jewish age in which the worship of God through literal incense and offerings will be reinstituted.

Dr. John F. Walvoord gives an example of the dispensational interpretive mind set:

> The idea that Gentiles should be on exactly the same plane as Israelites and furthermore, in intimate relationship as being members of the same body, is absolutely foreign to the Old Testament. According to Isaiah 61:5, 6, the Gentiles are pictured as being the servants and Israel as the priests of God. While it is true that the Gentiles were promised blessings in the future millennial kingdom, they are never given equality with the Jews in the Old Testament. What was new and unpredicted as far as the Old Testament is concerned, here forms the content of the special revelation given Paul concerning the church, the body of Christ. A Jew or a Gentile who through faith in Christ becomes a member of the body of Christ, by so much is detached from his former situation, and his prophetic program then becomes that of the church rather than that of Jews or Gentiles as such. It is only as the prophetic program of the church as the body of Christ is distinguished from that of Israel or that of the Gentiles that confusion can be avoided in the interpretation of unfulfilled prophecy.[7]

Dr. Walvoord is commenting on Isaiah 61:5-6:

> And strangers shall stand and feed your flocks, and the sons of the alien shall be your plowmen and your vinedressers. But ye shall be named the Priests of the Lord: men shall call you Ministers of our God: ye shall eat of the riches of the Gentiles, and in their glory shall ye boast yourselves.

He is saying that this prophecy can be fulfilled only in the Jewish millennial age where there will be literal Gentile servant status before national Israel and where there will be a revival of the literal Old Testament priesthood. Does not servant mean servant and does not priest mean priest? Is this not the normal meaning of the language as understood by the original recipients? Is this not the fulfillment that many Jews were expecting at the time of Christ? So reasons the dispensationalist. He sees this passage as the prophecy of an age that stands in contrast to the Christian church where believing Jew and Gentile are spiritual equals.

---

[7]See end of chapter, Long Footnote, p. 207.

The Reformed interpreter understands the above prophecy, not in contrast to, but in the light of the New Testament truth that believing Jews and Gentiles are spiritually equal in this age. The prophecy is not teaching that there will be literal Old Testament priests and literal Gentile subservience before national Israel at the time of its fulfillment. The prophecy is not teaching an absolute functional and religious dichotomy between Jews and Gentiles in the Messianic age. The prophecy is simply contrasting the coming age with the Old Testament era during which the Gentiles rejected the God of Israel and generally were hostile toward Israel. In the Messianic age the previously pagan Gentiles will serve the God of Israel as their God. The Jews will exercise a priestly ministry in that salvation will come from the Jews (John 4:22) through the Messiah. And the believing Gentiles will bring, through their service and finances, new outward strength to the people of God. In his exhortation in Romans 15:27 to the Christians at Rome to help the "poor saints which are at Jerusalem," Paul gives an example of a New Testament fulfillment of this prophecy: "For if the Gentiles have been made partakers of their spiritual things, their duty is also to minister unto them in carnal things."

For another example of the contrast in dispensational and Reformed interpretation of prophecy, I shall examine the prophecy found in Zechariah 2:4-5: "Jerusalem shall be inhabited as towns without walls for the multitude of men and cattle therein: for I, saith the Lord, will be unto her a wall of fire round about, and will be the glory in the midst of her." Is the final fulfillment of this prophecy dependent on the literal, earthly city of Jerusalem? There was a partial fulfillment of this prophecy under the old covenant in the city's divine protection during the vulnerable days when her walls were being rebuilt under the leadership of Nehemiah and in the future growth of the city's population.

There is, however, a more significant fulfillment in this age and in the age to come. In this age of the Messiah the forces of hell are the ones in need of defensive walls (Matthew 16:18). Today the Lord Jesus Christ has all authority in heaven and on earth, and the wicked one cannot touch His people (1 John 5:18), for "greater is He who is in them than he who is in the world" (1 John 4:4). The church is no longer on the defensive but is on the Great Commission offensive. The church is no longer isolated from the pagan nations by a wall of ceremonial law but is under orders to go and to disciple the pagan nations. Christ has bound Satan the strong man (Matthew 12:29), and the church is now plundering Satan's treasures as men are translated from the kingdom of darkness to the kingdom of the Son of God's love.

In the New Testament era God's kingdom has expanded from the confining walls of Jewish Jerusalem to include people, together with their possessions, from the uttermost parts of the earth. In the New Testament physical Jerusalem was judged by God to become a desolation (Luke 21:20) and ceased to have significance for God's people (John 4:21; Galatians 4:25; Hebrews 13:14). In the new covenant era God's people are citizens of the antitypical heavenly Jerusalem (Hebrews 12:22; Galatians 4:26; compare Hebrews 11:10,16; Revelation 21:2). Every citizen of the heavenly city is also a living stone in the temple and is filled with the glory of God through the indwelling Spirit. And the blessings of this age are but a foretaste of the blessings of eternity when the heavenly city will descend to the new earth and the glory of the Lord will be its light. These new covenant fulfillments of this prophecy are not dependent on the existence of a literal, earthly, Jewish city. A prophecy spoken in terms of Old Testament physical Jerusalem can be fulfilled in terms of the antitypical heavenly Jerusalem, of which all the elect become members at salvation. There is no need for a future Judaistic age in which Old Testament Jerusalem is rebuilt for the sake of a "literal" fulfillment of prophecy.

I will quickly mention one more prophecy and that from Zechariah. The following is taken from the Messianic prophecy associated with the royal crowning of Joshua the priest:

> Behold, the man whose name is *the Branch*; and he shall grow up out of his place, and he shall build the temple of the Lord: even he shall build the *temple* of the Lord; . . . . And they that are *far off* shall come and build in the temple of the Lord, . . . Zechariah 6:12b-13a,15a

Notice the striking similarity between this prophecy and the message of Paul in Ephesians chapter 2:

> But now in Christ Jesus ye who sometimes were *far off* are made nigh by the blood of Christ. . . . And are built upon the foundation of the apostles and the prophets, Jesus Christ himself being the chief corner stone; in whom all the building fitly framed together groweth unto an *holy temple* in the Lord (Ephesians 2:13, 20-21).

Is the above prophecy from Zechariah directly fulfilled through Jesus Christ building up the spiritual temple of His church with Gentile living stones? Or will Jesus have to build a literal Jewish temple out of literal stones in a future age to fulfill this prophecy? Which of these do you think the Apostle Paul would have regarded as the "normal" interpretation of Zechariah chapter six?

Types

Another profitable area to examine is the "normal" interpretation of prophetic types. If a sportscaster made a comment about a football team recruiting a Goliath for their defensive line, what would be the "normal" understanding of this statement? Should we expect the rookie lineman to be a literal Philistine? Should we expect to see him on the playing field in ancient armor and with a spear whose shaft is like a weaver's beam? Should we expect the rookie to be the resurrected original with his head stitched on? Or should we understand this comment only to mean that the new lineman is an unusually big, powerful and intimidating opponent on the football field and possibly also, depending on the statement's broader context, boastful, disrespectful, defiant, and showy? What would be the "normal" interpretation of the sportscaster's statement?

This figure of speech used by our hypothetical sportscaster is called a prophetic type when used in Biblical prophecy. In using a prophetic type, one takes an event or a person or an institution from the past and uses it to speak of the present or future. The chosen event, person, or institution has both a form and a substance. The substance of Goliath includes being a big, strong, formidable foe. The form of Goliath includes such things as his being a Philistine and an ancient warrior. The substance is the outstanding general characteristic and the real essence of the matter, and the form involves all the detailed but incidental specifics. When a prophetic type is used to divinely predict the distant future, it is not normal to expect an exact reproduction of all the incidental details or a reappearance of the literal original.

An example of a prophetic type is found in the prophecy in Amos 9:11-12 about the resurrection of the fallen booth of David. In a previous chapter we noticed the use of this prophecy in Acts 15 and the controversy over whether it refers to the church age or to the dispensational Jewish millennium. There is also controversy over who is meant by the name *David* in the prophecy. Reformed theologians believe that this prophecy which mentions King David will be fulfilled through his antitype, King Jesus. Some leading dispensational interpreters who are genuinely striving to be consistently literal instead believe that this and other similar prophecies which mention David in the context of the Messianic age[8] must be fulfilled through the literal, resurrected Old Testament David who will be given a millennial viceroyship. For example, observe what Dr. John F. Walvoord says:

> One of the interesting aspects of the millennial government is the fact that resurrected David will apparently be a prince under Christ in administering the millennial kingdom in so far as it relates to Israel. According to Ezekiel, David will act as a shepherd over the people of Israel. . . . Some have interpreted this mention of David as a reference to Christ. However, there is no good reason for not taking it in its ordinary sense inasmuch as David will certainly be raised from the dead and will be on the scene. What would be more natural than to assign him a responsible place in the government of Christ in relation to the people of Israel?[9]

And Dr. J. Dwight Pentecost believes similarly to Walvoord:

> Newell represents this view when he says:

> We must never confuse in our minds this situation. We must believe the plain words of God. David is not the Son of David. Christ, as Son of David, will be King; and David, His father after the flesh, will be *prince*, during the millennium.

> There are several considerations which support this interpretation. (1) It is most consistent with the literal principle of interpretation. (2) David alone could sit as regent in the millennium without violating the prophecies concerning David's reign. . . . It would be concluded that in the government of the millennium David will be appointed a regent over Palestine and will rule over the land as prince, ministering under the authority of Jesus Christ, the King. The prince thus might lead in worship, offer memorial sacrifices, divide the land allotted to him among his faithful seed without violating his position by resurrection.[10]

Literally speaking, David is no more Jesus than Israel is the church. If the prophet had meant Jesus, why did he not say "Son of David"? And if typological interpretation such as this is valid in Amos, then why not elsewhere? To admit its validity here is truly to

---

[8]Isaiah 55:3-4; Jeremiah 30:9; 33:15-17; Ezekiel 34:23-24; 37:24-25; Hosea 3:5.

[9]John F. Walvoord, *Israel in Prophecy* (Grand Rapids: Zondervan Publishing House, 1962), page 121; see also John F. Walvoord, *The Millennial Kingdom*, pages 300-301.

[10]J. Dwight Pentecost, *Things to Come, A Study in Biblical Eschatology* (Grand Rapids: Zondervan Publishing House, 1958), pages 500-501; quotation from William R. Newell, *The Revelation*, page 323.

allow the Reformed camel's nose into one's hermeneutical tent.

Another good example is the prophecy found in the last two verses of the Old Testament (Malachi 4:5-6) that Elijah would precede the coming of the Christ: "Behold, I will send you Elijah the prophet before the coming of the great and dreadful day of the Lord: And he shall turn the heart of the fathers to the children, and the heart of the children to their fathers, lest I come and smite the earth with a curse."

Was this prophecy to be fulfilled through the reappearance of the literal Old Testament Elijah or through a prophet who would come in the spirit and power of Elijah? We read in Luke 1:17 what an angel told Zacharias the following about his yet to be born son, John the Baptist: "And he shall go before [God] in the spirit and power of Elias, to turn the hearts of the fathers to the children, and the disobedient to the wisdom of the just; to make ready a people prepared for the Lord."

This passage indicates that John the Baptist was the fulfillment of both the Elijah prophecy of Malachi 4:5-6 and the preparatory messenger prophecy of Malachi 3:1 and Isaiah 40:3. Later Jesus Christ said the following about John the Baptist and Elijah after John sent his message from prison and after the three disciples saw literal Elijah on the mount of transfiguration:

> For all the prophets and the law prophesied until John. And if ye will receive it, this is Elias, which was for to come (Matthew 11:13-14).

> And [Jesus'] disciples asked him, saying, Why then say the scribes that Elias must first come? And Jesus answered and said unto them, "Elias truly shall first come, and restore all things. But I say unto you, that Elias is come already, and they knew him not, but have done unto him whatsoever they listed. Likewise shall also the Son of man suffer of them." And the disciples understood that he spake of John the Baptist (Matthew 17:10-13). (compare Mark 9:13)

Like Elijah, John the Baptist was a forceful preacher of repentance and judgment who at times lived in desert regions. The only possible exegetical argument against John being the fulfillment of Malachi 4:5-6 is in John 1:19-21; when some priests and Levites from Jerusalem asked John if he were the Christ or Elijah or the Prophet, John answered no. As John Calvin explains in his commentary on these verses, John the Baptist was answering the Jews' question in the spirit in which it was asked. The Jews were expecting the reappearance of the literal Old Testament Elijah before the coming of the Messiah; John the Baptist understood that the Jews by their question were asking him if he were the literal Old Testament Elijah, and John the

Baptist knew himself not to be the literal Old Testament Elijah. John the Baptist fulfilled the Malachi prophecy about the coming Elijah but not in the literal sense expected by the Jews. If "literalism" is correct, why doesn't "Elijah" mean "Elijah"? Is God trying to deceive us or is prophecy written differently?

There are dispensationalists who recognize that John the Baptist directly fulfilled Malachi 4:5-6,[11] but some do not. As evidenced by the following quotation, some dispensationalists, in the name of literalism, are looking for the literal Old Testament Elijah to appear and to fulfill this prophecy before the second coming of Christ:

> We affirm that John's coming does not literally fulfill Malachi's prophecy but typifies and foreshadows the yet-future coming of Elijah the Tishbite. . . . John did not fulfill Malachi's prophecy regarding the coming of Elijah the Tishbite; he is a type and prefigurement of the yet-future Elijah. . . . John the Baptist would have been the personal, literal Elijah had the Jews accepted Christ and His offer of the kingdom.[12]

As I have said, not all dispensationalists accept this interpretation. Even though this interpretation is the most literal and the most consistent with the popular Jewish understanding of the kingdom, it is much like the two-covenant view of the new covenant — difficult to reconcile with the testimony of the New Testament. Dr. Dwight Pentecost, for example, makes this concession:

> . . . the prophecy is interpreted by the Lord as being fulfilled, not in literal Elijah, but in one who comes in Elijah's spirit and power. If literal Elijah must appear Christ could not be making a *bona fide* offer of the kingdom, inasmuch as literal Elijah had to come and John could not have fulfilled that requirement.[13]

That some dispensationalists would defend the literal Elijah interpretation in spite of the witness of the New Testament about John the Baptist does reveal the inadequacies of the dispensational assumptions on prophetic interpretation. Literally speaking, Elijah is no more John

---

[11]Charles Caldwell Ryrie, *The Ryrie Study Bible: The New Testament* (Chicago: Moody Press, 1976), page 25, note on Matthew 11:14; J. Dwight Pentecost, *Things to Come*, pages 309-311.

[12]Paul Lee Tan, *The Interpretation of Prophecy*, pages 185-187; compare C. I. Scofield, editor, *The Scofield Reference Bible* (New York: Oxford University Press, 1909), page 1023, note on Matthew 17:10; J. Dwight Pentecost, *Things to Come*, pages 311-312.

[13]J. Dwight Pentecost, *Things to Come*, page 312.

the Baptist than Israel is the church. If the prophet had meant "someone in the spirit and power of Elijah," then why did he not literally say so? If a "spiritualized" interpretation such as this is valid in Malachi, then why not elsewhere? Considerations such as these and the desire for consistency explain why some dispensationalists are drawn to the literal Elijah theory.

Old Testament in the New Testament

Another interesting area of study is the New Testament's use of Old Testament prophecy. Dispensationalists routinely claim that every fulfillment of prophecy in the New Testament is a strictly literal fulfillment.[14] That claim simply is not true. Look at the fulfillments of prophecy in Matthew 2:13-18 (Mr. Crenshaw has adequately covered the various types, having broken down the types into various categories. However, I just want to summarize them now). Hosea 11:1 spoke of the exodus of Israel from Egypt, and Matthew saw Christ's return to Palestine from Egypt as a fulfillment of Hosea 11:1. Jeremiah 31:15 spoke of the weeping of a metaphorical Rachel, the mother of Benjamin, when Jewish captives were deported to Babylon from Ramah, a city in the territory of Benjamin. Matthew saw Herod's slaughter of the babes at Bethlehem (the place of Rachel's grave) as a fulfillment of Jeremiah 31:15. Matthew leaves no doubt that he is identifying a fulfillment of Old Testament prophecy:

> . . . that it might be fulfilled which was spoken of the Lord by the prophet, . . .(Matthew 2:15)

> Then was fulfilled that which was spoken by Jeremy the prophet, . . .(Matthew 2:17).

Were those literal fulfillments of prophecy? No, they were typological fulfillments in which national Israel was a type of Christ, the ultimate Seed of Abraham.[15] God protecting the nation Israel in Egypt in the nation's infancy during a perilous famine and then calling the nation out of Egypt to Canaan was typologically prophetic of

---

[14]J. Dwight Pentecost, *Things to Come*, pages 10, 61; John F. Walvoord, *The Millennial Kingdom*, page 131; Charles Caldwell Ryrie, *Dispensationalism Today*, page 88; Charles Caldwell Ryrie, *The Basis of the Premillennial Faith* (Neptune, N.J.: Loizeaux Brothers, 1953), page 44.

[15]See Patrick Fairbairn, *The Typology of Scripture Viewed in Connection with the Whole Series of the Divine Dispensations* (Grand Rapids: Baker Book House, 1900, 1975), 1.380-382.

Christ fleeing to Egypt as an infant until the death of Herod. Also, the grief at Ramah where the Babylonians assembled the last band of Jewish captives was typologically prophetic of Herod's attempt to destroy the Messianic Seed of Abraham. Not all the fulfillments of prophecy mentioned in the New Testament are strictly literal fulfillments.

Whenever a New Testament fulfillment of an Old Testament prophecy is not literal enough for the dispensationalist, the dispensationalist simply argues that the fulfillment really was not a fulfillment. Such fulfillments are classified as illustrations, foreshadowings, kingdom breakthroughs, prefigurements, types, and so on. They are said not to be either direct fulfillments or the event the prophet actually predicted. Only by classifying fulfillments in this way is the dispensationalist able to argue that all the fulfillments of the Old Testament found in the New Testament are literal fulfillments, which is, of course, circular reasoning.

Scripture Interprets Scripture

A last area to examine is the relative emphasis placed on Scripture interpreting Scripture in the two systems. Dr. Charles C. Ryrie charges the covenant theologian's use of this principle with the following:

> . . . as a result of the covenant of grace idea, covenant theology has been forced to place as its most basic principle of interpretation the principle of interpreting the Old Testament by the New. . . .
>
> Of course, there is everything right about letting the New Testament guide us in our understanding of the Old Testament, but everything wrong about imposing the New Testament on the Old. And this is exactly what the covenant theologian does under the guise of a basic hermeneutical principle which is allowable only if rightly used. The covenant theologian in his zeal to make Christ all in all is guilty of superimposing Him arbitrarily on the Old Testament. He does the same thing with the doctrine of the Church and with the concept of salvation through faith in Christ.[16]

Reformed prophetic interpretation does place a great emphasis on allowing Scripture to interpret Scripture. If Peter indicated that Joel's prophecy about the outpouring of the Spirit was fulfilled at Pentecost, then that should influence one's interpretation of Joel's prophecy. If Paul said that the true Seed of Abraham is Christ and those in covenant

---

[16]Charles Caldwell Ryrie, *Dispensationalism Today*, page 187.

union with Christ (Galatians 3:16, 29), then that should influence one's interpretation of the Abrahamic covenant. If the author of Hebrews associates the heavenly Jerusalem with the Abrahamic land promise (Hebrews 11:8-16) and if Paul associates the Abrahamic land promise with the entire world (Romans 4:13), then that should influence one's understanding of the Abrahamic land promise. The supposition here is that the only infallible interpreter of Scripture is Scripture itself, and the fallible human interpreter should study this infallible and inspired interpretation of prophecy as a guide to all prophetic interpretation. The dispensationalist, however, rejects this as reading the New Testament back into the Old Testament.[17]

The Reformed interpreter regards the New Testament as the source of an added clarity and fullness in the understanding of the Old Testament that was not available to the Old Testament saint. This position is consistent with the Scriptural teaching that God's truth is revealed with greatest clarity in the New Testament. Moses was said to be superior to the other Old Testament prophets in that God spoke clearly to him and not in dark sayings (Numbers 12:6-8). Not another prophet like Moses, "whom the Lord knew face to face" (Deuteronomy 34:10), arose until the Christ, who was counted worthy of more glory than Moses (Hebrews 3:3) and who was the prophesied Prophet like unto Moses (Deuteronomy 18:15, 18; Acts 3:22). In the Old Testament God spoke through the prophets "at sundry times and in divers manners," but He has "in these last days spoken unto us by His Son," who is "the express image of His person" (Hebrews 1:1-3), who has seen the Father (John 6:46), who has explained God (John 1:18), and who descended from heaven to bear witness to what He has seen (John 3:11-13). Through the inspiration of the outpoured Spirit, this apex of revelation continued with the Apostles (John 14:26; 16:13-14). The New Testament then is the final, full, and clearest revelation of God.

The Old Testament is the foundation and background of the New Testament and is indispensable for the proper understanding of the New Testament. The New Testament is the infallible revelation of the divine development of the Old Testament program in the fullness of time and is indispensable for understanding the Old Testament with new covenant clarity. The New Testament tells us about the Old Testament like an oak tree tells us about an acorn. The man who has

---

[17]See end of chapter, Long Footnotes, p. 208.

seen the fully grown oak can better understand the significance and meaning of the acorn.

To use another illustration, the New Testament aids in the understanding of the Old Testament like observing a specimen under a microscope with a higher magnification aids in understanding what is seen with a lower magnification. Let us say that two men are observing a specimen magnified twenty times but that one of them also has seen the same specimen magnified one hundred times. That man who has seen the greater magnification will be aware of details the other man cannot even see, and he will more accurately understand and interpret those details that both men can see with the lesser magnification. According to Reformed interpretation, we today, with the aid of the New Testament, can better understand the implications and meaning of the Old Testament than could the original recipients of that revelation because we have had the privilege of observing the same specimen (God's truth) under greater magnification (compare 1 Peter 1:10-12). Many prophets desired to see those things which we have seen but did not see them (Luke 10:24).

I have contrasted the basic differences between the Reformed and the dispensational understandings of Old Testament prophecy. These two schools disagree on prophetic interpretation, and the implications of this disagreement are great. If the Reformed principles are correct, then the church age is a continuing fulfillment of many Old Testament prophecies about the Messianic age and Old Testament prophecy applies directly to the Christian. If the dispensational principles are correct, then the church age becomes an unrevealed parenthesis in the prophesied Messianic program and Old Testament prophecy applies directly only to the tribulation, the millennium, and eternity. The Reformed interpretation is the only one that is consistent with Scripture!

LONG FOOTNOTES

[7] John F. Walvoord, *The Church in Prophecy* (Grand Rapids: Zondervan Publishing House, 1964), pages 46-47.

"That the Gentiles should be fellow heirs and of the same body is not a recognition of the Old Testament prediction that, during Israel's coming kingdom glory, Gentiles will be raised to a subordinate participation in those covenant blessings (Isa. 60:12). Those predictions were of an earthly calling, and, being revealed in very much Old Testament prophecy, could be no part of the heavenly calling — the 'mystery . . . hid in God.' This mystery is of a present uniting of Jews and Gentiles into one Body — a new divine purpose, and, therefore, in no sense the perpetuation of anything which has been before." Lewis Sperry Chafer, *Systematic Theology, 8 vols.* (Dallas: Dallas Seminary Press, 1948), 4:76-77.

Notice the long list of Old Testament prophecies about Gentiles that are said to be fulfilled in the millennium as opposed to the church age in the following quotation: "The universal aspects of the Abrahamic covenant, which promised universal blessing, will be realized in that age [the Millennium]. The Gentiles will be brought into relationship with the King. (1) The fact of the Gentiles' participation in the millennium is promised in prophetic Scriptures (Isa. 2:4; 11:12; 16:1-5; 18:1-7; 19:16-25; 23:18; 42:1; 45:14; 49:6; 22; 59:16-18; 60:1-14; 61:8-9; 62:2; 66:18-19; Jer. 3:17: 16:19-21; 49:6; 49:39; Ezek. 38:23; Amos 9:12; Mic. 7:16-17; Zeph. 2:11; Zech. 8:20-22; 9:10; 10:11-12; 14:16-19)." J. Dwight Pentecost, *Things to Come*, pages 507-508.

[17] "Nondispensational interpreters (of the covenant theology school) have been guilty of reading back (and sometimes forcing back) the teaching of the New Testament into the Old especially in order to try to substantiate their doctrine of salvation in the Old Testament. . . . Covenant theology allows for and even demands this reading back of the New Testament into the Old." C. C. Ryrie, *Dispensationalism Today*, page 34.

Chapter Seventeen

Dispensationalism: Rightly Dividing the Word

I can distinctly remember the time during my college days when a Christian whom God used in my life gave me a short introduction to dispensationalism. He quoted 2 Timothy 2:15 from the King James Version and pointed out the importance of "rightly dividing the word of truth." He then summarized the seven dispensations of the *Scofield Reference Bible*: 1) from creation to the fall, Innocency; 2) from the fall to the flood, Conscience; 3) from the flood to the Abrahamic covenant, Human Government; 4) from the Abrahamic covenant to the Mosaic covenant, Promise; 5) from the Mosaic covenant to the cross, Law; 6) from the cross to the rapture, Grace; and 7) from the second advent to eternity, Kingdom.[1] Now that I have rejected dispensationalism, I still regard this set of divisions, apart from any hidden significance that the names of the various dispensations might have, as a reasonable way to divide the dispensations, except that I am no longer a premillennialist or a pre-tribulation rapturist. I also no longer believe that 2 Timothy is directly referring to dividing Biblical history into different divine economies. The American Standard Version translates this verse "handling aright the word of truth," which better conveys the original Greek. Nevertheless, Christians have

[1]Charles Caldwell Ryrie, *Dispensationalism Today* (Chicago: Moody Press, 1965), page 84; C. I. Scofield, editor, *The Scofield Reference Bible* (New York: Oxford University Press, 1909), page 5 note 4 on Genesis 1:28.

recognized from earliest times that God has worked through different spiritual economies in different ages. Dividing Biblical history into different dispensational periods is not distinctive of dispensationalism. To say that all Christians who do not today offer animal sacrifices and who do not today worship on Saturday are at least incipient dispensationalists is extremely simplistic.[2] The particular number and choice of historical division points presented by Scofield do not define dispensationalism either. The true distinctives are found on a more subtle level.

I believe that we can see at least one real distinctive of dispensationalism's "rightly dividing the Word" by examining Scofield's definition of a dispensation: "A dispensation is a period of time during which man is tested in respect of obedience to some *specific* revelation of the will of God."[3] Now it is true that in every divine economy God gave further revelation of Himself and His will, and man was responsible for responding to that revelation in obedience. It is also true, as pointed out by dispensationalists, that man apart from God's saving grace will always fail the test of obedience because of man's depraved nature. God's judgment on man's disobedience is seen in the expulsion from the garden, in the flood, in the confusion of tongues at the tower of Babel, in the Babylonian captivity, in the Roman destruction of Jerusalem, and in the judgment on the final rebellion (Revelation 20:7-10). Although there is truth in Scofield's definition and scheme, there is also error. Dispensationalists and Reformed theologians disagree about the relationship that revelation given to past dispensations has to the present dispensation.

Dispensationalists teach that such past revelation is not binding today except to the extent that it is reaffirmed in the revelation given specifically for this present dispensation. Past revelation that is reaffirmed for the present is said to have a secondary and indirect application today because of the presence of timeless principles. In contrast Reformed theologians teach that past revelation continues to be binding today except to the extent that it was time bound or situation specific in its original application or to the extent that it has been modified by the more recent Biblical revelations because of the developments in God's program for the ages. An example of such a modification would be the New Testament teaching that the people of

---

[2]See end of chapter, Long Footnotes, p. 224.

[3]C. I. Scofield, editor, *The Scofield Reference Bible*, page 5 note 4.

God in this age are no longer to externally administer the Old Testament ceremonial laws, although the spiritual import and message of these laws continue to be valid. Like Christ, the Reformed theologian emphasizes the continuing relevance of God's former revelations (Matthew 5:17-19), whereas the dispensationalist puts the emphasis on the nonbinding nature of past revelation that is not specifically reaffirmed for today. This difference in emphasis is implied in Scofield's statement that each dispensation is related to "some *specific* revelation," as if each dispensation is limited to the revelation specifically directed to that dispensation.

The Law

To better appreciate the distinctives of dispensationalism's "rightly dividing the word," one needs to think through the dispensational explanation of Biblical history. A good place to start is the Abrahamic covenant and the dispensation of Promise. Here God provided a salvation administered on a by-faith basis and administered without moral conditions.[4] All went well for the people of God until Mount Sinai where a rash and tragic mistake occurred. There the people of God rashly abandoned their unconditional by-faith covenant position and instead tragically accepted the conditional and legalistic Mosaic covenant. Drs. Scofield and Chafer give us insight into the dispensational explanation of Mount Sinai:

> The Dispensation of Promise ended when Israel rashly accepted the law (Ex. 19.8). Grace had prepared a deliverer (Moses), provided a sacrifice for the guilty, and by divine power brought them out of bondage (Ex. 19.4); but at Sinai they exchanged grace for law.[5]

> When the Law was proposed, the children of Israel deliberately forsook their position under the grace of God which had been their relationship to God until that day, and placed themselves under the Law. . . .

> While it is certain that Jehovah knew the choice that the people would make, it is equally certain that their choice was in no way *required* by Him. . . . The surrender of the blessings of grace should have been allowed by these people on no condition whatsoever. Had they said at

---

[4] "This [Abrahamic] covenant, being without human condition, simply declares the unchanging purpose of Jehovah. It will be achieved in pure grace, apart from every human factor, and its accomplishments are eternal." Lewis Sperry Chafer, *Systematic Theology, 8 vols.* (Dallas: Dallas Seminary Press, 1948), 4:235.

[5] C. I. Scofield, editor, *The Scofield Reference Bible*, page 20 note 1 on Genesis 12:1.

the hearing of the impossible law, "None of these things can we do. We crave only to remain in that boundless mercy of God, who has loved us, and sought us, and saved us from all our enemies, and who will bring us to Himself," it is evident that such an appeal would have reached the very heart of God. And the surpassing glory of His grace would have been extended to them without bounds; for grace above all else is the delight of the heart of God. In place of the eagles' wings by which they were carried unto God, they confidently chose a covenant of works when they said: "All that the Lord hath spoken we will do." They were called on to face a concrete choice between the mercy of God which had followed them, and a new and hopeless covenant of works. They fell from grace. . . .

Upon the determined choice of law, the mountain where God was revealed became a terrible spectacle of the unapproachable, holy character of God. . . . He who had brought them to Himself under the unconditional blessings of grace, must now warn them lest they break through unto the Lord and perish. . . .

The children of Israel definitely chose the covenant of works, which is law, as their relationship to God.[6]

[ED. NOTE: What a weak view of God's holiness as revealed in His law. And the Jews allegedly had the option to reject this holy law in favor of "grace." And what law would they have followed for their morality? Why, their own, of course. They would have been as God, "knowing — or better, as the Hebrew means — *determining* (for themselves) good and evil." This is one of the greatest dangers of dispensationalism, that man is "free" to determine his own law, his own morality, to reject the Old Testament for a "greater" ethic. Mark it down that *whoever* makes the law for an individual, a family, a nation, that one is the god of the respective individual, family, or nation. Whomever one obeys, that one is his god. There is no compromising possible. Is one "free" to determine his own ethic or morality with impunity, as our pluralistic society would lead us to believe? Or is a nation "free" to determine its own morality with God's blessing, as the dispensationalists often argue?

I sat in their classes and churches and heard them say that the Christians have no "right" to force "their" morality on unbelievers,

---

[6]Lewis Sperry Chafer, *Systematic Theology*, 4:162-164. See also Charles L. Feinberg, *Millennialism: The Two Major Views, Third and Enlarged Edition* (Chicago: Moody Press, 1936), page 217. I might mention that the Bible's evaluation of Mount Sinai and the response of Israel to the law is in marked contrast to Dr. Chafer's evaluation (Deuteronomy 5:27-28).

which means that the government has the right to artificially manufacture its own "morality." Can one have or not have an abortion with
equal exemption from punishment? Or is there a God in heaven who
takes vengeance on the slighest deviation from His morality, His law,
and His ethic, who will not be mocked and who judges according to
man's works and His law (Gal. 6:7; James 2:8-12)? End Ed. note,
which was done by Curtis Crenshaw]

Contrast this traditional dispensational evaluation of Mount Sinai
with the Biblical evaluation of Mount Sinai:

> And Moses called all Israel, and said unto them, . . . The Lord our
> God made a covenant with us in Horeb. . . . The Lord talked with you
> face to face in the mount out of the midst of the fire. . . . And it came to
> pass, when ye heard the voice out of the midst of the darkness, (for the
> mountain did burn with fire,) that ye came near unto me, even all the
> heads of your tribes and your elders; and ye said, . . . Go thou near, and
> hear all that the Lord our God shall say: and speak thou unto us all that
> the Lord our God shall speak unto thee; and *we will hear it, and do it.*
> And the Lord heard the voice of your words, when ye spake unto me;
> and the Lord said unto me, I have heard the voice of the words of this
> people, which they have spoken unto thee: *they have well said all that
> they have spoken* (Deuteronomy 5:1, 2, 4, 23, 27-28).

According to dispensational authorities such as Dr. Chafer, by-
faith salvation based on an imputed righteousness was abandoned at
Mount Sinai and was not resumed until after Mount Calvary.[7] During
this period of law, there was no divine enablement and the people of
God obeyed the law in the power of the flesh.[8] Many, if not most,
dispensationalists teach that there was no enablement through a universal indwelling of the Holy Spirit among the Old Testament saints,[9]
and some also teach that there was no enablement through regeneration under the old covenant.[10] If the Old Testament saints did not have
the indwelling Holy Spirit or new power, then they were limited to
the energy of sinful flesh in obeying God's law.

---

[7] See end of chapter, Long Footnotes, p. 224.

[8] See end of chapter, Long Footnotes, p. 225.

[9] Dr. John F. Walvoord, *The Holy Spirit* (Grand Rapids: Zondervan Publishing House, 1954,1958), pages 71, 73, 75; Charles Caldwell Ryrie, *Dispensationalism Today*, page 120; C. I. Scofield, editor, *The Scofield Reference Bible*, page 982; J. Dwight Pentecost, *Things to Come, A Study in Biblical Eschatology* (Grand Rapids: Zondervan Publishing House, 1958), page 271.

[10] See end of chapter, Long Footnotes, p. 226.

[ED. NOTE: In other words, none were saved from Sinai to Calvary. Paul says, however, that David received imputed righteousness by faith (Rom. 4:5-8). Note by Curtis Crenshaw].

If one considers the period from the Abrahamic covenant to the end time church rapture, the Mosaic covenant was a legalistic parenthesis in a by-faith administration of grace that began in the dispensation of Promise and resumed in the dispensation of Grace.[11] If one considers the period from the Mosaic covenant to the end of the millennium, the church age is a parenthesis of grace in a meritorious administration of law since the post-rapture tribulation is a recontinuance of the dispensation of law and since the millennium will be a period of legalistic kingdom law that is similar to Mosaic law.[12] It is only fair to mention that some recent dispensationalists have, in various degrees, modified this excessively rigid dichotomy between law and grace in their explanations of redemptive history and have begun to drift toward the teachings on law and grace more traditionally held by Reformed theologians.

The Gospels and Acts

The next major development in the dispensational explanation of the Bible is the dispensational interpretation of the Gospels and the early chapters of Acts. According to dispensationalism John the Baptist was announcing and Jesus was offering a Judaistic political kingdom. Even though this was the sort of kingdom that the dispensationalists say the Jews were expecting and wanting, Israel as a nation rejected Christ and His offer. In judgment on Israel's unbelief, Christ postponed the Jewish kingdom and inaugurated the parenthetical and previously unrevealed church age. Because of this analysis of the ministry of Christ, dispensationalists see the Gospels as a complex combination of truth relating directly to three different dispensations: law, grace, and kingdom.[13] The preaching of John the Baptist[14] and Christ's Sermon on the Mount were legal discourses related to Jewish kingdom truth and not directly intended for the church age. For example, Dr. Chafer in his *Systematic Theology* gave the following

---

[11]See end of chapter, Long Footnotes, p. 226.

[12]See end of chapter, Long Footnotes, p. 226.

[13]See end of chapter, Long Footnotes, p. 227.

[14]Ibid., 4:214-215.

dispensational analysis of Christ's Sermon on the Mount:

There is in the Sermon on the Mount a recognition of the Father and the Messiah-Son, but no reference will be found to the Holy Spirit whose indwelling and limitless ministry is so great a factor in this age of the Church. There is no reference to the death of Christ with its redemption, reconciliation, and propitiation values. There is no regeneration and no mention of the faith principle as a way into the saving grace of God. There is a reference to faith as a life principle (Matt. 6:25-34), but this is in no way related to salvation from sin. The great truth of a New Creation procured and secured through the resurrection of Christ is wholly wanting in this address. The phrase "in Christ" with its infinite meaning relative to positions and possessions is not present, nor is even one of those positions or possessions hinted at throughout its more than one hundred verses. No enabling power whereby these great demands both in character and conduct may be realized is intimated. It represents a human responsibility. The great word *justification* could not possibly be introduced nor that imputed righteousness on which justification is founded. How far removed is a mere man-wrought righteousness which exceeds the righteousness of the scribes and the Pharisees (Matt. 5:20) from the "gift of righteousness" bestowed on those who receive "abundance of grace" (Rom. 5:17)! And how great is the difference between those who hunger and thirst after righteousness (Matt. 5:6) and those who are "made the righteousness of God in him" (2 Cor. 5:21)! Thus, also, great is the difference between those who are in danger of hell fire (Matt. 5:22, 29-30) and those who are justified on a principle of perfect divine justice who have done no more than believe in Jesus — even the ungodly (Rom. 3:26; 4:5). Thus, again, notice should be made of the divergence between those who obtain mercy by being merciful (Matt. 5:7) and those who have found everlasting mercy even when dead in sins (Eph. 2:4-5), likewise between those who hope to be forgiven on the ground of their own forgiveness of others (Matt. 6:12-15) and those who for Christ's sake have been forgiven (Eph. 4:32; Col. 3:13). And, yet again, consideration must be given to a distinction between those who follow a course — strait and narrow — with the goal in view that they may find life at the end of that path (Matt. 7:14) and those to whom eternal life has been given as a present possession (John 3:36; Rom. 6:23; 1 John 5:11-12). Finally, far removed is a situation in which some hear the Lord say, "I never knew you: depart from me, ye that work iniquity" (Matt. 7:23) and an assurance that one trusting in Christ "shall never perish" (John 10:28; Rom. 8:1).[15]

---

[15]Ibid., 5:112-113; compare 4:216f. "Sad, indeed, is the spectacle when Christians assume that the Sermon on the Mount represents the high calling of the Church and attempt to modify the character of sovereign grace to the end that it may conform to a merit system." Lewis Sperry Chafer, *Systematic Theology*, 5.109.

Dr. Scofield said:

> . . . the Lord's prayer is, dispensationally, upon legal, not church ground; it is not a prayer in the name of Christ . . .; and it makes human forgiveness, as under the law it must, the condition of divine forgiveness; an order which grace exactly reverses . . .[16]

Likewise Ryrie said:

> It is usually charged that dispensationalists teach that the Sermon on the Mount is all law and no gospel. To those who object to this claim, we merely ask, Where can one find a statement of the gospel in the Sermon?[17]

Dispensationalists regard the Sermon on the Mount as the Messiah's manifesto of the kingdom He would have then set up if Israel had accepted Him. Israel, however, did not accept Him, and Jesus began looking away from the prophesied Messianic age and the earthly people (the Jews) to the unrevealed, parenthetical church age and the heavenly people (the church). The parables of Matthew 13, which obviously refer to the church age, are interpreted by dispensationalists as an initial explanation of some of the unexpected mysteries of the coming age because of this postponement of the Jewish millennium and the unrevealed introduction of the church age. According to Dr. J. Dwight Pentecost:

> This thirteenth chapter holds a unique place in the development of the Gospel. . . . Christ shows that both He and His forerunner have been rejected (11:1-9), and this rejection will result in judgment (11:20-24). . . . In chapter 12 the rejection comes to a climax. . . . As the chapter closes (12:46-50) the Lord indicates that He is setting aside all natural relationships, such as Israel sustained to Him and to covenant promises by a physical birth, and establishes a new relationship, based on faith. . . . Since this kingdom was the subject of an irrevocable covenant it was unthinkable that it could be abandoned. The chapter gives the events in the development of the kingdom program from the time of its rejection until it is received when the nation welcomes the King at His second advent.[18]

---

[16]C. I. Scofield, editor, *The Scofield Reference Bible*, page 1089-1090 note 1 on Luke 11:1; see also page 1002 note 1 on Matt. 6:12. Compare Lewis Sperry Chafer, *Systematic Theology*, 4:221-222.

[17]Charles Caldwell Ryrie, *Dispensationalism Today*, page 108.

[18]J. Dwight Pentecost, *Things to Come*, pages 140-142.

The mystery form of the kingdom, then, has reference to the age between the two advents of Christ. The mysteries of the kingdom of heaven describe the conditions that prevail on the earth in that interim while the king is absent. These mysteries thus relate this present age to the eternal purposes of God in regard to His kingdom.[19]

Dr. Pentecost gives his dispensational interpretation of these parables of the kingdom in mystery form. The parable of the wheat and the tares "has primary reference to Israel during the tribulation period." The parable of the mustard seed teaches that the church age "is characterized by abnormal external growth." "That which was to be an herb has become a tree — it has developed into a monstrosity" and has become the resting place for metaphorical birds representing the enemies of God's program. The parable of the leaven reveals "that there will rise a religious system that will introduce a corrupting element into the doctrine of the person of Christ." The parable of the hid treasure depicts "the relationship of Israel to this present age" and the parable of the pearl of great price relates to the Christ's church which, "like a pearl, can only become His adornment by being lifted out of the place in which it was formed [i.e., the rapture]."[20]

After giving the parables of the kingdom in mystery form, Christ began speaking of both the coming parenthetical church age and the future Jewish tribulation and millennium when the prophesied but postponed kingdom program would be resumed. Matthew 16:18 is where Christ first openly revealed His plans to establish the church.[21] As we noted in a previous chapter, dispensationalists argue that Christ's statement "I will build My church" is a strong argument that the church was then an absolutely new spiritual entity. Matthew 18:17 is where Christ gave church truth on discipline. The Olivet Discourse (Matthew 24) is a detailed prophecy of the seven year Jewish tribulation period after the church rapture. The upper room discourse (John 14-16) that occured a few days later is church truth. The apostles in Acts 1:6 represented the Jewish remnant when they asked the risen Christ if He were then going to restore the kingdom to Israel. In Acts 2 on Pentecost the disciples preached church truth. On the other hand, according to some dispensationalists, the apostles in Acts 3:12-26 again offered the Judaistic kingdom to the Jewish nation one last

---

[19]Ibid., page 143.

[20]Ibid., pages 146-149.

[21]Ibid., page 201

time.[22] If the Jews had accepted this reoffer, the church rapture would have then occurred and the seven year Jewish tribulation period would have begun after an extremely short church age. [The moderate dispensationalists tend not to believe in a millennial offer.]

After Pentecost, Paul, the apostle to the Gentiles, was called and the emphasis progressively turned away from Israel to the formation of the largely Gentile church. The rest of the book of Acts is viewed by dispensationalists as definitely church truth. A problem for the dispensationalist is the frequent reference to the kingdom both in Acts and in the epistles written during that period. Dispensationalists explain that the kingdom referred to is not the theocratic Messianic kingdom of Old Testament prophecy but instead is either God's nontheocratic sovereign rule of providence or is "the kingdom in mystery form" of Matthew 13, which dispensationalists interpret as a name applicable to the non-kingdom church age. Dispensationalist Dr. Paul Lee Tan explains the present relevance of the kingdom as follows:

> It is true that the kingdom promised by the prophets was pos-tponed when the Messiah in the person of Jesus Christ was rejected. Nevertheless, during the present inter-advent age, the kingdom is anticipatorily present and has its present outworkings.[23]

Explanations such as these do not satisfy the ultradispensationalists who view Acts and the epistles of that period as Jewish truth and not as truth for the later Gentile Pauline Body and Bride of Christ.

Most dispensationalists believe that the parenthetical church age will end with a secret rapture before the beginning of a seven-year Jewish tribulation period which is identified as the seventieth of the seventy weeks of Daniel 9. The saints who are alive at that time will be translated into resurrection bodies and then be caught up to meet the Lord in the air (1 Thessalonians 4:16-17). Dispensationalists define the "dead in Christ" who are resurrected just before the rapture as the deceased saints who were saved after the Pentecost of Acts 2. According to Dr. John F. Walvoord: "The expression 'the dead in Christ shall arise first' (1 Thess. 4:16) seems to include only the church. The Old Testament saints are never described by the phrase

---

[22]C.I. Scofield, editor, *The Scofield Reference Bible*, page 1153 note 1 on Acts 3:20; J. Dwight Pentecost, *Things to Come*, page 469.

[23]Paul Lee Tan, *The Interpretation of Prophecy* (Rockville, Maryland: Assurance Publishers, 1974), page 311.

'in Christ'."[24]

After the tribulation Christ will return and resurrect the saved of all ages, except, of course, the "in Christ" saints who were resurrected or raptured seven years earlier. The earth will be populated by the believers who survived the tribulation period, and all the resurrected saints of all ages will go to abide in the heavenly Jerusalem that will descend to hover over Palestine during the millennium.[25] Christ will bind Satan, set up a national, Jewish kingdom and reign both on earth and from the heavenly city for 1000 years. Death will be rare or even non-existent except as a penal measure for overt sin.[26] The spirits of wicked millennial residents who die will go to hell to await the final judgment, and I have heard the opinion that millennial saints who die during the millennium will be immediately resurrected and will enter the heavenly city as resurrected saints. At the end of the millennium Satan will be loosed and will inspire a military revolt which Christ will quickly put down. The earthly millennial saints will be judged and translated into resurrected bodies and the eternal state.[27] Then the unsaved dead of all ages will be resurrected and condemned with Satan to the lake of fire at the great white throne judgment. The earth will be purged with fire, the new heavens and the new earth will be formed, the heavenly city will descend to earth, and eternity will begin.

This is the dispensational explanation of redemptive history. A significant difference between this view of redemptive history and the Reformed view is the unifying theme. In Reformed interpretation, the unifying theme that is the key to understanding the development of redemptive history is the saving work of Jesus Christ. God created Adam and gave him the earth to rule and to subdue. Because of Adam's fall into sin, the earth was cursed and man became a servant of sin and Satan. God immediately promised a coming Seed of woman who would overcome Satan and reverse the effects of the fall. The rest

---

[24] John F. Walvoord, *The Rapture Question* (Grand Rapids: Zondervan Publishing House, 1957), page 154; compare John F. Walvoord, *The Millennial Kingdom* (Grand Rapids: Zondervan Publishing House, 1959), page 280; J. Dwight Pentecost, *Things To Come*, p. 407; C. C. Ryrie, *Dispensationalism Today*, p. 136.

[25] John F. Walvoord, *The Millennial Kingdom*, pages 291, 302, 317, 324-326; J. Dwight Pentecost, *Things to Come*, pages 411, 414-415, 542, 546; Charles Caldwell Ryrie, *Dispensationalism Today*, pages 146-147.

[26] J. Dwight Pentecost, *Things to Come*, page 277; John F. Walvoord, *The Millennial Kingdom*, pages 317-318.

[27] John F. Walvoord, *The Millennial Kingdom*, pages 277, 328.

of redemptive history is the developing story of the restoration of fallen man's earthly inheritance and authority through the work of the Seed Redeemer on behalf of His people. The theocracy of Old Testament Israel fits into this redemptive drama as a localized pledge and prefiguration of the coming perfect kingdom rule and everlasting earthly inheritance that the Christ will establish for His people and as the national means through which the Christ was brought into the world. Through the historical work of Jesus Christ, Satan was defeated and Jesus of Nazareth, who is fully man as well as fully God, was exalted to the place of all authority in heaven and on earth. In this age Christ is exercising His authority, the nations are being discipled, and Christ's universal rule over men is being extended to the uttermost parts of the earth. The drama of redemption will find its ultimate and final fulfillment in the glorified new earth of Revelation 21 after Christ returns.

The dispensationalist rejects this concept of a Christological-soteriological unity to redemptive history and also claims to be the only one to have an adequate concept of progressive revelation. Walvoord and Ryrie respectively comment:

> Covenant theology is the view that all the dispensations from Adam to the end of human history are aspects of God's soteriological program. In other words, the dispensations are different pre-sentations of the way of salvation in a gradually unfolding progression. The tendency of this viewpoint is to regard God's general purpose as essentially that of saving the elect, to blend the various Biblical revelations regarding Israel, the Gentiles, and the church into one stream, and to minimize the differences between the various dispensations. In contrast, the dispensational theology, while not disputing the view of the unity of God's plan of salvation, finds in the various dispensations periods of stewardship which are not directly related to salvation. In a word, the dispensationalist does not consider the program of God for salvation as the sole purpose of God, and in fact denies that some of the dispensations are basically soteriological.[28]

> The covenant theologian in his zeal to make Christ all in all is guilty of superimposing Him arbitrarily on the Old Testament. He does the same with the doctrine of the Church and with the concept of salvation through faith in Christ.[29]

---

[28]Ibid., pages 79-80.

[29]Charles Caldwell Ryrie, *Dispensationalism Today*, page 187.

The hermeneutical straitjacket which covenant theology forces on the Scriptures results in reading the New Testament back into the Old Testament and in an artificial typological interpretation.[30]

Only dispensationalism does justice to the proper concept of the progress of revelation. . . . Covenant theology . . . because of the rigidity of its unifying principle of the covenant of grace can never show within its system proper progress of revelation. . . . Only dispensationalism can cause historical events and successions to be seen in their own light and not to be reflected in the artificial light of an overall covenant.[31]

Dispensationalism alone has a broad enough unifying principle to do justice to the unity of the progress of revelation on the one hand and the distinctiveness of the various stages in that progress on the other. Covenant theology can only emphasize the unity, and in so doing overemphasizes it until it becomes the sole governing category of interpretation.[32]

Despite Dr. Ryrie's bold claims, dispensationalism provides an inadequate basis for demonstrating the unity of the Word of God.

What is the unifying theme that holds together the dispensational explanation of redemptive history? I believe it is the theocratic kingdom. Dr. Lewis Sperry Chafer traces the theocratic kingdom from the time of the judges to eternity,[33] and Dr. J. Dwight Pentecost traces it from Eden to eternity.[34] The church age fits in this explanation of redemptive history as a parenthesis in the progression. It would even be hypothetically possible to omit the church age altogether. Dr. Chafer describes the parenthetical nature of the church age:

But for the Church intercalation — which was wholly unforeseen and is wholly unrelated to any divine purpose which precedes it or which follows it — Israel would be expected to pass directly from the crucifixion to her kingdom; for it was not the death of Christ and His resurrection which demanded the postponement, but rather an unforeseen age. It should require no great effort to notice that the recognition of this age — wholly unforeseen, wholly unrelated, and itself a strict intercalation — is the key to the understanding of the entire program of God in the ages, and

---

[30]Ibid., page 190.

[31]Ibid., pages 19-20.

[32]Ibid., page 35.

[33]Lewis Sperry Chafer, *Systematic Theology*, 5:333-358.

[34]J. Dwight Pentecost, *Things to Come*, pages 433-494.

without that key only confusion would result.[35]

My opinion is that a unifying theme that can logically omit a most important and significant stage of development is not an adequate unifying theme.

Dr. Charles C. Ryrie teaches that the glory of God is the unifying theme in redemptive history:

> No dispensationalist minimizes the importance of God's saving purpose in the world. But whether it is God's total purpose or even His principle purpose is open to question. The dispensationalist sees a broader purpose in God's program for the world than salvation, and that purpose is His own glory. For the dispensationalist the glory of God is the governing principle and overall purpose, and the soteriological program is one of the principal means employed in bringing to pass the greatest demonstration of His own glory. Salvation is part and parcel of God's program, but it cannot be equated with the entire purpose itself. . . . the unifying principle of covenant theology is in practice, soteriological. The unifying principle of dispensationalism is doxological, or the glory of God as He manifests His character in the differing stewardships given to man.[36]

Reformed theologians believe that the glory of God is the final purpose in all that happens but not the unifying theme that ties together the drama of redemptive history. Because God's glory is the final purpose in all that happens, every segment of redemptive history is related to God's glory. But finding a common factor in those segments is not the same thing as demonstrating that a certain theme is progressively developed and revealed in those segments.

Dr. Ryrie lists five purposes through which God's glory is manifest in redemptive history: "the program of redemption, the program of Israel, the punishment of the wicked, the plan for the angels, and the glory of God through nature."[37] Closer examination will reveal that these are not five independent purposes whose only common link is the glory of God. "The punishment of the wicked, the plan for the angels, and the glory of God through nature" are related progressively and developmentally to "the program of redemption." In redemptive history the angels function as "ministering spirits, sent forth to minister for them who shall be heirs of salvation" (Hebrews 1:14) and as

---

[35] Lewis Sperry Chafer, *Systematic Theology*, 5:348-349.

[36] Charles Caldwell Ryrie, *Dispensationalism Today*, pages 102-103.

[37] Ibid., pages 211-212.

agents of the punishment of the wicked and as members of the divine court. The "plan for the angels" in redemptive history is primarily a sub-purpose under "the program of redemption" and "the punishment of the wicked." Even when the angels appear in redemptive history as members of the divine court, they are a part of some vision of God that is a revelatory part of "the program of redemption." "The pun-ishment of the wicked" is but the other side of the coin of "the program of redemption." And "the glory of God through nature" is a basis of judgment for the wicked (Romans 1:20) and a basis of praise for the redeemed (Psalm 19). It is also related to "the program of redemption" in that the glorified new earth will be the eternal inheritance of the saints. When one gets to the real kernel of this doxological unifying theme with its five sub-purposes, one finds a theocratic kingdom program for Israel and a soteriological program with four sub-purposes. The theocratic kingdom program for Israel is inadequate as a unifying theme of redemptive history, and the dispensationalists reject the soteriological program as a unifying theme. To accept the soteriological program as the unifying theme would logically result in a soteriologically united people of God, which would destroy dispensationalism.

Dividing Biblical history into a progression of dispensations is not unique to dispensationalists. All theologians do that. What is characteristic of the consistent dispensationalist is that he suffers from an acute case of "hardening of the categories." Having in practice rejected the typological and organic union of the two testaments that is found in Christ and His saving work, the consistent dispensationalist has instead adopted a two-program, two-people view of Biblical history in which the church age is a logically unnecessary parenthesis in the divine program and, from the perspective of the Old Testament prophets, a divine afterthought and adjustment. My own opinion is that consistently interpreting Scripture through the rigid grid of dispensational assumptions has the potential for turning Biblical bread into theological shredded wheat. Fortunately, many dispensationalists today are mild dispensationalists who are not that rigid when it comes to dispensational interpretation and theology and who have had little actual exposure to the classical and definitive dispensational works by men such as Chafer and Scofield where these dispensational dichotomies are more rigidly pressed.

LONG FOOTNOTES

2 "(1) Any person is a dispensationalist who trusts the blood of Christ rather than bringing an animal sacrifice. (2) Any person is a dispensationalist who disclaims any right or title to the land which God covenanted to Israel for an everlasting inheritance. And (3) any person is a dispensationalist who observes the first day of the week rather than the seventh. To all this it would be replied that every Christian does these things, which is obviously true; and it is equally true that, to a very considerable degree, all Christians are dispensationalists. However, not all Christians, though sincere, are as well instructed in the spiritual content of the Scriptures as others, nor have they seen the necessity of recognizing other and deeper distinctions which do confront the careful student of the Word of God." Lewis Sperry Chafer, *Dispensationalism* (Dallas: Dallas Seminary Press, 1936), page 9.

7 "Men were *just and righteous* as related to the Mosaic Law, but none had the righteousness of God imputed to them on the ground of faith except Abraham, he who was so evidently marked out and raised up of God to anticipate and illustrate (cf. Romans and Galatians) the New Testament doctrine of imputed righteousness; so of Abraham alone Christ said, 'Abraham rejoiced to see my day: and he saw it, and was glad' (John 8:56)." [Emphasis added] Lewis Sperry Chafer, *Systematic Theology*, 6:74.

"A distinction must be observed here between just men of the Old Testament and those justified according to the New Testament. *According to the Old Testament men were just because they were true and faithful in keeping the Mosaic Law. . . . Men were therefore just because of their own works for God, whereas New Testament justification is God's work for man in answer to faith* (Rom. 5:1)." [Emphasis added] Lewis Sperry Chafer, *Systematic Theology*, 7:219.

Dr. Chafer has here made the same error of interpretation that was common in Judaism: "God expects those who are within the covenant, and who on this basis have been declared to be in right relationship with him, to live as children of the righteous Lord. . . . Where a mistake could be made, and in fact was made in later Judaism, was to think that God's declaration of righteousness was dependent upon an individual Jew's meticulous fulfillment of the laws within the covenant made with Moses on Mount Sinai. Actually, righteousness as an ethical quality of blamelessness came as a result of God's declaration of right standing before him within his covenant of grace, and not the opposite way around. The Pharisee in Luke 18 represents the way in which the whole pursuit of righteousness can go wrong. He stopped looking to the Lord as the giver of righteousness and concentrated on seeking to achieve righteousness to present to the Lord at the end of his life." Peter Toon, *Justification and Sanctification* (Westchester, Illinois: Crossway Books, 1983), page 18.

[8] "The law, being a covenant of works and providing no enablement, addressed itself to the limitations of the natural man. No more was expected or secured in return from its commands than the natural man in his environment could produce. The requirements under the law are, therefore, on the plane of the limited ability of the flesh. On the other hand, grace, being a covenant of faith, and providing the limitless enablement of the power of the indwelling Spirit, addresses itself to the unlimited resources of the supernatural man." Lewis Sperry Chafer, *Systematic Theology*, 4:247.

"The law system provided no enabling power for its achievement." Ibid., 4:51.

". . .but one of these three divine economies [i.e. law, grace, kingdom] provides directly and purposefully divine enablement for every require-ment which it places upon the individual; that is, no mention is made in two of these economies of a provision of divine enablement for their fulfillment. However, in the present economy, both supernatural stan-dards of action are announced and complete ability by the Spirit is provided for their fulfillment." Ibid., 4:156.

"The Law of Moses presents a covenant of works to be wrought in the energy of the flesh; the teachings of grace present a covenant of faith to be wrought in the energy of the Spirit." Ibid., 4:211; compare Ibid., 4:234.

"This same indwelling of the Holy Spirit becomes, as well, an age-char-acterization. This is a dispensation of the Spirit, a period of time in which the Holy Spirit is the believer's all-sufficient Resource both for power and guidance. In this age the Christian is appointed to live by a new life-principle (cf. Rom. 6:4). The realization of the Spirit's presence, power, and guidance constitutes a wholly new method of daily living and is in contrast to that dominance and authority which the Mosaic Law exercised over Israel in the age that is past." Ibid., 6.122-123.

"The basis of Law is a covenant of works; that of grace is a covenant of grace. Human merit is the foundation stone of the Law; the merit of Christ is the foundation of grace. . . . A covenant of works is grounded in what the flesh can do; a covenant of grace is based upon faith in what God has done and is willing to do." Charles L. Feinberg, *Millennialism: The Two Major Views*, pages 216-217.

Dispensationalist Dr. Charles C. Ryrie acknowledges the error of the above: "Dispensationalists have often pictured the Law as a period when enablement was completely lacking. It is true that there was a sharp contrast between the enablement under the law and the work of the Holy Spirit (John 14:17), but it is not accurate to say that there was no enablement under the law." Charles Caldwell Ryrie, *Dispensationalism Today* (Chicago: Moody Press, 1965), page 120.

[10] "At this point the question of what constituted the right relation of a Jew to God within the scope and purpose of Judaism might be asked. It is the Covenant theologian who advances at this point the assumption that the saints of the old order were regenerated and on the same basis of relationship to Jehovah as is accorded the saints of the New Testament. Such an assumption is needful if their theory is to be sustained." Lewis Sperry Chafer, *Systematic Theology*, 6:104-105; compare 3:215 and 6:111.

[11] "Since the covenant of grace which is based on human faith was established in the promise made to Abraham, the covenant of law, made four hundred years later, and added only for a temporary purpose, cannot disannul it. The reign of law, with its covenant of works, ceased with the death of Christ. Its purpose had been accomplished, and its appointed time had expired. Thus the by-faith principle which was announced in the Abrahamic covenant is brought again into force, through the death of Christ." Ibid., 4:229.

"The example of Abraham who *believed* Jehovah and it (his faith) was counted unto him for righteousness (Gen. 15:6) was ever before Israel, and David has described the blessedness of the man unto whom God imputeth righteousness without works (Romans 4:6); nevertheless, Israel stumbled over the stumbling stone of human merit . . . Their [Israel's] trouble was *ignorance*. They did not know the truth that faith in God would, as witnessed by Abraham, David, and the prophets, bring about, through divine grace, an adjustment all-satisfying to God — even a righteousness as perfect as Himself." Ibid., 3:79.

"Let it be restated that Abraham is the pattern of a Christian under grace and not of a Jew under law." Ibid., 3:84.

"The Law of Moses, to be sure, was an ad interim dealing in effect only until Christ should come. For the time being it gave to sin the character of transgression (Rom. 5:13; Gal. 3:19). It was preceded (Ex. 19:4) and followed (John 1:17) by grace." Ibid., 7:225-226.

[12] "The nature of a covenant which is based on human works is obvious. Whatever God promises under such a covenant, is conditioned on the faithfulness of man. Every blessing under the Law of Moses was so

conditioned, and every blessing in the kingdom relationship will be found to be so ordered. Turning to the kingdom teachings of Christ wherein the issues of personal conduct and obligation in the kingdom are taken up, it will be seen that all the kingdom promises to the individual are based on human merit. . . . It is a covenant of works only and the emphatic word is *do*. "This do, and thou shalt live" is the highest promise of the law. . . .

"Turning to the Law of Moses, we discover that it presents no other relation to God than this same covenant of works:. . . .

"By these references to the Law of Moses and the law of the kingdom, it may be seen that both of these systems are based wholly on a covenant of works." Ibid., 4:211-212.

". . . The kingdom teachings, like the Law of Moses, are based on a covenant of works. The teachings of grace, on the other hand, are based on a covenant of faith. In the one case, righteousness is demanded; in the other it is provided, both imputed and imparted, or inwrought. One is of a blessing to be bestowed because of a perfect life, the other of a life to be lived because of a perfect blessing already received." Ibid., 4:215-216.

"The tribulation period, also, seems to revert back to Old Testament conditions in several ways; and in the Old Testament period, saints were never permanently indwelt except in isolated instances, though a number of instances of the filling of the Spirit and of empowering for service are found. Taking all the factors into consideration, there is no evidence for the indwelling of the Holy Spirit in believers in the tribulation." Dr. John F. Walvoord, *The Holy Spirit*, page 230.

[13] "The Gospels are complex almost beyond any other portion of Scripture, since they are a composite of the teachings of Moses, of grace, and of the kingdom." Lewis Sperry Chafer, *Systematic Theology*, 4:172.

"The Synoptic Gospels, though on the surface presenting a simple narrative, are, nevertheless, a field for careful, discriminating study on the part of the true expositor. In these Gospels Christ is seen as loyal to and vindicating the Mosaic Law under which He lived; He also anticipates the kingdom age in connection with the offer of Himself as Israel's King; and, when His rejection is indicated, He announces His death and resurrection and the expectation concerning a heavenly people (Matt. 16:18) for whom He gave Himself in redeeming love (Eph. 5:25-27)." Ibid., 4:12.

"If critical scholars assume it possible to claim two Isaiahs on the evidence afforded in the difference in style and subject matter which the two parts of Isaiah's writing set forth, there would be by far more conclusive proof of at least three Christs. It seems not to occur to a certain group of theologians that these discourses not only introduce principles which, for a doctrinal standpoint, are irreconcilable, but also happen to be addressed to classes which are differently related to God and to Christ." Ibid., 5:96.

Chapter Eighteen

Dispensationalism: Christian Zionism

The dispensational system promotes Zionism among Christians, the conviction that physical Jews today have a Biblical right to possess the land of Palestine. The point of discussion in this chapter is not Zionism as a political issue but Zionism as a Biblically based theological issue. The typical dispensationalist does have a passionate commitment to theological Zionism and a religious regard for the Zionistic events of 1948 and 1967: the modern establishment of the Jewish state of Israel and the Israeli conquest of Jerusalem. These two events are viewed as the two most dramatic fulfillments of prophecy since the destruction of Jerusalem in 70 A.D. and as signs of the soon return of Christ. Many dispensationalists are also anticipating a third imminent Zionistic fulfillment of prophecy: the rebuilding of the temple at Jerusalem.[1]

The following statement by Dr. John F. Walvoord is typical:

> One of the most dramatic evidences that the end of the age is approaching is the fact that Israel has re-established her position as a nation in her ancient land. Israel today is in proper place to enter into the covenant anticipated in Daniel 9:27 which will begin the last seven-year period leading up to the second coming of Christ. Even the modern city of Jerusalem built by Israel is occupying the precise area predicted in Jeremiah 31:38-40 and constitutes a fulfillment of this prophecy given twenty-five hundred years ago and never before fulfilled. Jeremiah states that when Jerusalem is built in the area described, as it

---

[1]Hal Lindsey with C. C. Carlson, *The Late Great Planet Earth* (Grand Rapids: Zondervan Publishing House, 1970), pages 50-58; Dwight Wilson, *Armageddon Now! The Premillenarian Response to Russia and Israel Since 1917* (Grand Rapids: Baker Book House, 1977), pages 199-201.

has been in our generation, it will be a sign of the final chapter in the history of Jerusalem, in preparation for the millennial kingdom of our Lord.[2]

Hal Lindsey has even gone so far as to indulge cautiously in some prophetic date setting based on the 1948 event in his best selling book *The Late Great Planet Earth*, copyrighted in 1970:

> When the signs just given begin to multiply and increase in scope it's similar to the certainty of leaves coming on the fig tree. But the most important sign in Matthew has to be the restoration of the Jews to the land in the rebirth of Israel. Even the figure of speech "fig tree" has been a historic symbol of national Israel. When the Jewish people, after nearly 2,000 years of exile, under relentless persecution, became a nation again on 14 May 1948 the "fig tree" put forth its first leaves.

> Jesus said that this would indicate that He was "at the door," ready to return. Then He said, "Truly I say to you, *this generation* will not pass away until all these things take place" (Matthew 24:34 NASB).

> What generation? Obviously, in context, the generation that would see the signs — chief among them the rebirth of Israel. A generation in the Bible is something like forty years. If this is a correct deduction, then within forty years or so of 1948, all these things could take place. Many scholars who have studied Bible prophecy all their lives believe that this is so.[3]

Mr. Lindsey is saying that the 1948 establishment of the state of Israel has given him reason to anticipate that the events of the seven year Jewish tribulation period that culminates in the second coming of Christ could all occur by 1988. Since Mr. Lindsey, like most dispensationalists, places the church rapture seven years before the second coming, he would have expected the rapture by 1981 if he had looked for the second coming to occur by 1988.

Of course, the really careful dispensationalist neither sets dates nor regards 1948 and 1967 as direct fulfillments of prophecy. According to dispensational theory, no Jewish prophecy can directly refer to the unrevealed and parenthetical church age. Also, dispensationalists argue for their pre-tribulation rapture by insisting that "the prospect of being taken to heaven at the coming of Christ is not qualified by description of any signs or prerequisite events."[4] These Zionistic

---

[2] See end of chapter, Long Footnotes, p. 244.

[3] See end of chapter, Long Footnotes, p. 245.

[4] John F. Walvoord, *The Rapture Question* (Grand Rapids: Zondervan Publishing

events are instead regarded as dramatic preparations for the Jewish fulfillment of prophecy that will begin to occur after the rapture of the church. For the dispensationalist the supposed preparation of the end-time stage in this generation is a strong indication that the end-time drama is now imminent.

Dispensational Zionism is founded on the dispensational interpretation of the Abrahamic covenant. Dispensationalists argue that the Abrahamic covenant is Jewish, unconditional and unfulfilled. Since the covenant is unconditional, it must be fulfilled at some point in history. Since it has not been fulfilled in the past, then it must be fulfilled in the future. And since it is Jewish, it must be fulfilled in a future Jewish dispensation. Therefore, the Abrahamic covenant mandates a coming Jewish age, the millennium, for the fulfillment of Jewish prophecy. We will examine in this chapter the dispensational understanding of the Abrahamic covenant as Jewish and unfulfilled.

We will begin with the teaching that the Abrahamic covenant is Jewish. Using their "literal" hermeneutic, dispensationalists interpret the seed associated with the Abrahamic covenant to be the physical Jews. A difficulty with this interpretation is that in Galatians 3, verses 7 and 29, the Christian, regardless of his race, is said to be the seed of Abraham and the heir of the promise made to Abraham. The dispensational answer to this is that the individual Christian is a spiritual seed of Abraham and heir of the universal spiritual aspects of the Abrahamic covenant but not the physical seed to which the national promises were made. This dispensational solution is typical in that it stresses a rigid dichotomy between the earthly and the spiritual, the Jewish and the Gentile, the national and the individual aspects of the Abrahamic covenant.

According to Dr. Charles C. Ryrie:

> It is quite obvious that Christians are called the spiritual seed of Abraham, but the New Testament nowhere says that they are the heirs of the national promises made to the physical descendants. . . . the term "Israel" is not the appellative given to the spiritual seed of Abraham. It is correct to call *some* of the spiritual seed of Abraham spiritual Israel, but not all. . . . Only when a believer belongs to the race of Israel can he in any sense be called a spiritual Israelite.[5]

House, 1957), pages 78-79.

[5]Charles Caldwell Ryrie, *Dispensationalism Today* (Chicago: Moody Press, 1965), page 149.

Faith and justification are personal and individual matters, and belonging to the spiritual seed of Abraham is also a personal and individual matter unrelated to race. The spiritual seed of Abraham does not mean Israel, for Abraham is related to Israel as a national father, and he is related to believing individuals of all nations (including the Jewish) who believe, as a spiritual father. But believers *as a group* are not called spiritual Israel.[6]

According to Dr. John F. Walvoord:

There are, then, three different senses in which one can be a child of Abraham. First, there is the natural lineage, or natural seed. This is limited largely to the descendants of Jacob in the twelve tribes. To them God promises to be their God. To them was given the law. To them was given the land of Israel in the Old Testament. With them God dealt in a special way. Second, there is the spiritual lineage within the natural. These are the Israelites who believed in God, who kept the law, and who met the conditions for the present enjoyment of the blessings of the covenant. Those who ultimately possess the land in the future millennium will also be of spiritual Israel. Third, there is the spiritual seed of Abraham who are not natural Israelites. Here is where the promise to "all the families of the earth" comes in. . . . the children of Abraham (spiritually) who come from the "heathen" or the Gentiles fulfill that aspect of the Abrahamic covenant which dealt with Gentiles in the first place, not the promises pertaining to Israel. . . .

While premillenarians can agree with amillenarians concerning the fact of a spiritual seed for Abraham which includes Gentiles, they deny that this fulfills the promises given to the natural seed or that the promises to the "seed of Abraham" are fulfilled by Gentile believers. To make the blessings promised to all the nations the same as the blessings promised the seed of Abraham is an unwarranted conclusion.[7]

This dispensational explanation of the spiritual and physical seeds of Abraham does not adequately integrate all the Biblical data about Abraham's seed. Even as early as the Genesis 17 covenant of circumcision, there were provisions for including Gentiles and excluding physical seed of Abraham from the covenant community (Genesis 17:12-14).[8] Gentile proselytes such as Rahab the harlot and Ruth the

---

[6]Ibid., pages 149-150.

[7]John F. Walvoord, *The Millennial Kingdom* (Grand Rapids: Zondervan Publishing House, 1959), page 145-146.

[8]Dr. Walvoord's response is "Circumcision is wider in its application than the term 'seed,' as far as the use in Genesis is concerned." John F. Walvoord, *The Millennial*

Moabitess, ancestors of King David (Matthew 1:5), inherited the national promises of the Abrahamic covenant in the Old Testament. Physical descendants of Abraham such as Ishmael and Esau did not. Ishmael did receive his own national promise because of his physical descent from Abraham, but the seed of covenant blessing was reckoned only through Isaac (Genesis 21:12-13). Esau and Jacob were twin brothers, and yet only Jacob became a father of God's chosen nation and an heir of the land promise. This data suggest that the dispensational teaching that the physical seed will inherit the national promises is not an adequate explanation of the Biblical administration of the Abrahamic covenant.

In Reformed interpretation, the land-inheriting seed of Abraham are defined not strictly in terms of racial descent but in terms of a continuing covenant community.[9] Physical descent and genealogies were important under the old covenant because the coming Messianic seed was to be a physical descendent of both Abraham and David, but the developing covenant community both excluded unfaithful physical descendants of Abraham and assimilated believing Gentiles. The historical administration of the covenant can be explained from the Reformed perspective by using Paul's Romans 11 olive tree illustration. The olive tree represents God's covenant community and its roots represent God's gracious covenant. The physical seed within the covenant community are the natural branches who all partake of the roots' sap to some degree, who all enjoy covenant blessings such as exposure to the means of grace and special temporal blessings. Gentiles or branches from the wild olive tree of paganism can be grafted into the covenant community through a profession of faith. And any branch unrepentantly exhibiting obvious high-handed evidences of unbelief should be pruned off in discipline. After being cut off from the covenant community in judgment, the natural branches and their descendants remain beloved of God on account of their fathers and are prime prospects for grafting in through a profession of faith. In terms of this motif, Isaac and Jacob were persevering natural branches, Rahab and Ruth were persevering grafted on branches, Ishmael and Esau were pruned off natural branches that continued to experience certain temporal divine blessings, and the Edomites who became

Kingdom, page 141.

[9] J. Dwight Pentecost, *Things to Come, A Study in Biblical Eschatology* (Grand Rapids: Zondervan Publishing House, 1958), pages 86-87.

proselytes during the inter-testamental period were grafted in descendants of Esau, a pruned off branch.

The spiritual seed of Abraham are all those who truly share Abraham's faith (Romans 4:11-12), and these alone are the seed of Abraham in the most fundamental sense of the term (John 8:39; Romans 9:6-7; 2:28). Only these will inherit the promises of the covenant in terms of real spiritual rest and an eternal inheritance. This definition of the seed of Abraham, which is from the perspective of God's secret decrees and sovereign work of grace, is simple and easily understood. Defining the seed of Abraham from within the context of history and human relations, however, is much more complex because of human limitations. In administering the covenant the church is not to seek to pry into God's secret plans or to presume to be able to infallibly gauge everyone's true spiritual condition. The church's limited responsibility is to function in terms of God's revealed will, the Biblically defined rules for administering the covenant. The seed of Abraham from this perspective of historical covenant administration is a complex phenomenon best defined in terms of a continuing covenantal community rather than in terms of racial descent alone.

As we have seen, the dispensational position also stresses that the spiritual seed of Abraham as defined in Galatians 3 have no claim to the national land promise of the Abrahamic covenant. Paul's teaching on the Christian and the Abrahamic covenant will not allow such a conclusion. Paul argues in Galatians 3 that God intentionally used *seed* as a collective noun that has both a singular and plural reference so that the singular reference could refer to Christ and the plural reference could refer to those who are in Christ. Paul's point is that the Abrahamic promises were made to Abraham and to his seed (verse 16), that the seed of Abraham is Christ (verse 16) and all who are in Christ (verse 29), and that therefore the promise given to Abraham belongs to all who are in Christ (verse 29). In his argumentation Paul specifically quotes from the Old Testament the phrase "and to thy seed," the "thy" referring to Abraham (Galatians 3:16; see also Romans 4:13). The Greek phrase in Galatians 3:16 translated "and to thy seed" could have come from only two passages in the Septuagint: Genesis 13:15-17 and Genesis 17:8.[10] And in both of these Old Testament passages, that which is promised to Abraham's seed is the covenanted land

---

[10]The phrase "and to your seed" is found in both verses 15 and 17 of Genesis 13 in the LXX but only in verse 15 in the Hebrew.

promise.[11] Beyond this every time the phrase "to your seed" is used in the book of Genesis in the context of a divine promise to give something to somebody, the reference is to the Abrahamic land promise (See Gen. 12:7; 13:15; 15:18; 17:8; 24:7; 26:3, 4; 28:4, 13; 35:12; 48:4). When Paul was explaining the Old Testament promise that belongs to the Christian, he was referring specifically to the land promise, the one promise that dispensationalists argue that Paul could not have been referring to.

The Old Testament quotation in Galatians 3 that the dispensationalists stress is the statement "In thee shall all nations be blessed" (Genesis 12:3; Galatians 3:8). The dispensationalists acknowledge that this portion of the Abrahamic covenant has reference to the spiritual blessings that are now enjoyed by Gentiles in Christ Jesus.[12] There are many Old Testament prophecies that expand on this universal statement of the Abrahamic covenant,[13] and it is instructive to notice the dispensational position on their fulfillment. Since dispensationalists define the church age as an unrevealed parenthesis in the Jewish prophetic program, they cannot with consistency teach that these prophecies have a direct reference to the church age; these prophecies must be fulfilled in the future Jewish millennium. Under the heading "The Gentiles in the Millennium," Dr. J. Dwight Pentecost states: "The universal aspects of the Abrahamic covenant, which promised universal blessing, will be realized in that age."[14] That the universal aspect of the Abrahamic covenant finds its direct fulfillment, not in the church age, but in the coming Jewish earthly millennium, demonstrates how thoroughly Jewish the Abrahamic covenant is in dispensational interpretation.

The dispensationalist also argues that the Abrahamic covenant is unconditional in contrast to the conditional Mosaic covenant. Dispen-

---

[11]William Everett Bell, Jr., "A Critical Evaluation of the Pre-tribulation Rapture Doctrine in Christian Eschatology" (dissertation, School of Education of New York University, 1967), pages 125-126.

[12]John F. Walvoord, *The Millennial Kingdom*, page 145; Charles Caldwell Ryrie, *The Basis of the Premillennial Faith* (Neptune, N. J.: Loizeaux Brothers, 1953), page 62.

[13]Compare Psalm 22:27-30; 68:29-31; 72:8-11, 17; Isaiah 2:2-5; 11:10, 14; 19:24-25; 42:1-4; 45:14; 49:6-7, 22-23; 52:10; 54:1-3; 60:3f.; 65:1; 66:19; Jeremiah 16:19; Amos 9:11-12; Zechariah 2:3-13; 8:20-23; Malachi 1:11.

[14]J. Dwight Pentecost, *Things to Come*, page 507; compare Charles Caldwell Ryrie, *Dispensationalism Today*, page 134.

sationalists teach that the unconditional Abrahamic covenant was expanded into three other unconditional Jewish covenants: the Palestinian covenant, the Davidic covenant and the new covenant. The expanded covenant dealing with the land promise portion of the Abrahamic covenant is the Palestinian covenant, which dispensationalists identify with Deuteronomy 30:1-10. It does seem strange that anyone would teach that a section of Deuteronomy contains a separate covenant that is not a part of the Mosaic covenant and that differs from the Mosaic covenant in its basic nature. The Palestinian covenant is supposed to be unconditional in the dispensational sense of the word. Deuteronomy chapter 30, verses 1-3 and 10, however, contain statements that reflect moral conditions:

> And it shall come to pass when all these things are come upon thee, the blessing and the curse, which I have set before thee, and thou shalt call them to mind among all the nations, whither the Lord thy God hath driven thee, and shalt return unto the Lord thy God, and shalt obey his voice according to all that I command thee this day, thou and thy children, with all thine heart, and with all thy soul; that then the Lord thy God will turn thy captivity, and have compassion upon thee, and will return and gather thee from all the nations, whither the Lord thy God hath scattered thee.

> If thou shalt harken unto the voice of the Lord thy God, to keep his commandments and his statutes which are written in this book of the law, and if thou turn unto the Lord thy God with all thine heart, and with all thy soul.

Lastly, dispensationalists also argue that the Abrahamic covenant is unfulfilled. They claim to prove the covenant to be unfulfilled by examining the chronological and geographic boundaries of the covenant promise. Chronologically, the Abrahamic covenant is a forever promise (Genesis 13:15; 17:8), and the Jews possessed Palestine for only a limited time in the Old Testament. Geographically, the promised land was to include the land from the river of Egypt to the Euphrates River (Genesis 15:18). Dispensationalists argue that the Jews never possessed all the land within these boundaries. In 1 Kings 4:21, we learn that Solomon ruled over all the land from the border of Egypt to the Euphrates River, but the dispensationalists argue that the "border of Egypt" is not the "river of Egypt" and that Solomon merely ruled over much of this territory by collecting tribute, not by actually possessing it.[15] So, if the dispensationalists are right, the land promise of the Abrahamic covenant is Jewish, unconditional and unfulfilled, and therefore there must be a yet future Jewish possession of the land of Palestine.

If this is so, then exactly when and how is the Abrahamic covenant's land promise to be fulfilled? In searching out the details of this question, one encounters some interesting divergencies in dispensational answers. In the earlier dispensational writers like Chafer, the Abrahamic covenant had a truly eternal Jewish fulfillment. According to Dr. Chafer:

> Jehovah's fivefold covenant with Israel is everlasting in every respect — (1) a national entity (Jer. 31:36), (2) a land in perpetuity (Gen. 13:15), (3) a throne (2 Sam. 7:16; Ps. 89:36), (4) a King (Jer. 33:21), and (5) a kingdom (Dan. 7:14). These earthly promises are confirmed by the oath of Jehovah and extend *forever*, else language ceases to be a dependable medium for the expression of truth.[16]

In that system the resurrected Old Testament saints together with the resurrected millennial saints were to inherit eternally a Judaistic new earth after the Judaistic millennium and the church saints were to inherit a Christian new heavens for eternity. According to Dr. Chafer:

> . . . there is an eschatology of Judaism and an eschatology of Christianity and each, though wholly different in details, reaches on into eternity. One of the great burdens of predictive prophecy is the anticipation of the glories of Israel in a transformed earth under the reign of David's Son, the Lord Jesus Christ, the Son of God. There is likewise much prediction which anticipates the glories of the redeemed in heaven.[17]

> . . . Israelites, as a nation, have their citizenship now and their future destiny centered only in the earth, reaching on to the new earth which is yet to be, while Christians have their citizenship and future destiny centered only in heaven, reaching on into the new heavens that are yet to be . . . .[18]

---

[15]John F. Walvoord, *The Millennial Kingdom*, pages 156-157; Charles Caldwell Ryrie, *The Basis of the Premillennial Faith*, pages 60-61.

[16]Lewis Sperry Chafer, *Systematic Theology*, 8 vols. (Dallas: Dallas Seminary Press, 1948), 4:30.

[17]Lewis Sperry Chafer, *Systematic Theology*, 4:27; Dr. Lewis Sperry Chafer, *Dispensationalism* (Dallas: Dallas Seminary Press, 1936), page 65.

[18]Lewis Sperry Chafer, *Systematic Theology*, 4:30.

Every covenant, promise, and provision for Israel is earthly, and they continue as a nation with the earth when it is created new. Every covenant or promise for the Church is heavenly, and she continues in heavenly citizenship when the heavens are recreated.[19]

It should be asserted, however, that the entire system known as Judaism, along with all its component parts, is, in the purpose of God, in abeyance throughout the present age, but with the definite assurance that the entire Jewish system thus interrupted will be completed by extension into the kingdom, the new earth, and on into eternity to come.[20]

Among those who stand in eternal favor with God are the earthly citizens whose destiny it is to go on into eternity as the dwellers on the earth . . ., and the heavenly citizens whose destiny it is to occupy the new heaven . . . .[21]

The dispensationalist believes that throughout the ages God is pursuing two distinct purposes: one related to the earth with earthly people and earthly objectives involved, which is Judaism; while the other is related to heaven with heavenly people and heavenly objectives involved, which is Christianity. Why should this belief be deemed so incredible in the light of the facts that there is a present distinction between earth and heaven which is preserved even after both are made new; when the Scriptures so designate an earthly people who go on as such into eternity; and a heavenly people who also abide in their heavenly calling forever?[22]

In this older dispensational system, there was an eternal dichotomy of destinies between Israel, the earthly seed of Abraham, and the church, the heavenly seed of Abraham.

Some more recent dispensationalists disagree with these details of Chafer's view. They teach that the eternal Jewish land promise is to be completely fulfilled in the 1000 year Judaistic millennial period. According to Dr. Charles C. Ryrie:

The earthly purpose of Israel of which dispensationalists speak concerns the national promise which will be fulfilled by Jews during the millennium as they live on the earth in *UN*resurrected bodies.[23]

Dr. J. Dwight Pentecost concurs:

---

[19]Ibid., 4:47.

[20]Ibid., 4:248.

[21]Ibid., 4:401.

[22]Dr. Lewis Sperry Chafer, *Dispensationalism*, page 107.

[23]Charles Caldwell Ryrie, *Dispensationalism Today*, page 146.

The promises in the Abrahamic covenant concerning the land and the seed are fulfilled in the millennial age (Isa. 10:21-22; 19:25; 43:1; 65:8-9; Jer. 30:22; 32:38; Ezek. 34:24; 30-31; Mic. 7:19-20; Zech. 13:9; Mal. 3:16-18).[24]

The promises in the Palestinic covenant concerning the possession of the land are fulfilled by Israel in the millennial age (Isa. 11:11-12; 65:9; Ezek. 16:60-63; 36:28-29; 39:28; Hos. 1:10-2:1; Mic. 2:12; Zech. 10:6).[25]

It will thus be observed that the millennial age finds the complete fulfillment of all that God promised to the nation Israel.[26]

Elsewhere Dr. Pentecost argues that the eternal nature of the covenants with Israel requires that they be fulfilled in eternity on the new earth.[27] If, however, the land promise finds its ultimate fulfillment in eternity on the new earth, then there is no real mandate for a Jewish millennium in the Abrahamic covenant.

Some more recent dispensationalists also teach that the promised land is to be inhabited during the millennium only by unresurrected living Jews and Gentiles and not by the resurrected Old Testament saints.[28] During the millennium the resurrected Old Testament saints together with the resurrected church saints are to be in the new Jerusalem, which will be a millennial satellite city hovering over Palestine.[29] At the end of the millennium the new Jerusalem will descend to earth, and the saints of all ages will inhabit together the new earth. In this system, the strictly Jewish inheritance of the land promise is limited to the millennial years and to unresurrected millennial saints. The land promise specifically promised the land inheritance to Abraham as well as to his seed,[30] but Abraham, together with the other Old Testament saints, will be in the heavenly city with the

---

[24] J. Dwight Pentecost, *Things to Come*, page 476.

[25] Ibid., page 477.

[26] Ibid., page 477; compare William Everett Bell, Jr., "A Critical Evaluation of the Pre-tribulation Rapture Doctrine in Christian Eschatology," page 85.

[27] J. Dwight Pentecost, *Things to Come*, pages 491-494; 561-562.

[28] Ibid., pages 536-537, 542, 546.

[29] J. Dwight Pentecost, *Things to Come*, pages 546, 576-580; John F. Walvoord, *The Millennial Kingdom*, pages 327-330; Charles Caldwell Ryrie, *The Ryrie Study Bible: The New Testament* (Chicago: Moody Press, 1976), page 482, note on Revelation 21:2.

[30] See Lewis Sperry Chafer, *Systematic Theology*, 4:320, 406-407.

church saints during the time of the land inheritance.

Here we have the dispensational understanding of the Abrahamic covenant's land promise. Was Scripture truly allowed to interpret Scripture? Was there a sensitivity to progressive revelation? Is there any evidence that the dispensational interpreters recognize their fallibility and have a willingness to adjust, if necessary, their initial understanding of the Abrahamic covenant if it does not harmonize well with further infallible revelation on the subject? Or do we see evidence of a willingness to artificially bend further revelation in order to vindicate a particular understanding of the Abrahamic covenant's land promise?

My understanding of the Abrahamic land promise is different from the dispensationalist's. I believe the Jewish inhabitation of Palestine in the Old Testament was a temporary typological symbol and pledge of the ultimate eternal inheritance of the saints. I also believe that the land promise applies to the Christian today in the spiritual rest and heavenly position that is his in Christ Jesus. The following is a seven point explanation of my understanding of the fulfillment of the land promise.

The Land Promise

First, there is some sense in which the land promise had a real fulfillment in the Old Testament:

> And the Lord gave unto Israel all the land which he sware to give unto their fathers; and they possessed it, and dwelt therein. . . . There failed not ought of any good thing which the Lord had spoken unto the house of Israel; all came to pass (Joshua 21:43, 45).

> . . . not one thing hath failed of all the good things which the Lord your God spake concerning you; all are come to pass unto you, and not one thing hath failed thereof (Joshua 23:14b).

> Blessed be the Lord, that hath given rest unto his people Israel, according to all that he promised: there hath not failed one word of all his good promise, which he promised by the hand of Moses his servant (1 Kings 8:56).

> Thou art the Lord the God who didst choose Abram, and broughtest him forth out of Ur of the Chaldees, and gavest him the name of Abraham; And foundest his heart faithful before thee, and madest a covenant with him to give the land of the Canaanites, the Hittites, the Amorites, and the Perizzites, and the Jebusites, and the Girgashites, to give it, I say, to his seed, and hast performed thy words; for thou art righteous (Nehemiah

9:7-8).

This data must be integrated into one's total understanding of the land promise. There were many elements in the Old Testament Jewish economy other than the land promise that were said to be eternal. For the consistent literalist this requires a belief in an eternity involving resurrected Old Testament rites and rituals and institutions. Another possibility is that these Old Testament rites and rituals and institutions were temporary types of eternal spiritual realities. These found a fulfillment as types in the Old Testament and also anticipated a future fulfillment in terms of the antitype. According to Patrick Fairbairn:

> The occupation of the earthly Canaan by the natural seed of Abraham was a type, and no more than a type, of this occupation by a redeemed Church of her destined inheritance of glory; and consequently every thing concerning the entrance of the former on their temporary possession, was ordered so as to represent and foreshadow the things which belong to the Church's establishment in her permanent possession.[31]

Second, as we have already mentioned, the ultimate fulfillment of the land promise is an eternal fulfillment (Genesis 13:15; 17:8). The Hebrew word translated "forever" is at times contextually limited and does not always refer to a literal eternity (compare Deuteronomy 15:17), but God's covenants do have an eternal, forever reference. When the forever nature of God's covenant is compared to the life span of the sun, one can be certain that the divinely inspired writer had more in mind than a mere 1000 years (Psalm 89:34-37; compare Jeremiah 31:35-36; 33:20-21; Isaiah 54:10).

Third, the ultimate fulfillment of the land promise involves the whole world and not just Palestine. Notice what Paul said in Romans 4:13: "For the promise, that he should be the heir of the world (*kosmos*) was not to Abraham, or to his seed, through the law, but through the righteousness of faith." We have already shown the terminology about a promise given by God to Abraham and his seed can only refer to the land promise. Paul identified the land promise given to Abraham and his seed not merely with Canaan but with the whole world.

Fourth, the ultimate heirs of the land promise will be the elect of all the ages. As we have already seen, there are New Testament

---

[31]Patrick Fairbairn, *The Typology of Scripture Viewed in Connection with the Whole Series of the Divine Dispensations* (Grand Rapids: Baker Book House, 1900, 1975), 1:359.

passages which relate the language of the land promise to Christians as the spiritual seed of Abraham (Galatians 3; Romans 4:13). In the Sermon on the Mount Christ identified the heirs of the land promise as the spiritually meek (Matthew 5:5; compare Psalm 37:11), which is an appropriate description of God's people in general. In the book of Hebrews the land promise is associated with citizenship in the heavenly Jerusalem:

> By faith Abraham, when he was called to go out into a place which he should after receive for an inheritance, obeyed; and he went out, not knowing whither he went. By faith he sojourned in the land of promise, as in a strange country, dwelling in tabernacles with Isaac and Jacob, the heirs with him of the same promise: For he looked for a city which hath foundations, whose builder and maker is God. . . . But now they desire a better country, that is, an heavenly: wherefore God is not ashamed to be called their God: for he hath prepared for them a city (Hebrews 11:8-10, 16).

The saints of all ages are citizens of the heavenly Jerusalem (Hebrews 12:22-23; 13:14; Galatians 4:26), which is further evidence that the saints of all ages will inherit the land promise.

Fifth, this association of the land promise with citizenship in the heavenly Jerusalem means that during the inter-advent age, the land promise finds fulfillment in "an inheritance incorruptible and undefiled and that fadeth not away, reserved in heaven" (1 Peter 1:4). From the moment of conversion the Christian is a comer unto Mount Zion and a citizen of the heavenly Jerusalem (Hebrews 12:22), has spiritual rest in Christ Jesus (Matthew 11:28), and is seated with Christ in the heavenlies (Ephesians 2:6). We, today, in Christ Jesus have a foretaste of the heavenly rest that was pictured by Joshua's conquest of the promised land (Hebrews 4:8-9).

Sixth, the Christian today is in a position analogous to Israel under Joshua when they ccnquered the promised land. The difference is that our weapons are not physical (2 Corinthians 10:4) and our task is to conquer the whole world. We know that the Abrahamic land promise ultimately refers to the whole world (Romans 4:13). Adam was originally given dominion over the whole world (Genesis 1:26-28). This inheritance was lost in the fall and Satan became the prince of this world,[32] but God promised that a Seed Redeemer would ultimately defeat Satan (Genesis 3:15) and that this new Adam would

---

[32]John 12:31; 14:30; 16:11; compare Ephesians 2:2.

regain world dominion (Psalm 8:6). This Seed Redeemer would be a Seed of Abraham through whom Abraham would be a blessing to all nations (Genesis 12:3). This Seed Redeemer would be a son of David who would have the nations for His inheritance and the ends of the earth for His possession (Psalm 2:8). This Seed Redeemer would be a Son of Man who would be given dominion and glory and a kingdom that all peoples, nations, and languages should serve him (Daniel 7:14). Through His resurrection-ascension, Christ has received all authority in heaven *and on earth* (Matthew 28:18). Christ, from His heavenly throne, is today fulfilling Psalm 2 (Revelation 2:26-27; 12:5) and Psalm 8 (Hebrews 2:6-8; 1 Corinthians 15:25-27). Even as God gave Palestine to Israel under Joshua and told them to conquer it, so God has given the nations to new covenant Israel under Jesus and has told us to disciple them.

And seventh, when Christ returns the heavenly Jerusalem will descend to the new earth (Revelation 21:1-2), which then becomes the eternal locus of the land promise fulfillment. In Hebrews 4:8-9 we learn that the rest under Joshua after the conquest of the promised land was a type of the heavenly Sabbath rest of the eternal inheritance. The ultimate fulfillment of the land promise will be the eternal inheritance of the new earth by the saints of all ages. Only in this eternal context can Abraham and all his true seed inherit the land forever.

Before closing this chapter on the Abrahamic land promise, I want to comment on the Old Testament prophecies about dispersed Jews returning to the land. Dispensationalists tend to refer these prophecies to an end-time regathering of the Jews to Palestine, but it seems much more logical that these prophecies primarily referred to the Babylonian exile and the return of the Jewish captives, first under Zerubbabel and Joshua the priest, and later under Ezra. In opposition to this the dispensationalist can point out that these prophesied regatherings were a second return to the land (Isaiah 11:11) and a regathering from a world-wide dispersion, not from a localized Babylonian exile (Isaiah 49:12). This objection ignores the Biblical fact that the exiled Jews were scattered all over the civilized world of that day (Esther 3:8). And return from Babylonian exile was the second return to the land since the first was the exodus under Moses (Isaiah 11:15-16). There are elements in the restoration prophesies that go beyond what was experienced under the old covenant. This is because the fulfillment of prophecies of blessing can be limited (Joshua 1:4; 7:11-12) or postponed (Numbers 14:30-31) or canceled (Jeremiah 18:9-10) because of covenant disobedience and because these prophecies have continuing and progressively greater fulfillments in the church age and in eternity. As I discussed in the previous chapter on literalism, a prophecy can be given in terms of the old covenant economy and fulfilled in terms of the new covenant economy and eternity.

I no longer believe in a Zionistic interpretation of the Abrahamic land promise, but it is possible to retain a Zionistic element in one's understanding of prophecy without going to dispensational extremes. One needs to recognize that the Abrahamic covenant is primarily a spiritual covenant that relates to all the elect of all the ages. If there is any specific Jewish inheritance of Palestine in the Abrahamic covenant, this should be seen as secondary to the ultimate fulfillment in the eternal inheritance of all the saints. And such a limited Palestinian fulfillment should be conditioned on the physical Jews being converted in mass to Christianity and being regrafted into spiritual Israel. Nowhere does the Bible promise to God's covenant people blessings and return from judgmental exile when they are still living in rebellion.[33] The blessing of return to the land from exile is always conditioned on repentance and spiritual revival.

The major difference between the dispensational and the Reformed view of the land promise is that dispensationalists view it as having primary reference to physical Jews. This strong Jewish emphasis in the dispensational interpretation of the Old Testament covenants is probably best demonstrated by a statement made by Dr. J. Dwight Pentecost about the dispensational interpretation of the new covenant: ". . . there is one point of agreement: the new covenant of Jeremiah 31:31-34 must and can be fulfilled only by the nation Israel and not by the church."[34] If the dispensationalists have such a strongly Zionistic interpretation of the new covenant, is it any great surprise that their interpretation of the Abrahamic covenant's land promise is largely, primarily, and ultimately Zionistic?

LONG FOOTNOTES

[2] John F. Walvoord, *Israel in Prophecy* (Grand Rapids: Zondervan Publishing House, 1962), page 130; compare Dwight Wilson, *Armageddon Now!,* pages 123-143; 188-214.

[33] Louis A. DeCaro, *Israel Today: Fulfillment of Prophecy?* (Grand Rapids: Baker Book House, 1974), pages 31-42.

[34] J. Dwight Pentecost, *Things to Come*, page 124.

Dispensationalists interpret Daniel 9:27 as teaching that in the middle of the future Jewish tribulation period, the Anti-Christ will break a covenant made with national Israel that had allowed them to have temple worship with sacrifices and will desolate the temple by there proclaiming himself divine. This act is to mark the beginning of the three and one half year *great* tribulation.

[3] Hal Lindsey with C. C. Carlson, *The Late Great Planet Earth*, pages 53-54.

Contrary to Mr. Lindsey, the fig tree species was not "a historic symbol of national Israel." The only possible evidence for such a view is the barren fig tree in Matthew 21 which Christ cursed. That tree was used by Christ as a symbol of national Israel, not because it was a fig tree, but because its abundance of foliage gave reason to expect the presence of fruit when there was none. This was analogous to national Israel whose abundant foliage included the temple, the priesthood, and religious tradition, but which lacked the fruit of faith in God's Messiah. That Jesus did not regard the fig tree species as a symbol of Israel in the Olivet Discourse is evident from the wording in Luke 21:29: "Behold the fig tree, and all the trees." The grape vine (John 15) and the olive tree (Romans 11) were historic symbols of Israel.

Dispensationalism: "Thy Kingdom Come"

The Presbyterian Church in America *Book of Church Order* begins with the statement, "Jesus Christ . . . sits upon the throne of David." Most people raised with the teachings of the Reformed faith would take this fundamental truth for granted. Who, after all, would question this essential teaching? A dispensationalist would not only question this teaching, but would take strong exception to it. The Davidic throne is another Biblical subject concerning which dispensationalists and Reformed interpreters disagree. If Jesus is not on David's throne, whose throne is He on?

The Davidic kingdom in Scripture is founded on the Davidic covenant of 2 Samuel 7:12-16. This covenant promise obviously involved Solomon, David's immediate seed and heir to the throne, since it spoke of the seed building God's temple and of the seed sinning. The promise, however, also involved a greater antitypical fulfillment since it spoke of an eternal kingdom. The prophets later associated the eternal Davidic kingdom with the Messiah, who would inherit the throne of David and rule eternally over the kingdom in righteousness and justice (Isaiah 9:6-7; Jeremiah 23:5-6; 33:15-16). This Messianic kingdom was to become a universal kingdom over all the kingdoms of the world (Psalm 2; Daniel 2:44). According to Reformed interpretation, these Messianic kingdom prophecies were initially fulfilled by Christ at His first advent, are being progressively fulfilled by Christ throughout this age, and will be perfectly and

completely fulfilled by Christ at His second advent. Reformed interpreter Patrick Fairbairn has spoken succinctly concerning the nature
of Christ's fulfillment:

> Jesus of Nazareth needed no outward enthronement or local seat of
> government on earth, to constitute Him the possessor of David's king-
> dom, as He needed no physical anointing to consecrate Him priest for
> evermore, or material altar and temple for the due presentation of his
> acceptable service.[1]

> No more should it have been expected, that the Messiah was to be
> a king on the earthly model of David, than that he should be a prophet
> on the same level with Moses, or a priest after the imperfect type of those
> who presented their fleshly offerings on a brazen altar.[2]

Dispensationalists disagree with this evaluation of the kingdom
prophecies and their fulfillment. They teach that Christ at His first
advent offered the Jewish nation an earthly political kingdom. If the
Jews had accepted Jesus as the Messiah, He would have re-established
the old Davidic political kingdom, exalted its majesty and extended
its rule to the uttermost parts of the earth. Because the Jewish nation
rejected the Christ, this kingdom offer was retracted and the earthly,
political, re-established Davidic kingdom was postponed until the
future Jewish millennium. Between the withdrawal of the kingdom
offer and the future millennium the church age was inserted, a parenthesis in God's prophesied program for Israel and the nations. The
present age and the present reign of Christ have no direct relationship
to the Davidic covenant or to Messianic prophecy, according to
dispensationalism. The following comments by Dr. John F. Walvoord
on the fulfillment of the Davidic covenant are representative of
dispensational thought:

> If a literal interpretation be adopted, the present session of Christ is not
> a fulfillment of the covenant and it must be referred to the future. It is
> clear that at the present time Christ is not in any literal sense reigning
> over the kingdom of David.[3]

A literal promise spiritualized is exegetical fraud. The point of the

---

[1] Patrick Fairbairn, *Prophecy Viewed in Respect to Its Distinct Nature, Its Special
Function, and Proper Interpretation* (n.p.: T.&T. Clark, 1865; reprint ed., Grand
Rapids: Baker Book House, 1976), pages 230-231.

[2] Patrick Fairbairn, *Prophecy*, page 229.

[3] John F. Walvoord, *The Millennial Kingdom* (Grand Rapids: Zondervan Publishing
House, 1959), page 199.

Davidic covenant is that the Son of David will possess the throne of His father David. To make His person literal but His throne a spiritualized concept is to nullify the promise.[4]

The New Testament is totally lacking in positive teaching that the throne of the Father in heaven is to be identified with the Davidic throne. The inference is plain that Christ is seated on the Father's throne, but that this is not at all the same thing as being seated on the throne of David.[5]

Which of these two understandings of the Davidic covenant and kingdom is correct? I was once committed to the dispensational understanding of the Messianic kingdom but now am convinced that the Reformed understanding is correct. In my change of conviction on this subject, three areas of study were crucial. First, I came to a better understanding of the word "kingdom." Second, I re-examined the New Testament's testimony about the establishment of the kingdom at Christ's first advent. And third, I came to see some of the problems associated with the dispensational explanation of the kingdom.

First, there is the meaning of the word "kingdom." Formerly I could not understand why anyone would believe that Christ is now ruling over His Messianic kingdom. When I thought of the Messianic kingdom, I pictured Christ ruling from earth over a territorial realm and exercising authority over political subjects after the pattern of King David in the Old Testament. I could see the Davidic kingdom in the Old Testament and I could visualize a Messianic kingdom rule in the coming Jewish millennium, but I could not see any direct associa- tion between the Messianic kingdom and the church age. Part of my problem was the common association of the English word "kingdom" with realm and subjects. The following definitions of the word "king- dom" given in the *Oxford English Dictionary*:

> 2. An organized community having a king as its head; a monarchical state of government.

> 3. The territory or country subject to a king; the area over which a king's rule extends; a realm.[6]

These definitions are what we normally associate with the word "kingdom," and these definitions are consistent with the dispensa-

---

[4]Ibid., page 200.

[5]Ibid., page 203.

[6]*The Compact Edition of the Oxford English Dictionary* (Oxford University Press, 1971), s.v. "kingdom."

tional interpretation in which "kingdom" must refer to a political kingdom. These definitions, however, are secondary definitions. The primary meaning of the English word "kingdom" is the following: "1. Kingly function, authority, or power; sovereignty, supreme rule; the position or rank of a king, kingship."[7]

This primary definition is obsolete, which explains why we seldom associate it with the word, but this obsolete definition is the primary meaning of both the Hebrew and the Greek words that are translated kingdom in our Bibles.[8] According to the *Theological Dictionary of the New Testament*, the "essential meaning" of the Greek equivalent of "kingdom" "is reign rather than realm."[9] And the Hebrew equivalent of "the kingdom of heaven" is "an abstract construction to denote the fact that God is King . . . ."[10] The term "can never mean the kingdom of God in the sense of a territory ruled by Him. For the expression denotes the fact that God is King, i.e., His kingly being or kingship."[11] Both the Greek and the Hebrew words mean primarily the majesty and authority of the king. This abstract meaning is the primary meaning of the word, and the concrete aspects of a realm and subjects are secondary meanings.

This understanding of the word "kingdom" is well demonstrated in a parable which Christ gave in Luke 19:11-27 when he was about to enter Jerusalem and some "thought that the kingdom of God should immediately appear" (verse 11):

> A certain nobleman went into a far country to receive for himself a kingdom, and to return. And he called his ten servants, and delivered them ten pounds, and said unto them, "Occupy till I come." But the citizens hated him, and sent a message after him, saying, We will not have this man to reign over us.

Notice that this man left both his realm and his subjects to receive his kingdom. Leaving one's realm and subjects to receive one's kingdom makes little sense if "kingdom" refers primarily to a realm

---

[7] *The Compact Edition of the Oxford English Dictionary*, s.v. "kingdom."

[8] George Eldon Ladd, *Crucial Questions about the Kingdom of God* (Grand Rapids: Wm. B. Eerdmans Publishing Company, 1952), pages 77-81.

[9] Gerhard Kittel, editor; Geoffrey W. Bromley, translator and editor, *Theological Dictionary of the New Testament* (Grand Rapids: Wm. B. Eerdmans Publishing Company, 1964), 1:582.

[10] Gerhard Kittel, editor, *Theological Dictionary of the New Testament*, 1:572.

[11] See end of chapter, Long Footnotes, p. 261.

and subjects. But if the word "kingdom" refers primarily to the authority to rule, this usage of the word in the parable is lucid. This parable is allegorically referring to Jesus ascending to the Father to receive His kingdom.

This proper understanding of the word "kingdom" clarifies the meaning of many passages. For example, in Matthew 6:33, Christ said, "But seek ye first the kingdom of God, and His righteousness; and all these things shall be added unto you." What is the Christian to seek in order to obey this commandment, a theocratic kingdom in a future age or God's rule and authority in all of life now? Also, notice the second petition of the Lord's prayer: "Thy kingdom come" (Matthew 6:10). With this proper understanding of the word "kingdom," this second petition is almost synonymous with the third petition, "Thy will be done, on earth as it is in heaven."

When one realizes that the word "kingdom" has a primary reference to an abstract reign and a secondary reference to a concrete realm, he can easily understand how Christ's kingdom is simultaneously past, present and future. It is past in that the old Davidic political kingdom prefigured and anticipated the coming Messianic reign and in that Christ at His first advent actively established and exercised His authority to rule and to reign. It is future in that it is not until the time of the new heavens and the new earth that Christ's kingdom will be fully and perfectly realized in the concrete elements of realm (the new earth) and subjects (the elect of all ages). It is present in that the Lord Christ now has all authority in heaven and on earth and now is progressively concretizing His reign as the nations are discipled. As nations and peoples acknowledge and submit to the lordship of Jesus Christ, He is progressively possessing in practice what is already His in principle. The Messianic kingdom relates to the here and now as well as to the past and future. This is not an age of kingdom parenthesis and postponement.

The second area of study that caused me to change my concept of the Messianic kingdom from dispensational to Reformed was a general study of the New Testament teaching on the kingdom. To begin with, the language of Scripture does not say that Christ at His first advent offered a kingdom that could potentially be postponed. The language of Scripture indicates that Christ at His first advent established a kingdom. Both John the Baptist and Jesus proclaimed that the kingdom was near at hand (Matthew 3:2; 4:17), not that it was potentially near at hand. Jesus told his disciples to seek the kingdom because "it is your Father's good pleasure to give you the kingdom" (Luke 12:32). Jesus gave specific instructions on how to enter the kingdom (John 3:3, 5; Matthew 5:20; 7:21) and stated that "every man presseth into it" (Luke 16:16). In His Beatitudes, Jesus proclaimed that the kingdom belonged to those "which are persecuted for righteousness's sake" (Matthew 5:11). Christ spoke of the kingdom as an *actuality* that He was establishing, *not* as a *potentiality* that He might postpone.

Further, Jesus spoke as if the establishment of His kingdom was especially manifested in the casting out of demons (Matthew 12:28-30). In the casting out of demons, Satan, the strong man, was bound and his property was plundered (Matthew 12:29). When the disciples reported that "even the devils are subject unto us through Thy name," Jesus proclaimed that Satan was falling from heaven like lightning (Luke 10:17-18). The power of the name of Jesus over demons demonstrated that Satan was a defeated foe whose power was being grounded out. The kingdoms of this world had been in bondage to demonic paganism and under the lordship of Satan, who was called the prince of this world (John 12:31; 14:30; 16:11). Satan had come to regard the world's glory and domain as his own (Luke 4:6). But Christ invaded the kingdom of Satan and won the deciding victory. As Christ anticipated His plundering of Satan's treasure through the drawing of people from all nations unto Himself, he declared, "Now is the judgment of this world: now shall the prince of this world be cast out" (John 12:31).[12] This coming victory over Satan was so clearly manifested by the casting out of demons that Jesus said: "But if I cast out devils by the Spirit of God, then the kingdom of God is come unto you" (Matthew 12:28). This verse is especially significant in that it occurs in the very chapter in which, according to the dispensationalists, Christ was withdrawing His kingdom offer. George Ladd's insight into this verse is poignant:

> While the kingdom as the realm in which God's will is perfectly done continues to be future, the kingdom as the active saving power of God has come into the world in the person and activity of Christ to redeem men from the kingdom of Satan.[13]

Jesus also clarified the nature of the kingdom He was establishing

---

[12]Compare Colossians 2:15; Hebrews 2:14; 1 John 3:8; Revelation 12:9.

[13]George Eldon Ladd, *Crucial Questions about the Kingdom of God*, page 89.

in the parables of Matthew 13. Christ gave these parables, not to explain that He would not be establishing the Davidic kingdom spoken of in prophecy, but to correct some popular misconceptions about the prophesied Messianic kingdom. The mystery or previously unrevealed truth about the kingdom was not that God was going to postpone the kingdom program and temporarily engage in a church program that would be altogether different from the prophesied program. The mystery of the kingdom was that the kingdom would be established, not with cataclysmic suddenness and flaming judgment, but gradually and slowly. The kingdom was not to be established swiftly with military might, but peaceably through the sowing of the Word and the patient waiting for spiritual fruit. Kingdom success would not be immediate or sudden or conspicuous. Many would reject the kingdom like hardened soil rejects seed, and others would profess allegiance only to fall away like a plant in shallow soil or among thorns. The enemies of the kingdom were not to be immediately destroyed, but were to remain in this age like tares in a wheat field. The wicked were not to be fully removed from this world until the end of the age when their judgment will be like the burning of tares after a wheat harvest or the disposal of inedible fish after a harvest from the sea. The kingdom was to have a small and inconspicuous beginning, like a mustard seed, but it was gradually to grow into a great and remarkable entity. The kingdom was eventually to affect the whole world like a small bit of leaven brings life to a large and inert mass of dough. Though the kingdom had a small beginning, it was of great value and was worth giving one's life for. It was like a small pearl of great value or some treasure inconspicuously hidden in a field. Though these are small in size, men will sell all to obtain them. The kingdom parables taught that the kingdom was extremely valuable and that the kingdom had a great future even though its outward success would not be immediate or always apparent.

Jesus continued to refer to His kingdom work throughout His ministry. Jesus told the Pharisees that the kingdom was in their midst by virtue of His presence (Luke 17:20-21). Jesus gave Peter the keys of the kingdom of heaven (Matthew 16:19) and told His disciples that some of them would not taste death "till they see the Son of man coming in His kingdom" (Matthew 16:28). Jesus explained the principles of kingdom greatness (Matthew 18:1ff.), kingdom forgiveness (Matthew 18:21ff.) and the first and the last in the kingdom (Matthew 19:30ff.; 20:20ff.). The Lord expounded the relationships of spiritual eunuchs (Matthew 19:12), covenant children (Matthew 19:14), and the materially rich (Matthew 19:23) to the kingdom. Jesus warned the chief priests and elders of Israel that the publicans and harlots were entering the kingdom ahead of them (Matthew 21:31) and that the kingdom would be taken away from them and given to others (Matthew 21:43; 22:1ff.).

Near the end of His earthly ministry, the Lord entered Jerusalem and was acclaimed as the Messianic King of prophecy (John 12:13). Soon afterward, at His trial, He was accused of being a political king and a rival of Caesar (John 18:33; 19:12). Jesus denied this, saying that His kingdom was not of this world and arguing that if His kingdom were of this world, His followers would have fought to have prevented His arrest (John 18:36). Earlier in His ministry Christ had rejected a move to force Him to be such a king (John 6:15). It is noteworthy that Christ did not argue before Pilate that He had indeed come to establish a political kingship modeled after King David's, nor did He state that He had postponed an earthly kingdom and was not a rival to Caesar at this time. Caesar's soldiers mocked the kingship of Jesus (John 19:1-3), and He was crucified under the indictment: "Jesus of Nazareth the King of the Jews" (John 19:19). Jesus had given no evidence that He had offered a political kingdom to Israel. Instead this was the misinformation His enemies had used to have Him crucified.

After His crucifixion Jesus was resurrected from the dead and ascended to the right hand of the Father. The New Testament stresses that this resurrection-ascension established in a special way Jesus' Messianic kingship. The resurrected Christ appeared to the disciples and made the regal claim, "All power (or authority) is given unto me in heaven and in earth" (Matthew 28:18). He then promised to be with the church till the end of the age and gave the church the royal responsibility of discipling the nations, thereby securing for Christ His rightful realm. After giving the Great Commission, Christ ascended into heaven in a cloud in fulfillment of Daniel 7:13-14:

> I saw in the night visions, and, behold, one like the Son of man came with the clouds of heaven and came to the Ancient of days, and they brought him near before Him. And there was given Him dominion, and glory, and a kingdom, that all people, nations, and languages, should serve Him: His dominion is an everlasting dominion, which shall not pass away, and His kingdom that which shall not be destroyed.

Through His resurrection and ascension, Jesus was declared to be the Messianic Son of God in power (Romans 1:4).[14] Jesus' divine Sonship as the second Person of the Godhead had no beginning or need for exaltation, but His Messianic Sonship as a human Son of David was established in power when Christ entered into His glorified resurrection status. This Messianic Sonship had a beginning, a time at which God said, "Thou art My Son; this day have I begotten thee" (Psalm 2:7).[15] Therefore Peter could say on Pentecost regarding the resurrection and ascension of Jesus: "Therefore let all the house of Israel know assuredly, that God hath made that same Jesus whom ye have crucified both Lord and Christ" (Acts 2:36). The title "Christ," which is the Greek equivalent of the Hebrew "Messiah," means "the anointed one," which is the Old Testament title for God's chosen king over Israel (1 Samuel 24:6; 2 Samuel 23:1; Psalm 2:2).

At the synagogue of Pisidian Antioch, Paul proclaimed a similar message about the Messianic rule of Jesus:

> And we declare unto you glad tidings, how that the promise which was made unto the fathers, God hath fulfilled the same unto us their children, in that he hath raised up Jesus again; as it is also written in the second psalm, Thou art My Son, this day have I begotten thee (Acts 13:32-33).

This second Psalm was written in terms of the Davidic kingdom as evidenced by the statement, "Yet have I set My king upon My holy hill of Zion." And yet the New Testament nowhere teaches that this Psalm awaits fulfillment in a future Jewish age. Instead, the New Testament gives repeated indication that the Messianic coronation proclaimed in this Psalm was fulfilled at the resurrection and ascension of Jesus Christ.

In Acts 4:25-28 the second Psalm is again spoken of as fulfilled by "Thy holy Child (or Servant) Jesus whom Thou hast anointed." The book of Revelation also testifies that Jesus Christ by His resurrection-ascension and present heavenly reign has fulfilled and is fulfilling the second Psalm:

> And he that overcometh and keepeth My works unto the end, to Him will I give power over the nations: And he shall rule them with a rod of

---

[14]John Murray, *The Epistle to the Romans* (Grand Rapids: Wm. B. Eerdmans Publishing Company, 1959, 1965), 1:9-12.

[15]H. C. Leupold, *Exposition of the Psalms* (Grand Rapids: Baker Book House, 1959), pages 50-51; Gerhard Kittel, editor, *Theological Dictionary of the New Testament*, 8:367.

iron; as the vessels of a potter shall they be broken to shivers (Psalm 2:9): *even as I received of My Father* (Revelation 2:26-27).

And she brought forth a man child, who was to rule all nations with a rod of iron (Psalm 2:9); and her child was caught up unto God, and to his throne (Revelation 12:5).

And the author of Hebrews inscripturates the same:

So also the Christ glorified not Himself to be made a high priest; but He that said unto Him, Thou art My Son, to day have I begotten Thee (Hebrews 5:5).

Another Psalm that clearly refers to the Messianic kingdom is the 110th Psalm, which begins as follows:

The Lord said unto My Lord, Sit thou at My right hand, until I make Thine enemies Thy footstool. The Lord shall send the rod of Thy strength out of Zion: rule thou in the midst of thine enemies.

The dispensationalists claim that there is no basis for teaching that "the throne of the Father in heaven is to be identified with the Davidic throne,"[16] and yet this Psalm clearly identifies the Messianic throne with the right hand of the Father. And Peter quoted this very Psalm in his Pentecost sermon in which he sought to prove that God had made Jesus "both Lord and Christ" through His resurrection-ascension (Acts 2:29-36). The New Testament contains significant additional testimony that the fulfillment of this Messianic Psalm began with the resurrection, ascension and heavenly seating of the Lord of glory.[17]

That Jesus is now exercising His prophesied Messianic rule is further confirmed by the apostolic church's total ignorance of any kingdom postponement. At Samaria "Philip preached the things concerning the kingdom of God, and the name of Jesus Christ" (Acts 8:12). Paul and Barnabus encouraged newly formed churches with the message: "We must through much tribulation enter into the kingdom of God" (Acts 14:22). The unbelieving Jews at Thessalonica charged that Paul and Silas were acting "contrary to the decree of Caesar, saying that there is another king, one Jesus" (Acts 17:7). At Ephesus, Paul spoke "boldly for the space of three months, disputing and persuading the things concerning the kingdom of God" (Acts 19:8; compare 20:25). Throughout Paul's imprisonment at Rome, he

---

[16]John F. Walvoord, *The Millennial Kingdom*, page 203.

[17]Hebrews 1:13; 5:6; 7:17, 21; 10:12-13; Matthew 22:41-46; 1 Corinthians 15:25-27a.

"preached the kingdom of God" (Acts 28:31; compare verse 23). If Paul were aware that the kingdom had been postponed, he gave no indication of it. Perhaps this is why ultra-dispensationalists conclude that the kingdom was not postponed until after the book of Acts and that Acts and all the epistles written during the time of the Acts are Jewish books and not Christian books!

The kingdom is also mentioned often in the New Testament epistles. For example, Paul spoke of salvation as deliverance from the domain of Satan into the kingdom of God's dear Son (Colossians 1:13). In Colossians 4:10-11 Paul referred to Aristarchus, Mark, and Justus as "fellowworkers unto the kingdom of God." There are many other similar passages.[18] The dispensationalist reasons that since these verses definitely refer directly to the church age and since the kingdom Christ offered to Israel was entirely unrelated to the church age, then the word "kingdom" in the above verses must refer to something entirely different from the word "kingdom" in the preaching of Christ. They argue that the word "kingdom" refers to "the universal and spiritual kingdom or rule of God."[19] But where was the word "kingdom" redefined in Scripture? What is the Scriptural basis for claiming that the "normal" meaning of the word "kingdom" in the New Testament episties is entirely different from the "normal" meaning of the word in the Gospels? To use a criticism which Dr. Ryrie used against an amillennialist, the reason that the dispensationalist does not see the kingdom which Christ offered in the above verses is because "he feels, of course, that he has found justifiable reasons for spiritualizing the concept of the kingdom."[20] The "justifiable reason" here is that a consistent interpretation of the word "kingdom" would greatly contradict some basic dispensational assumptions.

Lastly, we must observe some of the difficulties associated with the dispensational view of the Messianic kingdom. We will do this by analyzing the dispensational explanation of the simple promise in the Davidic covenant, "I will establish the throne of his kingdom for ever" (2 Samuel 7:13b). Does the word "forever" mean David's throne

---

[18] 1 Corinthians 6:9-10; Galatians 5:21; Ephesians 5:5; 2 Thessalonians 1:5; 2 Timothy 4:18.

[19] Charles Caldwell Ryrie, *Dispensationalism Today* (Chicago: Moody Press, 1965), page 172; J. Dwight Pentecost, *Things to Come, A Study in Biblical Eschatology* (Grand Rapids: Zondervan Publishing House, 1958), pages 471-472.

[20] Charles Caldwell Ryrie, *Dispensationalism Today*, page 93.

would always be literally extant? Dispensationalists teach that this covenant will be fulfilled literally and unconditionally. If this is the case, then dispensationalists need to explain how the throne of David remained literally established during the time of the Babylonian exile. Verses 38, 39 and 44 of the eighty-ninth Psalm reveals the status of the Davidic covenant during times of divine chastisement:

> But Thou hast cast off and abhorred, Thou hast been wroth with Thine anointed. Thou hast made void the covenant of Thy servant: Thou hast profaned his crown by casting it to the ground.

> Thou hast made his glory to cease, and cast his throne to the ground.

There are only two ways the dispensationalist could handle this. On the one hand, he could acknowledge that the Davidic covenant is conditional in the sense that God blesses in accordance with holiness. Dr. J. Dwight Pentecost takes this route and says:

> The only conditional element in the covenant was whether the descendants of David would continually occupy the throne or not. Disobedience might bring about chastening, but never abrogate the covenant. Peters says:

> Some . . . wrongfully infer that the entire promise is conditional over against the most express declarations to the contrary as to the distinguished One, the pre-eminent Seed. It was, indeed, conditional as to the ordinary seed of David . . ., and if his seed would have yielded obedience, David's throne would *never* have been vacated until the Seed, par excellence, came; but being disobedient, the throne was overthrown, and will remain thus "a tabernacle fallen down," "a house desolate," until rebuilt and restored by the Seed.[21]

Dr. Pentecost then proceeds to argue that the Davidic covenant is unconditional because:

> . . . the covenant was reaffirmed after repeated acts of disobedience on the part of the nation. . . . These reaffirmations would and could not have been made if the covenant were conditioned upon any response on the part of the nation.[22]

I disagree with the dispensational teaching on conditional and unconditional covenants, but I am in basic agreement with what Dr. Pentecost has said about the Davidic covenant. The blessings of the

---

[21]J. Dwight Pentecost, *Things to Come*, pages 103-104.

[22]Ibid., page 104.

Davidic covenant were conditioned on obedience by the seed of David. This, however, did not mean that the Davidic covenant could have been abrogated because the covenant ultimately had reference to the sinless Christ who through His obedience merited the full blessings of this covenant for His people. I believe Dr. Pentecost has inaccurately handled the problem of the Babylonian exile by compromising the usual dispensational teaching on the nature of an unconditional covenant. (I will examine the dispensational dichotomy between conditional and unconditional covenants in the next chapter.)

On the other hand, a dispensationalist could dispense with the problem of the Babylonian exile by defining the Davidic throne in such a non-literal fashion that the throne may be said to be established while unoccupied. This is the solution suggested by Dr. John F. Walvoord:

> By the term "throne" it is clear that no reference is made to a material throne, but rather to the dignity and power which was sovereign and supreme in David as king. The right to rule always belonged to David's seed. By the term "kingdom" there is reference to David's political kingdom over Israel. By the expression "for ever" it is signified that the Davidic authority and Davidic kingdom or rule over Israel shall never be taken from David's posterity. The right to rule will never be transferred to another family, and its arrangement is designed for eternal posterity. Whatever its changing form, temporary interruptions, or chastisements, the line of David will always have the right to rule over Israel and will, in fact, exercise this privilege. This then, in brief, is the covenant of God with David.[23]

> It is, then, not necessary for the line to be unbroken as to actual conduct of the kingdom, but it is rather that the lineage, royal prerogative, and right to the throne be preserved and *never lost*, even in sin, captivity, and dispersion. It is not necessary, then, for continuous political government to be in effect, but *it is necessary that the line not be lost.*[24]

If the Davidic throne only refers to "the right to rule," then the seed of David did retain the throne even when in Babylonian exile. This brings us to an interesting question: Does not Christ now possess "the dignity and power which was sovereign and supreme in David as king" and "the right to rule"? If the more immediate seed of David could possess the Davidic throne even when in Babylon by retaining

---

[23]John F. Walvoord, *The Millennial Kingdom*, page 196.

[24]Ibid., page 201.

the "right to rule," then why does not Jesus now possess the Davidic throne? If one accepts Dr. Walvoord's definition of the Davidic throne, then how can one possibly hold that Christ does not now possess it because He is not literally ruling from earthly Jerusalem?

In arguing that Christ does not now possess the throne of David, dispensationalists insist that the true throne of David must be an earthly throne. They have insisted that a heavenly throne (Revelation 12:5) and a heavenly Mount Zion (Hebrews 12:22) do not fulfill the prophecy of the Davidic covenant. For example, Dr. Lewis Sperry Chafer has said: ". . . the throne of David is precisely what David believed it to be, an earthly institution which has never been, nor will it ever be, in heaven."[25]

More recently some dispensationalists have begun to teach that the Messianic rule will be exercised from both an earthly throne and a heavenly throne, as evidenced by the following quotations from Dr. J. Dwight Pentecost:

> According to the established principles of interpretation the Davidic covenant demands a literal fulfillment. This means that Christ must reign on David's throne on the earth over David's people forever.[26]

> This heavenly city will be brought into a relation to the earth at the beginning of the millennium, and perhaps will be made visible above the earth. It is from this heavenly city that David's greater Son exerts His Messianic rule, in which the Bride reigns, and from which the rewarded Old Testament saints exercise their authority in government.[27]

In closing this chapter I would like to summarize the practical difference between the Reformed and the dispensational views of the kingdom. When one accepts the Reformed understanding of the Davidic kingdom, it is meaningful to the Christian today. It relates to the "here and now," not to a future Jewish age. The prayer "Thy kingdom come" makes sense for today in the Reformed system. The dispensational view of the kingdom neglects the full significance of the present reign of Christ and can lead to a pietistic, other-worldly sort of Christianity that is culturally impotent. Some dispensationalists have said, "Why polish the brass on a sinking ship?" and "My job is to fish for men, not to clean up the goldfish bowl." Dr. John F.

---

[25] Lewis Sperry Chafer, *Systematic Theology*, 4:315.

[26] J. Dwight Pentecost, *Things to Come*, page 112.

[27] Ibid., page 546.

Walvoord has expressed this mentality well in his book *The Millennial Kingdom*:

> The premillennial concept of the present age makes the inter-advent period unique and unpredicted in the Old Testament. The present age is one in which the gospel is preached to all the world. Relatively few are saved. The world becomes, in fact, increasingly wicked as the age progresses. The premillennial view holds no prospects of a golden age before the second advent, and presents no commands to improve society as a whole. The apostles are notably silent on any program of political, social, moral, or physical improvement of the unsaved world. Paul made no effort to correct social abuses or to influence the political government for good. The program of the early church was one of evangelism and Bible teaching. It was a matter of saving souls out of the world rather than saving the world. It was neither possible nor in the program of God for the present age to become the kingdom of God on earth.[28]

LONG FOOTNOTES

[11] Gerhard Kittel, editor, *Theological Dictionary of the New Testament*, 1:571-572. According to Ridderbos, "in Jewish eschatological literature the '*malkuth shamaim*' [kingdom of heaven] is understood to be the coming universal revelation of the kingship of God with which the appearance of the Messiah is intimately connected." Herman Ridderbos, *The Coming of the Kingdom* (The Presbyterian and Reformed Publishing Company, 1962), page 13.

---

[28]John F. Walvoord, *The Millennial Kingdom*, page 134.

Chapter Twenty

Dispensationalism: Old Testament Salvation

According to dispensationalist Ryrie, the most frequent criticism of dispensationalism is that dispensationalism teaches different ways of salvation in different ages.[1] And the most probable basis for this criticism is the dispensational teachings on salvation in the Old Testament and the millennial kingdom. Certain dispensational writers have made statements that give the impression they are advocating Old Testament and millennial salvation by a meritorious system of works. For example, Dr. Lewis Sperry Chafer has boldly proclaimed:

> A distinction must be observed here between just men of the Old Testament and those justified according to the New Testament. According to the Old Testament men were just because they were true and faithful in keeping the Mosaic Law.... *Men were therefore just because of their own works for God whereas New Testament justification is God's work for man in answer to faith* (Rom. 5:1)[emphasis added].[2]

> The Law of Moses presents a covenant of works to be wrought in the energy of the flesh; the teachings of grace present a covenant of faith to be wrought in the energy of the Spirit.[3]

[1] Charles Caldwell **Ryrie**, *Dispensationalism Today* (Chicago: Moody Press, 1965), page 110.

[2] Lewis Sperry Chafer, *Systematic Theology, 8 vols.* (Dallas: Dallas Seminary Press, 1948), 7:219.

[3] Ibid., 4:211.

The law, being a covenant of works and providing no enablement, addressed itself to the limitations of the natural man. No more was expected or secured in return from its commands than the natural man in his environment could produce.[4]

It is to be concluded that the preaching of John the Baptist was wholly new, and was according to his mission as herald of the King; *but that message is legalistic and not gracious.* It is a covenant of works and not a covenant of faith. . . . Into that kingdom, men are said to be "pressing in." "To crowd oneself in" is the literal meaning, and the word suggests intense human effort, and implies the need of merit for entrance into the kingdom [emphasis added].[5]

The Sermon on the Mount is the expansion of the full meaning of the personal righteousness which is required in the kingdom. The great words in this age are *believe* and *grace*. Not once do these words appear in connection with the kingdom teachings of Matthew 5-7.[6]

The kingdom teachings, like the Law of Moses, are based on a covenant of works. The teachings of grace, on the other hand, are based on a covenant of faith. In the one case, righteousness is demanded; in the other it is provided, both imputed and imparted, or inwrought. One is a blessing to be bestowed because of a perfect life, the other is a life to be lived because of a perfect blessing already received.[7]

Under grace, the fruit of the Spirit *is*, which indicates the present possession of the blessing through pure grace; while under the kingdom, the blessing *shall be to such as merit it by their own works* [emphasis added].[8]

In this age, God is dealing with men on the ground of His grace as it is in Christ. His dealings with men in the coming age are based on a very different relationship. At that time, the King will rule with a rod of iron. There is no word of the cross, or of grace, in the kingdom teachings.[9]

It is strange, indeed, that men who have won honors as theologians of the first magnitude do not see the difference between the proclamation of an earthly kingdom addressed to one elect nation to be established on

[4]Ibid., 4:247.
[5]Ibid., 4:214-215.
[6]Ibid., 4:215.
[7]Ibid., 4:215-216.
[8]Ibid., 4:219.
[9]Ibid., 4:222.

legal grounds, and the proclamation of a grace message which concerns only individuals with Jews and Gentiles, on an equal footing, under sin and offers in sovereign grace to the one who believes on Christ that he will be made meet to be a partaker of the inheritance of the saints in light.[10]

"The straight and narrow way" is an outworking of personal merit and righteousness and is far removed from salvation, which provides a perfect and eternal justification based on an acceptance in the Beloved. The Christian has been saved by an act of faith and *not by relentless persevering in a narrow path.* . . . There is no rest here in the finished work of Christ (cf. Heb. 4:9); *all is personal merit* as the basis of hope for entrance into the kingdom of heaven.[11]

Thus it may be concluded that the teachings of the law, the teachings of grace, and the teachings of the kingdom are separate and complete systems of divine rule which are perfectly adapted to the varied conditions of three great dispensations. *The teachings of Moses and the teachings of the kingdom are purely legal, while the instructions to the believer of this dispensation are in conformity with pure grace* [emphasis added].[12]

Dr. Chafer does appear to have taught different ways of salvation in different ages, and yet Dr. Charles C. Ryrie, who studied under Dr. Chafer, claims the following:

Neither the older nor the newer dispensationalists teach two ways of salvation, and it is not fair to attempt to make them so teach. . . . Straw men are easy to create, but the huff and puff it takes to demolish them are only huff and puff.[13]

Such a claim in the blinding light of the above quotations demonstrates that the dispensational teachings on Old Testament salvation are a sensitive area for dispensationalists and an interesting area for study.

In this chapter I will examine the teachings on Old Testament salvation of the older and the newer dispensationalists, as Dr. Ryrie labels them, and contrast these dispensational teachings with that of Reformed theology. I will first discuss an inherent weakness in the dispensational teaching on Old Testament salvation and then examine

---

[10]Ibid., 5:101.

[11]Ibid., 5:110-111.

[12]Ibid., 4:225.

[13]Charles Caldwell Ryrie, *Dispensationalism Today*, page 207.

the specifics of their teaching on this subject.

This inherent weakness results from the foundational assumption that there is a strong dichotomy between Israel and the church such that the Old Testament saints will not be in the Body and Bride of Christ in eternity. This means that the dispensational system contains a presuppositional prejudice against the Old Testament saints being *in Christ* and under the covenant headship of Christ. The dispensational system imposes on its consistent adherents the necessity of explaining Old Testament salvation in such a way that Old Testament salvation does not involve covenant membership in the Body of Christ. To be in covenant union with Christ is to be in the Body and Bride of Christ, and to be in the Body and Bride of Christ is to be in the church universal, and for the Old Testament saints to be in the church universal is to deny dispensationalism. According to Dr. Paul Lee Tan: "To see the church as the Body of Christ, an organism different from Old Testament Israel, is to read Scripture dispensationally and to qualify as a dispensational interpreter."[14] According to Dr. J. Dwight Pentecost:

> The marriage of the Lamb is an event which evidently involves only Christ and the church. . . . While it would be impossible to eliminate these groups [Old Testament saints and tribulation saints] from the place of observers, they can not be in the position of participants in the event itself.[15]

According to Dr. Lewis Sperry Chafer:

> There is probably no word of Scripture which more clearly defines the essential fact concerning the Christian than the phrase "in Christ"; and as the Christian is the most important fact of all creation, there has never been a word uttered which was so far-reaching in all its implication, or which is fraught with greater meaning to humanity than the phrase "in Christ". . . . Over against the emphasis which is given to this truth in the teachings of grace, is the corresponding fact that there is no hint of a possible position in Christ in any teaching of law or of the kingdom.[16]

> Much of divine blessing is determined for Israel all of which is anticipated in her covenants and prophecies; but no covenant or pro-

---

[14]Paul Lee Tan, *The Interpretation of Prophecy* (Rockville, Maryland: Assurance Publishers, 1974), page 251.

[15]J. Dwight Pentecost, *Things to Come, A Study in Biblical Eschatology* (Grand Rapids: Zondervan Publishing House, 1958), page 227.

[16]Lewis Sperry Chafer, *Systematic Theology*, 4:98.

phecy brings that nation into heavenly citizenship or into marriage union with Christ.[17]

Dispensationalists recognize that if Old Testament saints are in Christ as Paul used that term, then Old Testament saints are in the church universal (1 Corinthians 12:13), and that would effectively destroy the dispensational dichotomy between Israel and the church. A salvifically unified people of God through the ages is a concept antithetical to the foundational presuppositions of dispensationalism. This fundamental dispensational bias against the salvific unity in Christ of the people of God through the ages is, I think, the most basic weakness in the dispensational teaching on Old Testament salvation.

Now that we have discussed this preliminary consideration, I will examine the specific details of the dispensational teachings on Old Testament salvation. Since dispensational teaching in this area has evolved over the years, I will first look at the older dispensational teaching as represented by Dr. Lewis Sperry Chafer and then at the newer dispensational teaching as represented by Drs. John F. Walvoord, Charles C. Ryrie, and J. Dwight Pentecost.

Historic Dispensationalism

The older dispensational teaching on Old Testament salvation is extensively explained in the fourth volume of Dr. Chafer's *Systematic Theology*, the primary source for my understanding on this subject. Fundamental to Dr. Chafer's system is his concepts of conditional and unconditional covenants. A conditional covenant, according to Dr. Chafer, is a covenant in which God agrees to do His part only on the condition that man does his part. It is a meritorious, by-works, "be good, and I will bless you" proposition. In contrast, Dr. Chafer defines an unconditional covenant as a covenant in which God has bound Himself to do something regardless. There is no human responsibility involved. It is a gracious, by-faith, "I have blessed you, now be good" proposition.[18]

In Dr. Chafer's system the nation Israel after Mount Sinai was under both a conditional and an unconditional covenant. The Abrahamic covenant with its land promise to Abraham and his Seed was Israel's unconditional covenant: "This [Abrahamic] covenant, being

---

[17]Ibid., 4:142.

[18]See end of chapter, Long Footnotes, p. 288.

without human condition, simply declares the unchanging purpose of Jehovah. It will be achieved in pure grace, apart from every human factor, and its accomplishments are eternal."[19]

When the nation Israel was redeemed from Egypt, they were in an ideal position. They had been redeemed as a nation, and, on the basis of the Abrahamic covenant, they had an unconditional right to the promised land which was contingent on no human responsibilities. But then, according to Dr. Chafer, Israel made a foolish and rash mistake at Mount Sinai by accepting the meritorious Mosaic covenant.[20] [Ed. Note: The assumption is that God offered a bad covenant. Dr. Chafer never addresses the impugned character of God such a bad offer would entail.]

Dr. Chafer regarded the Mosaic covenant as a meritorious covenant of works in which divine blessing was conditioned strictly on human faithfulness.[21] It was the antithesis of a covenant of grace.[22] Its byword was "This do and thou shalt live." It was a legal relationship by which one entered God's blessings by means of personal self-righteousness.[23] In a covenant of works like the Mosaic covenant, there is no divine enablement and man must depend on the energy of the flesh.[24]

We now have the nation Israel under both the conditional, "Be good, and I will bless you," meritorious, by-works, and temporary Mosaic covenant and the unconditional, "I have blessed you, now be good," gracious, by-faith and eternal Abrahamic covenant. This, of course, seems logically impossible. How could the same people simultaneously be related to God through two such antithetical covenants? The dispensational solution is to posit a strong dichotomy between national and individual promises and blessings and hopes. According to Dr. Chafer:

> What Jehovah has covenanted to His elect nation is one thing, and what He covenants to individuals within that nation is quite another thing. The national entity has been and will be preserved forever according to

[19]Lewis Sperry Chafer, *Systematic Theology*, 4:235.

[20]Ibid., 4:162-163.

[21]See end of chapter, Long Footnotes, p. 289.

[22]See end of chapter, Long Footnotes, p. 289.

[23]See end of chapter, Long Footnotes, p. 290.

[24]See end of chapter, Long Footnotes, p. 292.

covenant promises (Isa. 66:22; Jer. 31:35-37; Gen. 17:7-8). The individual Israelite, on the other hand, was subject to a prescribed and regulated conduct which carried with it a penalty of individual judgment for every failure (Deut. 28:58-62; Ezek. 20:33-44; Matt. 24:51; 25:12, 30).[25]

Israel as a nation was secure in its national salvation under the unconditional Abrahamic covenant, but the individual Israelites had an unsure salvation under the conditional Mosaic covenant. Dr. Chafer contrasted this with the universal church in which both the corporate body and all the individuals in the corporate body are secure.[26]

We now have the background necessary to examine Dr. Chafer's understanding of the way of salvation in the Old Testament. There are four elements in Dr. Chafer's explanation of Old Testament salvation.[27] The first element is physical birth into Judaism. According to Dr. Chafer:

> Whatever may have been the divine method of dealing with individuals before the call of Abraham and the giving of the law of Moses, it is evident that, with the call of Abraham and the giving of the law and all that followed, there are two widely different, standardized, divine provisions whereby man, who is utterly fallen, might stand in favor of God, namely, (a) by physical birth into Judaism or (b) by spiritual birth into Christianity or the kingdom of God.[28]

> Distinction would also be made between the blessings and pri-vileges within the covenants and the terms of admission into the covenants. In the case of the Israelite, entrance into the covenants was by physical birth; while in the case of the Christian it is by spiritual birth.[29]

> Israelites become what they are by physical birth. They are each one begotten of human parents and their inheritance is transmitted by human generation. Christians become what they are by spi-ritual birth. They are begotten directly by God and are therefore His legitimate offspring. Their inheritance is that each is a child of God.[30]

---

[25]Lewis Sperry Chafer, *Dispensationalism*, page 43; Lewis Sperry Chafer, *Systematic Theology*, 4:15.

[26]See end of chapter, Long Footnotes, p. 292.

[27]Lewis Sperry Chafer, *Systematic Theology*, 4:181.

[28]Lewis Sperry Chafer, *Dispensationalism*, page 41; Lewis Sperry Chafer, *Systematic Theology*, 4:14-15.

[29]Lewis Sperry Chafer, *Dispensationalism*, page 76.

[30]Lewis Sperry Chafer, *Systematic Theology*, 4:48.

Too much importance cannot be placed on the fact that an Israelite was physically born into an elect race, a redeemed nation, and made heir of the everlasting covenants. While an Israelite was inducted by his physical birth into all privileges of the chosen people, there was in the law an element of merit because its attending blessings for compliance and judgments for failure.[31]

The Jew, though under the legalistic Mosaic law, was still an heir by birth to the gracious and unconditional Abra-hamic covenant. The Abrahamic covenant was a national covenant, and since a Jew became a member of the Jewish nation by birth, he became an heir of the promised national blessing at birth. Therefore, according to Dr. Chafer, the Jew became a member of God's earthly people through physical birth just as the Christian becomes a member of God's heavenly people through spiritual birth. This gracious admission into the covenant relationships through physical birth meant that Old Testament salvation was not entirely through the law.[32] After all, the law did not make one a Jew. That was done by physical birth.

The second element in Dr. Chafer's system of Old Testament salvation is the sacrificial system. The Jew as an individual was under the meritorious covenant of law and he was responsible for keeping the law in full. That, however, was impossible. No one could keep the law fully, especially not in the power of the flesh with no divine enablement. The only reason salvation was possible for the Jew was because he had the sacrificial system as a means for obtaining forgiveness for his transgressions of the law. As Dr. Chafer explains it:

> The final standing of any Jew before God was not based on law observance alone, but contemplated that Jew in the light of the sacrifices he had presented in his own behalf.[33]

> In case of failure to do the law, sacrifices were accepted as a means to restoration. As the Christian may be forgiven and cleansed on the ground of confession of his sin to God (1 John 1:9), so Israelites both individually and nationally were restored by sacrifices.[34]

When looking back on his experience in Judaism, the Apostle Paul could say that he had been, as 'touching the righteousness which is in

---

[31]Ibid., 4:159.

[32]See end of chapter, Long Footnotes, p. 293.

[33]Ibid., 4:182.

[34]Ibid., 4:159.

the law, blameless' (Phil. 3:6). This did not imply sinless perfection, but rather that he had always provided the requisite sacrifices. On that basis the faithful Jew lived and was accepted of God in the Mosaic system.[35]

Old Testament salvation in Dr. Chafer's system involved forgiveness of sins through the sacrificial rituals and personal righteousness through keeping the law. Dr. Chafer stated that neither the by-faith principle of grace nor the imputed righteousness of Christ was a part of Old Testament salvation.[36] He taught that the Jews did not use the by-faith principle because they were ignorant of the possibility of a by-faith imputed righteousness — in spite of the example of Abraham and David in Romans 4![37] Dr. Chafer said that Abraham was "the pattern of a Christian under grace and not of a Jew under law."[38] He stated that "the by-faith principle which was announced in the Abrahamic covenant is brought again into force, through the death of Christ,"[39] and that the Mosaic law "was preceded (Ex. 19:4) and followed (John 1:17) by grace."[40] Dr. Chafer boldly states that there was no imputed righteousness in the Old Testament: "Israel, as a nation, is never seen in heaven, nor are they as a people, as is true of the Church, constituted righteous. Though termed 'a holy nation,' that holiness is relative rather than absolute."[41]

Similarly Dr. Chafer remarks about imputed righteousness in the Sermon on the Mount and in the millennial kingdom:

No reference, here or elsewhere, in this sermon, is made to imputed righteousness. The kingdom saint's righteousness under Messiah's reign will exceed the righteousness of the scribes and Pharisees. Indeed, such personal quality and merit are demanded for entrance into that kingdom at all. Many Jews will be judged unworthy to enter the kingdom, and those who will be judged will include Jews of the past dispensation who are raised to this judgment (cf. Dan. 12:1-3) as well as the last generation living who will enter that judgment. A reminder at this point may be in order, which asserts again that the believer is provided in this age with

---

[35] Lewis Sperry Chafer, *Dispensationalism*, page 92.

[36] Lewis Sperry Chafer, *Systematic Theology*, 4:215-216.

[37] Ibid., 3:79-80.

[38] Ibid., 3:84.

[39] Ibid., 4:229.

[40] Ibid., 7:226.

[41] Ibid., 4:131.

righteousness which is a gift from God made possible through the sweet
savor aspect of Christ's death and on the ground of the believer's position
in Christ.[42]

Old Testament salvation as explained by Dr. Chafer is a legalistic
system based on ritualistic and moral obedience. Dr. Chafer, however,
argues that Old Testament salvation as he has explained it is a by grace
system:

> Since human faithfulness in whatever degree could never be the exact
> compensation or exchange for the values of eternal life or for unending
> blessings in the kingdom, there is a very large measure of divine grace
> to be seen in the salvation of the elect earthly people.[43]

> [Ed. Note: Likewise the Roman Catholics explain salvation as by
> works but also ultimately by "grace," for no work could ever totally merit
> salvation. The Roman Catholic Church states: "If anyone saith that
> justifying faith is nothing else but confidence in the divine mercy which
> remits sin for Christ's sake alone; or, that this confidence alone is that
> whereby we are justified, let him be anathema" (Sess. VI, Can.12). Dr.
> Chafer displayed his weak theology in Old Testament salvation, being
> basically Roman Catholic at this point. Note by Curtis Crenshaw]

The third element in Dr. Chafer's system of Old Testament
salvation is the teaching that a Jew could be disowned from the nation
and thereby from the gracious Abrahamic covenant by neglecting to
keep the law and to offer sacrifices. Dr. Chafer expressed it as follows:

> The individual Jew might so fail in his conduct and so neglect the
> sacrifices as, in the end, to be disowned of God and cast out (Gen. 17:14;
> Deut. 28:58-61; Ezek. 3:18; Matt. 10:32-33; 24:50-51; 25:11-12, 29-30).[44]

> Thus it is disclosed that the salvation of an Israelite, who lived in the
> Mosaic age, which age will be completed in the coming Tribulation, was
> guaranteed by covenant; yet the individual could, by failing to do God's
> revealed will as contained in the Mosaic Law, sacrifice his place in the
> coming Kingdom and be cut off from his people (cf. Luke. 10:25-28;
> 18:18-21; Matt. 8:11, 12; 24:50, 51; 25:29, 30). Jehovah's salvation of
> Israel will be on the ground of Christ's death. *The human terms, because
> of the covenant promise regarding their salvation, are not the same as*

---

[42]Ibid., 5:106.

[43]See end of chapter, Long Footnotes, p. 293.

[44]Lewis Sperry Chafer, *Systematic Theology*, 4:181. "Of the election of the Church
which is individual, not one could ever be lost. On the other hand, the elect nation
will be purged and out of them will be removed all that offend." Ibid., 4:321.

that required by Abraham or an individual in this age, whether Jew or Gentile [emphasis added].[45]

And Dr. Chafer also gave insight to his thinking on this point in his comments of the Sermon on the Mount:

Thus, also, great is the difference between those who are in danger of hell fire (Matt. 5:22, 29-30) and those who are justified on a principle of perfect divine justice who have done no more than believe in Jesus — even the ungodly (Rom. 3:26; 4:5). . . . And, yet again, consideration must be given to a distinction between those who follow a course — strait and narrow — with the goal in view that they may find life at the end of that path (Matt. 7:14) and those to whom eternal life has been given as a present possession (John 3:36; Rom. 6:23; 1 John 5:11-12). Finally, far removed is the situation in which some hear the Lord say, "I never knew you: depart from me, ye who work iniquity" (Matt. 7:23) and an assurance that one trusting in Christ "shall never perish" (John 10:28; Rom. 8:1).[46]

Of course, Reformed interpreters agree that the Old Testament Jew could be disinherited from the nation for unrepented, high-handed sin. The Reformed interpreter, however, does not make physical birth into Israel the Old Testament equivalent to new covenant regeneration. For the Reformed interpreter, this Old Testament pruning of the unfaithful from the olive tree of Israel is in the same category with New Testament church discipline and is not to be contrasted with new covenant security in Christ.

The last element in Dr. Chafer's system is the national salvation of the nation Israel. Dr. Chafer held that this national salvation was a main objective in Christ's death.[47] This national salvation is to take place during the futuristic dispensational seven-year tribulation period after the church has been raptured and in connection with the post-tribulational return of Christ. During the tribulation, Israel will be regathered to the land of Palestine and many Jews will turn to God through the renewed preaching of the kingdom gospel.[48] The kingdom gospel, according to Dr. Chafer, was what John the Baptist and Jesus had preached at the first advent before Jesus turned from Israel to the Gentiles. Dr. Chafer quoted the following definition of the kingdom

---

[45]Lewis Sperry Chafer, "Inventing Heretics Through Misunderstanding," *Bibliotheca Sacra*, volume 102, number 405 (January - March, 1945), 4-5.

[46]Lewis Sperry Chafer, *Systematic Theology*, 5:112-113.

[47]Ibid., 3:108.

[48]Ibid., 4:318-322; 3:105-108.

gospel from the *Scofield Reference Bible*:

> This is the good news that God purposes to set up on earth, in fulfillment of the Davidic Covenant (2 Sam. 7:16. . .) a kingdom, political, spiritual, Israelitish, universal, over which God's Son, David's heir, shall be King, and which shall be, for one thousand years, the manifestation of the righteousness of God in human affairs . . .

> Two *preachings* of this Gospel are mentioned, one past, beginning with the ministry of John the Baptist, continued by our Lord and His disciples, and ending with the Jewish rejection of the King. The other is yet future (Matt. 24:14), during the great tribulation, and immediately preceding the coming of the King in glory.[49]

At the post-tribulational return of Christ, He is to deliver the nation of Israel from all her enemies and to save Israel as a nation from all her sins by applying the efficacy of His death to the many Jewish sins that for ages have been temporarily covered by animal sacrifices. There is to be a national judgment in which all the Old Testament Jews who were unfaithful to the Mosaic law will be cut off and purged from the people. Then the Holy Spirit will work in the hearts of the remaining faithful Jews, who then will be moved to accept in faith Christ's death for their national salvation. Thus, "all Israel will be saved" (Rom. 11:26).[50] As a result of the return of Christ and this national salvation, the Jews of every age, except the parenthetical church age, who were faithful to Judaism will inherit the land promised to Abraham.[51] These Jews, together with the Gentile nations that treated Israel well during the tribulation period, will enter the earthly millennium and the church will remain in heaven. In the millennium the Gentile nations will be inferior to Israel as Israel's servants.[52] And Israel will have a millennial inheritance that is inferior to the church, which will reside in heaven and rule as Christ's consort.[53] Implying problems with one way kind of salvation, Dr. Chafer expressed uncertainty about "the eternal estate of such patriarchs as Adam,

---

[49]Ibid., 7:175.

[50]Ibid., 3:105-107.

[51]See end of chapter, Long Footnotes, p. 294.

[52]Ibid., pages 20-22; Lewis Sperry Chafer, *Systematic Theology*, 4:5-6, 416; 3:108; 5:355-356. See also John F. Walvoord, *The Millennial Kingdom* (Grand Rapids: Zondervan Publishing House, 1959), page 304.

[53]See end of chapter, Long Footnotes, p. 294.

Enoch, Noah, Job and Melchizedek."[54] I do not know if Dr. Chafer believed these would inherit the earth with Israel or heaven with the church.

At the end of the millennium, there will be the creation of the new heavens and the new earth. In this new creation the separation between Israel and the church will continue throughout eternity. The new heavens will be the eternal inheritance of the heavenly people, the church, and the Judaistic new earth will be the eternal inheritance of the earthly people, Israel.[55]

There are three obvious problems with Dr. Chafer's system. First, though he denied that he taught divergent ways of salvation in different ages,[56] he did make many statements that appeared to justify this criticism.

Second, Dr. Chafer interpreted the phrase "heaven and earth" as referring to two separate spheres that are to remain eternally distinct. The phrase "heaven and earth" is a common Hebrew figure of speech (a merism) used to refer to all created reality.[57]

And third, Dr. Chafer's teaching that the resurrected Old Testament saints would be on earth during the millennium and that resurrected church saints would not be on the new earth during eternity contradicts the New Testament teachings on the New Jerusalem.

This third point about the New Jerusalem needs further explanation. A close examination of Revelation 21 will show that the New Jerusalem does not come to planet earth until after the creation of the new heaven and the new earth (Rev. 21:1-2, 9-10). As was demonstrated in Chapter Nine, the teaching of Revelation 21, Hebrews 11:39-40 and Hebrews 12:22-23 indicates that the New Jerusalem is symbolic for the saints of all the ages. This New Testament teaching

---

[54]"Whatever may be the eternal estate of such patriarchs as Adam, Enoch, Noah, Job, and Melchizedek, who are classed as the original stock which Gentiles perpetuate, a very distinct company of Gentiles are being called out and saved by God's grace into an eternal likeness to Christ and are destined to share His glory forever." Lewis Sperry Chafer, *Systematic Theology*, 4:416.

[55]See end of chapter, Long Footnotes, p. 294.

[56]Lewis Sperry Chafer, "Inventing Heretics Through Misunderstanding," Bibliotheca Sacra, volume 102, number 405 (Jan. - March, 1945),1. Quoted in Charles Caldwell Ryrie, *Dispensationalism Today* (Chicago: Moody Press, 1965), page 113.

[57]Merism: a form of synecdoche in which a totality is expressed by two contrasting parts.

on the New Jerusalem contradicts two aspects of Dr. Chafer's system. Both the resurrected Old Testament saints and the resurrected church saints are in the New Jerusalem. The New Jerusalem has a heavenly location during the dispensational millennium but is on the new earth during eternity. This makes it impossible for the resurrected Old Testament saints to be on earth during a millennial age and for the resurrected church saints not to be on the new earth during eternity.

Neo-Dispensationalism

These three problem areas with Dr. Chafer's teaching are the areas in which the newer dispensationalists have departed from Dr. Chafer's system. The neo-dispensationalists have eliminated the first problem by clearly teaching an Old Testament by-faith salvation. Dr. Charles C. Ryrie explains this position as follows:

> The *basis* for salvation in every age is the death of Christ; the *requirement* for salvation in every age is faith; the *object* of faith in every age is God; the *content* of faith changes in the various dispensations. It is this last point, of course, which distinguishes dispensationalism from covenant theology, but it is not a point to which the charge of teaching two ways of salvation can be attested. It simply recognizes the obvious fact of progressive revelation. When Adam looked on the coats of skins with which God had clothed him and his wife, he did not see what the believer today sees looking back on the cross of Calvary. And neither did other Old Testament saints see what we can see today.[58]

Dr. Ryrie quotes the Dallas Theological Seminary doctrinal statement:

> ... we believe that it was *historically impossible* that [the Old Testament saints] should have had as the conscious object of their faith the incarnate, crucified Son, the Lamb of God (John 1:29), and that it is evident that they did not comprehend as we do that the sacrifices depicted the person and work of Christ. We believe also that they did not understand the redemptive significance of the prophecies or types concerning the sufferings of Christ (1 Peter 1:10-12); therefore, we believe that their faith toward God was manifest in other ways as it is shown by the long record in Hebrews 11:1-40. We believe further that their faith thus manifest was counted unto them for righteousness (cf. Rom. 4:3 with Gen. 15:6; Rom. 4:5-8; Heb. 11:7).[59]

---

[58]Charles Caldwell Ryrie, *Dispensationalism Today*, pages 123-124.

[59]"We Believe . . . Doctrinal Statement" (Dallas: Dallas Theological Seminary,

Since dispensationalists cannot allow the Old Testament saints to have a position in Christ, it seems consistent that they would deny that the Old Testament saint's faith was in the coming Christ.

Dr. Ryrie has stated that the object of faith in every age has been God and that the content of faith was different in the Old Testament. This statement allows great latitude in interpreting the content of faith in the Old Testament. For example, it would accommodate the following analysis of the faith of Abraham by Dr. Chafer:

> Abraham believed God respecting a son whom he would himself generate. . .
>
> . . . God imputes righteousness to those in this age who believe, which righteousness is the foremost feature of salvation, on the one demand that they *believe*; but this belief is not centered in a son which each individual might generate, as in the case of Abraham, but in the Son whom God has given to a lost world, who died for the world and whom God has raised from the dead to be a Savior of those who believe. In Romans 4:23, 24 it is written, "Now it was not written for his sake alone, that it was imputed to him; But for us also, to whom it shall be imputed, if we believe on him that raised up Jesus our Lord from the dead." From this it will be seen that, though the specific object of faith — Isaac in the case of Abraham and Jesus Christ in the case of Christians — varies, both have a promise of God on which to rest and both believe *God*.[60]

Christ, however, said that Abraham saw His day and was glad (John 8:56). Paul said that God preached the gospel to Abraham (Galatians 3:8). This is not to say that Abraham understood God's covenant promise as well as we do today. This is to say that the content of Abraham's faith went beyond the belief that he would have a son in his old age. It is also to say that the object of Abraham's faith was a progressive revelation of the covenant promise which God began to reveal in the Seed-Redeemer promise of Genesis 3:15.

In regard to the object and content of faith, I would say that the object of saving faith for God's people has always been God as the giver of His covenant promise and that the covenant people's knowledge and understanding of God's covenant promise has progressively changed through the ages. Paul refers to the "covenants of promise" (Ephesians 2:12), which implies that all the various covenants which

---

n.d.), page 11.

[60]Lewis Sperry Chafer, "Inventing Heretics Through Misunderstanding," Bibliotheca Sacra, volume 102, number 405 (Jan. - March, 1945), 2-3.

God has administered throughout redemptive history are united by a common promise. Here we have the developmental diversity (many covenants) and the organic unity (one promise) of progressive revelation. God's covenant promise has never changed but man's knowledge and understanding of God's covenant promise has greatly progressed through the ages and will greatly progress in the future when all the saints see the risen and glorified Christ face to face at the second advent. That we today know and understand God's covenant promise better than did the Old Testament saints does not mean that the object of their faith was not the same covenant promise.

The Christian today has faith in the Christ who has already historically come and manifested Himself through the first advent. Faith in the Christ who has come, however, is but faith in the promise of Genesis 3:15 with a progressed knowledge and understanding of the promise of Genesis 3:15. The object of Adam and Eve's faith was the Seed-Redeemer promise, and the ultimate referent of that promise was Jesus of Nazareth, regardless of the level of their understanding of the promise. The ultimate referent of the sacrificial system and much of the Mosaic ceremonial law was Christ. To have believed in these Old Testament promises and institutions was to have believed in the Messianic promise to the extent that it had been revealed. The content of saving faith has not changed through the ages; man's understanding of that content has progressively changed through the ages. This explanation of the content of Old Testament salvation is better adapted to progressive revelation since progression implies an organic unity as well as diversity and developmental change.

In spite of Dr. Ryrie's teaching about the changing content of faith through the ages, Dr. Ryrie appears in his discussion of the Old Testament sacrificial system to teach that the dimly seen content of the Old Testament saint's faith was the coming Christ:

> And yet the law contained the revelation which brought men to a realization that their faith must be placed in God the Saviour. How did it do this? Primarily through the worship which it instituted through the sacrificial system. The sacrifices were part of the law; the keeping of them did not save; and yet a man could respond to what they taught so as to effect eternal salvation.[61]
>
> . . . there seemed to have been in the offerings that which could point a believing worshipper to a better sacrifice which would deal finally with

---

[61]Charles Caldwell Ryrie, *Dispensationalism Today*, page 126.

the entire sin question. This might be called an ulterior efficacy in the sacrifices which did not belong to them as sacrifices but as prefigurations of a final dealing with sin. However, it cannot be implied that the Israelite understood what that final dealing was. . . . *Christ was not the conscious object of their faith,* though they were saved by faith in God as He had revealed Himself principally through the sacrifices which He instituted as a part of the Mosaic law.[62]

There is little difference between what Dr. Ryrie has stated and the general Reformed position on the content of Old Testament faith. To distinguish himself from the Reformed position, Dr. Ryrie has to characterize the covenant theologian as presuppositionally inclined toward the teaching that the Old Testament saint understood Christ's work as typified in the sacrifices as clearly as does the New Testament saint:

> The obvious fallacy in the covenant theologian's solution to this problem is that it is an a priori approach which has yielded artificial results. The assumption is that everything about salvation must be the same; therefore, the conscious object of the faith of old Testament saints must have been Christ. This is not to imply that covenant theologians do not recognize a limitation on the revelation of the Old Testament, but they do everything possible to obliterate the resulting effect that any limitation of revelation might have on the doctrine of Old Testament salvation.[63]

The above may be a valid criticism of certain statements by individual Reformed interpreters,[64] but Dr. Ryrie should not accuse covenant theologians as a class with making this mistake. For example, examine the following statement by Reformed theologian Geerhardus Vos:

> Even though the defective provisional efficacy of the ceremonies might be to some extent perceived, it was far more difficult to tell what was intended to take their place in the future. Here the type needed the aid of prophecy for their interpretation (cf. Isa. 53). We must not infer from our comparatively easy reading of the types that Israelites of old felt the same ease in interpreting them. It is unhistorical to carry back into the Old Testament mind our developed consciousness of these matters. The failure to understand, however, does not detract from the objective

---

[62]Ibid., page 129.

[63]Ibid., page 123.

[64]Ibid., page 122.

significance these types had in the intent of God.[65]

Or examine the following statement by Patrick Fairbairn, a Reformed interpreter from a past age:

> It was comparatively an easy thing for the Jewish worshipper to understand how, from time to time, he stood related to a visible sanctuary and an earthly inheritance, or to go through the process of an appointed purification by means of water and the blood of slain victims applied externally to his body, — much more easy than for the Christian to apprehend distinctly his relation to a heavenly sanctuary and realize the cleansing of his conscience from all guilt by the inward application of the sacrifice of Christ and the regenerating grace of the Holy Spirit. But for the Jewish worshipper to do both his own and the Christian's part, — both to read the meaning of the symbol as expressive of what was already laid open to his eyes, and to descry its concealed reference to the yet undiscovered realities of a better dispensation, — would have required a reach of discernment and a strength of faith far beyond what is now needed in the Christian.[66]

[ED. NOTE]: The Bible and Old Testament Salvation (By Curtis Crenshaw)
THE APOSTLES DECLARE OLD TESTAMENT SALVATION TO BE BY FAITH IN CHRIST:

> Of Him all the prophets bear witness that through His name every one who believes in Him has received forgiveness of sins (Acts 10:43).

> By faith Moses, when he had grown up, refused to be called the son of Pharaoh's daughter; choosing rather to endure ill-treatment with the people of God, than to enjoy the passing pleasures of sin; considering the reproaches of *CHRIST greater riches than the treasures of Egypt* (Heb. 11:24-26).

> Seeking to know what person or time the Spirit of Christ within them was indicating as He predicted the sufferings of Christ and the glories to follow (1 Peter 1:11).

> All were baptized into Moses in the cloud and in the sea; and all ate

---

[65]Geerhardus Vos, *Biblical Theology: Old and New Testaments* (Grand Rapids: Wm. B. Eerdmans Publishing Co., 1948), pages 147-148.

[66]Patrick Fairbairn, *The Typology of Scripture Viewed in Connection with the Whole Series of the Divine Dispensations,* 2 vols. (New York, 1900; reprint, Grand Rapids: Baker Book House, 1975), 1:58.

the same spiritual food; and all drank the same drink, for they were drinking from a spiritual rock which followed them; and the rock was *CHRIST* (1 Cor. 10:2-4).

Paul ... set apart for the gospel of God, which He promised beforehand through His prophets in the holy Scriptures, *CONCERNING HIS SON* (Rom. 1:1-3).

Behold, I lay in Zion a stone of stumbling and a rock of offense, and he who *BELIEVES IN HIM* will not be put to shame (Rom. 9:33 quoting Isa. 28:16).

Remember that you were at that time separate from *CHRIST*, excluded from the citizenship of Israel, and strangers to the covenants of promise, having no hope and without God in the world (Eph. 2:12; if the Gentiles had been without Christ, then the implication is that the Old Testament Jews had not been without Him! On several occasions Paul states that the Prophets and Moses spoke of the death and resurrection of Messiah: Acts 26:22, 23; 28:23, 24; Rom. 1:1-3; 2 Tim. 3:14, 15).

CHRIST WITNESSES TO HIMSELF FROM THE LAW:

And He said to them, "O foolish men and slow of heart to believe all that the prophets have spoken. Was it not necessary for the *CHRIST* to suffer these things and to enter His glory?" And beginning with Moses and the prophets, He explained to them the things *CONCERNING HIMSELF IN ALL THE SCRIPTURES* (Luke 24:25-27).

Now He said to them, "These are My words which I spoke to you while I was still with you, that all things which are written about Me in the Law of Moses and the Prophets and the Psalms must be fulfilled." Then He opened their minds to understand the Scriptures, and He said to them, *"THUS IT IS WRITTEN THAT THE CHRIST SHOULD SUFFER AND RISE AGAIN FROM THE DEAD THE THIRD DAY*; and that repentance for forgiveness of sins should be proclaimed in His name to all the nations — beginning from Jerusalem" (Luke 24:44-47).

You search the Scriptures, because you think that in them you have eternal life; and it is these that bare witness of Me (John 5:39).

Your father Abraham rejoiced to see My day; and he saw it, and was glad (John 8:56).

MANY AT THE TIME OF JESUS' INCARNATION WERE LOOKING FOR THE MESSIAH:

(Without a doubt these passages demonstrate that the Messiah was the "conscious object of their faith.")

He found first his own brother Simon, and said to him, "We have found the Messiah" (John 1:41).

Philip found Nathanael, and said to him, "We have found Him, *OF WHOM MOSES IN THE LAW AND ALSO THE PROPHETS WROTE*, Jesus of Nazareth" (John 1:46).

The woman said to Him, "*I KNOW THAT MESSIAH IS COMING* (He who is called Christ); when that One comes, He will declare all things to us" (John 4:25).

And behold, there was a man in Jerusalem whose name was Simeon; and this man was righteous and devout, *LOOKING FOR* the consolation of Israel; and the Holy Spirit was upon him. And it had been revealed to him by the Holy Spirit that *HE WOULD NOT SEE DEATH BEFORE HE HAD SEEN THE LORD'S CHRIST* (Luke 2:25, 26).

And at that very moment she came up and began giving thanks to God, and continued to speak *OF HIM (CHRIST)* to all those *WHO WERE LOOKING FOR THE REDEMPTION* of Jerusalem (Luke 2:38).

AND EVEN FROM THE OLDEST BOOK IN THE BIBLE WE READ:

I know that my Redeemer lives, and at the last day He will take His stand on the earth (Job 19:25).

Even now, behold, my witness is in heaven, and my Advocate is on high (Job 16:19).

Genesis 3:15, spoken to Adam and Eve, presents the Messiah Himself as coming to destroy Satan and that He too would be bruised. Did Eve "unconsciously" know this? Even further, in Genesis 4:1 Eve says she has "gotten a man, even the *LORD*" (Hebrew text), which indicates several things: (1) She was joyfully looking for the Messiah; (2) she thought He would be deity — the *LORD*; and (3) she believed Him to come as incarnate, a Man. Even if we reject the above translation and render it "gotten a man with (the help of) the *LORD*" (which is done by most on theological grounds: "She could not have known that much of Messiah"), surely we can still say with George Bush on *Genesis* (vol. one, p. 95) that Eve was looking for the divine Redeemer, so that the meaning is essentially the same.

Or one can peruse Appendix IX of *The Life and Times of Jesus the Messiah* by Edersheim to observe in how many passages the Jews — before Christ's incarnation — saw their Messiah. He lists 349 passages and with the New Testament we know there were many more. Hengstenberg's massive two volumes on the *Christology of the Old Testament* are even more telling.

And was not the gospel preached beforehand to Abraham (Gal. 3:8; John 8:56) and to those in the wilderness (Heb. 4:1-6), and is not the gospel about Jesus and the resurrection (1 Cor. 15:3, 4)? And even more, the Gentiles are heirs of the *same promise* made to the Jewish fathers (Jer. 33:14-18 with Acts 7:17; 13:23, 32; 26:6; see also Rom. 15:8-13; Gal. 3:14-29; 4:21-31; Eph. 2:11-3:7), and that promise came through the gospel (Eph. 3:6). The list and arguments are endless. But who can convince those who have a "veil over their face when they read the Old Testament," which veil is taken away by Christ when He "opens our minds to understand Moses and the Prophets" by seeing Him (Luke 24:44-47). Those who see their Redeemer in the "volume of the Book" (Heb. 10:7) need no other arguments.

I think the dispensationalists do not want to see Christ as the "conscious object" of faith of the Old Testament saints because this would indicate too much covenantal unity, implying only one way of salvation. Centuries ago John Owen faced the same view among the Arminians:

First, then, they grant salvation to the ancient Patriarchs and Jews, before the coming of Christ, without any knowledge of or faith in Him at all; nay they deny that any such faith in Christ was ever prescribed unto them or required of them. "It is certain that there is no place in the Old Testament from whence it may appear that faith in Christ as a Redeemer was ever enjoined or found in any of them," say they jointly in their Apology; the truth of which assertion we shall see hereafter. Only they grant a general faith, involved under types and shadows, and looking on the promise as it lay hid in the goodness and providence of God, which indirectly might be called a faith in Christ: from which kind of faith I see no reason why thousands of heathen infidels should be excluded. Agreeable unto these are the dictates of their patriarch Arminius, affirming, "that the whole description of the faith of Abraham, Rom. 4, makes no mention of Jesus Christ, either expressly or so implicitly as that it may be of any one easily understood." And to the testimony of Christ Himself to the contrary, John 8:56, "Your father Abraham rejoiced to see My day; and he saw it, and was glad," he answereth, "He rejoiced to see the birth of Issac, who was a type of Me," — a goodly gloss, corrupting the text (vol. 10, p. 109).

[End Ed. Note]

A second area where neo-dispensationalists significantly differ from the older dispensationalism of Dr. Chafer is related to the concept of the New Jerusalem and to the interpretation of the new heavens and the new earth, the second and third problem points in Dr. Chafer's system. In the newer system as contained in the writings of Dr. J. Dwight Pentecost and Dr. John F. Walvoord, the church enters her eternal state in the heavenly Jerusalem at the rapture immediately before the beginning of a seven year tribulation period. During this tribulation period, God's program with Israel, which was interrupted by the church age, will be resumed. After this tribulation period, at the time of the second advent and the beginning of the dispensational millennium, the heavenly Jerusalem will descend to a hovering position over the land of Palestine.[67] This satellite city will have astonishing dimensions, being either a cube or a pyramid with a 1500 mile square base and a height of 1500 miles.[68]

At the time of the second advent, the dead Old Testament saints will be resurrected and will enter their eternal state in the heavenly Jerusalem along with the resurrected church saints. The living Jewish saints who survived the tribulation period, however, will enter the millennium in unresurrected bodies on earth along with select Gentiles.[69] The resurrected saints of the heavenly city will be free to travel to and from the earth during the millennial period.[70] At the end of the millennium, the new heavens and the new earth will be created, the heavenly city will descend to Palestine on the new earth, and the redeemed of all the ages will enjoy eternity together on the new earth.

This newer system does not have the specific problems previously pointed out in Dr. Chafer's system. In this neo-dispensational system, there is one eternal destiny for the saints of all ages in accordance with a proper interpretation of the phrase "heaven and earth." Also, this system does not contradict the New Testament's teaching on the New Jerusalem the way Dr. Chafer's system does. This new system, however, has generated new problems in its adjustments to compensate for the old problems in Dr. Chafer's system.

---

[67]See end of chapter, Long Footnotes, p. 296.

[68]See end of chapter, Long Footnotes, p. 297.

[69]John F. Walvoord, *The Millennial Kingdom*, pages 324-325; J. Dwight Pentecost, *Things to Come*, page 542, 415, 422; Charles Caldwell Ryrie, *Dispensationalism Today*, page 146.

[70]John F. Walvoord, *The Millennial Kingdom*, page 329; J. Dwight Pentecost, *Things to Come*, page 579.

First, the newer system does not allow the Old Testament saints to inherit the land promised to Abraham and his seed, which, according to Chafer, violates the plain, literal language given to Old Testament saints that they would inherit the land. Neo-dispensationalist Dr. John F. Walvoord has said the following:

> Much of the confusion that exists in regard to the millennium and the eternal state stems from a failure to distinguish between the promises that are given to the last generation of saints who are on the earth at the time of the second advent and the promises that are given resurrected or translated saints in both the Old and New Testaments. The prophecies of the Old Testament give adequate basis for the doctrine that Israel has an earthly hope. The prophets in Israel's darkest hours painted the most glowing picture of the coming earthly kingdom in which Israel would participate as a favored nation and possess their promised land under the reign of the Son of David. The promises given, however, clearly refer to those who were not resurrected and are directed to the nation of Israel as it is to be constituted at the time of the second advent, that is, the Israelites who will survive the great tribulation. They and their seed will inherit the promised land and fulfill the hundreds of prophecies that have to do with Israel's hope in the millennial kingdom. These promises are delineated in the Abrahamic, Davidic, Palestinian, and new covenants.[71]

Dr. Walvoord's explanation becomes obviously inadequate the moment one remembers that the Abrahamic covenant specifically stated that Abraham himself would inherit the land along with his seed. But Abraham, in this neo-dispensational scheme, will not be on earth during the millennium to inherit any land. He will be in the heavenly city. The speculation about the New Jerusalem hovering over Palestine during the millennium and its inhabitants being able to travel to and from planet earth may be meant to compensate for this flaw by at least giving the Old Testament saints such as Abraham access to the land they are supposed to inherit. In reality, this newer system does not allow Abraham to inherit any land during the millennium but instead makes him a millennial bond servant in the heavenly city.[72]

A second problem with this newer system is that the word "forever" no longer literally means forever but means a long duration or, to be specific, one thousand years. This is not consistent literalism,

---

[71] John F. Walvoord, *The Millennial Kingdom*, pages 324-325.

[72] See end of chapter, Long Footnotes, p. 297.

for God promised to give the land to Abraham and to his seed "forever." That is why in Dr. Chafer's system the Jews continued throughout eternity on earth with a distinctive Jewish inheritance. As Dr. Chafer said, "Those earthly promises are confirmed by the oath of Jehovah and extend 'forever', else language ceases to be a dependable medium for the expression of truth."[73]

If the dichotomy between the earthly people and the heavenly people is to be consistently maintained and if the Jewish covenants are eternal covenants, then the Jews must have a distinctively Jewish eternity separate from the church. But if the Jewish covenants find their complete fulfillment in eternity, as in Dr. Chafer's system, this de-emphasizes the millennium and makes it a mere addendum to the dispensational system. The dispensationalist's millennium is no longer mandatory and "an integral part of his entire scheme and interpretation of many Bible passages"[74] if the Jewish covenants find their final fulfillment in eternity, not in the millennium. Therefore, in neo-dispensational thought, these eternal covenants must find their fulfillment in the specifically Jewish millennium and not during the eternity on the new earth that will be shared with the church. "Forever," therefore, means one thousand years!

A third problem with the neo-dispensational system is the significant new strain that it puts on the dispensational dichotomy between national and individual promises. In Dr. Chafer's system, all the individuals within the nation were to receive the same promises, though admittedly on a conditional basis, but the nation as a whole was to receive its promises on an unconditional basis. All those individuals who remained members in good standing of the nation were heirs of the national land promise that was to be realized in a coming earthly kingdom. According to Dr. Chafer, "The glorious Messianic kingdom has been the hope of the Old Testament saints and in conformity to this hope they ordered their lives."[75]

In neo-dispensationalism *none* of the individuals who made up the nation in the Old Testament are to receive the promised national inheritance. The only individuals who will inherit land in this newer

[73]Lewis Sperry Chafer, *Systematic Theology*, 4:30.

[74]The language used here is from a criticism of nondispensational premillennialists by Dr. Ryrie. Charles Caldwell Ryrie, *Dispensationalism Today*, page 160.

[75]Lewis Sperry Chafer, *Systematic Theology*, 4:406. See also Lewis Sperry Chafer, *Dispensationalism*, page 91.

scheme are the living Jews of that future generation that will enter the millennium and their descendants. The individual hopes of all the individual Jews of the Old Testament era find their fulfillment not in the Jewish national inheritance but in the heavenly Jerusalem and in an eternity shared with the church.[76] Of what significance was a national promise to an Old Testament Jew if he as an individual were not to partake of it? Language would then "cease to be a dependable medium for the expression of truth."

A fourth problem is that the neo-dispensationalist gives the Old Testament saint an eternal destiny in common with the church but without giving the Old Testament saint a salvation based on covenant union with Christ. I see no justification for the Old Testament saint having the same eternal destiny as the New Testament saint apart from the Old Testament saint being in union with Christ in eternity. Not being in covenant union with Christ is not simply a quantitative difference in Old Testament salvation that allows the Old Testament saint to have the same inheritance as the church saint but with less honor. It is a qualitative difference that requires a separate inheritance altogether, assuming that any inheritance is possible apart from covenant union with Christ.

A dispensationalist might argue that Abraham had an imputed righteousness, and that Abraham, an Old Testament saint who had not experienced the baptism of the Spirit, was not and is not in covenant union with Christ. Was he not? Paul uses Abraham's imputed righteousness as a proof that the Christian has an imputed righteousness (Rom. 4:22-25), and the Christian's imputed righteousness is an "in Christ" imputed righteousness (2 Cor. 5:21). Did Abraham have an "out of Christ" imputed righteousness? That is not possible since the righteousness that is imputed in justification is the righteousness of Christ. And, assuming that there can be an "out of Christ" imputed righteousness, then it would be radically inferior to "in Christ" righteousness. And in correlation to this, the Old Testament saint must be given an eternal destiny that differs from the eternal destiny of the church like the earth differs from the heavens. This is how Dr. Chafer reasoned. To give the Old Testament saint an eternal destiny in accord with an "in Christ" righteousness is to put the Old Testament saint in the church, for the church consists of all those who are in Christ.

A fifth problem is that differences between the newer and the older

---

[76]See end of chapter, Long Footnotes, p. 298.

dispensationalism evidence a less consistent use of the dispensational hermeneutic by the neo-dispensationalists. On the basis of their hermeneutic, dispensationalists have long insisted that the seed which is to inherit the land is the physical seed of Abraham. Dr. Chafer put more emphasis on the significance of physical birth in Old Testament salvation, making physical birth an integral part of Old Testament salvation and playing down the importance of proselyte salvation apart from physical lineage in the Old Testament.[77] The newer dispensational emphasis on by-faith salvation in the Old Testament could also be called a reading of the New Testament back into the Old Testament.

After examining the dispensational concept of Old Testament salvation, it must be concluded that the dispensational theories on this subject are inadequate and objectionable. Several questions can be raised to show further this inadequacy: Is the rent veil of the temple to be repaired for the millennium and eternity? Is worship again to be centered in Jerusalem (John 4:21)? Is the dividing wall that was destroyed by Christ to be rebuilt (Eph. 2:14)? Are all church saints going to be superior in eternity to Old Testament saints such as Abraham, Moses and David? It is true that Jesus said that the least in the kingdom of heaven would be greater than John the Baptist, but was he not referring to spiritual privileges enjoyed in this life and not to eternal destinies? Is Mary, the mother of our Lord, to be in a different eternal assembly from her husband Joseph simply because she lived a few years longer? Is the future to be a time of retrogression in God's program instead of a time of progression? These and other difficulties are the inevitable result of the dispensationalist's dogmatic dichotomy between Israel and the church as it is applied to Old Testament salvation.

LONG FOOTNOTES

[18] "Whatever God declares He will do is always a binding covenant. If He in no way relates His proposed action to human responsibility, the covenant is properly termed 'unconditional.' If He relates it to human responsibility or makes it to depend on cooperation on the part of any

[77] "Apart from the privilege accorded proselytes of joining the congregation of Israel — which seemed to bear little fruitage — entrance into the right to share in the covenants of blessing designed for the earthly people was and is by *physical* birth." Lewis Sperry Chafer, *Systematic Theology*, 4:15.

other being, the covenant is properly termed 'conditional'. . . . A covenant which is unconditional cannot be conditional and a conditional covenant cannot be unconditional." Lewis Sperry Chafer, *Dispensationalism* (Dallas: Dallas Seminary Press, 1936), page 73.

"If God has made a covenant declaring what He will do provided man does his part, it is conditional and the human element is not one of walking worthy of what God's sovereign grace provides, but rather one of *being* worthy to the end that the promise may be executed at all. When the covenant is unconditional, God is limited in what He will do only by the knowledge-surpassing bounty of His infinite grace. When the covenant is conditional, God is restricted by what man is able or willing to do. As an efficacious appeal, the obligation to walk worthy, though in no way conditioning the sovereign purpose, secures more normal and spiritual response than all the meritorious systems combined. The human heart is far more responsive to the proposition couched in the words 'I have blessed you, now be good,' than it is to the proposition couched in the words 'Be good, and I will bless you.' The element of human conduct thus appears in each form of the divine covenant but in such a manner that one is rendered unconditional and the other conditional." Lewis Sperry Chafer, *Dispensationalism*, page 75.

"In relation to His earthly people, Israel, and their blessings God has made various covenants. Some of these are conditional, and some unconditional, which terms suggest that in some covenants God has them to depend on human faithfulness, while in others He merely declares what He will do wholly apart from the question of human worthiness or faithfulness." Lewis Sperry Chafer, Systematic Theology, 7:97.

21 "The law covenant was strictly a conditional agreement which conditioned divine blessings upon human faithfulness." Ibid., 3:77.

"The Law of Moses presents a covenant of works to be wrought in the energy of the flesh; the teachings of grace present a covenant of faith to be wrought in the energy of the Spirit. . . . The nature of a covenant which is based on human works is obvious. Whatever God promises under such a covenant, is conditioned on the faithfulness of man. Every blessing under the Law of Moses was so conditioned, and every blessing in the kingdom relationship will be found to be so ordered. Turning to the kingdom teachings of Christ wherein the issues of personal conduct and obligations in the kingdom are taken up, it will be seen that all the kingdom promises to the individual are based on human merit." Ibid., 4:211-212.

22 "In this context [Romans 8:2-8], the law stands as the representation of the merit system — that divine arrangement which, according to the

New Testament, is held as the antipodes of God's plan of salvation by grace." Ibid., 3:343.

"Since law and grace are opposed to each other at every point, it is impossible for them to coexist, either as the ground of acceptance before God or as the rule of life. Of necessity, therefore, the scriptures of the New Testament which present the facts and scope of grace, both assume and directly teach that the law is done away. Consequently, it is not in force in the present age in any sense whatsoever. This present nullification of the law applies not only to the legal code of the Mosaic system and the law of the kingdom but to every possible application of the principle of law. The larger conception of the law, as before defined, is threefold: (1) the actual written instructions of both the teachings of Moses and the teachings of the kingdom; (2) the law covenant of works in all of its applications, which conditions blessing and acceptance with God on the ground of personal merit; and (3) the law principle of dependence on the energy of the flesh, in place of the faith principle of a dependence on the power of the indwelling Holy Spirit." Ibid., 4:234.

"The kingdom teachings, like the Law of Moses, are based on a covenant of works. The teachings of grace, on the other hand, are based on a covenant of faith. In the one case, righteousness is demanded; in the other it is provided, both imputed and imparted, or inwrought. One is of a blessing to be bestowed because of a perfect life, the other is of a life to be lived because of a perfect blessing already received." Ibid., 4:215-216.

"The determining character of pure law is seen in the fact that it is a covenant of works wherein the divine blessing is conditioned on human merit. No semblance of this principle is to be found under grace, except that rewards are to be bestowed for faithful service upon those who have already entered into every present position and possession provided in grace. It therefore follows that, not only the written rules of the law, but the very principle of the law covenant of works, has been done away in this age of grace." Ibid., 4:247.

"According to the Old Testament men were just because they were true and faithful in keeping the Mosaic Law. . . . Men were therefore just because of their own works for God, whereas New Testament justification is God's work for man in answer to faith (Rom. 5:1)." Ibid., 7:219.

23 "The nature of a covenant which is based on human works is obvious. Whatever God promises under such a covenant, is conditioned on the faithfulness of man. Every blessing under the Law of Moses was so conditioned, and every blessing in the kingdom relationship will be found to be so ordered. Turning to the kingdom teachings of Christ wherein

the issues of personal conduct and obligation in the kingdom are taken up, it will be seen that all the kingdom promises to the individual are based on human merit. The kingdom blessings are reserved for the poor in spirit, the meek, the merciful, the pure in heart, and the peacemaker. It is a covenant of works only and the emphatic word is do. 'This do, and thou shalt live' is the highest promise of the law. As men judge, so shall they be judged. A tree is approved, or rejected, by it fruits. And not every one that saith Lord, Lord, shall enter into the kingdom of heaven; but he that doeth the will of 'my Father' which is in heaven. As the individual forgives, so will he be forgiven. And except personal righteousness shall exceed the righteousness of the scribes and Pharisees, there shall be no entrance into the kingdom of heaven. To interpret this righteousness which is required to be the imputed righteousness of God, is to disregard the teaching of the context, and to introduce an element which is not once found in this whole system of divine government. The kingdom teachings of the Sermon on the Mount are concluded with the parable of the house built on the rock. The key to this message is given in the words, 'Whosoever heareth these sayings of mine, and doeth them.'

"Turning to the Law of Moses, we discover that it presents no other relation to God for the individual than this same covenant of works: . . . By these references to the Law of Moses and the law of the kingdom, it may be seen that both of these systems are based wholly on a covenant of works." Ibid., 4:211-212.

"First, both the commandments and requirements of the Mosaic system and the commandments and requirements of the kingdom are wholly legal in their character, and, together, comprise the written statement of the law, which law, it will be seen, is set aside during the present reign of grace.

"Second, every human work, be it even the impossible, heaven-high beseeching of grace, which is wrought with a view to meriting acceptance with God, is of the nature of a legal covenant of works, and therefore belongs only to the law. Through the finished work of Christ, acceptance with God is perfectly secured; but that acceptance can be experienced only through faith which turns from dependence on merit, and rests in Christ as the sufficient Savior. In like manner, it will be seen, the whole proposition of legal, meritorious acceptance with God has passed during the reign of grace.

"Third, again, any manner of life or service which is lived in dependence on the flesh, rather than in dependence on the Spirit, is legal in character and has passed during the present period in which grace reigns." Ibid., 4:238. See also Ibid., 4:119-120.

24 "The Law of Moses presents a covenant of works to be wrought in the energy of the flesh; the teachings of grace present a covenant of faith to be wrought in the energy of the Spirit." Ibid., 4:211.

"The law, being a covenant of works and providing no enablement, addressed itself to the limitations of the natural man. No more was expected or secured in return from its commands than the natural man in his environment could produce. The requirements under the law are, therefore, on the place of the limited ability of the flesh. On the other hand, grace, being a covenant of faith, and providing the limitless enablement of the power of the indwelling Spirit, addresses itself to the unlimited resources of the supernatural man. The requirements to be met under grace are, therefore, on the plane of the unlimited ability of the Spirit. There is no divine injunction addressed to the unregenerate concerning his daily life. The gospel of the saving grace of God alone is offered to him. The only divine injunctions now in force in the world are addressed to those who are saved, and these heaven-high standards are to be realized on the principle of faith toward the sufficiency of the indwelling Spirit, and never by dependence on the energy of the flesh." Ibid., 4:247. See also Ibid., 4:51, 156, 234, 239.

26 "But this national election does not extend to every Israelite. That it does not, the Apostle proves in Romans 9:1-24. On the contrary, the individual Israelite, when under the Mosaic Law, was, in the matter of his personal blessing, under a secondary, meritorious covenant with gracious provisions in the animal sacrifices for the covering and cure of his sins and failures. In sharp distinction to this, the Church is, in respect to her corporate whole, an elect people also (Rom. 8:33), but her election and sovereign security is extended to every individual in that body (John 5:24; 6:37; 10:28; Rom. 8:1, A.R.V.)." Lewis Sperry Chafer, *Dispensationalism*, page 76.

"Of the election of the Church which is individual, not one could ever be lost. On the other hand, the elect nation will be purged and out of them will be removed all that offend." Lewis Sperry Chafer, *Systematic Theology*, 4:321.

"The national covenants with Israel do not extend to the individual; they guarantee the perpetuality of the race or nation and its final blessing. When under the Mosaic Law, the individual Israelite, it will be seen, was on an unyielding meritorious basis. Over against this, the divine purpose for the whole Church as a body do extend to the individual believer and every one predestinated will be called, and every one called will be justified, and every one justified will be glorified (Romans 8:30)." Lewis Sperry Chafer, *Dispensationalism*, page 90.

"The conclusion is that blessing under the Mosaic economy was conditioned on individual faithfulness to the law. This economy formed a secondary covenant which was meritorious in character — secondary in the fact that it was restricted to the problems concerning the individual's conduct and in no way compromising the primary covenants which determine the destiny of the nation. In contrast to this, the Christian, while given a rule of life which is in no way meritorious though his faithful service will win a reward or divine recognition (1 Cor. 3:12-15; 9:19-27; 2 Cor. 5:9-11), is in regard to his personal salvation — like the corporate whole to which he belongs — both secure and safe and destined to eternal glory from the moment he believes." Ibid., page 93.

[32] "Thus, in like manner, the Mosaic Law, even if observed, never had the function of creating Israelites; it was given as a consistent rule of life to those who were Israelites by physical birth." Lewis Sperry Chafer, *Dispensationalism*, page 91.

"They [the Jews in the old dispensation] were born into covenant relation with God wherein there were no limitations imposed upon their faith in Him nor upon their fellowship with Him. This fact was in itself a demonstration of superabounding grace." Lewis Sperry Chafer, *Systematic Theology*, 4:181.

[43] Lewis Sperry Chafer, *Dispensationalism*, page 91. "As before stated, whatever God does for sinful man on any terms whatsoever, being made possible through the death of Christ, is, to that extent, an act of divine grace; for whatever God does on the ground of Christ's death is *gracious* in character, and all will agree that a divine covenant that is void of all human elements is more gracious in character than one which is otherwise. These distinctions apply only to the divine side of any covenant. On the human side — a theme yet to be considered — there is no exercise of grace in any case; but the human requirements which the divine covenant imposes may be either absolutely lacking or so drastically imposed as to determine the destiny of the individual." Ibid., page 74.

"Once again and finally let it be asserted, that salvation of any character or of any people or upon any varied human terms is the work of God in behalf of man and is righteously executed by God on the sole basis of the death of Christ. It is puerile to intimate that there could be a salvation achieved alone by the power of either law-works or faith. It is only God's power set free through Christ's death that can save and it is always and only through Christ's death, whatever the human responsibility may be." Lewis Sperry Chafer, "Inventing Heretics Through Misunderstanding," *Bibliotheca Sacra*, volume 102, number 405 (Jan. - March, 1945), 5.

[51] "Quite in contrast to the experience accorded the Church (cf. John 5:24), the nation Israel must be judged, and it is reasonable to believe that this judgment will include all of that nation who in past dispensations have lived under the covenants and promises. Therefore a resurrection of those generations is called for and must precede their judgment. The glorious Messianic kingdom has been the hope of the Old Testament saints and in conformity to this hope they ordered their lives. . . . Their rewards will be for them when they 'return,' which term anticipates the day of Israel's regathering." Ibid., 4:406-407.

"As indicated before, Israel in all her generations — exclusive of those who have entered into the exalted privilege of the present age of grace — will come up for judgment, some to everlasting life and others to everlasting contempt (cf. Dan. 12:2; Ezek. 20:33-44; Matt. 24:37-25:30). The portion of this people who are destined to enter the kingdom become the 'all Israel' who will be saved (cf. Isa. 63:1) when the Deliverer comes out of Sion according to God's unalterable covenant (Rom. 11:26-27, 29). These, like all other creatures of God, are traced into eternity to come; for the kingdom is 'an everlasting dominion' (Dan. 7:13-14). Great grace from God will be upon those who enter the land (cf. Ezek. 20:44; Rom. 11:27)." Ibid., 4:416-417.

"As has been seen, the blessings proffered to the individual Israelites under the law were in two classifications: . . .

"(b) For faithfulness under the law they were promised a share in the future glories which Jehovah, with unconditional sovereignty, covenanted to the nation." Lewis Sperry Chafer, *Dispensationalism*, page 91.

[53] "Should the present king of Great Britain marry a woman of another nation he would bring her into his kingdom, not as a subject, but as a consort. The present divine purpose is the outcalling from both Jews and Gentiles of that company who are the Bride of Christ, who are, therefore, every one to partake of His standing, being in Him, to be like Him, and to reign with Him on the earth (Rev. 20:4, 6; 22:5)." Lewis Sperry Chafer, *Systematic Theology*, 4:10; Lewis Sperry Chafer, *Dispensationalism*, pages 30-31.

[55] "Such contrasts might be cited to great lengths, but the important objective has been gained if it has been made clear that there is an eschatology of Judaism and an eschatology of Christianity and each, though wholly different in details, reaches on into eternity. One of the great burdens of predictive prophecy is the anticipation of the glories of Israel in a transformed earth under the reign of David's Son, the Lord Jesus Christ, the Son of God. There is likewise much prediction which anticipates the glories of the redeemed in heaven." Lewis Sperry Chafer,

Dispensationalism, page 65; Lewis Sperry Chafer, *Systematic Theology,* 4:27.

"The dispensationalist believes that throughout the ages God is pursuing two distinct purposes: one related to the earth with earthly people and earthly objectives involved, which is Judaism; while the other is Christianity. Why should this belief be deemed so incredible in the light of the facts that there is in the present distinction between earth and heaven which is preserved even after both are made new; when the Scriptures so designate an earthly people who go on as such into eternity; and a heavenly people who also abide in their heavenly calling forever?" Lewis Sperry Chafer, *Dispensationalism,* page 107.

"The fact that revelation concerning both Israel and the Church includes the truth about God, holiness, sin, redemption by blood, does not eliminate a far greater body of truth in which it is disclosed that Israelites become such by a natural birth while Christians become such by a spiritual birth; that Israelites were appointed to live and serve under a meritorious, legal system, while Christians live and serve under a gracious system; that Israelites, as a nation, have their citizenship and future destiny centered only in the earth, reaching on to the new earth which is yet to be, while Christians have their citizenship and future destiny centered only in heaven, extending on into the new heavens that are yet to be . . . ." Lewis Sperry Chafer, *Systematic Theology,* 4:30.

"Every covenant, promise, and provision for Israel is earthly, and they continue as a nation with the earth when it is created new. Every covenant or promise for the Church is for a heavenly reality, and she continues in heavenly citizenship when the heavens are recreated." Ibid., 4:47.

"It should be asserted, however, that the entire system known as Judaism, along with all its component parts, is, in the purpose of God, in abeyance throughout the present age, but with definite assurance that the entire Jewish system thus interrupted will be completed by extension into the kingdom, the new earth, and on into eternity to come." Ibid., 4:248.

". . . each [Judaism and Christianity] has its sphere of existence — Israel in the earth for all ages to come, the Church in heaven." Ibid., 4:249.

"Among those who stand in eternal favor with God are the earthly citizens whose destiny it is to go on into eternity as the dwellers on the earth (cf. Rev. 21:3-4; Isa. 66:22), and the heavenly citizens whose destiny it is to occupy the new heavens (cf. Heb. 12:22-24; Rev. 21:9-22:7; John 14:1-3)." Ibid., 4:401.

"It is clear that Israel will dwell in their own land forever. If it is to be an unending residence, that dwelling in the land must transcend the

millennial kingdom and thus continue into the new earth that shall
be. . . . Earth has been the sphere of sin and corruption unsuited to the
presence of God; but it will then be as holy as heaven, and in the new
earth He will delight to dwell among men and to be their God. The term
'men' is evidently in contradistinction to the Biblical term 'saints.' Heaven
will be, as now, the abode of the saints, while earth will be the abode of
men. God is said to dwell among men too. Peter asserts that righteousness
will dwell in both the new heaven and the new earth alike (2 Pet. 3:13)."
Ibid., 5:365-366.

As demonstrated by the above, Dr. Chafer dogmatically and repeatedly
asserted in his writings that there is an eternal dicho-tomy between Israel
and the church with Israel inhabiting the new earth eternally and the
church inhabiting the new heaven eternally. Dr. Chafer, however, did on
occasion make statements contradicting this teaching and which anticipated the newer dispensational teachings. For example, Dr. Chafer in one
place suggested the possibility, and in another place stated the fact, that
the earthly people or Israel will be included together with the church in
the heavenly Jerusalem (Ibid., 4:131; 5:367). And in another place, Dr.
Chafer spoke as if he believed that the unconditional Old Testament
covenants would find their complete fulfillment in the one thousand year
millennium (Ibid., 1:41).

[67] "This heavenly city will be brought into a relation to the earth at the
beginning of the millennium, and perhaps will be made visible above the
earth." J. Dwight Pentecost, *Things to Come*, page 546.

"This dwelling place prepared for the bride . . . is moved down into the
air to remain over the land of Palestine during the millennium, during
which time the saints exercise their right to reign. These saints are in
their eternal state and the city enjoys its eternal glory. At the expiration
of the millennial age, during the renovation of the earth, the dwelling
place is removed during the conflagration, to find its place after the
recreation as the connecting link between the new heavens and the new
earth." Ibid., page 580.

"This view contemplates the heavenly Jerusalem as in existence during
the millennium over the earth as the habitation of the resurrected saints,
and is in contrast to the city Jerusalem located on the earth. The heavenly
Jerusalem apparently is withdrawn at the time of the destruction of the
present earth and heaven. Then as pictured in Revelation 21:2 it returns
to the new heaven and the new earth when the scene is ready for its
descent. This interpretation regards Revelation 21:9ff. as the heavenly
city in the eternal state though recognizing its existence in the millennium. This seems to solve most of the exegetical problems that are

involved and, in fact, answers many objections to the premillennial interpretation of Scripture as a whole. It provides a clear distinction between resurrected saints who inhabit the New Jerusalem and the millennial saints on the earth who will inhabit the millennial earth. It is assumed, though the Scriptures do not state it, that the millennial saints at the end of the millennium will be translated prior to their entrance into the eternal state and thus will qualify for entrance into the heavenly Jerusalem." John F. Walvoord, *The Millennial Kingdom*, page 328.

"If this interpretation be admitted, there is no particular reason why the New Jerusalem should not be in existence throughout the millennium and suspended above the earth as a satellite city. . . . If the heavenly Jerusalem is hovering over the earth during the millennial reign, it would be a natural dwelling place not only for Christ Himself but for the saints of all ages who are resurrected or translated and therefore somewhat removed from ordinary earthly affairs. Their position thus close to the earth would permit them to carry on their functions in earth in connection with the millennial reign of Christ and yet would remove them as far as residence is concerned from continuing or mingling with those in their natural bodies and would solve the problem of lack of reference to a dwelling place for resurrected beings on earth during the millennium." John F. Walvoord, *The Church in Prophecy* (Grand Rapids: Zondervan Publishing House, 1964), pages 159-160.

"During the millennium the new Jerusalem . . . apparently will be suspended over the earth, and it will be the dwelling place of all believers during eternity . . . ." Charles Caldwell Ryrie, *The Ryrie Study Bible: The New Testament* (Chicago: Moody Press, 1976), page 482 (note on Revelation 21:2).

[68] "A most astounding feature is the dimension of the city which is given as 1500 square miles and also 1500 miles high. . . . Expositors differ as to whether the city is in the form of a cube or a pyramid though the latter seems more likely. If in the form of a pyramid, it is possible that the throne of God will be at the top and the river of life will wind its way from the throne down the various levels of the city." John F. Walvoord, *The Millennial Kingdom*, page 334.

In a more recent work, Dr. Walvoord sets the dimensions at 1342 miles and mentions that the city also might be a sphere. John F. Walvoord, *The Church in Prophecy*, pages 161-162.

[72] "At the rapture and resurrection of the church the saints of this age are, after judgment and marriage, installed in that prepared place. They are joined by the saints of the Old Testament at the time of their resurrection at the second advent. This dwelling place prepared for the

bride, in which the Old Testament saints find their place as servants (Rev. 22:3), is moved down into the air to remain over the land of Palestine during the millennium, during which time the saints exercise their right to reign." J. Dwight Pentecost, *Things to Come*, page 580.

76 "There is no question in the mind of the literal interpreter of the Scriptures but that Israel's national promises will be fulfilled by the nation itself in the millennial age, which follows the advent of the Messiah. All the covenanted national promises are earthly in content and will be fulfilled in the time of the earthly reign of Messiah." J. Dwight Pentecost, *Things to Come*, page 535.

". . . the national promises were to be fulfilled but *at the time of* and in the millennium . . . ." Ibid., page 536.

"The living will realize the fulfillment of the national promises of the Old Testament in the millennium, while the resurrected will realize the fulfillment of the expectation of a 'city which hath foundations' during the millennial age." Ibid., page 542.

"The conclusion to this question would be that the Old Testament held forth a national hope, which will be realized fully in the millennial age." Ibid., page 546.

Chapter Twenty-One

Dispensationalism: Confronting It in the Real World

I began to question the dispensational system during my fifth year as a student in the Th. M. program at Dallas Theological Seminary. Until that time I had had a somewhat unquestioning faith in the teaching of my Dallas professors. I knew so little and they were so knowledgeable, and I thought that questioning their teaching seemed presumptuous. Through the influence of my seminary friend, Herb Swanson, who had then recently graduated from Dallas, I began reading Reformed literature on Calvinism. Thank you, Herb! Through this reading I came to disagree with a good bit of what I had been taught at Dallas regarding salvation. Although I continued to value much of the instruction I had received at Dallas, I came to view some of the theological instruction as shallow and inaccurate. Then I wanted to re-evaluate my commitment to dispensationalism. What was discouraging was the great difficulty in finding anyone who could show me Biblical passages that related to the basic issues at stake. I finally found the help I needed in a dissertation by William Everett Bell, Jr. entitled "A Critical Evaluation of the Pretribulation Rapture Doctrine in Christian Eschatology." This work is a much broader criticism of dispensationalism than the title would suggest. Dr. Bell, a Dallas graduate, wrote this while pursuing a doctorate in philosophy at New York University. Thank you, Dr. Bell! Ironically, the summer before my last year at Dallas, I had publicly challenged Dr. Bell at a Southern Baptist Sunday school class when Dr. Bell had criticized Dr. Ryrie's teachings on "Savior only" salvation.

I hope this book that has grown out of my own continuing study will help the Reformed pastor when someone comes to him and says, "Show me from Scripture why I should not be a dispensationalist. Show me from Scripture why I should accept Reformed or covenant theology."

How to Handle Dispensationalists

I offer the following suggestions to help the open-minded inquirer with a dispensational background:

1) Center your arguments on the teachings of specific Scriptures. Dispensationalists are sometimes taught that Reformed interpreters superimpose a rationalistic theological system onto Scripture that distorts its true message. Dispensationalists will probably be more open to arguments taken directly from the exegesis of specific passages than to general theological arguments.

2) Emphasize the foundational issues of the unity of God's people in Christ and the continuity of God's program. Don't get sidetracked on peripheral issues such as the definition of a dispensation or the pre-tribulation rapture.

3) Be content with arguing against dispensationalism in general and for Reformed theology in general. Don't feel that you also need immediately to convince the inquirer of your particular convictions on secondary prophetic issues.

4) Don't begin with arguments about the interpretation of genuinely difficult passages such as Daniel's seventy weeks prophecy, Ezekiel's temple vision, the man of sin passage, or the book of Revelation. I do not believe anyone could have convinced me to reject the dispensational interpretation of Daniel's seventy weeks vision until I had first begun to doubt the dispensational system in general and the parenthesis theory in particular. I had been well drilled in the dispensational understanding of Daniel 9 but had never really noticed or given thought to most of the clear New Testament passages on unity and continuity.

5) Be careful not to overstate your case. Acknowledge that there

is a real newness to the New Testament church, that the word "Israel" does often refer to the physical Jews in the New Testament, that the prophets in Ephesians 2:20 are New Testament prophets, and so on.

6) State your case with prayerful compassion and patience. Don't present your case with arrogance and emotion or with an "I'm right and your position is ridiculous" attitude. Sow the seeds of truth and leave the rest to the Lord of the harvest.

7) Know the basics of the dispensational system well and be able to document them if necessary. Some today who call themselves dispensationalists are very emotionally attached to that system but have done little actual research on the basics of the system. They would prefer not to believe what traditional dispensational teachers have taught.

Major Dispensational Errors

I also would like to list what I consider to be the really objectionable teachings associated with dispensationalism. There are other dispensational teachings with which I disagree, but I do not view them as foundational and basic. The following are the dispensational teachings that I personally regard as especially objectionable:

1) The belief that Old Testament salvation was not through faith in the coming Christ. The Reformed position is not, as it has been misrepresented on occasion, that the Old Testament saints understood as much about Christ and the Gospel as we do today. The Reformed position is that the object of saving faith in the Old Testament was the same as the object of saving faith in the New Testament, although the Old Testament saint had much less knowledge of Christ. He saw dimly through the Messianic prophecies and types. The object of faith has not changed through the dispensations; the degree of knowledge of the object has.

2) The belief that the Old Testament saint had a salvation that did not include union with Christ and that the Old Testament saints in eternity will not be members of the Body and Bride of Christ. Reformed theology does recognize that the New Testament era is of greater grace and spiritual fullness to the point that Scripture can contrast the New and Old Testament ages as light compared to darkness. This is not to say that the Old Testament was so lacking in grace that Old Testament salvation did not involve covenant union with Christ and the covenant headship of Christ.

3) The belief that there is a strong dichotomy of nature between the Abrahamic covenant and the Mosaic covenant in that one is unconditional and the other conditional. Related to this would be the dispensational teaching that the Sermon on the Mount and the Lord's Prayer are legal ground and thus not directly applicable to the Christian. Reformed theology views the Mosaic covenant as basically a nationally expanded version of the Abrahamic covenant, and its moral law elements are regarded as still valid. Since moral law is merely the expression of God's holiness as it relates to created reality, God's moral law can no more be invalidated than can God's holiness (cf. Matthew 5:17-20). There can be, and are, adjustments in the realm of case law and ceremonial law since case law is a time-bound, situation-specific application of moral law and ceremonial law is positive law.

4) The belief that the New Testament era is a parenthesis in the prophetic program for Israel to the point that no Old Testament prophecy can directly refer to the church age.

5) The conviction that the Abrahamic covenant and the Davidic covenant and the new covenant of Jeremiah 31 are primarily Jewish covenants that can relate to the Christian only in a secondary and indirect sense at most.

6) The belief that Christ's present reign at the right hand of the Father has no direct relationship to the fulfillment of the Davidic covenant and the Messianic kingdom prophecies.

7) The belief that there is no organic relationship of continuity between Old Testament Israel and the New Testament church. Reformed interpreters believe that the Christian church, and not the theological heirs of Phariseeism, are the true present heirs of the Old Testament covenants and kingdom promises.

The purpose of this list is not to stereotype all dispensationalists. These are objectionable beliefs from the perspective of Reformed theology, and these are beliefs that have been taught by leading dispensational theologians as basic elements in that system. If there are Christians today who think of themselves as dispensationalists and who disagree with some of the above listed beliefs, then I am thankful that they do disagree with at least some of these. What a person actually believes is more important than how he classifies himself theologically. Such people, however, should be challenged to think through their total theological systems. A person should accept with consistency all the implications of the dispensational presuppositions or else reject the dispensational presuppositions as invalid impositions on Scripture.

Why Dispensationalism is Popular

I would like to conclude with some suggestions as to why dispensationalism has been so popular among Bible believing American Christians in modern times. I know that I was a sincere student of God's Word when I was a dispensationalist, and I have no reason to doubt that this is true of dispensationalists in general. And yet dispensationalism so plainly contradicts the teachings of Scripture. Why do they continue to adhere to this system? I would suggest the following possible reasons.

First, many dispensationalists have never been exposed to the weaknesses of their system. I attended a dispensational seminary for four years without becoming aware that there were any significant weaknesses in the dispensational system. I was so confident in dispensationalism that I saw no need for wasting my time reading any unsympathetic critiques of the system. When I finally was exposed to some of these weaknesses, I had no answers.

Second, many dispensationalists have not consistently thought through the implications of their system's assumptions. How many realize that this theory, if applied consistently, excludes the Old Testament saints from the Body and Bride of Christ? How many realize the implications of this theory concerning the federal headship of Christ in Old Testament salvation? How many who accept the parenthesis theory realize that this theory, if applied consistently, denies any direct fulfillment of Old Testament prophecy in the church age?

Third, many have been attracted to dispensationalism because some dispensational predictions have seemingly materialized in the modern world. The rise of Russia, the establishment of the Israeli state, the formation of the European Common Market, the development of the World Council of Churches, and the growth of apostasy in the mainline denominations all fit in well with the dispensational end time scenario. This apparent spectacular modern day confirmation of the ancient Biblical prophecies is attractive to many sincere Christians because of its apparent apologetic value.

Fourth, the pessimism of dispensationalism explains the current world problems and also effectively relieves the Christian of his responsibility to work toward discipling the nations in this age. We are facing the repercussions of the age of reason in which man is philosophically elevated and God dismissed as a myth. This philosophical rebellion spawned the atheistic social scientists who have gained control over much of the world. There is presently a major ideological war to the death between Christianity and atheistic humanism. At a time such as this, it is convenient for the Christian to be eschatologically pessimistic. If the church is responsible for discipling the nations for Christ, then we have an awesome task on our hands. Wouldn't it be much more convenient to believe that the church age was prophesied to be a failure and that all the Christian can hope to accomplish today is to snatch a few souls from the fire? It is convenient to think that things are inevitably going to get worse and that there is little we can do except wait to be raptured out of the situation.

Fifth, we are approaching the year 2000. While this millennial date approaches, there will naturally be much prophetic speculation just as there was when the year 1000 approached a millennium ago. In such an atmosphere dispensationalism, with its direct identification of prophecy with current events, will have a popular appeal.

Sixth, dispensationalism appeals to some philosophical biases. As we have noticed, dispensationalism is pessimistic, and pessimism conforms to the existential spirit of our age. Also, there are some striking parallels between empirical philosophy and dispensationalism. They both prefer literal, precise language over figurative poetic expression. They both emphasize the diversity of truth, seeing each truth as a self-sufficient, encapsulated entity to the point of neglecting the organic unity of truth. British empiricism compared truths to billiard balls and rejected the concept that truths are related organically like a blossom is related to fruit. Similarly, dispensationalists reject the idea that the Old and New Testaments are related like a bud is related to a blossom. British empiricists also emphasized individual autonomous freedom, and a similar emphasis can be seen in the teaching of those dispensationalists who say that the Christian today is not under law in any sense. Dispensationalism is individualistic in its pessimistic attitude toward the organized church and in its relegation of kingdom truths, with their social implications, to a future age.

George M. Marsden has pointed out that dispensationalism developed in the nineteenth century when the empiricism of Francis Bacon was philosophically popular in America. Mr. Marsden made the following observations:

To whatever degree dispensationalists consciously considered themselves Baconians (it is rare to find reflections on philosophical first
principles), this closely describes the assumptions of virtually all of them.
They were absolutely convinced that all they were doing was taking the
hard facts of Scripture, carefully arranging and classifying them, and thus
discovering the clear patterns which Scripture revealed.[1]

The role of the interpreter, according to the same Baconian assumptions,
was not to impose hypotheses or theories, but to reach conclusions on
the basis of careful classification and generalization alone. This disposi-
tion to divide and classify everything is one of the most striking and
characteristic traits of dispensationalism.[2]

Dispensationalist leaders regarded these methods of dividing and classifying as the only scientific ones. Scofield, for example, contrasted his
work to previous "unscientific systems." Similarly, Reuben Torrey regarded ideas basically as things to be sorted out and arranged. One of
his major works, *What the Bible Teaches* (1898), is an incredibly dry
five-hundred-page compilation of thousands of Biblical "propositions"
supported by proof texts. The closest analogy would be to an encyclopedia or dictionary. Torrey explicitly defended this utter lack of style or
elegance. "Beauty and impressiveness," he said in the preface, "must
always yield to precision and clearness." As usual, his model was the
scientist. Torrey depicted his work as "simply an attempt at a careful
unbiased, systematic, thorough going, *inductive* study and statement of
Bible truth. . . . The methods of modern science are applied to Bible study
— thorough analysis followed by careful synthesis."

Induction had to start with the hard facts, and dispensationalists
insisted that the only proper way to interpret Scripture was in "the literal
sense," unless the text or the context absolutely demanded otherwise.[3]

The parallels between dispensational and empirical thought are
striking.

My prayer is that Bible believing dispensationalists will prayerfully reconsider their commitment to that system and prayerfully
analyze the reasons for their commitment to it. I have been through
the process, and I know that it is painful. Giving up familiar beliefs
and seeking new answers is not easy. Our ultimate loyalty, however,

---

[1] George M. Marsden, *Fundamentalism and American Culture: The Shaping of
Twentieth-Century Evangelicalism: 1870-1925* (New York/Oxford: Oxford
University Press, 1980), page 56.

[2] Ibid., page 59.

[3] Ibid., page 60

should not be to any system. It should be to Jesus Christ, for He is the Truth. And the Truth will make us free.

Conclusion

[by Curtis Crenshaw]

The dispensationalists have many theological problems to contend with. Among these problems are the hermeneutic that the Apostles use (not literal or figurative but biblical); the church called Israel and Israel the church; the prophesied Old Testament kingdom established by Christ when He came; the church engrafted into Israel in Ephesians 2 and Romans 11; Christ ruling now on David's throne; all saints of all ages united with Christ; no salvation apart from union with the Lord Jesus so that the Old Testament saints are members of His body by faith in Him; the New Covenant made with "Israel" is for us; Ezekiel's temple and sacrifices cannot be rebuilt since Christ's blood has nullified all animal sacrifices (Heb. 9 and 10). If the temple is rebuilt and used for memorial sacrifices, then Ezekiel is not taken literally, for Ezekiel's sacrifices were not memorial but expiatory. To take them as memorials is to read the New Testament into the Old Testament and to deceive the ancient readers of Ezekiel who thought they were more than memorials, as dispensationalists often remind us.

There are also many problem texts for the dispensationalists, such as Hebrews 2 (one people of the Old Testament and New Testament), Galatians 6:16 (church is the "Israel of God"), Revelation 21 (twelve Apostles and twelve tribes both members of the Bride of Christ), Matthew 21:43 (kingdom taken from the nation Israel and given to another "nation"), Joel 2:28 (Old Testament prophecy of the outpouring of the Spirit fulfilled in the church), Acts 15 (God is rebuilding His tabernacle now by adding Gentiles to it), Acts 13:44-48 (God promised that He would bless the Gentiles in the age of the Messiah; see Rom. 15:7-13), and many others.

Such a system leads to many severe theological problems such as antinomianism, the idea that one can have Christ as Savior while rejecting Him as Lord. They promote two ways of salvation, for if the Old Testament saints were not indwelt permanently by the Holy Spirit, did not believe in the coming Messiah, did not understand the Old Testament sacrifices as pointing to the one sacrifice, and were not in union with Christ, then it could not be clearer that they were saved by some other way than the Bible way. Antinomianism and Satan as lord of the world have also lead to a retreat from society that has allowed the humanists to take over America so that Christians are facing severe persecution with Christian-bashing already being popular. The whole nation is being judged now, and the dispensationalists love it, thinking that this means that Jesus is soon to return. As one dispensational woman said to a lady in my church: "I don't want to do anything in our culture, for the quicker things get worse, the sooner Jesus will return." She heard this from her dispensational pastor who has the largest church in her large metropolitan area.

The moderate dispensationalists have only slightly improved their theology, but they have left intact their antinomianism, Arminianism, two ways of salvation, and the problem of union with Christ. One wonders where they will end up; and if one wants an uncertain theology that sails in a ship with an unknown destination, he will be comfortable sailing with them. But we shall stay will the time-tested, stable Reformed Faith.

May the Lord be pleased to use our book to free many from such a system. Amen.

Appendix One

Warfield's Critique of Chafer

[researched by Curtis Crenshaw]

The following article by B. B. Warfield in 1918 is just one indication that the Reformed had many problems with dispensational theology, and that the perfectionistic tendency of dispensational thought is not my imagination. The article is taken out of *Bibliotheca Sacra*, which journal was at Princeton when Dr. Warfield wrote but now, ironically, is at Dallas Theological Seminary. The article is a critique of the still popular book by Lewis Chafer, *He That Is Spiritual*. We turn now to the great prince of Princeton, B. B. Warfield. All emphasis is his.

Mr. Chafer is in the unfortunate and, one would think, very uncomfortable, condition of having two inconsistent systems of religion struggling together in his mind. He was bred an Evangelical, and, as a minister of the Presbyterian Church, South, stands committed to Evangelicalism of the purest water. But he has been long associated in his work with a coterie of "Evangelists" and "Bible Teachers," among whom there flourishes that curious religious system (at once curiously pretentious and curiously shallow) which the Higher Life leaders of the middle of the last century brought into vogue; and he has not been immune to its infection. These two religious systems are quite incompatible. The one is the product of the Protestant Reformation and knows no determining power in the religious life but the grace of God; the other comes straight from the laboratory of John Wesley, and in all its forms — modifications and mitigations alike — remains incurably Arminian, subjecting all gracious workings of God to human determining. The two can unite as little as fire and water.

Mr. Chafer makes use of all the jargon of the Higher Life teachers. In him, too, we hear of two kinds of Christians, whom he designates respectively "carnal men" and "spiritual men," on the basis of a misreading of 1 Cor. 2:9ff (pp. 8, 109, 146); and we are told that the passage from the one to the other is at our option, whenever we care to "claim" the higher degree "by faith" (p. 146). With him, too, thus, the enjoyment of every blessing is suspended on our "claiming it" (p. 129). We hear here, too, of "letting" God (p. 84), and, indeed, we almost hear of "engaging" the Spirit (as we engage, say, a carpenter) to do work for us (p. 94); and we do explicitly hear of "making it possible for God" to do things (p. 148), — a quite terrible expression. Of course, we hear repeatedly of the duty and efficacy of "yielding" — and the act of "yielding ourselves" is quite in the customary manner discriminated from "consecrating" ourselves (p. 84), and we are told, as usual, that by it the gate is opened into the divinely appointed path (pp. 91, 49). The quietistic phrase, "not by trying but by a right adjustment," meets us (p. 39), and naturally such current terms as "known sin" (p. 62), "moment by moment triumph" (pp. 34, 60), "the life that is Christ" (p. 31), "unbroken walk in the Spirit" (pp. 53, 113), "unbroken victory" (p. 96), even Pearsall Smith's famous "at once": "the Christian may realize *at once* the heavenly virtues of Christ" (p. 39, the italics his). It is a matter of course after this that we are told that it is not *necessary* for Christians to sin (p. 125) — the emphasis repeatedly thrown on the word "necessary" leading us to wonder whether Mr. Chafer remembers that, according to the Confession of Faith to which, as a Presbyterian minister, he gives his adhesion, it is in the strictest sense of the term *not necessary* for anybody to sin, even for the "natural man" (ix, I).

Although he thus serves himself with their vocabulary, and therefore of course repeats the main substance of their teaching, there are lengths, nevertheless, to which Mr. Chafer will not go with his Higher Life friends. He quite decidedly repels, for example, the expectation of repetitions of the "Pentecostal manifestations" (p.47), and this is the more notable because in his expositions of certain passages in which the charismatic Spirit is spoken of he has missed that fact, to the confusion of his doctrine of the Spirit's modes of action. With equal decisiveness he repels "such man-made, unbiblical terms as 'second blessing', 'a second work of grace', 'the higher life', and various phrases used in the perverted statements of the doctrines of sanctification and perfection" (pp. 31, 33), including such phrases as "entire sanctification" and "sinless perfection" (pp. 107, 139). He is hewing here, however, to a rather narrow line, for he does teach that there are two kinds of Christians, the "carnal" and the "spiritual"; and he does teach that it is quite unnecessary for spiritual men to sin and that the way is fully open to them to live a life of unbroken victory if they choose to do so.

Mr. Chafer opens his book with an exposition of the closing verses of the second and the opening verses of the third chapters of 1 Corinthians. Here he finds three classes of men contrasted, the "natural" or unregenerate man, and the "carnal" and "spiritual" men, both of whom are regenerated, but the latter of whom lives on a higher plane. "There are two great spiritual changes which are possible to human experience," he writes (p.8), — "the change from the 'natural' man to the saved man, and the change from the 'carnal' man to the 'spiritual' man. The former is divinely accomplished when there is real faith in Christ; the latter is accomplished when there is a real adjustment to the Spirit. The 'spiritual' man is the divine ideal in life and ministry, in power with God and man, in unbroken fellowship and blessing." This teaching is indistinguishable from what is ordinarily understood by the doctrine of a "second blessing," "a second work of grace," "the higher life." The subsequent expositions only make the matter clearer. In them the changes are rung on the double salvation, on the one hand from the *penalty* of sin, on the other from the *power* of sin — "salvation into safety" and "salvation into sanctity" (p. 109). And the book closes with a long-drawn-out analogy between these two salvations. This "analogy" is announced with this statement: "The Bible treats our deliverance from the bond servitude to sin as a distinct form of salvation and there is an analogy between this and the more familiar aspect of salvation which is from the guilt and penalty of sin" (p. 141). It ends with this fuller summary: "There are a multitude of sinners for whom Christ has died who are not now saved. On the divine side everything has been provided, and they have only to enter by faith into His saving grace as it is for them in Christ Jesus. Just so, there are a multitude of saints whose sin nature has been perfectly judged and every provision made on the divine side for a life of victory and glory to God who are not now realizing a life of victory. They have only to enter by faith into the saving grace from the power and dominion of sin.... Sinners are not saved until they trust the Savior, and saints are not victorious until they trust the Deliverer. God has made this *possible* through the cross of His Son. Salvation from the power of sin must be claimed by faith" (p. 146). No doubt what we are first led to say of this is the quintessence of Arminianism. God saves no one — He only makes salvation *possible* for men. Whether it becomes *actual* or not depends absolutely on their act. It is only by their act that it is made *possible* for God to save them. But it is equally true that here is the quintessence of the Higher Life teaching, which merely emphasizes that part of this Arminian scheme which refers to the specific matter of sanctification. "What He provides and bestows is in the fullest divine perfection; but our adjustment is human and therefore subject to constant improvement. The *fact* of our possible deliverance, which depends on Him alone, does not change. We will have as much at any time as we make it possible for Him to bestow" (p. 148).

When Mr. Chafer repels the doctrine of "sinless perfection" he means, first of all, that our sinful natures are not eradicated. Entering the old controversy waged among perfectionists between the "Eradicationists" and "Suppressionists," he ranges himself with the latter — only preferring to use the word "control." "The divine method of dealing with the sin nature in the believer is by direct and unceasing *control* over that nature by the indwelling Spirit" (p. 134). One would think that this would yield at least a sinlessness of conduct; but that is to forget that, after all, in this scheme the divine action waits on man's. "The Bible teaches that, while the divine provision is one of *perfection* of life, the human appropriation is always *faulty* and therefore the results are *imperfect* at best" (p. 157). God's provisions only make it *possible* for us to live without sinning. The result is therefore only that we are under no *necessity* of sinning. But whether we shall sin or not is our own affair. "His provisions are always *perfect*, but our appropriation is always *imperfect*." "What He provides and bestows is in the fullest divine perfection, but our adjustment is human.... The fact of our possible deliverance, which depends on Him alone, does not change. We will have as much at any time as we make it possible for Him to *bestow*" (pp. 148, 149). Thus it comes about that we can be told that "the child of God and citizen of heaven may live a superhuman life, in harmony with his heavenly calling by an unbroken walk in the Spirit" — that "the Christian may realize *at once* the heavenly virtues of Christ" (p. 39); and that, in point of fact, he does nothing of the kind, that "all Christians *do* sin" (p. 111). A possibility of not sinning which is unillustrated by a single example and will never be illustrated by a single example is, of course, a mere postulate extorted by a theory. It is without practical significance. A universal effect is not accounted for by its possibility.

Mr. Chafer conducts his discussion of these "two general theories as to the divine method of dealing with the sin nature in believers" on the presumption that "both theories cannot be true, for they are contradictory" (p. 135). "The two theories are irreconcilable," he says (p. 139). "We are either to be delivered by the abrupt removal of all tendency to sin, and so no longer need the enabling power of God to combat the power of sin, or we are to be delivered by the immediate and constant power of the indwelling Spirit." This irreducible "either/or" is unjustified. In point of fact, both "eradication" and "control" are true. God delivers us from our sinful nature, not indeed by "abruptly" but by progressively eradicating it, and meanwhile controlling it. For the new nature which God gives us is not an absolutely new somewhat, alien to our personality, inserted into us, but our old nature itself remade — a veritable recreation, or making of all things new. Mr. Chafer is quite wrong when he says: "Salvation is not a so-called 'change of heart.' It is not a transformation of the old: it is a regeneration, or creation, of something wholly new, which is possessed in conjunction with the old so long as we are in the body" (p. 113). That this furnishes out each Christian with two conflicting natures does not appall him. He says, quite calmly: "The unregenerate have but one nature, while the regenerate have two" (p. 116). He does not seem to see that thus the man is not saved at all: a different, newly created, man is substituted for him. When the old man is got rid of — and that the old man has to be ultimately got rid of he does not doubt — the saved man that is left is not at all the old man that was to be saved, but a new man that has never needed any saving.

It is a temptation to a *virtuoso* in the interpretation of Scripture to show his mettle on hard places and in startling places. Mr. Chafer has not been superior to this temptation. Take but one example. "All Christian love," he tells us (p. 40) "according to the Scriptures, is distinctly a manifestation of divine love *through* the human heart" — a quite unjustified assertion. But Mr. Chafer is ready with an illustration. "A statement of this is found," he declares, "at Rom. 5:5, 'because the love of God is shed abroad (lit., gushes forth) in our hearts by (produced, or caused by) the Holy Spirit, which is given unto us.'" Then he comments as follows: "This is not the working of human affection; it is rather the direct manifestation of the 'love of God' passing *through* the heart of the believer out from the indwelling Spirit. It is the realization of the last petition of the High Priestly prayer of our Lord: 'That the love wherewith thou hast loved me may be in them' (John 17:26). It is simply God's love working *in* and *through* the believer. It could not be humanly produced, or even imitated, and it of necessity goes out to the objects of divine affection and grace, rather than to the objects of human desire. A human heart cannot *produce* divine love, but it can *experience* it. To have a heart that feels the compassion of God is to drink of the wine of heaven." All this *bizarre* doctrine of the transference of God's love, in the sense of His active power of loving, to us, so that it works out from us again as new centres, is extracted from Paul's simple statement that by the Holy Spirit which God has given us His love to us is made richly real to our apprehension! Among the parenthetical philological comments which Mr. Chafer has inserted into his quotation of the text, it is a pity that he did not include one noting that "ekcheo" is not "eischeo," and that Paul would no doubt have used "eischeo" had he meant to convey that idea.

A haunting ambiguity is thrust upon Mr. Chafer's whole teaching by his hospitable entertainment of contradictory systems of thought. There is a passage near the beginning of his book, not well expressed it is true, but thoroughly sound in its fundamental conception, in which expression is given to a primary principle of the Evangelical system, which, had validity been given to it, would have preserved Mr. Chafer from his regrettable dalliance with the Higher Life formulas. "In the Bible," he writes, "the divine offer and condition for the cure of sin in an unsaved person is crystallized into the one word 'believe'; for the forgiveness of sin with the unsaved is only offered as an indivisible part of the whole divine work of salvation. The saving work of God includes many mighty undertakings other than the forgiveness of sin, and salvation depends only upon *believing*. It is not possible to separate some one issue from the whole work of His saving grace, such as forgiveness, and claim this apart from the indivisible whole. It is, therefore, a grevious error to direct an unsaved person to seek forgiveness of his sins as a separate issue. A sinner minus his sins would not be a Christian; for salvation is more than subtraction, it is addition. 'I give unto them eternal life.' Thus the sin question with the unsaved will be cured as a part of, but never separate from, the whole divine work of salvation, and this salvation depends upon *believing*" (p. 62). If this passage means anything, it means that salvation is a unit, and that he who is invited to Jesus Christ by faith receives in Him not only justification — salvation from the *penalty* of sin — but also sanctification — salvation from the *power* of sin — both "safety" and "sanctity." These things cannot be separated, and it is a grievous error to teach that a true believer in Christ can stop short in "carnality," and, though having the Spirit *with* him and *in* him, not have Him *upon* him — to use a not very lucid play upon prepositions in which Mr. Chafer indulges. In his attempt to teach this, Mr. Chafer is betrayed (p. 29) into drawing out a long list of characteristics of the two classes of Christians, in which he assigns to the lower class practically all the marks of the unregenerate man. Salvation is a process; as Mr. Chafer loyally teaches, the flesh continues in the regenerate man and strives against the Spirit — he is to be commended for preserving even to the Seventh Chapter of Romans its true reference — but the remainders of the flesh in the Christian do not constitute his characteristic. He is in the Spirit and is walking, with however halting steps, by the Spirit; and it is to all Christians, not to some, that the great promise is given, "Sin shall not have dominion over you," and the great assurance is added, "Because ye are not under the law but under grace." He who believes in Jesus Christ is under grace, and his whole course, in its process and in its issue alike, is determined by grace, and therefore, having been predestined to be conformed to the image of God's Son, he is surely being conformed to that image, God Himself seeing to it that he is not only called and justified but also glorified. You may find Christians at every stage of this process, for it is a process through which all must pass; but you will find none who will not in God's own good time and way pass through every stage of it. There are not two kinds of Christians, although there are Christians at every conceivable stage of advancement towards the one goal to which all are bound and at which all shall arrive.

Appendix Two

The Pre-Tribulation Rapture Doctrine

[by Grover Gunn]

From experience I have learned that when I am discussing the dispensational pre-tribulation rapture doctrine, I need to be careful to explain that I do believe that the saints who are alive when Christ returns will be raptured to meet Him in the air. This is the clear teaching of 1 Thessalonians 4:16-17: "... the dead in Christ shall rise first: then we which are alive and remain shall be caught up together with them in the clouds, to meet the Lord in the air." The English word "rapture" is based on the Latin "rapere" which means to seize or snatch and is used in the Latin translation of 1 Thessalonians 4:17. Since I believe what 1 Thessalonians 4:16-17 teaches, I believe in the rapture of the saints. What I disagree with is the notion that the rapture will occur seven years before Christ's second coming and will involve only those saints who were saved after Acts 2. According to dispensationalist Dr. John F. Walvoord: "The expression 'the dead in Christ shall arise first' (1 Thess. 4:16) seems to include only the church. The Old Testament saints are never described by the phrase 'in Christ.'"[1]

For what purpose will the saints meet the Lord in the air? A study of the Greek word translated "meet" in 1 Thessalonians 4:17 answers

---

[1]John F. Walvoord, *The Rapture Question* (Grand Rapids: Zondervan Publishing House, 1957), page 154; see John F. Walvoord, *The Millennial Kingdom* (Grand Rapids: Zondervan Publishing House, 1959), page 280.

that question. That word was a technical term for a civil custom of antiquity whereby a public welcome was accorded by a city to important visitors.[2] If any dignitary were newly arriving in an ancient city, the great of the city would go out to meet him as he approached the city gates and then would personally escort him into the city. It was the ancient equivalent of rolling out the red carpet. This word translated "meet" does not always refer to this ancient custom, but, interestingly, this understanding of the word does fit each of its three occurrences in the New Testament. This word occurs in Matthew 25 in the parable of the foolish virgins:

> And at midnight there was a cry made, Behold, the bridegroom cometh; go ye out to *meet* him. Then all those virgins arose and trimmed their lamps. . . .the bridegroom came, and they that were ready went in with him to the marriage: and the door was shut.

This word also occurs in Acts 28 in the account of Paul's arrival at Rome:

> . . . we went toward Rome. And from thence, when the brethren heard of us, they came to *meet* us as far as Appii forum, and the three taverns . . . . And when we came to Rome . . . .

The use of this same Greek word, translated "meet," in 1 Thessalonians 4:17, would indicate that the resurrected saints will "meet" the Lord in the air to honor Him as the King of kings and the Lord of lords by providing Him with a royal escort for the remainder of His descent to earth. The saints, the truly royal citizens of planet earth, will meet Christ in the air at His second advent to give Him the "red carpet treatment" when He comes to earth to renew it and to rule over it for eternity.

I believe that the rapture of the saints will occur at the time of Christ's second advent and not seven years before. I know of no place in Scripture that teaches the rapture and the second advent are separated by a significant time span. And there are certain passages that are especially difficult to explain in terms of the dispensational pre-tribulation rapture doctrine. For example, in 2 Thessalonians 1:5-10, Paul comforts the church age saints at Thessalonica with the blessed hope of the rest that will be both theirs and Paul's when Christ returns in flaming fire and judges those who have been troubling the

---

[2]Gerhard Kittel, Editor, *Theological Dictionary of the New Testament* (Grand Rapids: Wm. B. Eerdmans Publishing Company, 1964), 1.380-381.

church. According to dispensational assumptions, however, this passage could not be referring to the Christian's blessed hope. In dispensational thinking there is no flaming judgment associated with the church return of Christ, which is a secret rapture. Flaming judgment is associated only with the Jewish return of Christ, which is the second advent. So the Christian church age recipients of 2 Thessalonians 1 were being taught Jewish truth. According to a consistent application of the dispensational distinctions and assumptions, the Christians at Thessalonica must have been acting as representatives of Jewish tribulation saints.[3]

Notice also Titus 2:13. Paul mentions "the blessed hope," which dispensationalists acknowledge to be the church return of Christ, the secret rapture. Paul, however, also mentions in this verse the appearing of the glory of Jesus Christ. To what end-time event does that refer? The most obvious answer is the second advent when Christ will openly come to earth in flaming glory, the opinion of Dr. John F. Walvoord in an early article.[4] The problem with this interpretation for the dispensationalist is that the Greek of Titus 2:13 strongly identifies "the blessed hope" and "the glorious appearing" as one event. This can be clearly seen in the New International Version which translates this phrase "the blessed hope — the glorious appearing." The dispensational answer that has appeared in the later writings of Dr. Walvoord is an argument that "the glorious appearing" must refer to the rapture. He points out that at least the raptured church saints will then see the glory of Christ.[5]

The main subject of the classic rapture passage (1 Thess. 4:16, 17) is not the rapture of living saints but the resurrection of the "dead in Christ." Paul wrote this passage primarily to assure Christians that those saints who are alive at the return of Christ will have no precedence over those saints who die before the return of Christ. Paul states, "We who are alive and remain until the coming of the Lord will by no means precede those who are asleep" and "the dead in Christ shall rise first." Paul's main point in this passage then is that the physically

---

[3]John F. Walvoord, *The Blessed Hope and the Tribulation* (Grand Rapids: Zondervan Publishing House, 1976) pages 122-124.

[4]J. Dwight Pentecost, *Things to Come*, page 157; quotation from John F. Walvoord, "New Testament Words for the Lord's Coming," Bibliotheca Sacra, 101:288, July 1944.

[5]John F. Walvoord, *The Rapture Question*, pages 81,157; John F. Walvoord, *The Blessed Hope and the Tribulation*, pages 57,165.

dead who are in covenant union with Christ will be resurrected prior to the rapture.

There are two passages of Scripture that dispensationalists commonly interpret to teach that OT saints will not be among those resurrected at the time of the pretribulation rapture: Isaiah 26:19 and Daniel 12:1, 2. I will discuss only the clearer of the two:

> At that time Michael shall stand up, the great prince who stands watch over the sons of your people; and *there shall be a time of trouble,* such as never was since there was a nation, even to that time. And at that time your people shall be delivered, every one who is found written in the book. And *many of those who sleep in the dust of the earth shall be awake,* some to everlasting life, some to shame and everlasting contempt (Daniel 12:1, 2).

This passage teaches that there will be a resurrection of saints after "a time of trouble, such as never was since there was a nation." Most dispensationalists identify this "time of trouble" with an end time tribulation and interpret this passage to teach that the Old Testament saints will be resurrected at the Second Advent. If the OT saints are resurrected at the Second Advent and if the "dead in Christ" are resurrected seven years before the Second Advent, then the OT saints cannot be included among the "dead in Christ." Dispensationalists will argue that the OT saints are included among "those who are Christ's" (1 Cor. 15:23) but not among the "dead in Christ" of 1 Thessalonians 4:16.

Dispensationalists must either give up the pretribulational rapture doctrine or teach that the OT saints were saved apart from union with Christ. As a rule they have held to their pretribulational rapture teaching. For confirmation of this, note these quotes:

> Concerning the completion of the Church when saints will be translated and resurrected, Paul uses the phrase "dead in Christ" (1 Thess. 4:16). This clearly distinguishes those who have died in this age from believers who died before Christ's first advent, thus marking the Church off as distinct to this age and a mystery hidden in Old Testament times but not revealed.[6]

> The Old Testament saints are never described by the phrase "in Christ."[7] . . . The best answer . . . is to concede the point that the

---

[6]Charles C. Ryrie, *Dispensationalism Today* (Chicago: Moody Press, 1965), p. 136.

[7]Editor: This is not true. See Gal. 3 where the true child of Abraham is the one who has faith in Christ, belongs to Christ, and is in Christ and especially verse 17 where

resurrection of Old Testament saints is after the tribulation and resurrection of the church.[8]

---

the Majority text (KJV) reads that the promise was "in Christ," indicating that the OT saints were also in Christ.

[8]John F. Walvoord, *The Rapture Question*, p. 154. Compare Walvoord's *The Millennial Kingdom*, p. 280 and J. Dwight Pentecost, *Things to Come*, p. 407.

Appendix Three

Conditional and Unconditional Covenants

[by Grover Gunn]

Dispensationalists stress a strong dichotomy between the unconditional Abrahamic covenant, which was expanded into the Palestinian covenant, the Davidic covenant, and the new covenant, and the conditional Mosaic covenant. What do the dispensationalists mean when they label the Abrahamic covenant unconditional and the Mosaic covenant conditional? Dr. Lewis Sperry Chafer explains:

> Whatever God declares He will do is always a binding covenant. If He in no way relates His proposed action to human responsibility, the covenant is *unconditional*. If He relates it to human responsibility or makes it to depend on cooperation on the part of any other being, the covenant is properly termed *conditional*.[1]

> In relation to His earthly people, Israel, and their blessings, God has made various covenants. Some of them are conditional and some unconditional, which terms suggest that in some covenants God has them to depend on human faithfulness, while in others He merely declares what He will do wholly apart from the question of human worthiness or faithfulness.[2]

---

[1]Lewis Sperry Chafer, *Dispensationalism* (Dallas: Dallas Seminary Press, 1936), page 73.

[2]Lewis Sperry Chafer, *Systematic Theology, 8 vols.* (Dallas: Dallas Seminary Press,

When any person becomes the beneficiary of God's unconditional, unalterable promise apart from any consideration of human merit, his obligation for righteous conduct becomes that of *adorning*, or *walking worthy*, of the position into which the covenant has brought him. If God has made a covenant declaring what He will do provided man does his part, it is conditional and the human element is not one of walking worthy of what God's sovereign grace provides, but rather of being worthy to the end that the promise may be executed at all. When the covenant is unconditional, God is limited in what He will do only by the knowledge-surpassing bounty of His infinite grace. When the covenant is conditional, God is restricted by what man is able or willing to do. As an efficacious appeal, the obligation to walk worthy, though in no way conditioning the sovereign purpose, secures more normal and spiritual response than all the meritorious systems combined. The human heart is far more responsive to the proposition couched in the words "I have blessed you, now be good," than it is to the proposition couched in the words, "Be good, and I will bless you." The element of human conduct thus appears in each form of the divine covenant but in such a manner that one is rendered unconditional and the other conditional.[3]

Dr. J. Dwight Pentecost has given the following explanation:

There are two kinds of covenants into which God entered with Israel: conditional and unconditional. In a conditional covenant that which was covenanted depends for its fulfillment on the recipient of the covenant, not on the one making the covenant. Certain obligations or conditions must be fulfilled by the receiver of the covenant before the giver of the covenant is obligated to fulfill that which was promised. It is a covenant with an "if" attached to it. The Mosaic covenant made by God with Israel is such a covenant. In an unconditional covenant that which was covenanted depends on the one making the covenant alone for its fulfillment. That which was promised is sovereignly given to the recipient of the covenant on the authority and integrity of the one making the covenant apart from the merit or response of the receiver. It is a covenant with no "if" attached to it whatsoever.

To safeguard thinking on this point, it should be observed that an unconditional covenant, which binds the one making the covenant to a certain course of action, may have blessings attached to that covenant that are conditioned on the response of the recipient of the covenant, which blessings grow out of the original covenant, but these conditioned blessings do not change the unconditional character of the covenant. The

---

1948), 7:97.

[3]Lewis Sperry Chafer, *Dispensationalism*, pages 74-75.

failure to observe that an unconditional covenant may have certain conditioned blessings attached to it has led many to the position that conditioned blessings necessitate a conditional covenant, thus perverting the essential nature of Israel's determinative covenants.[4]

It is difficult to analyze this dispensational dichotomy between conditional and unconditional covenants because it is difficult to understand. The conditional nature of the Mosaic covenant as described by dispensationalists makes the Mosaic covenant sound like a legalistic and meritorious system of salvation. Also, some of the dispensational descriptions of an unconditional covenant make the unconditional covenants sound like "cheap grace" licenses to sin. If the land promise were unconditional in the sense of involving no "ifs" or moral conditions of any sort, then why did God punish Israel's rebellion at Kadesh Barnea by not allowing that generation to enter the promised land and why did God later in judgment expel Israel from the land in the Babylonian captivity? Because of Biblical considerations such as these, some dispensationalists qualify the position that an unconditional covenant contains absolutely no moral conditions by suggesting a dichotomy between the covenant and the blessings of the covenant, as evidenced by the above quotation from Dr. Pentecost. To give another example, Dr. John F. Walvoord in one place states that an unconditional covenant "is not conditional upon the obedience of individuals or nations for its fulfillment," and then in another place in the same book argues that unconditional covenants involve "human contingencies."[5]

Instead of seeing a rigid dichotomy between the unconditional, gracious and national Abrahamic covenant and the conditional, meritorious and individualistic Mosaic covenant, Reformed interpreters view the Mosaic covenant as a national expansion of the promises, moral stipulations and ceremonial law found in the Abrahamic covenant. Both covenants were by-grace covenants and both involved moral stipulations with blessings promised for obedience and neither, when properly interpreted, were legalistic or meritorious.

Dr. Lewis Sperry Chafer argues that "A covenant which is unconditional cannot be conditional and a conditional covenant cannot be unconditional."[6] I disagree. God's covenants are all unconditional in

---

[4] J. Dwight Pentecost, *Things to Come*, page 68.

[5] John F. Walvoord, *The Millennial Kingdom*, pages 149, 177.

[6] Lewis Sperry Chafer, *Dispensationalism*, page 73.

their meritorious base and conditional in their normal instrumental means of administration. The meritorious base of God's covenant is the substitutionary suffering and the alien righteousness of Jesus Christ. The Christian is saved, not because of His own works, but because of the work of Christ in his place. The suffering of Christ satisfies God's wrath against the guilt of His people, and the righteousness of Christ is imputed to their legal account before God. And Christians do nothing to earn or to deserve this saving work of Christ on their behalf; it is all of grace, totally undeserved, completely gratuitous.

That the Christian's personal holiness is not the meritorious basis for his salvation, however, does not mean that personal holiness is not a necessary part of the Christian life or that God does not administer covenant blessings in accordance with the Christian's personal obedience. God normally administers His gracious covenant through a required response of genuine faith. I say normally because God saves without such a response in exceptional cases such as the death of an elect infant. I say genuine faith because not all professed faith is genuine faith. Genuine saving faith is faith that progressively bears the fruit of holiness and good works (James 2:17; Ephesians 2:10; Hebrews 12:14). The saved then are, as a rule, those who do good before God (John 5:29; Romans 2:7; Ephesians 2:10) but the saved are not saved by means of or because of the good they do (Titus 3:5; Ephesians 2:8-9).

These conditional and unconditional aspects of the covenant are not antagonistic dichotomies for two reasons. First, though an obedient faith is necessary for salvation, it is not meritorious. The only meritorious work in salvation is the saving work of Christ on behalf of His covenant people. In this essential question of covenantal merit, God's covenant is purely unconditional. And secondly, an obedient faith is necessary for salvation except in exceptional cases such as the death of an infant, but Christ gives His chosen people the spiritual life and ability needed to meet this requirement. As a part of His saving work, Christ redemptively purchased for His people deliverance from their bondage to unbelief and the gift of regeneration through the work of the outpoured Holy Spirit. Every professed Christian has the God-given responsibility to work out his own salvation with fear and trembling (Philippians 2:12), but God works in His people's lives to enable them to will and to work according to His good pleasure (Philippians 2:13). God unconditionally gives His chosen people the spiritual ability necessary to meet the conditions for receiving the blessings of the covenant.

In my estimation, the Calvinistic theology of rewards is the best explanation of how God's covenants can condition blessings on moral stipulations and still be totally unconditional and all of grace. Without faith, it is impossible to please God (Hebrews 11:6), and the natural, non-regenerate man is totally unable to please God (Romans 8:8). The person, however, whom God unconditionally chooses to bless, He regenerates and sanctifies and enables to believe with a dynamic faith that will lead to holy living. God then rewards this obedient holiness with blessings and rewards. The faith that works is not a meritorious condition for blessing but is the instrument through which God brings blessing on the saint in accordance with the divine principle, "to be carnally minded is death but to be spiritually minded is life and peace" (Romans 8:6). God's covenant blessings are but rewards on the effects of His own grace.

When God unconditionally chose Abraham to receive blessings, God regenerated him and enabled him to believe and to obey so that God could bless him in accordance with holiness. God chose to actively, personally know Abraham in order that Abraham might raise His family in the way of righteousness and thereby receive covenant blessings (Genesis 18:19). God rewarded Abraham for his obedience (Genesis 22:15-18; 26:2-5) and yet Abraham's salvation was unconditional and all of grace.

In regard to the land promise, the covenant blessing of rest in the land was historically conditioned on covenant obedience (Deuteronomy 4:25-26; chapter 28). This explains the wilderness wanderings and the exile and the times of unrest and the geographic limitations on the land inheritance in the Old Testament history of Israel. The land promise, however, will have a perfect, final, full, and eternal fulfillment when the saints are glorified and freed from all sin. The new earth will be inherited both unconditionally and in holiness since glorification will be a by-grace gift from God to His people.

Index of Major Persons, Passages, & Subjects